Corporate
Financial
Reporting

ROGER HUSSEY & AUDRA ONG

Former Dean of the Odette School of Business
University of Windsor, Canada

Odette School of Business
University of Windsor, Canada

CORPORATE

FINANCIAL

REPORTING

 macmillan education   palgrave

First published 2017 by
PALGRAVE

Palgrave in the UK is an imprint of Macmillan Publishers Limited,
registered in England, company number 785998, of 4 Crinan Street,
London, N1 9XW.

Palgrave® and Macmillan® are registered trademarks in the United States,
the United Kingdom, Europe and other countries.

ISBN: 978-1-137-52765-3 paperback

This book is printed on paper suitable for recycling and made from fully
managed and sustained forest sources. Logging, pulping and manufacturing
processes are expected to conform to the environmental regulations of the
country of origin.

A catalogue record for this book is available from the British Library.

A catalog record for this book is available from the Library of Congress.

Printed in China

SHORT CONTENTS

CONTENTS

LIST OF DIAGRAMS

LIST OF TABLES

LIST OF STANDARDS

ABOUT THE AUTHORS

 Roger Hussey is Emeritus Professor at both the University of the West of England and the University of Windsor, Canada. He is a Fellow of the Association of Chartered Certified Accountants and the Association of International Accountants. He holds an MSc and a PhD from Bath University, UK. After several years in industry, he was appointed Director of Research into Employee Communications at the Industrial Relations Unit of St Edmund Hall, University of Oxford. After six years at Oxford, Roger became Deloitte Professor at the University of the West of England. In 2000, Roger moved to Canada as Dean of the Odette School of Business, University of Windsor.

 Audra Ong, PhD, FCIS, is Associate Professor of Accounting at the University of Windsor, Canada. She received her PhD in Accounting from the University of the West of England, her MBA from the University of Wales, and BSc (Accounting) from Queen's University Belfast, UK. She has taught in the UK, Mexico and Canada. Audra is co-author of *Strategic Cost Analysis* (2012) and *Pick a Number: Internationalizing U.S. Accounting* (2014), published by Business Expert Press. *Pick a Number* was also chosen by Harvard Business Publishing as featured reading to pair with *Harvard Case Studies*. Audra is a Fellow of the Institute of Chartered Secretaries and Administrators (ICSA) in Canada.

PREFACE

Corporations are the lifeblood of world economies. They provide employment, products and services, and are the engine for economic growth. Their profits boost share prices and pay dividends. The financial muscle of global companies has transformed the social fabric and socio-economic status of countries.

We know that being financially knowledgeable assists in understanding companies' activities. International Financial Reporting Standards (IFRSs) are therefore extremely important, but the authority of the International Accounting Standards Board (IASB) is limited. It is a country, or a group of countries such as the European Union, that decides whether certain companies should comply with IFRSs and to enforce their compliance. A country also determines what additional information, if any, companies should disclose, and there may be a significant amount of additional information. In *Corporate Financial Reporting*, we provide a detailed but broad perspective on the information disclosed by companies.

Corporate Financial Reporting enables you to understand and analyze a variety of financial and non-financial information issued by companies. It is important to emphasize that financial statements are not just about numbers. A substantial amount of information is textual. The income statement, balance sheet and other 'numbers' statements mean little without the many pages of notes that support them. The financial pages are also only a minor part of company information and in this book we explain the reasons for and content of non-financial disclosures.

Throughout the years, corporate reporting has received its share of criticism because of some companies' financial excesses and scandals. The financial collapse in 2007/8 and the demise of Lehman Brothers resulted in several new and amended IFRSs. But there were financial frauds and scandals before this, and we are certain that there will be others in the future. It would be impossible to prevent all financial fraud but knowledge of corporate financial reporting enables us to identify it.

The goal of *Corporate Financial Reporting* is to expand understanding of the scope and impact of international accounting, but in the context of wider business activities. As this book is about international accounting, we illustrate our discussions with examples from companies in many different countries such as Australia, Canada, China, India, Russia and the U.K. Although the focus is the UK, over 100 other countries have adopted IFRSs.

Financial information remains a highly significant part of the communications given by large companies. But it is only one part of a wide array of disclosures, many of them not financial but narrative and not regulated by IFRSs but by national legislation. There has also been a significant growth in information being given voluntarily by companies. These practices have been encouraged by the use of the internet. In *Corporate Financial Reporting*, we explain and discuss these developments.

In the first three chapters of this book, we trace the growth of corporate financial reporting over the years, the regulatory developments and the foundations of the main financial statements produced by companies. Although UK experiences are used as an exemplar, we also trace developments in other countries.

Because of the importance of IFRSs in constructing the main financial statements, Chapters 4 to 10 explain in detail the relevant standards. We expand these explanations with company examples from many countries and worked examples.

Chapters 11 and 12 address the complications of financial instruments, and they are followed by Chapters 13 to 15 that explain the individual standards applying to certain events and transactions. Consolidated financial statements and other business relationships are covered in Chapters 16 and 17. This part of the book, concentrating on accounting standards, is completed by Chapter 18 covering interim financial reporting and events after the reporting period.

Chapter 19 describes the analysis of corporate reports. The introductory part of the chapter concentrates on the collection of relevant data and the process of conducting an analysis. The remainder of the chapter demonstrates the calculation and interpretation of various ratios

Chapter 20 expands our discussion of the corporate report. The introduction of narrative disclosures such as the strategic report, corporate governance and the stewardship code are described. We also address such issues as sustainability reporting and the growth of key performance indicators.

The final chapter considers possible future developments including integrated reporting, the use of XBRL and reporting on the internet. Our message is that corporate financial reporting is not only about understanding accounting standards, but also appreciating them in the context of all the other communications made by companies. These can be financial or narrative, regulated or voluntary, in print or digital.

TOUR OF THE BOOK

Learning objectives
Assist you in understanding the knowledge you should gain from each chapter and how you should apply it.

LEARNING OBJECTIVES

At the end of this chapter, you should be able to:

- Discuss the theoretical debate associated with the statement of comprehensive income
- Explain the purpose of a statement of comprehensive income
- Discuss the issues regarding changes in exchange rates
- Demonstrate the accounting for transactions in a foreign currency and translations to a presentation currency
- Identify the different types of employee benefits
- Describe and explain the accounting issues for the two main types of pension plans

Definitions
Concisely explain key terminology. These are shown in **bold** and in boxes to aid your recognition of them, with a full alphabetical glossary also featuring other useful terms at the end of the book.

accounting policies

Accounting policies are the specific principles, bases, conventions, rules and practices applied by an entity in preparing and presenting financial statements

Based on IAS 8, para. 5

As can be seen from the definition of **accounting policies**, the standard includes all the financial statements and the decisions or choices the board makes when it is selecting the way it accounts for and discloses financial transactions and events.

The standard sets out the criteria for selecting and applying accounting policies. IAS 1 *Presentation of Financial Statements* requires the disclosure of these policies and other sources of uncertainty.

Citations and References
Point to wider information sources, whose findings are summarized with in-chapter (author-date) citations and full publication details in the **References** at the end of the book.

THE 2007/8 CRISIS

A crisis frequently commences with a single, spectacular event. Most commentators would identify the collapse of Lehman Brothers as that event in the 2007/8 global financial crisis. The company had reported record revenue and earnings for 2007, but, in September 2008, it became the largest company in US history to file for bankruptcy.[1] On the day that Lehman Brothers Holdings Inc. (LBHI) filed for bankruptcy, its affiliates had over 930,000 derivative contracts outstanding. It is claimed that: 'The fate of these contracts illustrates the challenges facing those who work with derivatives' (Barkhausen 2010: 7).

Scenarios
Illustrate the application of accounting regulations to economic transactions and events. These are drawn from actual company examples or specially constructed to demonstrate the procedure.

Scenario 13.1   Change in doubtful debts estimate

An entity knows from experience that it will not be able to collect all the money from its customers. In the past, at the year-end it has always estimated these 'bad debts' at 2%. There has been a rapid economic decline and the entity is contemplating increasing the amount for doubtful debts from 2% to 3% of the accounts receivable. It is concerned, however, that if it changes the estimate it will have to revise the financial statements in previous years.

Under IAS 8, this is a change in the accounting estimate. The entity does not have to revise previous financial statements because they were constructed on the best information at that time, that is, when the economy was healthier.

Worked examples
Demonstrate the application of the specific requirements of standards with calculation-based examples. These are necessarily brief and simplified but offer valuable advice on working with financial figures and numbers. You will find it useful to reflect on these in the context of actual company practices.

Worked example 13.1   Change of asset life estimate

A company purchases machinery on 1 January 2012 for £100,000. The company considers that the machinery has a useful life of 10 years and no residual value. The annual depreciation charge using the straight line method is:

$$\text{Annual depreciation charge} = \frac{£100,000}{10 \text{ years}} = £10,000$$

Three years later, on 31 December 2014 the carrying amount of the machinery is £70,000.

On 1 January 2015, the company decides that the remaining useful life of the machinery is only 5 years and not 7 years. The annual depreciation charge from 1 January 2015 and for the following years will be:

$$\text{Annual depreciation charge} = \frac{£70,000}{5 \text{ years}} = £14,000$$

Company examples

Illustrate the application of IFRSs through extracts from the annual reports and accounts of real-life companies. Brief details of the companies' activities provide context for the financial statements.

Company example 20.7

Sustainability and Governance

CRH's strategy and business model is built around the principles of sustainable, responsible and ethical performance. The Group's organisational culture is rooted in a daily commitment to core values of honesty, integrity and respect in all business dealings.

CRH believes that combining these principles and values with best international practice, promotes good governance and provides a platform for the business to deliver superior returns over a sustained period of time, while also being sensitive and responsive to stakeholders and the environment in which the Group operates.

CRH has therefore placed sustainability and corporate social responsibility at the heart of its business model, strategy and activities worldwide.

CRH, Sustainability Report, 2014, p. 7

Notes

Identify other sources of information on particular topics at the end of the chapter, for further exploration.

NOTES

1 IFRIC was previously the Standards Interpretations Committee (SIC). Interpretations issued by SIC are still in force.

2 The progress of the relationship between the US and international standard setters has been documented by Kirsch (2012).

3 Hussey and Ong (2014) summarize the reasons for the ending of the relationship.

4 Information on the jurisdictions using IFRSs is on *www.ifrs.org/Use-around-the-world/Pages/Jurisdiction-profiles.aspx* (accessed 24 August 2016).

CONCLUSIONS

Conclusions

Draw together the main points of the chapter to help you consolidate your learning.

In this chapter, we have discussed financial reporting regulations. In the UK, this comes under the FRC. We would emphasize that the great majority of countries have a similar structure.

Although many countries have adopted international accounting standards, these usually apply to large companies that are listed on a stock exchange. One should take care when countries state that they have adopted IFRSs. It is for the country to determine the extent to which it adopts them. In addition, monitoring and enforcement at the national or even regional level can vary.

The greatest problem facing the IASB in constructing a standard is the lack of an agreed CF. We have explained some of the concepts and attributes in the 2015 ED. This document has been criticized, and it may be some considerable time before a final version is produced. Even then, there will probably be disagreement on its contents.

The ED has generated significant discussions, and it is impossible to summarize all of the issues raised. The FRC has questioned the way that the ED dealt with the concepts of stewardship, prudence and reliability, in particular, in a 47-page response (FRC 2015a).

In the pipeline

Looks ahead to future developments in the constantly changing environment of corporate financial reporting.

IN THE PIPELINE

It is clear that there are two major issues outstanding: the CF and materiality. Whatever the outcome, both are likely to have a significant impact on financial accounting and reporting, but we may not experience these changes for several years.

The ED for the CF has been criticized. The FRC has issued several documents regarding the establishment of a CF, with which it fully agrees. However, in the full response issued in November 2015, the FRC expressed its considerable unease with the IASB's proposals.

Companion website

www.palgravehighered.com/hussey-cfr
contains additional resources to aid learning and teaching, such as:

For students:
Multiple choice questions and answers
'In the pipeline' quarterly updates

For lecturers:
Multiple choice question test bank and answers
Short case studies
PowerPoint presentations for each chapter

ACKNOWLEDGEMENTS

Although authors' names always appear in a book, the product is a team effort. Our gratitude is therefore expressed to the reviewers, editors, designers and others that made this edition possible. In particular we wish to recognize the contributions of the following reviewers:

Christopher Coles (Senior Teaching Scholar, Accounting and Finance, University of Stirling, UK)
Andrew Ekuban (Principal Lecturer in Accounting and Finance, University of Bedfordshire, UK)
Natalie Forde-Leaves (Lecturer in Accounting and Finance, Cardiff University, UK)
Christiaan Lamprecht (Senior Lecturer, Accounting, University of Stellenbosch, South Africa)
Kelvin Leong (Principal Lecturer and Professional Lead, Finance, Glyndwr University, UK)
Jing Li (Senior Lecturer, Director of Studies BSc Accounting and Finance, University of
    Bradford, UK)
Brian Miller (Senior Teaching Fellow, Lancaster University, UK)
Rabih H. Nehme (Assistant Professor, Lebanese American University, Lebanon)
Faisal Sheikh (Head of Undergraduate Programmes, Accounting, Marketing, Tourism, York
    St John University, UK)

We also benefited from very sound advice from Sophie Dunbar on focussing our explanations. Finally, the support and guidance of Nikini Jayatunga and her team at Palgrave was invaluable and much appreciated.

Extracts on pp. 32, 33, 34–35, 41, 42, 45–49 from Exposure Draft ED/2015/3 paras 2.6–2.19; paras 2.22–2.36; para 1.22; paras 2.18 and 3.10; paras 6.19–6.46; para 8.1; para 10; p. 53 from IAS 1 para 54; pp. 59, 61, 66 from IAS 16 paras 11–13; para 31; para 67; p. 67 from IAS 23 para 8; BC 20; pp. 74, 76, 79 from IAS 38 para 3; paras 51–67; paras 48–50; pp. 80, 81, 83 from IAS 36 para 8; para 2; para 12; para 66; pp. 91, 97, 104–5 from IAS 1 para 106; para 79; para 106; pp. 120, 121 from IAS 18 para 18; para 30; pp. 125, 127, 128 from IFRS 15 para 9; paras 35–8; para 91; pp. 134, 137 from IAS 2 para 2; para 16; p. 140 from IAS 16 para 6; p. 145 from IFRS 2 para 1; pp. 154, 156, 157 from IAS 1 para 81A; para 82A; para 92; p. 159 from IAS 21 para 8; p. 166 from IAS 19 para 5; pp. 173, 174, from IAS 7 para 7; para 10; p. 190 from IAS 32 para 11; pp. 206, 207 from IAS 32 para 16; para 28; p. 209 from IAS 39; p. 218 from IFRS 9 para 6.1; p. 219 from IFRS 13 para 6; p. 231 from IAS 8 para 5; pp. 236, 237 from IAS 37 para 14; para 70; pp. 246–7 from IAS 12 para 5–6; pp. 252, 253, 254, 256 from IAS 17 para 4; para 8; para 20; para 58; p. 258 from IFRS 16 paras 9–33; pp. 264, 265 from IAS 40 para 16; paras 20 and 30; p. 268 from IAS 41 para 10; p. 272 from IFRS 6 para 9; para 18; pp. 274, 276 from IFRS 5 paras 33; paras 7–8; pp. 278, 279, 281 from IFRS 8 para 2; paras 12–13; paras 22–24; pp. 286, 291, 292–3, 296 from IFRS 3 para 5; para 39; para 18; para 32; para 10; pp. 299 and 305 from IFRS 10 para 2; para 27; p. 311from IAS 28 para 5; p. 317 from IAS 27 para 10; p. 319 from IFRS 11 para 5; p. 320 from IFRS 12 para 7; pp. 331, 333–4, 336 from IAS 34 para 5; paras 37–39; para 15B; p. 340 from IAS 10 paras 5–6; p. 369 from IAS 33 para 70.

GUIDE TO TERMINOLOGY

Accounting, like other disciplines, has its own terminology. Some words and phrases are in common usage; others require a specific definition. Where we have taken the term from IASB documents or elsewhere we have referenced the source.

Sometimes a term has an alternative or a different term is in common usage. We list below some main terms with an explanation of how we use them in this book.

Entity – Company

An entity is not necessarily a legal entity. It is an organization that chooses or is required to prepare general purpose financial statements. Usually, the term 'reporting entity' means the entity that is issuing an annual report and accounts. In this book both the terms 'entity' and 'company' refer to the organization issuing an annual report and accounts. We use the word 'entity' where we are explaining the requirements of a standard or other IASB document. When we are referring to a specific company or group of companies we use the word 'company'.

Annual report and accounts – Corporate financial reports

Companies are required to provide a printed annual report and accounts disclosing certain financial information to their shareholders. There are regulations determining the information and auditors must state their opinion on the contents. This is a public document and major companies have a website where anyone can download the annual report and accounts.

Over the years, company legislation has required more information that is not specifically financial. Major companies also disclose voluntarily information. Most annual report and accounts now consist of three distinct sections:

1   Strategic Report
2   Governance Report
3   Financial Statements and Notes

The financial statements and notes only now take up approximately one-third of the annual report and accounts. In addition, companies have websites that provide a substantial quantity of other information. Because of this explosion in disclosures, we use the terms 'corporate financial reporting' or 'corporate reporting' unless we are referring to the annual report and accounts.

International Accounting Standards – International Financial Reporting Standards

The International Accounting Standards Committee (IASC) first started issuing International Accounting Standards (IASs) in 1975 with IAS 1 *Disclosure of Accounting Policies*. The International Accounting Standards Board (IASB) replaced the Committee in 2000 and retained most of the IASs that had been issued. The IASB issued its first standard in 2003, entitled IFRS 1 *First-time Adoption of IFRSs*. We identify specific standards as either IAS or IFRS, whichever is appropriate. When we refer to standards in a general sense, we use the terms 'international standards' or 'accounting standards' to encompass both IASs and IFRSs.

Titles of the Financial Statements

The profit or loss account and the balance sheet had been major financial statements for decades. In 2007, the IASB revised IAS 1 to take effect from 1 January 2009. This standard introduced changes to the titles of some financial statements and added another required financial statement. The present position is that a company complying with international standards must publish annually a complete set of financial statements as follows:

- a statement of financial position (balance sheet) at the end of the period;
- a statement of profit or loss and other comprehensive income for the period (presented as a single statement, or by presenting the profit or loss section in a separate statement of profit or loss, immediately followed by a statement presenting comprehensive income beginning with profit or loss);
- a statement of changes in equity for the period;
- a statement of cash flows for the period;
- notes, comprising a summary of significant accounting policies and other explanatory information;
- comparative information prescribed by the standard.

A company can use titles other than the ones above. Our researches show that companies mainly use the following (with the chapters in which we discuss the statement in parentheses):

- Balance sheet (Chapters 4, 5 and 6) instead of Statement of financial position
- Income statement (Chapters 7 and 8) and Statement of comprehensive income (Chapter 9) instead of Statement of profit or loss and other comprehensive income
- Statement of changes in equity (Chapter 6)
- Statement of cash flows (Chapter 10)

We use the term 'statement of financial position' in the titles of Chapters 4, 5 and 6. We use the term 'balance sheet' in the main text unless we are referring specifically to IASB documentation.

'Income statement' is the name mostly used by companies for the profit or loss section of the Statement of profit or loss and other comprehensive income. We have mainly used the term, as in the standard, of 'profit or loss'. We have titled Chapters 7 and 8 'Statement of profit or loss' since these two chapters deal only with disclosures on that statement. Chapter 9 uses the title 'Statement of other comprehensive income'.

Students should take care when using the term 'income' because companies and others frequently use it without distinguishing between profit and other income. It is also sometimes used to mean revenue.

THE GROWTH OF CORPORATE REPORTING

At the end of this chapter, you should be able to:

- Describe the financial developments that led to company legislation in the UK
- Identify the important concepts that were established by legislation
- Explain the role of the Financial Reporting Council
- Explain the need for accounting standards and the introduction of International Financial Reporting Standards
- Describe the range of methods used by companies to report different types of corporate information

INTRODUCTION

corporate reporting

Corporate reporting is the provision of information that describes the activities of a company. The range of information can include, but not be limited to: financial statements and supporting explanations, directors' remuneration, corporate governance, sustainability reporting, ethical and environmental policies and other narrative reports. The information may be required by legislation, accounting standards, or stock exchange rules, or it may be provided voluntarily.

In this chapter, we discuss the events that led to the present corporate financial reporting by public limited companies. We start with a massive eighteenth-century UK scandal, the South Sea Bubble. This occurred at a time when there was little notion or practice of any form of **corporate reporting**. We then trace the development of company legislation and the introduction of the concepts of financial reporting, limited liability, the social responsibility of companies, and the true and fair view.

Until the twentieth century corporate reporting concentrated, almost exclusively, on financial information. This was a legislative response to the frauds and misdemeanours that were taking place. The establishment of a strong legal framework took many years and additions and improvements continue.

Legislation can compel the disclosure of financial information by companies, but it is not effective for specifying the form and detail. This requires a separate mechanism and we introduce the notion of standards for accounting in the second section of this chapter. Our discussion updates the legislative discussion by examining the current work of the Financial Reporting Council (FRC).

The FRC has authority for all accounting regulations in the UK and Northern Ireland. It is responsible for determining the accounting standards for all types of companies. These standards apply to companies listed on the London Stock Exchange and private limited companies, including very small ones.

The final section of the chapter considers the broadening reporting agenda. This underlines the legal basis of the annual report and accounts, and reviews the additional information disclosed by companies that falls within corporate reporting.

This chapter draws mainly on practices in the UK to describe the growth of corporate financial reporting. Many countries have experienced similar developments. The common factor in this chapter is our focus on companies in any country that comply with International Financial Reporting Standards (IFRSs) in producing their annual corporate reports.

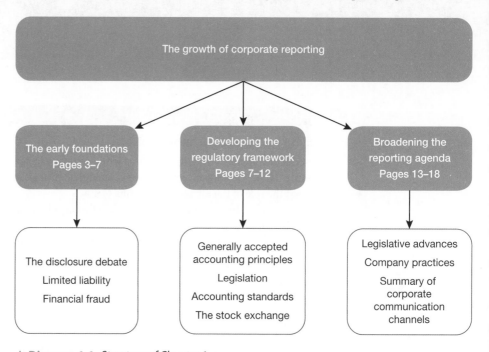

▲ **Diagram 1.1** *Structure of Chapter 1*

Individual countries also have their own legislative requirements. A company therefore must comply with IFRSs and any legal requirements of the country where they were incorporated. Even in the European Union (EU) this can lead to some differences, as shown in Company example 1.1 which quotes from the English version of the annual report of Carrefour, the French multinational retailer. Carrefour opened its first store in 1960, and is now one of the largest hypermarket chains in the world with 1,600 hypermarkets in more than 30 countries in Europe, the Americas, Asia and Africa.

We started this introduction with a scandal: the South Sea Bubble, and this is the first topic in this chapter. We finish the introduction with a drama: 'Brexit'. In June 2016, the people of the UK voted to leave the EU. In Chapter 2, we describe the impact of this decision on accounting regulations in the UK. In Chapter 21, we consider the implication for corporate reporting in the future.

Company example 1.1

Legislative requirements

This report should be read in conjunction with, and construed in accordance with, French law and professional auditing standards applicable in France.

Carrefour Annual Report and Accounts 2015, p. 1

THE EARLY FOUNDATIONS

The disclosure debate

In this section, we explain the reasons for the types of corporate reports issued by public limited companies (plcs). Our comments focus mainly on the document referred to as the annual report and accounts, and we start with a case of fraud from the eighteenth century. The South Sea Bubble contains all the elements of a great drama.[1] The term 'South Sea' referred to South America and other lands in the surrounding waters that were being colonized. The Lord Treasurer at that time, Robert Harley, with John Blunt, established the South Sea Company in 1711. Although it appeared to be a trading company, the primary objective was to fund government debt.

The British government believed that offering exclusive trading rights with Spain's colonies would be an effective incentive to convince the private sector to assume the government's current debts. Unfortunately, the company's trading rights were not extensive. However, stories of South American gold and silver ready to be imported to Europe attracted investors' attention.

The tales of boundless riches, understandably, had a very beneficial effect on the South Sea's share prices. In January 1720, the share price was £128. By May, this had reached the dizzy heights of £550. The South Sea Company's example had the effect of encouraging the growth of other companies offering business proposals that ranged from the doubtful to the totally implausible.

In an attempt to control these highly speculative ventures, Parliament passed the 'Bubble Act' in 1720. This Act required the legal incorporation of new joint-stock companies. These incorporated businesses allowed shareholders to buy different proportions of company stock. However, the businesses were unlimited; in other words, the shareholders were personally liable for all of the debts of the company should it fail.

The passing of the Bubble Act encouraged even more joint stock companies to be registered and there was a stock market frenzy. By August 1720, the South Sea Company's share price was £1,000 but the company's dismal profits could not support this enthusiasm. There was a crash and speculators who had purchased shares on credit and still held them often became bankrupt. In September 1720, the shares hit a low of £150.

Public outrage forced Parliament into holding an investigation. The final report revealed that there had been extensive fraud as well as corruption among members of the government.

The Bubble Act was repealed in 1825. Following this, company legislation started to address seriously the disclosure of financial information by companies. The discussions included consideration of the concept of limited liability.

Limited liability

> **limited liability**
>
> The liability of the shareholders of the company for its debts is limited to the amount they have agreed to invest. Generally, the liability of the shareholders is limited to the amount, if any, on any unpaid amount on their shares in the event of the company becoming bankrupt.

The Industrial Revolution and the need to build factories and develop canals and railways led to new businesses. Investment was needed to start these businesses. Canal and railway companies were generally incorporated by Act of Parliament, and this was a lengthy business. Many businesses adopted a more informal constitution: the Deed of Settlement. This did not give the business a corporate status and it was similar to a large partnership of many investors.

With such organizations, there was the very unsettling question of whether investors enjoyed **limited liability**. If you were very rich and the business failed, those owed money would be likely to come to you to pay the debt.

If people were to be attracted to investing in these new businesses, their legal liability had to be resolved. During the nineteenth century, several Acts of Parliament partially addressed this issue. The UK Joint Stock Companies Act 1844 was enacted to regulate these new types of businesses. It contained the following main principles:

1   A clear distinction between partnerships and joint stock companies. The joint stock company created a new type of business where investors owned the business but managers could run it on a daily basis.
2   Incorporation by registration as opposed to a special Act of Parliament or Royal Charter. Company registration in Scotland commenced in 1856.[2]
3   The disclosure of financial information as a safeguard against fraud. Until this time, investors received no financial information. The Act required directors to provide an annual balance sheet to shareholders and to give an auditor access to the company's records. However, there was no requirement for a profit or loss account.

The Companies Act 1844 was the first foundation stone of corporate reporting. It established who would be the providers of information – the joint stock company. It also detailed the type of information, namely a balance sheet. It is fair to say that the information in the balance sheet was basic and the role of the auditor did little to prevent fraud.

The Act did not address one important issue. The concept of limited liability was not discussed and thus there was a deterrent to investment. The balance sheet allowed the shareholder and lenders to obtain some guide to the solvency of the company, but the information was basic.

The Limited Liability Act 1855 introduced the concept of limited liability. This restricted the obligation of shareholders to the amount they had agreed to invest. Critics referred to the Act as the 'Rogues Charter' because unscrupulous entrepreneurs could abuse the system and avoid personal liability for a company's insolvency (Rose 1965). The Joint Stock Companies Act 1856 repealed the Rogues Charter and was itself succeeded by the Companies Act 1862.

The Companies Act 1862 introduced several important changes:

- Companies had to file the current year's audited balance sheet with the Registrar of Companies.
- The balance sheet had to disclose certain items separately (assets had to be classified into 'fixed' and 'floating', various intangible assets had to be shown, and investments in and balances due to and from subsidiaries had to be disclosed).
- A profit or loss account had to be presented to shareholders, but was not audited or filed.

Although it had taken many years, company legislation gradually set in place some of the foundations on which present-day corporate reporting sits. The concept of a joint stock company was introduced, with the shareholders having limited liability. Companies were obliged to disclose certain financial information, although the reliability of such information was sometimes in doubt. The Companies Act 1862 established:

- that the provider of information is the limited liability company;
- a rudimentary basis on the disclosure of certain financial information;
- that the recipients of the information are the investors.

Although these answers demonstrate an advancement at that time, fraud was to continue to be the main force for introducing further changes.

To summarize, in the nineteenth century the following developments in company legislation had arisen:

- A new type of business organization was introduced – the joint stock company.
- Incorporation could be made by registration as opposed to a special Act of Parliament or Royal Charter.
- The concept of limited liability was established.
- Companies had to file the current year's audited balance sheet with the Registrar of Companies. The balance sheet had to disclose certain items separately.
- A profit or loss account had to be presented to shareholders, but was not required to be audited or filed.

Financial fraud

Although legislation had made progress in corporate disclosures, such changes were not always met with enthusiasm. The Directors of the Peninsular and Orient Company contended in the nineteenth century that: 'Proprietors at a distance forming their opinion of the future position of the company from published accounts of past transactions could scarcely avoid arriving at erroneous conclusions' (Naylor 1960). Such conclusions could mean criticisms of the actions of the directors and demands for improved profits.

The obvious way to prevent such misunderstandings was to restrict the amount of financial information given. In 1925, a Company Law Amendment Committee reviewed company law. The Committee collected evidence and several commentators criticized the provision of financial information to investors. Some considered that giving investors more information would hamper the Directors from managing the business in the manner which they considered to be best.

The Law Society believed that: 'Too much disclosure should not be insisted on and the greatest possible freedom should be allowed to those responsible for the business' (Board of Trade 1925: X/IX). The Institute of Chartered Accountants in England and Wales supported this sentiment and argued: 'It is impossible by legislation to protect fools from their own folly' (Board of Trade 1925: LXVIII). However, the magazine, the *Economist*, adopted a more open approach. It argued that 'the growth, size and power of the great Joint Stock Companies made their accounts a subject of public economic interest. Accordingly, the revision of company law should not be approached merely from the point of view of the company itself, but from that of what the public ought to know' (*Economist* 1926: 1133).

This debate took place before the Companies Act 1929 was drawn up. In view of the controversies about the amount of financial disclosure and the recipients, it is not surprising that the 1929 Act made little advance in corporate disclosures. The Royal Mail Case exposed this failure in 1931 (see Company example 1.2).

Company example 1.2

The Royal Mail Case

In 1928, the Royal Mail Steam Packet Company issued a prospectus inviting potential investors to buy £2 million of 5% debentures. The prospectus stated that the company had produced an average yearly profit of £500,000 in the last decade. Despite these profit claims, only a year later the company asked for time to pay back loans owing to the Treasury.

Unfortunately, Lord Kylsant, the director of the Royal Mail Steam Packet Company, had falsified the trading prospectus with the aid of the company accountant, making the company appear profitable and thus attracting investors.

A Government-requested investigation revealed not only that the company was not profitable, but also that it had not made a trading profit since 1925. In the previous two years over £1.25 million had been drawn from reserves to enhance the profit or loss account.

The jury acquitted both Kylsant and Moreland of falsifying records but found Kylsant guilty of fraud in respect of the 1928 prospectus. Kylsant was sentenced to 12 months' imprisonment and his knighthood was removed.

The Royal Mail case is a prime example of financial fraud, but at that time companies could massage their profits. In the good years, there were ways they could hide some of the profits without the shareholders' knowledge. Then, it was easy in the bad years to bring the hidden profits forward, thus misleading the shareholders about the actual profit made in the current year.

> **financial accounting and reporting**
>
> Financial accounting and reporting is the branch of accounting concerned with the recognition and measurement of economic transactions and events, and their disclosure by organizations to external users.

After the significant Companies Act of 1862, for over 80 years company law did little to promote judicious and thorough corporate reporting. It was essential to take a more serious approach.

In 1945, the Board of Trade asked the Cohen Committee to review company law, tasking it to examine the 'safeguards afforded for investors and the public interest' (Board of Trade 1945: 2). For the first time, a committee on company law had a stated duty to be aware of companies' responsibilities to society, instead of only to investors and creditors. We return to this argument on responsibility to society in Chapter 2 and, at greater length, in Chapter 20.

In its final report the Cohen Committee stressed 'with robustness the importance of information to shareholders and society in general' (Rose 1965: 23). This sentiment was reflected in the Companies Act 1948 that required:

- Acting auditors to be registered members of a recognized accounting body. It is auditors' duty to report to shareholders on the accounts and their professionalism gave assurance to the reliability of the accounts.
- Auditors to state whether the balance sheet and income statement were in agreement with the books of the company, and that the books gave a full and fair view of the company's financial status and operating results. This requirement attempted to ensure information was not hidden, although in later chapters we will find that other techniques have been used.

- Consolidated accounts to be disclosed for the first time. Increasingly, some companies had been acquiring others. It was important therefore that shareholders received information on the finances of the group of companies by consolidating their financial statements into one group statement.

The 1948 Companies Act expanded the boundaries of financial accounting and reporting, and established the following important points:

- Limited liability encouraged investment because liability was limited to the amount invested.
- Financial statements should give a full and fair view. In other words, economic transactions and events should be fully disclosed.
- Consolidated accounts were required, thus allowing investors to understand the operations of an entire group of companies.
- A balance sheet and a profit or loss account were required. The balance sheet allowed users to assess the financial position of the company and the profit or loss account allowed users to assess the financial performance.
- Companies had a responsibility to society.
- Qualified auditors were required to examine the accounts of a company.

Since 1948, there have been several more Companies Acts, the latest being in 2006. The financial framework for regulating corporate reporting is firmly established.[3] The concept of financial statements giving a 'full and fair view', and what that means, is the basis for setting standards to determine the most appropriate accounting practices. The suggestion that companies have responsibilities to society leads on to determining the users of corporate reports and their information needs. We return in subsequent chapters to these important topics.

DEVELOPING THE REGULATORY FRAMEWORK

Generally Accepted Accounting Principles

Generally Accepted Accounting Principles

Generally Accepted Accounting Principles (GAAP) constitute the framework that determines how accountants and businesses record their economic transactions and events to produce and disclose financial statements and other corporate information. GAAP is a set of regulations with substantial authoritative support.

Generally Accepted Accounting Principles (GAAP) has three separate inputs, as shown in the Diagram 1.2 overleaf.

Company legislation

Parliament has the responsibility for passing Companies' Acts but the legislation needs to be made operational. Companies' Acts concentrate, among many other matters, on the structure, responsibilities and authority of companies. However, there is little in the legislation on the detail of financial information to be disclosed. In other words, a separate body is required to ensure the monitoring and enforcement of the legislation on a continuing basis. There must be some method for ensuring compliance with the legislation.

In the UK, the Financial Reporting Council (FRC) is the body with the prime responsibility for corporate reporting. The FRC was established in 1990 and its role has been expanded and strengthened over the years. In 2004, the UK government extended the authority of the FRC. It became the single independent regulator of the accounting and auditing profession, as well as being responsible for determining accounting standards and their enforcement.

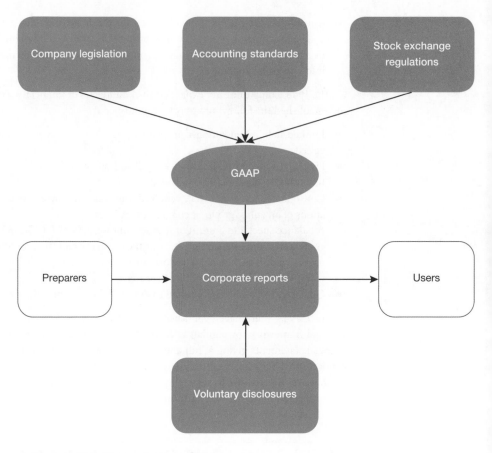

▲ **Diagram 1.2** *The application of GAAP*

The role of the FRC was strengthened further in 2012, following consultation with the Department for Business, Innovation and Skills on the improvement of its status and operations. The FRC now has responsibility for:

- Promoting high standards of corporate governance through the UK Corporate Governance Code.
- Setting standards for corporate reporting, audit and actuarial practice.
- Monitoring and enforcing accounting and auditing standards.
- Overseeing the regulatory activities of the actuarial profession and the professional accountancy bodies.
- Operating independent disciplinary arrangements for public interest cases involving accountants and actuaries.

The FRC's Board is responsible for the philosophy and overall strategy of the FRC, and for its management and culture. There are several committees and councils reporting to the Board of which the most important for our purposes are given below.

Codes & Standards Committee

This committee is responsible for advising the FRC Board on maintaining an effective framework of UK codes and standards for corporate governance, stewardship, accounting, auditing and assurance, and actuarial technical. The committee also advises on the wider regulatory framework and the FRC's research programme.

Accounting Council

The Accounting Council has responsibility for accounting standards. It reports to the Codes & Standards Committee and has the following responsibilities:

- Providing strategic input and thought leadership, both in the field of accounting and financial reporting and in the work-plan of the FRC as a whole.
- Advising the FRC Board upon draft codes and standards (or amendments thereto) to ensure that a high-quality, effective and proportionate approach is taken.
- Considering and commenting upon proposed developments in relation to international codes and standards and regulations.
- Advising on research proposals and other initiatives undertaken to inform the FRC on matters which are material to its remit and any resultant publications.

Conduct Committee

The Companies Act 2006 authorizes the Conduct Committee to ensure financial accounts and other reports, including annual reports and directors' reports, comply with the law and other relevant reporting requirements.

The Conduct Committee must follow a number of steps when it investigates a company. The Committee, if it decides that a company has not complied with the regulations, can request a company to make changes. If the company refuses, the Committee can make an application to court. The application will request a court declaration that the annual accounts of a company do not comply, or that a strategic report or a directors' report does not comply with the requirements of the 2006 Act. The court may order the directors of the company to prepare revised accounts or a revised report.

The main aim of the FRC is to contribute to trustworthy behaviour and trustworthy information. It achieves this by:

- Setting UK standards for accounting, audit and actuarial work.
- Providing guidance on narrative reporting.
- Contributing to high-quality international standards.
- Offering guidance and improvements through the work of the Financial Reporting Lab.

The FRC aims to be transparent, accountable, proportionate, consistent and targeted in its actions. To achieve these objectives, it collaborates with accounting standard setters from other countries and the International Accounting Standards Board (IASB). Importantly, it works closely with the European Financial Reporting Advisory Group (EFRAG) that advises the European Commission on International Financial Reporting Standards in Europe. Although the Companies Acts in the UK establish legislation in this country, at the time of writing the UK is a member of the EU, which has legal powers concerning corporate reporting and determines the adoption of IFRSs in member states.[4] Following the 'Brexit' (British exit) referendum result in June 2016, this is going to change, as we discuss in the next chapter.

Accounting standards

Legislation in the form of Companies Acts is not an efficient method for setting the detailed requirements for financial accounting and the disclosure of information in an entity's main financial statements. The legal process is time consuming and cumbersome. It is too slow to respond quickly to the complexity and dynamics of business activities so a more flexible and responsive system is needed to fill the void.

accounting standards

Accounting standards are the regulations issued by a recognized body setting out the rules and procedures relating to the recognition, measurement and disclosure of economic transactions and events. Either a national or an international standard-setting body issues standards. There is normally, at the national level, some mechanism to ensure that companies comply with the accounting standards.

The initial position was to leave it to accountants to determine how companies should undertake financial reporting. Unfortunately, there were problems with this approach. The accountancy profession had no central mechanism to ensure that all its members followed the same procedures and methods when preparing financial statements.

Recognizing this failure, in January 1970, the Institute of Chartered Accountants in England and Wales (ICAEW) established an Accounting Standards Steering Committee. Other accounting bodies joined the Committee in the following years.

The name of the Accounting Standards Steering Committee (ASSC) was later shortened to the Accounting Standards Committee (ASC) and its constitution was revised. Between 1970 and 1990, the ASC issued 25 Statements of Standard Accounting Practice (SSAPs), each of which dealt with a specific topic; for example, SSAP 1 *Accounting for Associated Companies* and SSAP 25 *Segmental Reporting*.

Although this system resolved weaknesses in financial accounting and reporting, it was not sufficiently robust. Its members were part-time and unpaid, and the task required greater resourcing. It required a move to a more formal process with standard setters who are independent of the professional accounting bodies and have unambiguous legal backing.[5]

On its creation in 1990, the Accounting Standards Board (ASB) adopted a number of the ASC's SSAPs, which brought them within the legal definition of **accounting standards**. From 1990, the ASB issued accounting standards under the title of Financial Reporting Standards (FRSs). This was only a change of name. Standards continued to contain directives on the recognition, measurement and disclosure of financial transactions and events.

The establishment of national standards with legal status greatly improved financial accounting and reporting. Unfortunately, the products of the standards – the financial statements – were frequently difficult to compare with those of an entity operating in another country.

In the latter half of the twentieth century, there were some highly publicized examples of very profitable entities in Europe that wanted to list shares on the New York Stock Exchange (NYSE). In order to do so, the entity had to redraft its financial statements in accordance with US GAAP. In some instances, the previously declared profit for a financial year turned into a loss, as in the famous case of Daimler Benz (Company example 1.3).

Company example 1.3

Profits at Daimler Benz?

Daimler Benz AG, a German company, wished to list its shares on the US Stock Exchange in the early 1990s. In order to do so, it had to reconcile the profit it had shown for 1993 using German GAAP with what the profit would have been if it had used US GAAP. The net income, or profit, the company had reported in its German financial statements was DM615 million.

After the company had made all the adjustments to comply with US GAAP the reported net income turned to a net loss of DM1839 million. Such a huge difference demonstrated that national accounting did not make sense when viewed at the international level. It was not acceptable to say that Daimler Benz either made a good profit or a massive loss depending on which country's regulations were used.

Examples such as Daimler Benz (see Company example 1.3) highlighted the problem, but the issue of significant differences in national accounting standards had been recognized at an earlier stage. In 1973, national accountancy bodies from Australia, Canada, France, Germany, Mexico, the Netherlands, the United Kingdom and Ireland, and the United States established the International Accounting Standards Committee (IASC) based in London, UK.

The IASC had limited resources and power. It chose a strategy of gradual harmonization of financial reporting on a worldwide basis and issued regulations in the form of International Accounting Standards (IASs). Its influence strengthened and, in 1995, the IASC embarked on an ambitious programme with the International Organization of Security Commissions (IOSCO) to issue a core set of standards.

The IASC was successful in the core standards project, but the major economies that had argued for international standards in 1973 continued to use their own national standards. To encourage the use of international standards either a complete overhaul of all aspects of the IASC or the formation of a new body was required. The latter was the course of action chosen.

International Financial Reporting Standards (IFRSs) have been a part of financial reporting in the UK since 2005 when an EU Regulation required companies to use international accounting standards where they:

- had securities in the form of either equity or debt;
- admitted to trading on a regulated market of any member state of the EU;
- issued consolidated financial statements.

In the next chapter, we discuss the workings of the IASB, the effect of IFRSs on the financial section of the corporate report and the likely consequences of Brexit. We also give an update on the seven countries that agreed to set up the IASC in 1973.

The stock exchange

stock exchange

A stock exchange is an institution, organization or association that serves as a market for trading financial instruments such as stocks, bonds and their related derivatives. Most modern stock exchanges have both a trading floor and an electronic trading system.

The London Stock Exchange (LSE), as with other **stock exchanges** around the world, has rules for companies wishing to list their shares. It has several markets, allowing different sized companies, including international ones, to list.

You must use some caution when referring to the LSE's listing rules because they clearly state: 'Please note that these listing rules are only a summary and it is important to understand that there are other 'unwritten' listing rules and requirements as well which are not published by the London Stock Exchange' (LSE 2016). However, for our purposes we need only summarize those that apply to the disclosure of financial information.

The main objective of the LSE is to ensure that corporate information that may affect a company's share price is made publicly available as soon as possible. Many of the rules are based on Directives issued by the European Parliament. We show the main rules relating to financial reporting below. Where appropriate we have added the chapter number in this book that addresses the issues.

Annual reports

- Companies must publish an audited annual report within four months of their year-end. The report must remain publicly available for at least ten years.
- European Economic Area (EEA) incorporated companies preparing consolidated accounts (Chapter 16) must comply with IFRSs as adopted in the EU. Other entities can use national GAAP (Chapter 2).
- There must be a management report providing a fair review of the issuer's business and a description of the principal risks and uncertainties facing the issuer (Chapter 20).

- There must be a responsibility statement setting out to the best of the directors' knowledge that the financial statements give a true and fair view.

Half-yearly reports (Chapter 11)

- Entities must prepare a half-yearly report within three months of the period-end, containing condensed financial statements.
- The condensed financial statements must comply with IAS 34 (Chapter 18) for EEA companies issuing consolidated accounts and national GAAP for others.
- There must be an interim management report containing an indication of important events that have occurred during the first six months of the financial year, and their impact on the condensed set of financial statements, and a description of the principal risks and uncertainties for the remaining six months of the financial year.
- There must be a responsibility statement.
- Issuers of equity shares must prepare an interim management statement (IMS) in the first and second six-month periods of a financial year.
- The IMS must be published in a period between ten weeks after the beginning, and six weeks before, the end of the relevant six-month period.
- The IMS must provide an explanation of material events and transactions that have taken place during the relevant period and their impact on the financial position of the issuer and its controlled undertakings.

Disclosure and control of inside information

Inside information:

- is not generally available;
- relates, directly or indirectly, to one or more issuers of the qualifying investments or to one or more of the qualifying investments;
- if generally available, would be likely to have a significant effect on the price of the qualifying investments or on the price of related investments;
- includes announcements that disclose an expected substantial decline in profits and are typically referred to as 'profit warnings'.

Issuers are required to disclose inside information to the market as soon as possible, except when doing so would not mislead the public and would prejudice the issuer's legitimate interests. Such interests might include negotiating an acquisition or disposal. However, issuers must then put in place controls to ensure that third parties that do become 'inside' (e.g. advisers and other parties to a deal) keep the material confidential, and that, when the matter is no longer prejudicial (or if it leaks), an announcement is made forthwith.

Corporate governance (Chapter 19)

UK incorporated companies with listed shares (or with shares traded on the Alternative Investment Market (AIM) and listed debt) must publish certain corporate governance information.

Companies must announce all of the above information to a regulatory information service (e.g., the LSE's Regulatory News Service). It must also be filed with the National Storage Mechanism – a free-to-access website operated on behalf of the United Kingdom Literacy Association (UKLA).

Most of the companies listed on the main LSE are registered in the UK, but some are registered in other countries. The non-British companies on the Exchange often have their primary listing on another exchange and a secondary listing in London.

Among the 48 Chinese companies listed on the LSE in 2016, 6 companies were listed in the main market and the other 42 were all listed in the AIM, as were several Indian companies.

BROADENING THE REPORTING AGENDA

Legislative advances

The previous sections mainly examined the regulations concerning financial accounting and reporting. If we consider the broader narrative information that companies have been legally required to provide in their annual report and accounts, there are three main documents (Chapter 20):

1 *Corporate Governance Report* explaining how the composition and organization of the entity's governance structures supports the achievement of the entity's objectives.
2 *Directors' Report* providing certain statutory and regulatory information about the company.
3 *Directors' Remuneration Report* setting out the directors' remuneration policy, how it has been implemented and the amounts awarded to directors.

In August 2013, the Government published new regulations introducing a Strategic Report. The regulations resulted in an amendment to existing company law requirements and became effective on 1 October 2013. The Strategic Report is separate from the Directors' Report, and forms part of the company's annual report and accounts.

As laid out by the FRC (*Guidance on the Strategic Report*, June 2014), the objectives of the Strategic Report are:

- To provide context for the related financial statements.
- To provide insight into the company's business model and its main objectives and strategy.
- To describe the principal risks the entity faces and how they might affect its future prospects.
- To provide an analysis of the company's past performance.
- To provide signposting to show the location of complementary information.

For many quoted companies, the Strategic Report may add significant information to their existing disclosures. The new requirements identified the following disclosures:

- A description of the company's strategy and business model.
- Information on social and community issues including human rights issues.
- Information on such issues as the gender spilt for directors, managers and employees.

The option for companies to issue a summary financial statement instead of the full annual report and accounts was withdrawn. Instead, companies can provide the strategic report with supplementary material, including the single total figure table for directors' remuneration. The change was, therefore, a move towards narrative disclosures and away from financial statement disclosures.

Company practices

The Institute of Chartered Accountants of Scotland (1988) argued that the provision of financial and appropriate non-financial information fulfils three roles for external users:

- assisting overall governance of corporations;
- allowing individuals and organizations to judge the performance of corporate management;
- aiding decision making.

▼ Table 1.1 *Growth in the annual report and accounts*

	2005		2014	
	Number of pages	Percentage of total	Number of pages	Percentage of total
Audit report	1	1	4	2
Financial statements	4	3	5	3
Notes to the accounts	39	34	48	29
Other disclosures	72	62	111	66
Total	**116**	**100**	**168**	**100**

Some 30 years after this observation, the boundaries of corporate reporting are still expanding. Gradually, companies have added a range of mainly non-financial information, both legally required and voluntarily given. We have taken ten companies listed on the Stock Exchange at random, and compared the length of their annual report and accounts in 2005 to those in 2014 (Table 1.1). The year 2005 was when public companies became legally obliged to comply with IFRSs.

Over the ten-year interval examined, the length of the annual reports increased substantially. The growth in the lengths of the audit report and financial statements are driven by regulation. Interestingly, the notes to the accounts showed an increase of 9 pages on average but, as a percentage of the total document, declined from 34% to 29%.

As one may have anticipated, the growth in the 'other disclosures' is due mainly to corporate governance requirements. In 2005, the average number of pages was 8 but by 2014 this had increased to 42 pages. It is more difficult to compare the number of pages that would come under the heading of Strategic review. The 2005 data is not collected under a single heading but we would estimate the average to be 12 pages. In 2014, the section entitled Strategic review or Strategic report averaged 36 pages.

We have analyzed the information contained in the annual report and accounts, but companies use other documents. For example, in 2013 Associated British Foods issued a separate 88-page Corporate Responsibility Report which had the themes outlined in Company example 1.4. Similar reports can be downloaded from the internet.

Company example 1.4

Associated British Foods

2013 Corporate Responsibility Report

Responsible stewardship of our environment
Being responsible for our people
Being a responsible neighbour
Being responsible for promoting good health
Working with others

Company example 1.5

WPP plc

The fast read
1   A six-minute read

Who we are
12   Our companies & associates

Why we exist
14   Our mission

Our 4 strategic priorities
16   New markets, new media, data investment management
       & application of technology, horizontality

WPP: a global company
18   Our growth markets

How we're doing
21   Financial summary
24   Strategic report to share owners

The annual report and accounts remains the main, single document. Whether printed or on the internet, many regard it as the cornerstone of corporate reporting because of the range and reliability of financial and other information. We show in Company example 1.5 the contents list of the first 24 pages of the printed 2014 Annual Report and Accounts of WPP plc. WPP plc has its main offices in London with 3,000 offices in 112 countries. It is the world's largest advertising company by revenues, and has 190,000 employees. WPP plc has received numerous awards for its annual report and accounts, which demonstrates the range and depth of information some companies disclose. Its 2014 annual report and accounts contains 248 pages.

Summary of corporate communication channels

Annual report and accounts

Requirements for the annual report and accounts are in the Companies Act 2006. The legislation requires (among many other things) the following disclosures for individual accounts:

- a balance sheet as at the last day of the financial year; and
- a profit or loss account.

Of course, the company is entitled to include in its published annual report and accounts any other information it believes will be of interest to users or will promote the company in some way. These disclosures are sometimes referred to as narrative reporting to distinguish them from the financial reports.

The directors of a quoted company must deliver to the Registrar of Companies for each financial year a copy of:

- the company's annual accounts;
- the directors' remuneration report;
- the directors' report;
- the auditor's report.

Annual general meeting

A public company must hold an annual general meeting within six months of its year-end. The main purpose of the meeting is for the directors to present the previous year's audited accounts and accompanying reports. Shareholders do not have the authority to accept or reject the accounts, but they do have the opportunity to question the directors. The business press will usually cover meetings they consider newsworthy.

Summary financial statements/Strategic report

The Companies Act 1989 introduced provisions allowing companies to issue summary financial statements. These were re-enacted in the Companies Act 2006, which gave companies the option of issuing a summary financial statement instead of the full accounts if shareholders had agreed to receive them.

The option for companies to provide summary financial statements to shareholders was withdrawn by The Companies (Receipt of Accounts and Reports) Regulations 2013. Instead, companies may provide shareholders with a strategic report, along with 'supplementary material'. The supplements include some administrative particulars, information on the auditor's report and, for quoted companies, the 'single total figure table' for directors' remuneration required by the 2013 Directors' Remuneration Regulations.

The supplementary material does not have to include any additional financial information. The consequence is that shareholders are increasingly reliant on the more narrative-style information provided in the strategic report. We discuss the strategic report in Chapter 20.

Preliminary profit announcements

In the UK, companies listed on the LSE are required to issue a preliminary statement of annual results and dividends (generally known as the preliminary announcement), without delay, after board approval. The statement then becomes a public document.

Preliminary announcements are companies' primary vehicle for the first public communication of their full-year results and year-end financial position to the markets.

Interim financial reporting

UK companies are required to issue interim financial reports at semi-annual intervals. This is unlike the USA, which requires quarterly reporting. The ASB issued a standard, IAS 34, which offered suggestions for best practice, and the FRC has since endorsed this standard. As we will discuss in Chapter 18, half-yearly reporting raises some issues regarding the timing of events and the information companies should disclose.

Corporate governance report

The Corporate Governance Code sets out good practice covering issues such as board composition and effectiveness, the role of board committees, risk management, remuneration and relations with shareholders. In 2010, the FRC issued an updated corporate governance code for UK companies. We discuss corporate governance in Chapter 19.

Regulatory News Service

The LSE has a Regulatory News Service which provides detailed market information for companies and investors. Originally a twice-weekly paper publication, it is now distributed online and covers a wide range of corporate information.

Employee reporting

Distributing non-statutory financial reports to all employees is a voluntary practice adopted by some companies. Companies in the US started the practice early in the twentieth century, and there was increased interest in the late 1930s and early 1940s (Lewis et al. 1982).

In the 1950s, the UK Board of Trade was encouraged by US counterpart funds to ask the British Institute of Management (BIM) to undertake an investigation into the disclosure of financial information to employees. Given US practices, the experiences of some UK companies, the progressive approach of the Companies Act 1948 and changes in society, it was not surprising that the BIM report had no hesitation in lauding financial disclosure to employees (BIM 1957).

The practice of a printed financial report for employees was very popular in the 1960s and 1970s.[6] Companies' enthusiasm has apparently declined, possibly partly because of the availability of corporate information on their websites.

Press releases

Companies issue press releases for a number of reasons; some to comply with the Stock Exchange requirement for the timely announcement of price-sensitive information, others to put in the public domain the activities of the company. WPP's contents page (Company example 1.5) notes that news releases are available on its website, and an extract from one of many is given in Company example 1.6.

Company example 1.6

WPP Digital launches Polestar in China
24 September 2014

New Joint Company to provide integrated solutions in country's fast-growing e-commerce space

SHANGHAI — WPP Ventures, the investment division of WPP Digital, announces the launch of a new joint company in China, Polestar Co. Ltd., a start-up company offering integrated e-commerce solutions in China's booming e-commerce sector.

WPP Digital takes a minority stake in Polestar. The new company will be led by its principal investors – founder, Figo Yang, who will serve as CEO, and Allen Liu, COO. Both are successful entrepreneurs who bring together years of e-commerce expertise gained at Alibaba, Netease, Yahoo!, HP and UTC. Yang was also a founder of Wang Cang, China's first company to automate and systematize critical warehousing operations in the e-commerce sector.

China's e-commerce market is the world's largest, having surpassed the US in 2013, with Chinese online shoppers forecast to spend RMB3.3 trillion in 2015 (US$540 billion), according to Bain & Co. Despite the country's fast-growing e-commerce sector, China lacks companies that currently provide integrated e-commerce solutions.

http://www.wpp.com/wpp/investor/financialnews/2014/sep/24/
wpp-digital-launches-polestar-in-china/ (accessed 7 September 2016)

Analysts' briefings

Listed companies hold meetings with analysts that correspond with the release of financial results, providing opportunities for questions. They also hold briefings that give updates on business activities. There is clearly a danger that the information disclosed could be price sensitive and the Stock Exchange has regulations for the timing of these briefings. Company example 1.7 is taken from a Regulatory News Service notice for Greene King plc.

Company example 1.7

GREENE KING plc

01 May 2014

NOTICE OF ANALYST BRIEFING

Greene King plc will be presenting a business update to sell-side analysts today at 1100. The presentations will include an update on our strategy and will be available to download from the company website at 1200.

Many companies make the details of the analysts' briefings, presentation slides and notes available on their websites.

Internet reporting

The internet has brought about an explosion in communications by companies. Not only is legally required information disclosed, but a range of material of possible interest to external audiences is provided. The range of disclosures is now so extensive that we discuss internet reporting in detail in Chapter 21.

NOTES

1 There is an immense amount of literature on the subject. A detailed and authoritative source is *The Secret History of the South Sea Bubble: The World's First Great Financial Scandal* (2003) by Malcolm Balen. A much shorter and very readable description is an article 'The South Sea Bubble' by John Gill in the *Chartered Accountants Journal* (New Zealand), October 2010, pp. 46–47.

2 All limited companies in England, Wales, Northern Ireland and Scotland are now registered at Companies House. There are more than 3 million limited companies registered in the UK, and more than 400,000 new companies are incorporated each year.

3 Napier (1993) provides a useful summary of the development of company legislation.

4 *The FRC and its Regulatory Approach* (January 2014) provides details of the structure and operations of the FRC.

5 Financial Reporting Council (2012) *Financial Reporting Standard 100: Application of Financial Reporting Requirements* (November).

6 The history and practice of employee reporting is described in R. Hussey and A. Marsh (1983) *Disclosure of Information and Employee Reporting*, Gower.

CONCLUSIONS

Cases of fraud and doubtful practices by companies, and the legislative response of disclosure of financial information led to the beginning of corporate reporting. Starting in the mid-nineteenth century, a succession of Companies Acts compelled companies to publish, first a balance sheet, and many years later a profit or loss account. In the early years, the information value of these statements was debatable.

It was not until the Companies Act 1948 that there was a robust commitment to disclosure of financial information. This was a focal stage in corporate reporting and the following concepts were established:

- Limited liability companies.
- Financial statements giving a full and fair view.
- Consolidated accounts.
- A balance sheet and a profit or loss account.
- Companies having a responsibility to society at large.

- Qualified auditors required to examine the accounts of a company.

The most recent Companies Act was enacted in 2006 and the application of this legislation is the remit of the Financial Reporting Council. Recent legislation has broadened the information that companies should disclose publicly. Much of this information is in a narrative form and introduces issues such as a company's strategy and corporate governance. We discuss these disclosures in later chapters.

Financial disclosures were the kick-start for corporate reporting and remain an essential and important element. In the next chapter, we explain the procedures for ensuring the reliability of the financial information issued by listed companies, and we discuss the conceptual and practical issues that confront those attempting to set standards for financial accounting and reporting.

ADDITIONAL RESOURCES

Go online to the companion website for this book to access further teaching and learning materials for this chapter.
www.palgravehighered.com/hussey-cfr

LEARNING OBJECTIVES

At the end of this chapter, you should be able to:

- Describe the role of the Financial Reporting Council
- Discuss standard setting at the international level
- Explain the importance of a conceptual framework
- Identify and evaluate proposals in the 2015 Exposure Draft on the Conceptual Framework
- Discuss terms in the conceptual framework that are difficult to define

INTRODUCTION

financial reporting

Financial reporting is the communication of the financial information
of the entity's business activities
to external users. The communication is usually in the form of
structured financial statements
accompanied by notes.

In this chapter, we concentrate only on **financial reporting** and leave other
forms of corporate reporting until later chapters. In many countries, the regulation of financial accounting and reporting operates at two levels. At the national level, the government sets the broad framework, including the way that
accounting standards are set. At the international level, the International Accounting Standards Board (IASB) is responsible for setting detailed accounting standards. By 2016, more than 140 jurisdictions had adopted international
standards, and that number is expanding.

In the first section of this chapter, we look at the legal structure in the UK
and the Republic of Ireland. This involves deciding which types of entities are
required to follow International Financial Reporting Standards (IFRSs), those that can choose
to do so, and what others must do. The European Union (EU) made the decision to adopt
IFRSs from 2005. Because the UK is part of the EU, it complies with the EU's decision, although this will change as and when the UK's 2016 decision to leave the EU is implemented.

The second section of the chapter looks at the international position for setting accounting
standards. We discuss the role and structure of the IASB and the IFRSs it issues. We put the

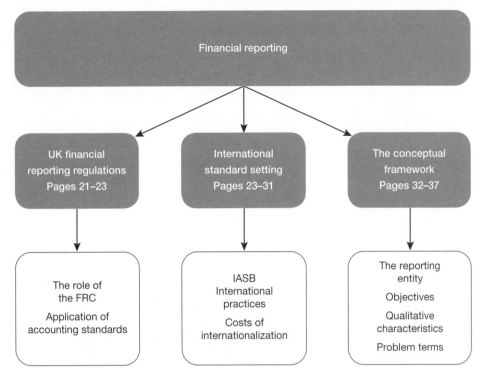

▲ Diagram 2.1 *Structure of Chapter 2*

international accounting dimension in context by explaining accounting practices in Australia, Canada, Mexico and the US. We also comment on practices in some other countries.

The third section expands on some of the issues we discussed in Chapter 1. We analyze the standard setters' struggle to establish concepts that will help them to determine how to account for economic transactions and events. If standards are to ensure that the disclosure of the financial information is of value to the user, there must be some basis from which to draw. The basis which the standard setters aim to establish is the Conceptual Framework (CF).

The final section of this chapter analyzes four terms that cause considerable difficulties to standard setters and entities: stewardship, true and fair view, prudence and going concern. We cannot give complete and specific definitions of these terms because various accounting bodies are still debating the meanings, but we do explain their importance to financial accounting and reporting.

UK FINANCIAL REPORTING REGULATIONS

The role of the FRC

From 2012 to 2014, the Financial Reporting Council (FRC) revised financial accounting and reporting standards in the UK and Republic of Ireland. It introduced substantial changes that came into effect in January 2015.

The FRC has responsibility for financial accounting and reporting by all types of limited liability companies. In this book, we concentrate on public limited companies listed on a stock exchange. In many countries, these companies follow IFRSs.

Countries that have adopted IFRSs for their large companies can decide the regulations for smaller companies. Smaller companies have two options.

1   The IASB's International Financial Reporting Standard for small and medium-sized entities (IFRS for SMEs), issued in 2009. This is one comprehensive standard of less than 250 pages. The IASB's objective was to meet the needs and capabilities of small and medium-sized entities (SMEs) which are estimated to account for over 95 per cent of all companies around the world.
2   The standards set in their own country for smaller entities. In the UK, this is the Financial Reporting Standard for Smaller Entities (FRSSE)

Application of accounting standards

Diagram 2.2 shows the regulations introduced by the FRC. It also issued FRS 104 *Interim Financial Reporting* and FRS 105 *Financial Reporting Standard applicable to the Micro-entities Regime*. Our interest is in FRS 100 and FRS 102.

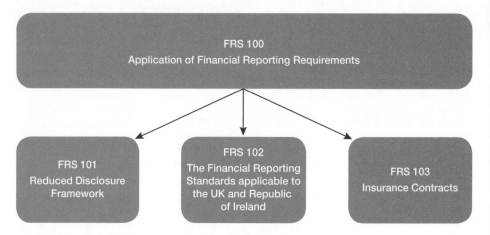

▲ Diagram 2.2 *FRC financial reporting requirements*

FRS 100 Application of Financial Reporting Requirements

This standard, effective from 1 January 2015, sets out the financial reporting regime for UK entities. It explains which standards apply to which entity, when an entity can apply the reduced disclosure framework, and when an entity should follow a Statement of Recommended Practice (SORP).

SORPs are recommendations for specialized industries, sectors or areas of work. They can also provide guidance if there are special factors or transactions that are not adequately covered in an accounting standard issued by the FRC. Our own interests do not include SORPs, and they will not be discussed further in this book.

The requirements of FRS 100 are:

1   If the financial statements are those of an entity that is eligible to apply the FRSSE, they may be prepared in accordance with that standard.
2   If the financial statements are those of an entity that is not eligible to apply the FRSSE, or of an entity that is eligible to apply the FRSSE but chooses not to do so, they must be prepared in accordance with one of the following:

- o EU-adopted IFRSs;
- o FRS 101 if the financial statements are the individual financial statements of a qualifying entity;
- o FRS 102.

FRSSE came into force in 1997 and the latest revision was in 2015. An EU Accounting Directive led the FRC to issue proposals to amend UK and Irish accounting standards. These changes affected 1.5 million of the smallest companies by simplifying their reporting requirements. Listed groups should find that there is greater flexibility and efficiency in reporting formats. The proposals were effective for financial periods beginning on or after 1 January 2016.

FRS 101 Reduced Disclosure Framework

This standard permits groups that report under EU-adopted IFRS to have their subsidiaries report under the same recognition and measurement regulations, but without all the disclosures required by the EU-endorsed IFRS. This standard only applies to 'qualifying entities'. In order to qualify, an entity must be a member of a group for which the parent company prepares publicly available consolidated financial statements intended to give a true and fair view and the entity is included in the consolidation. FRS 101 cannot be applied to any consolidated financial statements.

FRS 102 Financial Reporting Standard applicable in the UK and Republic of Ireland

This standard became mandatory for accounting periods commencing on or after 1 January 2015. FRS 102 is a single reporting standard of 350 pages, which replaced most of the FRSs and other instruments that formed the previous regulations.

FRS 102 draws from the IASB's standard, the IFRS for SMEs. However, it amends significantly the text of the IASB's standard. The most important differences are that:

- enterprises must comply with the Entities Act UK legislation;
- the standard permits additional accounting policy choices.

Entities listed on the London Stock Exchange or Alternative Investment Market (AIM) and issuing consolidated financial statements must follow IFRSs as adopted by the EU. We concentrate on these entities in this book.

The entities listed below may, if they wish, opt to follow IFRSs as adopted by the EU:

- listed entities – individual financial statements;
- AIM entities – individual financial statements;
- unlisted group – consolidated financial statements;
- unlisted entities – individual financial statements.

INTERNATIONAL STANDARD SETTING

International Accounting Standards Board (IASB)

The International Accounting Standards Board succeeded the IASC in April 2001, with greater funding and a reorganized structure. It 'adopted' the IASs issued by the IASC and commenced issuing its own standards entitled International Financial Reporting Standards (IFRSs). On page xviii, we have listed all the standards, both IASs and IFRSs, which were in force in 2016.

The IASB's role is a technical one of setting standards. It has no authority to compel entities to adopt standards, to monitor their compliance or to take action to remedy practices with which it disagrees. National governments determine whether they will adopt IFRSs and to what extent.

Some examples of the limits on the IASB's authority include:

1 It cannot compel companies or countries to adopt IFRS.
2 If a country adopts IFRSs, the IASB cannot determine the type of companies to which IFRSs should apply.
3 It cannot prevent countries amending IFRSs to meet their own needs.
4 It cannot dictate the contents of corporate reports – it can only set standards.
5 The IASB has no enforcement powers.

Diagram 2.3 illustrates the international standard-setting structure.

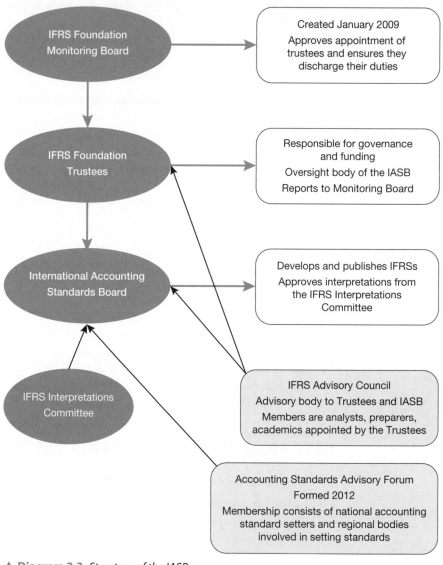

▲ Diagram 2.3 *Structure of the IASB*

The role of the IFRS Interpretations Committee (IFRIC) is a crucial one.[1] It examines newly identified financial reporting issues that are not specifically dealt with in IFRSs, and issues where unsatisfactory or conflicting interpretations have developed, or seem likely to develop in the absence of authoritative guidance. IFRIC interpretations are subject to IASB approval and have the same authority as a standard issued by the IASB.

Not all of the issues brought to IFRIC will lead to an interpretation. The Committee may decide to pass the issue to the IASB or conclude that the standard does not require any interpretation. The Committee does not give advice to individual entities and firms of accountants who may have difficulties in understanding a particular standard.

The development of an IFRS is a lengthy process and follows the sequence depicted in Diagram 2.4. This is an exhaustive, time-consuming process. Once issued, standards may be revised if there are changes in business practices or deficiencies in the standard. If the issues are extensive, the existing standard may be withdrawn and replaced with a new standard with a new IFRS number. In addition to these major changes, the IASB annually conducts an improvement project, which may make minor changes to some standards.

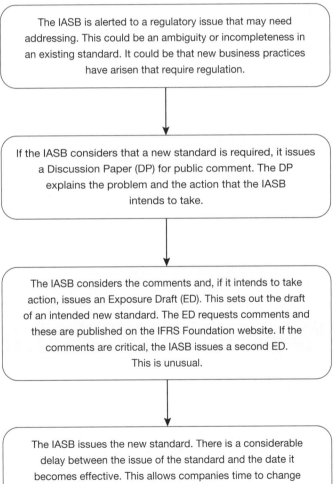

▲ **Diagram 2.4** *Developing an IFRS*

International practices

Practices in using IFRSs at the international level vary. There is a mixture ranging from full adoption of IFRSs, through partial adoption to no adoption.[2] If you are uncertain whether a specific company is using IFRSs, you should check by reading the auditor's report. This will clearly state whether the financial statements are IFRS compliant.

The extract in Company example 2.1 states that the financial statements are in accordance with IFRSs. It also confirms the company's compliance with the regulations in which the country was incorporated. Aluminium Bahrain B.S.C. (Alba) is one of the largest and most modern aluminium smelters in the world, employing over 2,900 people.

Company example 2.1

Extract from Auditor's Report

Opinion

In our opinion, the financial statements present fairly, in all material respects, the financial position of the Company as of 31 December 2015 and its financial performance and its cash flows for the year then ended in accordance with International Financial Reporting Standards.

Report on other regulatory requirements

As required by the Bahrain Commercial Companies Law we report that:

(a) the Company has maintained proper accounting records and the financial statements are in agreement therewith; and

(b) the financial information contained in the Report of the Board of Directors is consistent with the financial statements.

We are not aware of any violations of the Bahrain Commercial Companies Law, the Central Bank of Bahrain (CBB) Rule Book (applicable provisions of Volume 6) and CBB directives, regulations and associated resolutions, rules and procedures of the Bahrain Bourse or the terms of the Company's memorandum and articles of association during the year ended 31 December 2015 that might have had a material adverse effect on the business of the Company or on its financial position. Satisfactory explanations and information have been provided to us by the management in response to all our requests.

Aluminium Bahrain B.S.C., Annual Report, 2015, p. 35.

This book uses as its main example the UK experience in complying with international standards. As the adoption of international standards took place at the European level, all member states of the EU should comply with international standards. However, it is usually only the larger companies listed on a stock exchange that uses IFRSs.

We take the UK as representative of EU international accounting practices, but also give the examples of four non-European countries: Australia, Canada, Mexico and the United States. All were present at the meeting in 1973 that agreed to establish international accounting. Australia and Canada have adopted IFRSs, and we use examples from some of their entities in subsequent chapters. We also consider the position of the United States that has not adopted IFRSs, and the practices in some other major countries.

Australia

The Institute of Chartered Accountants first issued its Recommendations on Accounting Principles in 1946. It is argued that 'these were virtually copies of similarly titled documents produced by the Institute of Chartered Accountants in England and Wales' (Walker 1987: 269). Possibly this similarity helped Australia to transfer to IFRSs.

Currently, the Australian Accounting Standards Board (AASB) issues accounting standards. The AASB is an Australian government agency that develops and maintains financial reporting standards that legally apply to entities in the private and public sectors of the economy.

When the AASB first started to adopt IFRSs as Australian Accounting Standards, it made some modifications. This resulted in the removal of some alternative accounting methods and the addition of required disclosures for the financial statements.

In 2007, the AASB modified Australian Accounting Standards so that their requirements were identical to international standards with some additional disclosures. Compliance with Australian Accounting Standards ensures that the financial statements and notes of the entity comply with IFRSs.

Company example 2.2 is an extract from Wesfarmers Limited Annual Report 2014, and shows how Australian entities comply with national and international requirements.

Company example 2.2

Opinion

In our opinion:

a. the financial report of Wesfarmers Limited is in accordance with the *Corporations Act 2001*, including:

  i.   giving a true and fair view of the consolidated entity's financial position as at 30 June 2014 and of its performance for the year ended on that date; and

  ii. complying with Australian Accounting Standards and the *Corporations Regulations 2001*; and

b. the financial report also complies with *International Financial Reporting Standards* as disclosed in the Notes to the financial statements.

Wesfarmers, Extract from Independent Auditor's Report, 2014, p. 148

Canada

Prior to 1946, there were no accounting regulations. The Canadian Institute of Chartered Accountants (CICA) commenced issuing bulletins that codified existing practice largely as a service to its members.

In 1967, the bulletins appeared in the form of an official handbook. In 1975, revisions to the Canada Business Corporations Act specified that GAAP in Canada were the practices and guidance within the CICA Handbook.

The period of 1981–1998 was an unusual one in Canada when two competing standard-setting bodies existed: the Canadian Institute of Chartered Accountants and the newer Accounting Standards Authority of Canada. It is contended that the 'alternative standard-setter, the Accounting Standards Authority of Canada, experienced significant implementation issues and was unable to overcome advantages accruing to the CICA by virtue of locked-in users, first mover advantage and reputation advantage' (Richardson 2011: 110–111). It may be that other countries experience similar implementation issues if they are attempting to adopt IFRSs.

The CICA established The Accounting Standards Oversight Council (AcSOC) in 2000. The role of AcSOC is to serve the public interest by overseeing and providing input to the activities of the Accounting Standards Board (AcSB) which is responsible for establishing standards of accounting and reporting by Canadian entities and not-for-profit organizations.

In January 2006, the AcSB published a strategic plan to implement IFRSs. These have been mandatory in Canada since 2011 for publicly accountable enterprises. The application of IFRSs in Canada, therefore, is broader than in Europe because it applies to many more types of entities.

Publicly accountable enterprises are profit-orientated enterprises that have responsibilities to a large or diverse group of stakeholders, and include:

- publicly listed entities;
- enterprises with fiduciary responsibilities, such as banks, insurance entities, credit unions, securities firms, mutual funds and investment banks;
- certain government corporations.

Several Canadian entities have listed on US stock exchanges for many years. The regulations provide an option to those entities to apply US GAAP rather than Canadian GAAP.

Certain entities in Canada known as rate-regulated entities had some technical difficulties in complying with IFRSs. The issue of IFRS 14 Regulatory Deferred Accounts resolved the issues and compliance with IFRSs commenced for annual periods beginning on or after 1 January 2015.

As with Australia, the evidence of compliance with IFRSs is in the auditor's report. Company example 2.3 is from a large Canadian company.

Company example 2.3

Opinion

In our opinion, the consolidated financial statements present fairly, in all material respects, the consolidated financial position of Empire Company Limited as at May 3, 2014 and May 4, 2013, and its consolidated financial performance and its consolidated cash flows for the 52 week fiscal years then ended, in accordance with International Financial Reporting Standards.

Empire Company Limited, Extract from Independent Auditor's Report, 2013, p. 70

The UK from the European perspective

The consolidated financial statements of UK-listed entities must be prepared in accordance with 'EU-adopted International Financial Reporting Standards'. The procedure for adoption (or endorsement) of a new standard is:

- The European Financial Reporting Advisory Group (EFRAG) holds consultations, examines the potential impact and advises the Commission on endorsement.

- The Commission drafts an endorsement regulation.
- The Accounting Regulatory Committee (ARC), which comprises government representatives from each of the member states, votes and gives an opinion.
- The European Parliament and Council examine the standard.
- The Commission adopts the standard and publishes it in the Official Journal of the European Union.

In assessing whether the EU should adopt a particular IFRS, the regulation requires that it:

- be consistent with the true and fair view;
- be conducive to the public good in Europe;
- meet basic criteria on the quality of information required for financial statements to satisfy users' needs.

The time to review and adopt a new standard is lengthy. However, the only difference between IFRSs and EU-adopted IFRSs has been a 'carve-out' of a few sentences in IAS 39 that barred the use of a form of hedge accounting applied by a minority of European banks.

Company example 2.4 shows an extract of the independent auditor's report in the annual report and accounts of Burberry Group plc.

Company example 2.4

Our opinion

In our opinion the Group financial statements:

- give a true and fair view of the state of the Group's affairs as at 31 March 2014 and of the Group's profit and cash flows for the year then ended;
- have been properly prepared in accordance with International Financial Reporting Standards (IFRSs) as adopted by the European Union; and
- have been prepared in accordance with the requirements of the Companies Act 2006 and Article 4 of the IAS Regulation.

This opinion is to be read in the context of what we say in the remainder of this report.

Burberry Group plc, Annual Report and Accounts,
Independent Auditor's Report, 2014, p. 111

The UK outside the EU

In a referendum in 2016, the populations of the United Kingdom of Great Britain, which consists of England, Scotland, Wales, and Northern Ireland, voted to leave the EU. The EU consists of 28 countries that operate as one economic and political group.

The UK's decision to leave the EU has political and economic consequences. Understandably, in the immediate aftermath of the referendum there was considerable volatility on the share markets amid warnings of economic collapse. These events and predictions were worrying but they have no immediate impact on setting accounting regulations. They may, however, have an impact on a company's financial statements, and we discuss the issues in Chapter 21.

The 2016 referendum result did not mean that the UK immediately left the EU. However, it did give the Prime Minister the right to invoke Article 50 of the Treaty of Lisbon, which is the legal basis for the EU.

The process of invoking Article 50 and negotiating the terms of the UK's exit from the EU is likely to take several years. During that period, the UK will continue to apply the same accounting standards as the EU. We do not, therefore, expect to see any changes to current practices in the near future. If the UK does eventually leave the EU there will be political and economic consequences, and, as far as corporate financial reporting is concerned, we discuss these in Chapter 21.

Mexico

In 2009, the Mexican Banking and Securities Commission (Comisión Nacional Bancaria y de Valores, or CNBV) amended the country's securities and exchange laws to make the use of IFRSs mandatory for listed companies. The only exception to this is financial institutions.

The commencement date was 2012, after which financial statements had to be audited under International Standards on Auditing instead of Mexican Auditing Standards.

United States

The stock market collapse in 1929 destroyed public confidence in the financial markets. Congress decided that the best way to restore confidence was to establish the Securities and Exchange Commission (SEC).

The SEC ensures that entities publicly offering securities to investors must disclose to the public the truth about their businesses, the securities they are selling, and the risks involved in investing. To achieve this, the SEC requires public entities to disclose meaningful financial and other information to the public.

The Financial Accounting Standards Board (FASB) originated in 1973. It is answerable to the SEC and has the responsibility of acting in the interests of financial statement users. It is the standard setter.

The FASB Accounting Standards Codification is the official source of authoritative, non-governmental US generally accepted accounting principles (US GAAP). The Codification does not change US GAAP but orders and structures thousands of pronouncements issued by the FASB, the AICPA, and other standard-setting bodies into approximately 90 accounting topics. It also includes relevant SEC guidance that follows the same topical structure in separate sections in the Codification. New additions to US GAAP are issued by means of a FASB document called an Accounting Standards Update (ASU)

In August 1991, the FASB published its plan for international activities, and in 2002, the FASB and the IASB signed the Norwalk Agreement whose objective was the convergence of US and international standards.[2]

The two parties worked successfully for several years on joint projects. IFRSs and those of the FASB were, on a one-by-one basis, gradually converged. This does not mean that the US adopted IFRSs. It retained its own standards but amended them to agree with the converged international standard.

As the years progressed, so total agreement on each standard became harder to achieve. A comparison of international standards and US standards showed that there were similarities, but some differences remained. In 2012, it was evident that the relationship was not working, and the two parties reverted to developing their accounting standards separately. The search for convergence ended and the US decided to follow its own course. It will retain an international presence but the emphasis is on satisfying the needs of its domestic market.[3]

China

The Accounting Regulatory Department of the Ministry of Finance of China is the official standard setter in that country. In February 2006, the Chinese Accounting Standards for Business Enterprises (ASBEs) were substantially converged with international standards. At the end of 2015, the Chinese Ministry of Finance and the IFRS Foundation agreed to work jointly towards the greater use of IFRS standards in China. This was particularly relevant for internationally orientated Chinese companies.

Currently, domestic companies cannot use IFRSs but must use ASBEs. A limited number of Chinese companies use IFRSs because they trade on the stock exchanges in Europe, Hong Kong and the US. Foreign companies currently do not trade on Chinese markets so the use of IFRSs does not apply to them.

India

India has confronted some difficulties in adopting IFRSs. The intention was to use a phased approach to converge with IFRSs, beginning in 2011. The burden of the change placed on entities and the accounting profession proved to be too great, and the decision was made to delay the transition.

The Indian Ministry of Corporate Affairs (MCA) released a roadmap with a series of requirements depending on the net worth of companies. From 1 April 2016 companies over a certain size had to comply with Indian Accounting Standards (Ind AS). These are substantially, but not totally, converged with IFRSs. From 1 April 2017, the same requirements apply to smaller companies that are listed or are in the process of being listed. Banks, insurance and non-banking finance companies will follow a phased approach, with Ind AS adoption beginning on 1 April 2018.

Costs of internationalization

Setting accounting standards at the national level is expensive. For many smaller jurisdictions, the ability to use standards set by the IASB can represent a cost saving. For larger countries, there may be a reduction in the expense of setting their own standards, but there can be a cost for the individual entities.

A survey of publicly traded Australian entities concluded that there was an increase of audit costs in the year of the transition to IFRSs (De George et al. 2013). Further investigations revealed that entities with greater audit complexity experience greater increases in compliance costs for the transition to IFRSs

Experiences in Canada support the findings in Australia. A survey by the Canadian Financial Executives Research Foundation (CFERF) (2013) examined the transition costs and the recurring costs. The average total transition cost for larger-sized entities was Can$4,041,177. The lowest amount spent by a large company was Can$80,000 and the highest cost was Can$25.5 million. The significance of the cost can be gauged by a comparison to revenue: costs as a percentage of revenues were 0.006% for the lowest spender and 0.08% for the highest spender.

The experiences of Australia and Canada do not necessarily represent the experiences of other countries. If a country, on adoption of IFRSs, has to make substantial changes to its regulations then significant costs are to be expected. In addition, if the adoption of IFRSs requires much fuller disclosures of financial information to the users, an increased cost is likely to arise.

There is also a further factor at the country level. It is likely that on adoption of IFRSs the national standard-setting process will end, meaning that a large cost burden will be relieved and transferred to the international level. In 2015, the IFRS received total contributions of £21,302,000 to support its activities, confirming that standard setting at any level is expensive.[5]

THE CONCEPTUAL FRAMEWORK (CF)

Conceptual Framework

The Conceptual Framework has the primary purpose of assisting the IASB in setting and revising accounting standards by identifying the concepts that underlie the preparation and presentation of financial statements.

Based on Exposure Draft ED/2015/3, 2015

The search at the international level for a **Conceptual Framework** (CF) has been long and exhausting, and is continuing at the time of writing.[6] The benefits of a CF are that it helps:

- the IASB to develop and revise standards;
- preparers to understand standards and develop their own consistent accounting policies;
- users to understand and interpret financial statements.

In other words, all those involved in financial accounting and reporting have sound and consistent guidance from a CF.

The International Accounting Standards Committee (IASC) published its *IASC Framework for the Preparation and Presentation of Financial Statements* in 1989, and it was adopted by the IASB in 2001 on assuming the role of the IASC.

In the US, part of the agreement between the FASB and the IASB to converge their standards involved a joint project to construct a new conceptual framework. The two Boards, not having achieved agreement, deferred the project in 2010. In 2012, the IASB commenced its own revision of the 1989 framework.

The Exposure Draft (ED) issued by the IASB in 2015 is a lengthy document. In this chapter, we explain three key terms that set the scene for our discussions in subsequent chapters:

- *reporting entity* (Chapter 3 of the Exposure Draft);
- *objectives of general purpose financial reporting* (Chapter 1 of the Exposure Draft);
- *qualitative characteristics of useful financial information* (Chapter 2 of the Exposure Draft).

After our discussion of the above three terms, we identify some specific words that are causing particular problems because there are difficulties in reaching agreement as to their meaning and their application. These are not merely academic discussions, but issues that determine the financial information disclosed by companies.

Reporting entity

reporting entity

A reporting entity is an entity that chooses, or is required, to prepare general purpose financial statements. A reporting entity is not necessarily a legal entity. It can comprise a portion of an entity, or two or more entities.

Based on IASB Exposure Draft ED/2015/3, 2015, paras 3.11 and 3.12

The importance of the ED definition is that parts of an entity or two or more entities can be **reporting entities**, even if they are not legal entities. This broad definition captures those 'entities' that some companies formed in the past to obscure their performance by not having to report to stakeholders.

In this book we examine general purpose financial statements which are not specific to any particular purpose or the narrow needs of any one group of users. Their purpose is to disclose financial information that is useful to existing and potential investors, lenders and other creditors in making decisions about providing resources to the entity.

In considering general purpose financial statements, we are examining the most highly regulated and highly technical part of corporate reporting. At the end of this chapter, we introduce the main financial statements. Chapters 4 to 18 explain in detail the international accounting requirements.

Objectives of financial statements

objectives

The objective of general purpose financial reporting is to provide financial information about the reporting entity that is useful to existing and potential investors, lenders and other creditors in making decisions about providing resources to the entity. Those decisions involve buying, selling or holding equity and debt instruments, and providing or settling loans and other forms of credit.

IASB Exposure Draft ED/2015/3, 2015, p. 22

Although the definition of **objectives** has clarity, some would dispute it. They would argue, first, about the anonymity in the term 'reporting entity'. The IASB can fit many different types of organization under this definition. Mainly, we are interested in large companies with thousands of employees, producing goods and services for a large section of the population. Their activities have a substantial impact on society, the economy and the environment, and these companies wield considerable powers. Understandably, some users are particularly interested in the role in society of these reporting entities and their financial activities.

The second criticism relates to the limited range of users and their reasons for requiring the information. This dispute has been with us for many years. The IASB's opinion is that users are existing and potential investors, lenders and other creditors who will use the information in making decisions about providing resources to the entity. Others claim that the significance of large companies in society leads to other groups being very interested in their activities. The growth from financial reporting to corporate reporting is evidence of that interest.

The ED's emphasis is on general purpose financial statements. These cannot provide all of the information needs of the users it identifies. Consequently, those users, and others, will have to obtain relevant information from other sources. In Chapter 20, we identify such sources.

The ED makes clear that the reporting entity can include any additional information it wishes. This explains the expansion of information in the annual report and accounts, both required by legislation and voluntarily provided by companies.

The financial statements and the accompanying notes now do not take up the most pages of the annual report and accounts. There are legal requirements for companies to disclose strategy, business models and corporate governance practices. In recent years, we have seen the development of a document – the annual report and accounts – that is concerned with wider corporate reporting. In Chapters 20 and 21, we explain these developments.

Qualitative characteristics of financial information

There are two fundamental qualitative characteristics: relevance and faithful representation. The characteristic of relevance has two aspects, and we illustrate the fundamental characteristics in Diagram 2.5 overleaf.

Diagram 2.5 is only an introduction to the discussions in the ED. There may be changes before the publication of the final document. Materiality, in particular, has resulted in strong debate. We review the issues regarding the definition of materiality in the next chapter.

In addition to fundamental characteristics, there are other qualitative characteristics that enhance the usefulness of financial information:

- *Comparability* enables users to identify and understand similarities in, and differences among, items.
- *Verifiability* helps assure users that information faithfully represents the economic phenomena it purports to represent.
- *Timeliness* means having information available to decision-makers in time to be capable of influencing their decisions.
- *Understandability* is achieved by classifying, characterizing and presenting information clearly and concisely.

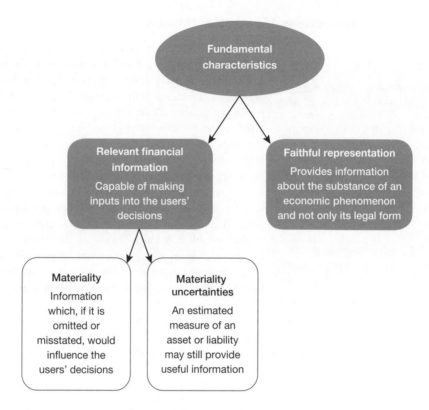

▲ **Diagram 2.5** *Fundamental characteristics of financial information*

Problem terms

In accounting, there are words and terms whose meaning is not immediately clear, ambiguous or even controversial. We briefly explain four of these. Both the IASB and the FRC either have issued or will be issuing their thoughts on these terms and others.

Stewardship

The word 'stewardship' is not in common usage internationally but, generally, can be taken to mean 'responsibility'. The IASB puts forward the view that information can help users to assess management's stewardship of the reporting entity's economic resources. These are reflected in the ED for the CF, which states that financial information assists users on:

- the nature and amounts of a reporting entity's economic resources and claims;
- the reporting entity's financial strengths and weaknesses.

True and fair view

The FRC (2014d) has issued its views on true and fair because this is not a concept shared by every country in relation to financial statements. The FRC argues that both UK and EU law require company accounts to give a true and fair view. The CF uses the term 'fair presentation'. The FRC opinion is that this is equivalent to a true and fair view.

This is a conceptually difficult area. Our interpretation is that, in complying completely with an accounting standard, an entity may produce financial statements that do not provide a full picture of the situation. In these circumstances, the company can depart from the detailed requirements of the standard to give a 'true and fair view'. This would be extremely unusual but the EU retains this concept.

The concept of true and fair is not restricted to EU countries. Company example 2.5 is taken from the annual report and accounts of an Indian company. Essar was founded in 1969. It was India's first private company to buy an oil tanker in 1976, and has since invested in a diverse shipping fleet and oil rigs. In the 1990s, it diversified its shipping fleet, started oil and gas exploration and production, laid the foundation of its oil refinery at Vadinar in Gujarat, and set up a power plant near the steel complex in Hazira. It has continued to consolidate and grow its businesses on a global basis.

Company example 2.5

True and fair view

In our opinion and to the best of our information and according to the explanations given to us, the aforesaid financial statements give the information required by the Act in the manner so required and further to the matters described in paragraph 8 below give a true and fair view in conformity with the accounting principles generally accepted in India, of the state of affairs of the Company as at March 31, 2015, and its profit and its cash flows for the year ended on that date.

Essar Oil Limited, Annual Report, 2015, p. 67

Prudence

The IASB's original discussion paper did not use the term 'prudence' but, based on the comments it received, the IASB has made it clear that it will include the term in the final document.

Some argue that, if the financial information is prepared so that it is 'neutral', then there is no need for the concept of 'prudence'. Others disagree, presumably holding the opinion that directors may be overly optimistic in making their estimates and assumptions at the year-end.

The FRC is a strong advocate of prudence and has stated its views very clearly. Most likely, it will be defined as 'caution when making judgements under conditions of uncertainty' and advocated as an important tool for achieving neutrality.

Going concern

When we scrutinize financial statements, we assume that they are prepared on the basis that the reporting entity is a going concern; in other words, the entity will continue in operation for the foreseeable future. If we believed that an entity was about to become bankrupt, we may change our conclusion of the information in the financial statements.

The concept has been in force for many years and was included in the 1989 CF. However, the FRC argued that the wording in later CFs had become much weaker than in the original framework. In April 2016, the FRC issued guidance for directors of companies that brings together the requirements of company law, accounting standards, auditing standards, other regulations and existing FRC guidance relating to the going concern basis of accounting. The guidance also covers, within the context of principal risks and uncertainties disclosed in the strategic report, solvency and liquidity risks.

NOTES

1 IFRIC was previously the Standards Interpretations Committee (SIC). Interpretations issued by SIC are still in force.
2 The lengthy and arduous progress of the relationship between the US and international standard setters has been extremely well documented by Kirsch (2012).
3 Hussey and Ong (2014) summarize the reasons for the ending of the relationship.
4 Information on the jurisdictions using IFRSs is on *http://www.ifrs.org/Use-around-the-world/Pages/Juris-diction-profiles.aspx* (accessed 24 August 2016).

5 A list of contributions from various sources for 2015 is shown on pages 42–46 of the IFRS Foundation Annual Report 2015. *http://www.ifrs.org/Alerts/Governance/Pages/IFRS-Foundation-publishes-2015-Annual-Report.aspx* (accessed 7 September 2016).
6 Zeff (2013) provides a scholarly exposition of the search for a conceptual framework at the international level.

CONCLUSIONS

In this chapter, we have discussed financial reporting regulations. In the UK, this comes under the FRC. We would emphasize that the great majority of countries have a similar structure. They have a body, established by the government, that has legal powers to decide on the application of accounting standards, and the authority to monitor and enforce them.

Although many countries have adopted international accounting standards, these usually apply to large companies that are listed on a stock exchange. One should take care when countries state that they have adopted IFRSs. It is for the country to determine the extent to which it adopts them, or even makes changes. In addition, the monitoring and enforcement at the national or even regional level can vary.

We have given the present position of the seven countries which agreed in 1973 that internationalization of accounting would be of benefit. We have also identified the status of some other countries. Undoubtedly, the adoption of IFRSs by the EU in 2005 boosted the international movement, and many countries now claim to use international standards.

The greatest problem facing the IASB in constructing a standard is the lack of an agreed CF. We have explained some of the concepts and attributes in the 2015 ED. This document has been criticized, and it may be some considerable time before a final version is produced. Even then, there will probably be disagreement on its contents.

The ED has generated significant discussions. Not all of these are, by any means, fully in agreement with the ED, and it is impossible to summarize all of the issues raised. The FRC has questioned the way that the ED dealt with the concepts of stewardship, prudence and reliability, in particular, in a full 47-page response in November 2015 (FRC 2015a).

IN THE PIPELINE

At the time of writing this chapter (July 2016), it is clear that there are two major issues outstanding: the CF and materiality. Whatever the outcome, both are likely to have a significant impact on financial accounting and reporting, but we may not experience these changes for several years.

The ED for the CF has been criticized. The FRC has issued several documents regarding the establishment of a CF, with which it fully agrees. However, in the full response issued in November 2015, the FRC expressed its considerable unease with the IASB's proposals (2015a).

At the end of June 2016, the IASB did not anticipate issuing the CF document for at least six months. Our opinion is that it will be longer than this, and the next document may not present a complete framework. The most likely scenario is an 'interim' document with the IASB planning to continue its work on the more contentious issues.

The IASB anticipates publishing an Exposure Draft on the definition of a business in the latter half of 2016.

ADDITIONAL RESOURCES

Go online to the companion website for this book to access further teaching and learning materials for this chapter.

www.palgravehighered.com/hussey-cfr

PREPARATION AND PRESENTATION OF FINANCIAL STATEMENTS

LEARNING OBJECTIVES

At the end of this chapter, you should be able to:

- Identify and evaluate proposals in the current Exposure Draft on the Conceptual Framework
- Explain the application of recognition, derecognition, measurement and disclosure
- Discuss the issues and importance of materiality
- Analyze the concepts of capital and capital maintenance
- Identify and summarize the main financial statements

INTRODUCTION

In Chapter 2, we introduced the Conceptual Framework Exposure Draft (ED) published by the IASB in May 2015. Previously, we concentrated on Chapter 1 of the ED, which was mainly concerned with the objectives of financial reporting, and Chapter 2 on the qualitative characteristics of financial information. We will examine in detail Chapters 3 and 4 of the ED when we discuss individual standards later in this book.

In this chapter, we concentrate on Chapters 5–8 of the ED, where the focus is on recognition, derecognition, measurement, disclosure and concepts of capital and capital maintenance. We will apply these terms when we analyze individual standards in subsequent chapters.

The penultimate section of this chapter is a short examination of the word 'materiality'. This concept is critical in determining the financial information that users receive. Both the IASB and the FRC have expressed their opinions, which we summarize, but the public debate is continuing.

The final section introduces the financial statements that IFRS-compliant entities must issue:

- Statement of financial position;
- Statement of comprehensive income;
- Statement of changes in equity;
- Statement of cash flows.

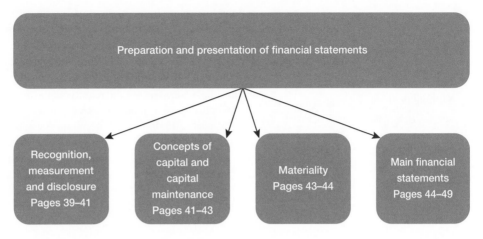

▲ **Diagram 3.1** *Structure of Chapter 3*

RECOGNITION, MEASUREMENT AND DISCLOSURE

Chapters 5, 6 and 7 of the ED cover the essential processes of recognizing economic transactions and events, selecting an appropriate measurement method and then disclosing the relevant information to users. In later chapters, we examine these issues in detail as we explain specific economic transactions and events. In this section, we establish a foundation, based on the Conceptual Framework (CF) to illustrate the decisions the reporting entity must make in recognition, measurement and disclosure.

Recognition and derecognition

recognition

Recognition is the process of capturing, for inclusion in the statement of financial position or the statement(s) of financial performance, an item that meets the definition of an element.

IASB Exposure Draft ED/2015/3, 2015, para. 5.2

The elements of a statement of financial position or financial performance are assets, liabilities, equity, income and expenses. **Recognition** determines what should be included in the financial statements and when that should occur. Some elements cause few recognition problems. The day-to-day operations of a business are easy to recognize. Entities may purchase raw materials, pay the workforce for converting them into finished goods and then sell them. There may be liabilities for items such as rent and insurance. Production, distribution, administration and many other activities incur large expense.

In recognizing economic transactions and events, we use the accruals concept of accounting. This means that recognition takes place when the event occurs and not when payment is either made or received.

Although many elements cause no recognition difficulties, other elements may cause more problems. Usually, the IASB issues a specific standard to resolve any difficulties. For example, what should we do if we are being sued, but the case has not yet come to court? (The standard is IAS 37 – see our Chapter 13.) What action should we take if our factory burns down two weeks after the year-end? (The standard is IAS 10 – see our Chapter 18.)

For these transactions and events, both accountants and the users of information must be confident that the proper accounting treatment is applied. Users will also wish to be certain that the basis an entity has used for the production of financial information is comparable to that produced by other entities and is comparable from one year to the next.

As the CF sets out the regulations for recognizing the elements it is reasonable that it also sets out the requirements for **derecognition**.

An entity's asset is normally derecognized when the entity loses control of all or part of the previously recognized asset. For example, a company may own some machinery which appears on its balance sheet. If the company sells the machinery, it will derecognize it and remove it from the balance sheet. An entity usually derecognizes a liability when it no longer has a present obligation for all or part of the previously recognized liability. In simple terms, the entity has paid the debt or an agreement has been reached that it is no longer due.

> **derecognition**
>
> Derecognition is the removal of all or part of a previously recognised asset or liability from an entity's statement of financial position.
>
> *Based on IASB Exposure Draft, 2015, para. 5.25*

Initial and subsequent measurement

We may have been able to recognize our economic phenomenon but the next question is whether we can measure it with reliability. The traditional **measurement** method has been historical cost accounting. An entity measures the economic transaction or event at the time it recognizes it. This method has the great advantage of being very reliable (you know what was paid), but unfortunately it has some weaknesses.

> **measurement**
>
> Measurement is the process of quantifying, in monetary terms, information about an entity's assets, liabilities, equity, income and expenses.
>
> *Based on IASB Exposure Draft ED/2015/3, 2015, para. 6.2*

Imagine that you had purchased a computer and a house on the same date five years ago. It is definite that the value of your computer will be a lot less than you paid for it because developments in technology will have made it redundant. On the other hand, it is likely that the value of the house has increased if there is an extremely active housing market. In both cases, the historical cost is different from the present value of the items shown in the financial statements. The statements are of little use for any decisions you wish to make now. (For information on these, refer to Chapter 4 on revaluations, Chapter 5 on impairments and Chapter 19 on analysis.)

With some transactions and events, we may have great difficulty in measuring the value. For example, you have purchased the right to drill for oil, and you have struck lucky. How much is that oil worth? It is obviously worth less whilst it is still in the ground, but how much less? (Refer to Chapter 15 on specific business activities.)

Another example of difficulties in measurement is with brand names. Many of us will purchase clothes or equipment because it has a 'brand' name. If that name attracts us to buying the item, then the brand must have value for the entity that owns it. But how do we measure that value? (Refer to Chapter 5.)

Because of the weakness of historical cost accounting, the CF identifies the alternative method of current value which updates the values at the measurement date. This reflects any positive or negative changes since the previous measurement date. The CF identifies two current value methods, illustrated in Diagram 3.2.

Unfortunately, measurement remains an uncertain concept. Historical cost has been the main method for many years and remains so. In subsequent chapters, we discuss the alternatives and their applications.

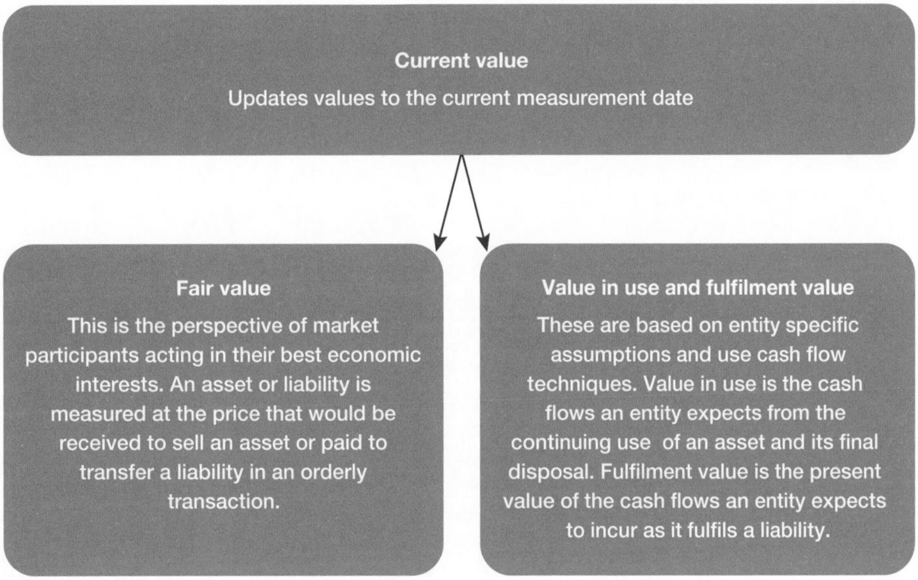

Current value
Updates values to the current measurement date

Fair value
This is the perspective of market participants acting in their best economic interests. An asset or liability is measured at the price that would be received to sell an asset or paid to transfer a liability in an orderly transaction.

Value in use and fulfilment value
These are based on entity specific assumptions and use cash flow techniques. Value in use is the cash flows an entity expects from the continuing use of an asset and its final disposal. Fulfilment value is the present value of the cash flows an entity expects to incur as it fulfils a liability.

▲ **Diagram 3.2** *Current value methods*

Disclosure

disclosure

Disclosure is the communication of financial information to those who have a right to receive it or an interest in the activities of the entity.

All businesses, even the smallest ones, will have to prepare some form of accounts to satisfy the tax authorities in the country where the business is situated. The larger the business entity, the more people are likely to be interested in seeing financial information. Entities that have shares or other securities quoted on a stock exchange will be required by the exchange to publish financial statements, at least annually, and possibly interim financial statements half-yearly or every three months.

The CF contains several pages on presentation and **disclosure**. We address these more fully in Chapters 20 and 21 when we look at corporate reporting in its entirety. At that stage, we also review the 'Disclosure Initiative' being undertaken by the IASB, and other approaches to making the full corporate report useful to its recipients.

CONCEPTS OF CAPITAL AND CAPITAL MAINTENANCE

In this section, we examine Chapter 8 of the ED. Some have claimed that the concepts of capital and capital maintenance emphasize the role of financial accounting and reporting as a main responsibility to shareholders. The purpose of capital maintenance is to demonstrate that the company protects the financial investment made by shareholders. As Page, among others, has argued: 'There is an implicit, sometimes explicit, view that the primary users of financial statements are investors or their advisers' (Page 2005: 573).

There are other opinions on the role of the limited company in society, but we leave those discussions to our later chapters on corporate reporting. In this section, we concentrate on the

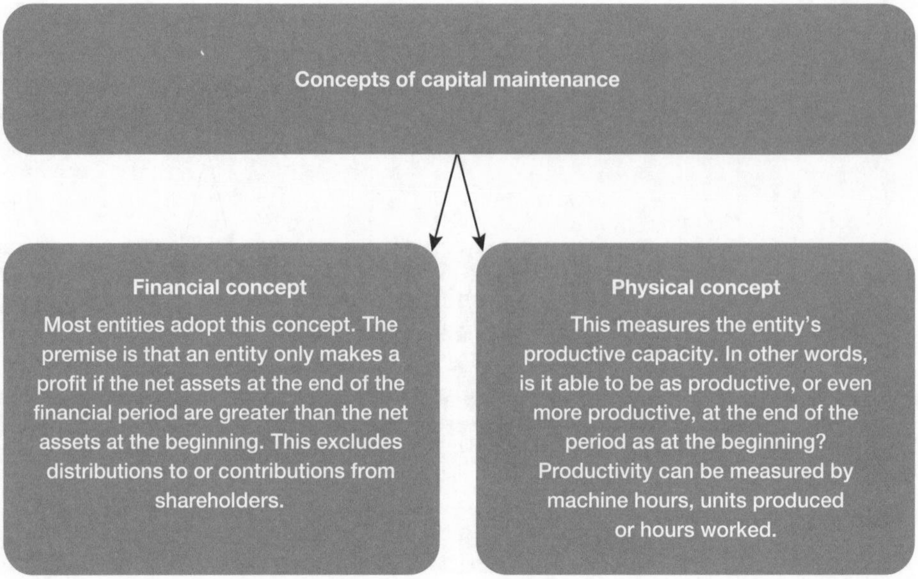

Concepts of capital maintenance

Financial concept
Most entities adopt this concept. The premise is that an entity only makes a profit if the net assets at the end of the financial period are greater than the net assets at the beginning. This excludes distributions to or contributions from shareholders.

Physical concept
This measures the entity's productive capacity. In other words, is it able to be as productive, or even more productive, at the end of the period as at the beginning? Productivity can be measured by machine hours, units produced or hours worked.

▲ **Diagram 3.3** *Concepts of capital maintenance*

definitions and explanations in the 2015 ED. We will introduce the result of the accounting equation that Net assets = Total assets – Total liabilities and the alternative terminology that Net assets = Equity. The ED tends to use both 'net assets' and 'equity'.

There are two concepts of capital maintenance: financial and physical, as illustrated in Diagram 3.3. With both of these approaches, the problem is the impact of inflation on assets and liabilities and our measurement of profit. With the financial concept, an increase in the net assets over the period represents a profit. With the physical concept, an increase in the physical productive capacity over the period represents a profit. Because most entities use the financial concept, we concentrate on this approach.

Inflation is a sustained increase in the general price level of goods and services over a period. Each unit of currency buys progressively fewer goods and services. In other words, there is a reduction in the purchasing power per unit of money. Worked example 3.1, although simplistic, demonstrates the issues.

Worked example 3.1

Note: Assume all transactions are for cash.

Drinks Company raises £60,000 and buys a store for £50,000. It now has £10,000 cash in hand. It manufactures and sells cups. The materials cost for one cup is £1.00. The financial activities are as follows.

First three months. Manufactures 10,000 cups at £1.00 and sells them for £1.50 each to give a total income of £15,000. The profit is £5,000 and the company has £10,000 cash in hand.

Second three months. Due to inflation, the manufacturing cost is £1.25 for a cup. If the profit from the first three months has been distributed in full, the company has only £10,000 to purchase materials for cups. Therefore, it can only manufacture 8,000 cups (£10,000/£1.25).

The company in Worked example 3.1 has a problem. Does it increase the selling price of cups? The consumers may not like this. Does it keep the same selling price but earn lower profits? The shareholders may not like this.

Inflation data for a country is usually based on the Consumer Price Index or similar measure. However, within a country, there are likely to be significant variations in different areas of the economy. For example, in Canada the inflation rate in 2013 was running below the 2% level. Nationally, the price of Canadian farmland from coast to coast increased by an average of 12% per year from 2008 to 2013 (Pittis 2013).

Small movements in inflation rates may be of no consequence but when the country's inflation rate hits double digits, as in the UK in the late 1970s (see Table 3.1), accountants need to do something to avoid the financial statements being misleading. It does not appear that the ED directly addresses this issue.

▼ **Table 3.1** *UK inflation rates 1976–1980*

Year	Inflation rate
1976	16.5%
1977	15.8%
1978	8.3%
1979	13.4%
1980	18.0%

Source: http://www.whatsthecost.com/historic.cpi.aspx
(accessed 24 August 2016).

MATERIALITY

materiality

Information is material if omitting it or misstating it could influence decisions that the primary users of general purpose financial reports make on the basis of financial information about a specific reporting entity.

IASB Exposure Draft, 2015, para. 2.11

We have put this topic in a separate section because **materiality** is a critical concept in financial accounting and reporting. It determines what financial information the user receives. When preparing general purpose financial statements, management must determine the information that should be included, excluded, or aggregated with other information. As well as deciding the information to be disclosed, the concept of materiality assists management in deciding how best to make the information understandable by the user.

If management includes immaterial information, the user may become confused or overwhelmed by the amount of information disclosed. Management must be as careful in identifying and excluding immaterial information as in disclosing material information.

The IFRS issued an Exposure Draft Practice Statement on the application of materiality in 2015, covering the following topics:

- the characteristics of materiality;
- applying materiality when making decisions about presenting and disclosing information;
- deciding whether omissions and misstatements of information are material.

Although the draft Practice Statement is helpful, management always considers materiality in respect of a specific entity. Management is considering whether specific events or transactions may affect the decision made by the users of those particular financial statements. Responses to the ED had to be submitted by February 2016 and the IASB reviewed the project in July 2016. The Board aims to finalize the revised Conceptual Framework in early 2017 (*http://www.ifrs.org/Current-Projects/IASB-Projects/Conceptual-Framework/Pages/Conceptual-Framework-Summary.aspx*, accessed 8 September 2016).

The FRC issued a document on the Strategic Report (2014c) pointing out that the Companies Act 2006 does not use the term 'material'. The FRC argues, however, that materiality is implicit in many of its requirements.

Although the FRC's document is concerned with the Strategic report, its comments are applicable to many aspects of the full corporate report. For example, it states that company law or other legislation requires some disclosures. Materiality is therefore not applicable to the legal requirements for disclosure or non-disclosure. In addition, most of the requirements for the directors' report are legally required.

As a final reminder to the IASB, the FRC concludes that a company's shareholder base can include separate groups; for example, retail investors and institutional investors. These shareholders can have their own different needs and interests, so the materiality of information may differ among the groups. Management must satisfy the needs of all significant shareholder groups, advice which holds good for all types of information.

THE MAIN FINANCIAL STATEMENTS

The requirements on which financial statements and their content are given in IAS 1 *Presentation of Financial Statements*. The standard has been amended and revised several times and, assuming that the CF we discussed earlier is a solid foundation, IAS 1 will be revised again.

Table 3.2 highlights the most significant revisions to IAS 1. IAS 1 *Presentation of Financial Statements* is a surprisingly brief standard in view of the information it has to provide. The reason is that the standard concentrates on the presentation of the financial statements and not issues of recognition, measurement and detailed disclosure requirements.

▼ Table 3.2 *Timeline of IAS 1*

Date	Comment
1975	Standard first issued
1997	Revised standard issued
2003	Revised standard issued
2014	Revised standard issued
Interpretations issued	IFRIC 17 Distribution of Non-cash Assets to Owners
	SIC 27 Evaluating the Substance of Transactions in the Legal Form of a Lease
	SIC 29 Disclosure – Service Concession Arrangements

Recognition and measurement are two key concepts in constructing financial statements. In Chapter 1, we discussed the channels of communication entities use to disclose financial information. This section examines the requirements of IAS 1 regarding the content and presentation of the main financial statements.

The following financial statements are required:

- Statement of financial position as at the end of the period;
- Statement of profit or loss and other comprehensive income for the period;
- Statement of changes in equity for the period;
- Statement of cash flows for the period;
- Notes, comprising a summary of significant accounting policies and other explanatory information.

IAS 1 requires that the financial statements should contain comparative information in respect of the preceding period. However, entities are not obliged to use the titles of the statements given in the standard, and some prefer to use their own terminology.

At this stage, we refer only to the main presentation requirements. Diagrams 3.4 to 3.7 show the chapters in this book that explain the detailed requirements for each statement. We also add some brief comments on what you may find in practice.

Statement of financial position (balance sheet)

The statement of financial position was formerly called the balance sheet, and many entities have kept that heading. In our sample of 25 UK listed entities, only 3 used the new title; of the 10 Australian and Canadian entities sampled, 5 used the new title. In the rest of the book, for reasons of brevity, we use the term 'balance sheet'.

The information, if applicable, required by the standard is as follows:

(a) property, plant and equipment;
(b) investment property;
(c) intangible assets;
(d) financial assets;
(e) investments accounted for using the equity method;
(f) biological assets;
(g) inventories;
(h) trade and other receivables;
(i) cash and cash equivalents;
(j) the total of assets classified as held for sale and assets included in disposal groups classified as held for sale;
(k) trade and other payables;
(l) provisions;
(m) financial liabilities (excluding amounts shown under (k) and (l));
(n) liabilities and assets for current tax;
(o) deferred tax liabilities and deferred tax assets;
(p) liabilities included in disposal groups classified as held for sale;
(q) non-controlling interests, presented within equity; and
(r) issued capital and reserves attributable to owners of the parent.

This is a somewhat bewildering array of items. Entities can also include additional line items, headings and subtotals when such presentation is relevant to an understanding of their financial position.

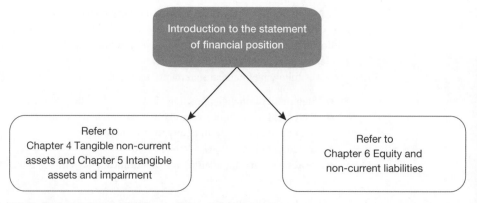

▲ **Diagram 3.4** *The statement of financial position*

There is no particular format for the balance sheet and entities usually use a format with headings and subtotals based on the accounting equation or a variation. The basic accounting equation is

Assets = Capital + Liabilities

A simplified typical format is as follows:

Balance sheet as at ….		
Assets	£	£
Non-current assets	50	
Current assets	30	
Total assets		80
Liabilities		
Current liabilities	20	
Non-current liabilities	25	
Total liabilities		45
Net assets		**35**
Equity		**35**

Some entities prefer to use a format, which emphasizes working capital defined as current assets minus current liabilities. In such instances, the balance sheet is similar to the following simplified layout:

Balance sheet as at …		
	£	£
Non-current assets		50
Current assets	30	
Less current liabilities	20	10
		60
Non-current liabilities		25
Equity		35
		60

Statement of comprehensive income

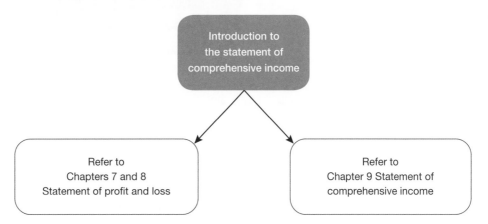

▲ **Diagram 3.5** *The statement of comprehensive income*

For many years, people had been content with merely a statement of profit or loss. However, there was a growing opinion that such a statement was, in itself, insufficient to inform the user of the total financial performance of the entity.

On 6 September 2007, the IASB issued a revised IAS 1 which became effective for annual periods beginning on or after 1 January 2009. In IAS 1 an entity must present in its annual report and accounts:

- One statement of comprehensive income; or
- Two separate statements comprising:
  1 An income statement displaying components of profit or loss.
  2 A statement of comprehensive income. This statement begins with profit or loss shown on the bottom line of the income statement. The items of other comprehensive income for the reporting period follow.

In Chapter 9, we discuss the debate that has surrounded the introduction of the statement of comprehensive income.

Statement of changes in equity

Shareholders, understandably, are very interested in any changes in the equity shown in the balance sheet. The reasons for the changes are not always easy to discern. There are several reasons why the amount of equity can change through the financial period which fall into two distinct categories. First, there are the changes that occur from transactions with shareholders, such as issue of new shares and payment of dividends. Secondly, there are changes that occur due to matters such as the net income for the period and the revaluation of fixed assets.

In 2007 IAS 1 introduced a statement of changes in equity, which is a summary of the changes that have taken place during the financial reporting period. The standard requires the balances of equity accounts at the beginning of the financial period to be reconciled with the closing balances. As there is a requirement for the previous year's disclosures as a comparison, this can result in a considerable amount of information.

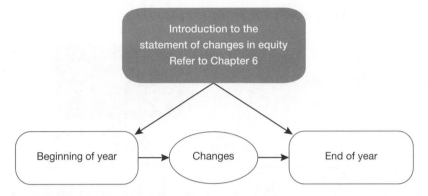

▲ **Diagram 3.6** *The statement of changes in equity*

The statement must disclose the following information:

- Total comprehensive income for the period, showing separately the total amounts attributable to owners of the parent and to non-controlling interests.
- For each component of equity, the effects of retrospective application or retrospective restatement.
- For each component of equity, a reconciliation between the carrying amount at the beginning and the end of the period, separately disclosing changes resulting from:
  1 profit or loss;
  2 other comprehensive income;
  3 transactions with owners in their capacity as owners, showing separately contributions by and distributions to owners and changes in ownership interests in subsidiaries that do not result in a loss of control.

Statement of cash flows

It took standard setters many years to decide – or possibly entities to accept – that cash is very important to users of financial statements, so the introduction of a statement of cash flows was long overdue. The standard now requires the provision of information about the historical changes in cash and cash equivalents of an entity in a statement of cash flows. This statement classifies cash flows during the period from operating, investing and financing activities.

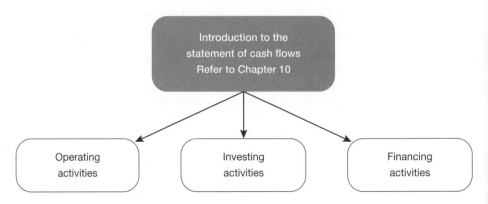

▲ **Diagram 3.7** *The statement of cash flows*

Cash flow from operating activities is a key indicator of an entity's ability to generate sufficient cash without needing external finance. Some would argue that the standard could have been tougher in its approach to the calculation of cash from operating activities. The standard setters allow a choice of methods:

- the direct method which shows major classes of gross cash receipts and payments; or
- the indirect method which adjusts the profit or loss for the period by transactions of a non-cash nature.

In Chapter 10, we demonstrate the calculations required by the indirect method.

CONCLUSIONS

The greatest problem facing the IASB in constructing a standard is the lack of an agreed robust Conceptual Framework (CF). We have explained some of the concepts and attributes in the 2015 Exposure Draft (ED). This document has been criticized and it may be some considerable time before a final version is produced but, even then, there is likely to be disagreement over its contents.

The methods of measurement are debatable. The use of historic cost does not necessarily give the most useful information to the user. Other methods may provide information that is more relevant but the question arises as to whether it is reliable. In debating these issues, the complex concept of materiality constantly appears.

We discussed the CF in the previous chapter and this one. If we look at the comments and criticisms made by various groups, we must conclude that the 2015 proposals are not fully acceptable. As we argued in the previous chapter, we anticipate that the IASB will need to rethink parts of the ED.

We finished the chapter by introducing the main financial statements required by IAS 1 *Presentation of Financial Statements*. In Chapters 4 to 10, we explain the main financial statements in detail. This is also an opportunity for us to define and explain more fully some of the details in the conceptual framework.

IN THE PIPELINE

Materiality is high on the agenda of the FRC. In a document issued in June 2014 concerning the Strategic Report (FRC 2014c), the FRC spent considerable time explaining the importance, concept and legal background of the term. In our opinion, the IASB should take into its considerations some of the arguments made by the FRC.

In July 2016 the IASB identified a research project entitled the Primary Financial Statements project, which focuses on:

- the structure and content of the statement(s) of financial performance;
- the potential demand for changes to the statement of cash flows and the statement of financial position;
- the implications of digital reporting for the structure and content of the primary financial statements.

The IASB anticipated that it would decide the scope of the project before the end of 2016 (*http://www.ifrs.org/Current-Projects/IASB-Projects/Pages/IASB-Work-Plan.aspx*, accessed 8 September 2016).

ADDITIONAL RESOURCES

Go online to the companion website for this book to access further teaching and learning materials for this chapter.
www.palgravehighered.com/hussey-cfr

STATEMENT OF FINANCIAL POSITION – TANGIBLE NON-CURRENT ASSETS

IAS 16 Property, plant and equipment
IAS 23 Borrowing costs

LEARNING OBJECTIVES

At the end of this chapter, you should be able to:

- Explain the accounting equation
- Identify the recognition criteria for a tangible non-current asset
- Explain the requirements of IAS 16
- Discuss the concept of depreciation
- Describe the procedure for revaluing tangible non-current assets
- Calculate the amount of borrowing costs that can be capitalized under IAS 23

INTRODUCTION

The accounting equation is the basis of the statement of financial position, also referred to as the balance sheet. The relationship between the assets, liabilities and capital in a business is given by:

> Assets – Liabilities = Capital

The purpose of the balance sheet is to enable users to identify an entity's financial strengths and weaknesses. The straightforward balance sheet remains an output from the double entry bookkeeping system, but the complexity of modern business transactions and the perceived information needs of users demand a more complex financial statement. This chapter explains current regulations and practices.

In this chapter and the following one, we concentrate on non-current assets. These are items held by the entity to generate future benefits, and can include tangible assets, such as property, equipment, machinery and vehicles, and intangible non-current assets, such as patents and goodwill. We examine the accounting treatment of tangible assets in this chapter, and we discuss intangible assets in Chapter 5.

In the first section of this chapter, we differentiate between tangible non-current and current assets. Non-current assets are a very substantial category of items on the balance sheet for all entities. To provide useful information there must be clear and unambiguous regulations on the recognition and measurement of non-current assets, and we explain in detail the main regulations for the standards relevant to tangible non-current assets.

IAS 16 *Property, Plant and Equipment* sets out the criteria for recognizing a non-current asset and the measurement methods. The standard contains two measurement methods: initial cost and subsequent measurement using revaluation. The standard also explains the procedure for charging depreciation of the asset.

Strongly linked to IAS 16 is IAS 23 *Borrowing Costs*. IAS 23 requires entities to charge borrowing costs as part of the initial cost of a non-current asset. This has been a contentious issue as some argue that interest should not be recognized as a construction cost. The standard is very specific on which assets are eligible and how the borrowing costs are to be calculated.

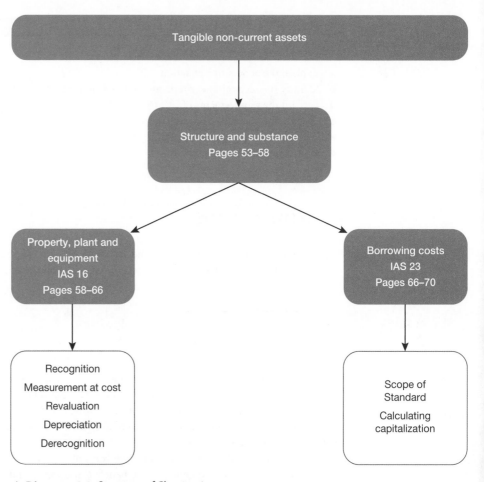

▲ **Diagram 4.1** *Structure of Chapter 4*

STRUCTURE AND SUBSTANCE

Structure

IAS 1 *Presentation of Financial Statements* states that financial statements are general purpose documents designed to meet the needs of various users. One of the financial statements is the statement of financial position, also known as the balance sheet. The standard permits companies to use either term. Our research shows that most companies use the term 'balance sheet', and we will do so, unless we refer specifically to the standard.

The balance sheet shows the economic resources of an entity and the claims on those resources. This information helps the user to decide the entity's liquidity and solvency, as well as the potential need for additional financing and the likelihood of obtaining it.

Table 4.1 shows the line items to be included on the statement of financial position (IAS 1 para. 54). We have also included, where appropriate, the relevant standard and the chapter in this book that discusses the item.

▼ Table 4.1 *Contents of balance sheet*

Line item	Standard	Chapter
Property, plant and equipment	IAS 16	4
Investment property	IAS 40	15
Intangible assets	IAS 38	5
Financial assets	IFRS 7 and IFRS 9	12
Investments accounted for using the equity method	IFRS 10	16
Biological assets	IAS 41	15
Inventories	IAS 2	8
Trade and other receivables		
Cash and cash equivalents	IAS 7	10
The total of assets classified as held for sale	IFRS 5	15
Trade and other payables		
Provisions	IAS 37	13
Financial liabilities	IFRS 7/9	12
Current tax	IAS 12	14
Liabilities and assets for deferred tax	IAS 12	14
Liabilities included in disposal groups classified as held for sale	IFRS 5	15
Non-controlling interests, presented within equity	IFRS 10	16
Issued capital and reserves attributable to owners of the parent	IFRS 10	16

A balance sheet can list the items in Table 4.1 in any order. An entity, depending on the nature of its operations, can show further sub-classifications of the items. It can include these in either the balance sheet or the notes to the accounts.

We explained in the previous chapter that the objective of presenting information is to make it understandable. The Board, with the advice of the Finance Director, can include other line items and headings if this assists in the users' understanding.

The two main standards regulating tangible non-current assets are IAS 16 and IAS 23. However, both standards link to other standards, as illustrated in Diagram 4.2. The unshaded boxes indicate the relevant standards discussed in later chapters.

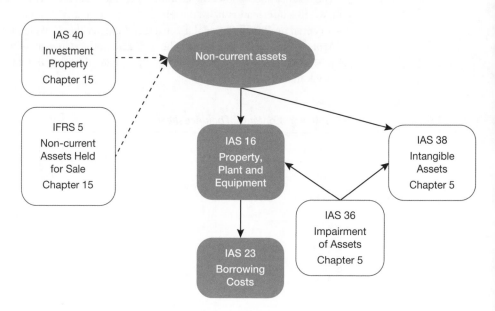

▲ **Diagram 4.2** *Standards applying to non-current assets*

Substance

asset

An asset is a resource controlled by the enterprise as a result of past events and from which future economic benefits are expected to flow to the enterprise.

Based on IASB, Exposure Draft ED/2015/3, 2015, para. 4.4

At one time it was possible to refer to assets as 'things which the business owns'. Life has become more complicated and now we recognize an **asset** by applying the quoted definition, without insisting on the right of ownership.

For an asset to be recognized on the balance sheet it should meet the following recognition criteria:

1 *Entity control of the asset*: An entity may not own a particular asset but has an agreement with another party that it can use or has control of an asset. Control is through an event in the past, for example, entering into a formal agreement.

2 *Expectation of future economic benefits*: A business will acquire control of premises, machinery, equipment, vehicles and other assets in the expectation that they will generate future benefits. This may be cash or other benefits. For example, the purchase of a more efficient machine may lead to a reduction in manufacturing costs.

3   *Reliable measurement*: In this instance, measurement means placing a monetary value on the asset. If an asset is recognized, the amount shown in the balance sheet is termed the 'carrying amount'. This is the original measurement less all depreciation charged to date. If an asset's *carrying amount* exceeds the amount that could be recovered through use or sale of the asset it is impaired. Finally, in the case of property plant and equipment, entities can choose to revalue the asset if they wish.

Non-current assets are classified either as tangible, and come under IAS 16, or intangible, and come under IAS 38 that we discuss in the next chapter. The title of IAS 16 – property, plant and equipment – describes the nature of tangible assets. Intangible assets are more difficult to describe but are becoming more important. They are identifiable assets without physical substance such as goodwill, patents, brands, and computer software.

IAS 16 requires the classification of assets into current assets and tangible non-current assets. They must be shown separately on the balance sheet.

In order to be classified as current, an asset must meet any one or more of the following criteria:

● It is expected to be sold or used in the entity's normal operating cycle. Examples are raw materials used in production and goods bought and resold at a profit.
● It is held primarily for the purposes of trading.
● It is expected to be realized within 12 months after the balance sheet date. For example, money owing to the company will be paid.
● It is cash.

There is no definition of a non-current asset. If an asset does not meet the criteria for recognition as a current asset, it must be non-current.

Because of the structure given in the standard, you may consider that all balance sheets will look very similar. Certainly, balance sheets individually have a superficial similarity. However, there will be considerable variations between companies in different industries because of the nature of the industry. Table 4.2 shows four companies, their industry and their total non-current assets in 2014.

If you take the companies in Table 4.2 and convert the financial amounts for the line items into percentages, there are significant differences. Diagram 4.3 shows the total assets categorized into intangible assets, property, plant and equipment (PPE), other non-current assets, and current assets. The different categories are expressed in percentages.

Not surprisingly, Associated British Foods has substantial property, plant and equipment. The media company, WPP, has few PPE assets but a significant investment in intangible assets. In fact, goodwill comprises 38% of the 45% investment in intangibles.

▼ Table 4.2 *Company, industry and total non-current assets*

Company	Industry	Total assets
Associated British Foods plc (UK)	Food	£10,472 million
BAE Systems plc (UK)	Military	£19,788 million
Incitec Pivot Limited (Australia)	Manufacturing	Au$7,970 million*
WPP plc (UK)	Media	£25,005 million

* Approx. £4,6000 million in September 2016.

Source: Data from companies' published annual reports and accounts.

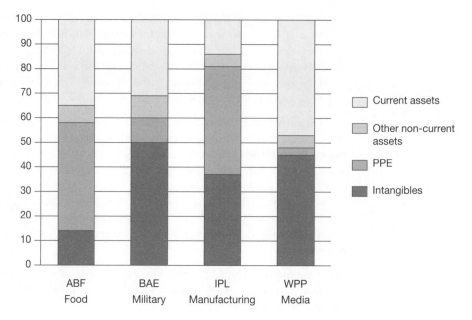

▲ **Diagram 4.3** *Examples of asset classifications from various industries*
Source: Based on data from companies' published annual reports and accounts.

BAE has the highest percentage of intangible assets at 50% of the total assets. BAE develops, delivers and supports advanced defence and aerospace systems, including the manufacture of military aircraft, surface ships, submarines, and fighting vehicles. One might anticipate that these activities would lead to most of the assets being in PPE, but that is not the case. Company example 4.1 contains a note from BAE's annual report and accounts which illustrates the growing importance of intangible assets in all industry sectors. We discuss intangible assets in detail in the next chapter.

Company example 4.1 demonstrates the range of intangible assets companies may hold. It also provides some comments on the basis for capitalization.

The analysis of the substance of balance sheets demonstrates that, for the user to benefit from the information, three aspects need to be appreciated:

1 The requirements of the accounting standards.
2 The nature of the business.
3 The danger of comparing the balance sheets of entities in different industries.

There are still problems not revealed on the balance sheet such as:

1 Entities usually have policies on the minimum amount they will treat as a non-current asset. It may be that one entity treats expenditure on equipment under £5,000 as a current asset. The expense of the asset goes to the profit or loss account and therefore reduces the profit by this amount. Another may decide to capitalize the acquisition, in other words, put it on the balance sheet as a non-current asset. The auditors should refer to the company any classifications that they consider unreasonable.

2 There is no information on how well the non-current asset is maintained. One hopes that in a properly managed entity, a regular maintenance programme is followed and the asset has not declined substantially in value. IAS 36 *Impairment of Assets* addresses this issue and is discussed in the next chapter.

Company example 4.1

BAE

Intangible assets

Goodwill

Goodwill on acquisitions of subsidiaries is included in intangible assets. Goodwill on acquisitions of joint ventures and associates is included in the carrying value of equity accounted investments. Gains and losses on the disposal of an entity include the carrying amount of goodwill relating to the entity sold.

Programme and customer-related

The most significant intangible assets recognised by the Group are in relation to on-going programmes within businesses acquired, mainly in respect of customer relationships and order backlog.

Other intangible assets

Other intangible assets include:

- Computer software licences acquired for use within the Group are capitalised as an intangible asset on the basis of the costs incurred to acquire and bring to use the specific software;
- Software development costs that are directly associated with the production of identifiable and unique software products controlled by the Group, and that will probably generate economic benefits exceeding costs beyond one year, are recognised as intangible assets;
- Group-funded expenditure associated with enhancing or maintaining computer software programs for sale is recognised as an expense as incurred;
- Research and development expenditure funded by the Group on development activities applied to a plan or design for the production of new or substantially improved products is capitalised as an internally generated intangible asset if certain conditions are met. The expenditure capitalised includes the cost of materials, direct labour and related overheads; and
- Patents, trademarks and licences.

BAE, Annual Report and Accounts, Note 9, 2014, p. 118

3   The carrying amount in the balance sheet is the cost less depreciation and impairments in value to date. This carrying amount is not what the non-current asset may be worth on the open market. IAS 16 partially addresses this issue by permitting entities to revalue their assets if they choose.

4   Intangible assets, as demonstrated in Diagram 4.3, are very important in demonstrating an entity's financial strength. IAS 38 *Intangible Assets,* explained in the following chapter, sets out the requirements but there is still disagreement over the accounting treatment, particularly of goodwill.

We explore these issues in connection to the accounting standards that relate to them in this and subsequent chapters, but a simple example of asset valuations (Worked example 4.1) will highlight the problems. It also illustrates the danger of conducting comparisons without having the full information.

Worked example 4.1   Asset valuations

Company A has only two assets. One is a machine it purchased for £200,000 5 years ago with an estimated total life of 10 years. It also has an intangible asset shown in the balance sheet that it acquired 5 years ago for £200,000.

As the machine has been depreciated, it will be shown in the balance sheet at £100,000. This does not necessarily represent what the machine could be sold for or the cost of replacing it. The amount is the original cost less the amount of depreciation. The intangible asset has not been depreciated and the original cost of £200,000 appears on the balance sheet.

Company B is a new company in the same industry that has purchased similar machinery for £200,000 but has only depreciated for 1 year. In its balance sheet, the machinery will appear at £180,000. It may, or may not, have any intangible assets.

To understand the financial actions taken by the companies in Worked example 4.1, we need to know the accounting regulations. In this chapter, we explain the basis for depreciation of tangible non-current assets. In the following chapter, we describe the accounting regulations for intangible assets.

IAS 16
PROPERTY, PLANT AND EQUIPMENT (PPE)

▼ **Table 4.3** *Timeline of IAS 16*

Date	Comment
1982	Standard first issued
1993	Standard revised
2003	Current version of standard issued
2014	Latest amendment
Interpretations issued	IFRIC 20 Stripping Costs in the Production Phase of a Stripping Mine

property, plant and equipment

These are tangible items held for the purpose of generating profits. These items may be used in the production or supply of goods or services, for rental to others, or for administrative purposes. Property, plant and equipment are assumed to be used by the organization for more than one financial period and therefore they are non-current assets.

The objective of IAS 16 is to set out the accounting treatment for most types of **property, plant and equipment**. Non-current assets meeting the PPE definition should be recognized if:

- it is probable that there will be future economic benefits; and
- the cost of the item can be measured reliably.

Although IAS 16 has the title 'Property, Plant and Equipment', the standard does not apply to all PPE and Diagram 4.4 shows the items excluded.

One particular feature of IAS 16 is the requirement for measurement to be originally at cost but subsequently the asset can be carried at either cost or a revalued amount. The revalued amount arises when a company

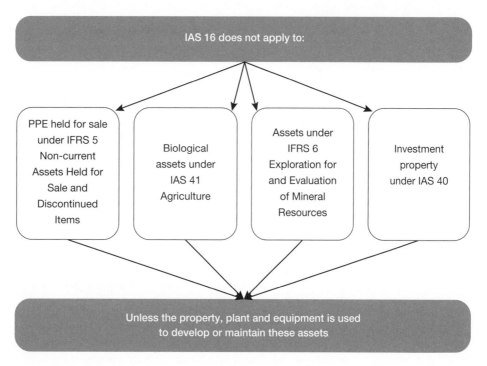

IAS 16 does not apply to:

PPE held for sale under IFRS 5 Non-current Assets Held for Sale and Discontinued Items

Biological assets under IAS 41 Agriculture

Assets under IFRS 6 Exploration for and Evaluation of Mineral Resources

Investment property under IAS 40

Unless the property, plant and equipment is used to develop or maintain these assets

▲ **Diagram 4.4** *Limitations on the scope of IAS 16*

considers that the carrying amount of an asset shown in the balance sheet is misleading. In practice, the great majority of entities use cost but it is important to remember that revaluation of the non-current assets is an option.

Measurement at cost

There are two categories of cost:

1 Initial costs incurred to acquire or construct an item of PPE to bring it to working condition for its intended use.
2 Subsequent costs for additions to the original PPE or to replace part of it.

Service costs that improve the asset leading to additional economic benefits can be recognized but not normal servicing costs. For example, a major overhaul of a piece of machinery to obtain greater efficiency would lead to economic benefits. The cost of the major overhaul can be capitalized.

Examples of cost for items of PPE are:

● Land – purchase price, legal fees and preparation of site for intended use.
● Buildings – purchase price and costs incurred in putting the buildings in a condition for use.
● Plant and machinery – purchase price, transport and installation costs, testing costs

Abnormal costs such as rectifying installation errors, design errors, wastage and idle capacity are not part of the original cost of the asset but a charge to the profit or loss account.

The stage is reached when the item can be used in the manner for which it was intended. However, the entity may incur some subsequent costs related to the asset. It will charge these costs to the profit or loss account. An entity cannot add the following to the carrying amount of the item.

- Initial operating losses, if any. For example, an entity may not be enjoying economic benefits until it achieves a certain level of production. The losses it initially makes cannot be capitalized.
- Costs incurred whilst waiting to bring the item into full use. For example, a hotel may be ready for opening but incurs security costs before the first guests arrive.
- Costs incurred in relocating or reorganizing part or all of an entity's operations. For example, a factory may be reorganized to move some heavy machinery so that it fits better into the production flow. This cost cannot be added to the value of the machinery.
- Incidental operations that are not relevant to an item being at the location and in a fit condition for operations. For example, with the introduction of new machinery, a company may decide to move its storage facilities of raw materials. It cannot add this cost to the cost of the new machinery.

With some items, it is possible that, when the activity has reached the end of its useful economic life, the entity will be obliged to dismantle the equipment and restore the site to its original state. These expected future costs can be included in the original cost of the asset.

The basis for conclusions in IAS 16 states 'that the cost of an item should include the costs of dismantlement, removal or restoration, the obligation for which an entity has incurred as a consequence of having used the item during a particular period other than to produce inventories during that period' (para. 15). Essentially, the standard requires a company to make good any damage it has caused through its operations.

The complexity and time frame of these calculations is considerable. Company example 4.2 shows the notes to the annual report of Centrica plc, a company in the energy industry, and demonstrates the issues very well.

Company example 4.2

Decommissioning costs

The estimated cost of decommissioning at the end of the producing lives of fields (including storage facility assets) is reviewed periodically and is based on reserves, price levels and technology at the balance sheet date. Provision is made for the estimated cost of decommissioning at the balance sheet date. The payment dates of total expected future decommissioning costs are uncertain and dependent on the lives of the facilities, but are currently anticipated to be incurred until 2055, with the majority of the costs expected to be paid between 2020 and 2030. Significant judgements and estimates are also made about the costs of decommissioning nuclear power stations and the costs of waste management and spent fuel. These estimates impact the carrying value of our Nuclear investment. Various arrangements and indemnities are in place with the Secretary of State with respect to these costs, as explained in note S2.

Centrica plc, Annual Report, 2014, p. 100

During the life of a non-current asset, it is possible that some parts need replacement. In this case, we are considering substantial replacements and not routine servicing and upkeep. Examples of substantial replacements are the heating system of a factory, the power trains for machinery, the interior fittings and equipment in buildings.

In these cases, the entity recognizes the full cost of the replacement as an addition to the carrying amount of the original non-current asset. It will depreciate the replacement part over its expected useful life. This could be different from other components of the asset.

Revaluation

IAS 16 permits the revaluation of non-current assets. This is a significant departure from the long-established measurement method of historical cost. The argument for introducing revaluations was that they would provide more valuable information to the users of financial statements. The concerns were the amount of work that would be required and the reliability of the revaluation. Whether a revaluation should take place is at the discretion of management. They decide whether to revalue, when to revalue and, with some restrictions, which assets to revalue.

One might suppose that, where an asset has increased in value, an entity would be keen to demonstrate this. It would reveal financial strength and an ability to meet claims, and, possibly, prevent a hostile takeover.

However, relatively few entities use the option in IAS 16 to revalue some of their assets. There are three reasons for this. First, by revaluing their assets, the ratio known as *return on assets* declines, and users might interpret this as a decline in company performance. We discuss accounting ratios in Chapter 19.

Second, the revalued asset has to be depreciated over its useful economic life. The revaluation is likely to result in an increased depreciation charge. This could have a negative effect on profits.

The third reason for entities not rushing to revalue assets is that, if they choose to do so, they must comply with the following regulations:

- Revaluations should be carried out regularly, so that the carrying amount of an asset does not differ materially from its fair value at the balance sheet date.
- The entire class of assets to which that asset belongs should be revalued. A class of PPE is a grouping of assets of a similar nature and use in an entity's operations. Examples are buildings, machinery, motor vehicles, furniture and fixtures. An entity must revalue all buildings and not just a few.
- Depreciation is charged in the same way as under the cost basis.
- Increases in revaluation value should be credited to equity under the heading of 'Revaluation surplus'. If the increase is a reversal of a revaluation decrease of the same asset previously recognized as an expense, it should be recognized as income.
- Decreases as a result of a revaluation should be recognized as an expense to the extent that it exceeds any amount previously credited to the revaluation surplus relating to the same asset.
- Disposal of revalued assets can lead to a revaluation surplus which may be either transferred directly to retained earnings or left in equity under the heading 'Revaluation surplus'.
- The revaluation model can only be used if the fair value of the item can be measured reliably.

The requirement to review revaluations regularly can apply annually or at least when there are indications that there have been changes in the prices in the market. Each class of assets must be revalued to prevent what is known as 'cherry picking'; that is, the revaluation of only those particular assets in a class which have increased in value and excluding those in a class which have not increased in value.

Where fixed assets are revalued this comes within the scope of IFRS 13 *Fair Value Measurements*, both in terms of measurement and disclosure (refer to Chapter 12). Note that IAS 16 regulates the process of the revaluation of items.

Despite the work required to conduct a revaluation, companies do so. The reasons for this have attracted the interest of researchers. A study by Lin and Peasnell (2000) analyzed UK companies for the years 1989 and 1991. Some of their conclusions are no longer applicable because accounting regulations have changed or are not relevant to our discussions in this chapter. However, the authors found that entities tended to use revaluations when they faced borrowing constraints. By increasing the value of their assets, they appeared richer! Entities also only carried out revaluations if they had a large stock of fixed assets which would make an impact on the balance sheet.

A later study by Barlev et al. (2007) confirmed for the UK and Australian markets many of the findings from previous research. However, the authors argued that the motivations and effects of revaluations differ depending on the country and its cultural, economic and legal environments.

These variables can affect both the motivation and subsequent effects of the revaluation decision. This is important both to international standard setters attempting to determine regulations that are used by many different countries and for users attempting to make financial comparisons of entities in different countries.

Users of financial statements must be cautious where there is a revaluation but, undoubtedly, the action by the entity is sending messages to the users of financial statements. If an asset is revalued upwards; the sum of the total assets will be increased by that amount. The entity will appear wealthier and the shareholders' stake will increase.

The revaluation impacts directly on the accounting equation of Assets − Liabilities = Capital. Although there is no 'profit' because the asset has not been sold, the increase is credited to comprehensive income. We discuss this topic in Chapter 9. The increase appears on the balance sheet under equity with the heading of 'Revaluation surplus'. Worked example 4.2 demonstrates this.

Worked example 4.2   Revaluation of land

Endow Co. owns land originally purchased for £150,000. The Board believes that a rival company intends to launch a hostile bid. To deter this action it decides to use the regulations in IAS 16 that permit revaluations. The work is carried out and the revaluation figure is £180,000.

The accounting actions are as follows. The land is on the balance sheet at the revalued amount. There is a difference between the original cost and the revaluation amount of £30,000. The land appears on the balance sheet at the revalued amount of £180,000. The balance of £30,000 goes to the Statement of Comprehensive Income as a revaluation surplus.

A problem arises where there has already been depreciation of the asset. In these circumstances, the standard allows two approaches (as shown in Worked example 4.3). The accumulated depreciation can be adjusted to equal the difference between the gross carrying amount

---

Worked example 4.3   **Revaluations and depreciation**

Digby Co. purchased machinery for £50,000 in January 2013 and depreciates it at £10,000 per annum. The carrying amount at the end of 2015 is £20,000 (£50,000 – (3 years x £10,000)).

The machinery is revalued at the beginning of 2016 at £28,000. The revalued amount of £28,000 is shown on the balance sheet and the surplus of £8,000 goes to comprehensive income as a revaluation reserve. The company can either:

1 Restate the gross amount of the asset at £50,000 and restate the accumulated depreciation at £22,000. This gives the carrying amount as £28,000 on the balance sheet.

or:

2 Show the revised carrying amount at £28,000 and reverse the accumulated depreciation. The annual depreciation charge for the remaining 2 years of the asset will be

$$\frac{£28,000}{2 \text{ years}} = £14,000 \text{ per annum.}$$

The increase in the depreciation charge of £4,000 annually can be written off against the revaluation surplus that was created as a part of the surplus that is being realized. This is a movement in owner's equity and will not go to the profit or loss account.

---

and the carrying amount of the asset. Alternatively, the accumulated depreciation is eliminated against the gross carrying amount of the asset.

A revalued asset is carried on the balance sheet at its revaluation amount, less depreciation and subsequent impairment losses, if any. A downwards revaluation is accounted for as an expense in the profit or loss account if there has been no previous revaluation upwards. Any subsequent revaluation downwards can be offset against any previous upwards increase in value of the same asset.

The user interpreting revaluations needs, firstly, to assess the possible reasons for the entity making revaluations and, secondly, to consider how this relates to their own interests in the entity.

Depreciation

depreciation

Depreciation is the systematic allocation of the *depreciable amount* of an asset over its *useful life*.

Based on IAS 16, para. 6

When an entity acquires a non-current asset, it affects both the balance sheet and the profit or loss account. We explain accounting for **depreciation** more fully in Chapter 8, but it is useful at this stage to consider the impact on the balance sheet.

If an entity purchases a machine for cash, the initial accounting is simple. There is a credit to the cash account and a debit to the machinery account. At the year-end, the asset appears on the balance sheet. However, non-current assets do not last for ever; they have finite useful economic lives.

The entity will use the machine to generate profits. It seems sensible that the cost of the machine is shown as a cost on the profit or loss account. However, it would be misleading to users of financial statements if the full cost was shown in the year of purchase. If the entity considers that the machine has an economic useful life of five years, it makes sense to spread the initial cost or depreciable amount over the five years' profit or loss accounts.

IAS 16 requires the depreciation of PPE on a systematic basis over the asset's useful economic life. Depreciation applies to both the cost and revalued bases for assets. The depreciation charge commences when the asset is available for use and continues until the asset is derecognized regardless of periods of idleness.

There are several depreciation methods. The standard identifies three main methods: the straight line method, the diminishing balance method (also known as the reducing balance method) and the units of production method.

The last method is used in those circumstances where the organization is able to estimate satisfactorily the number of units the asset is able to produce during its useful economic life. This method is not used frequently and therefore we concentrate on the straight line method and the diminishing balance method.

The straight line method

The annual depreciation to be charged using the straight line method is:

$$\text{Annual depreciation charge} = \frac{\text{Cost of asset} - \text{Residual value}}{\text{Estimated life of asset}}$$

The accumulated annual depreciation charge is deducted from the cost of the asset to give the carrying amount, which appears in the balance sheet. At the end of its useful economic life the carrying amount should equal the asset's residual value.

The diminishing balance method

The diminishing balance method applies a set percentage rate annually over the life of the asset. Depreciation charged each year decreases. Some prefer this method because the asset becomes less productive and costs more in repairs as it ages. The depreciation charge is decreasing as the charge for repairs is increasing thus, one hopes, resulting in the total charge being consistent over the life of the asset.

Depreciation in practice

Worked example 4.4 uses the straight line method to help to clarify the basic process of applying depreciation.

Worked example 4.4   Straight line depreciation

Dibdobs Company purchases a machine for £26,000 on 1 January 2017. It estimates that it will be able to use the machine profitably for 6 years. At the end of that time, it should be able to sell the machine for £2,000. This amount is the residual or scrap value.

The amount that Dibdobs needs to charge to the profit or loss account each year is £26,000 – £2,000 = £24,000. This is the total amount, termed the depreciable amount, to be charged to the profit or loss account over the 6-year period. The formula is:

$$\frac{\text{Cost} - \text{Residual value}}{\text{Number of years}} = \text{Annual depreciation charge}$$

$$\frac{£26,000 - £2,000}{6 \text{ years}} = £4,000 \text{ per year}$$

Worked example 4.4 raises several questions, the obvious ones being:

What if the machine does not last 6 years?
What if the residual value is greater or less than £2,000?
If there is inflation should this be accounted for in the residual value estimate?

But there are even more complications. One relates to the number of decision-makers involved. The entity decides the useful economic life of the asset. The manufacturers may give guidance. The entity's own engineers may have the knowledge to assist. The company may have a stated policy, for example, that all motor vehicles are depreciated over 3 years and then sold. Finally, the finance director and auditors will be making comparisons with practices by other entities.

The other issue is the estimate of the residual value of the asset at the end of its useful economic life. Once again, the entity decides. IAS 16 requires entities to reassess the useful life of assets on an annual basis.

An increase in the economic life has several implications for the user of the accounts. The first concern is how long the useful economic life is in reality. Secondly, the carrying amount in the balance sheet reduces at a slower rate annually as the asset is depreciated over a longer time. Thirdly, the annual charge to the profit or loss account will be smaller, thus enhancing the profit.

It is critical for the user to understand what period an entity sets for the useful lives of assets, and how this is reassessed. Company example 4.3 from British Telecom (BT) demonstrates the considerable work an entity undertakes in making such decisions. It is worth mentioning that the carrying amount for PPE on the balance sheet is the significant figure of £13,840 million. British Telecom uses the term 'amortization' which, for the purposes of this chapter, is the same as depreciation.

Company example 4.3

Useful lives for property, plant and equipment and software

The plant and equipment in our networks is long lived with cables and switching equipment operating for over ten years and underground ducts being used for decades. We also develop software for use in IT systems and platforms that supports the products and services provided to our customers and that is also used within the group. The annual depreciation and amortisation charge is sensitive to the estimated service lives allocated to each type of asset. Asset lives are assessed annually and changed when necessary to reflect current thinking on the remaining lives in light of technological change, network investment plans (including the group's fibre rollout programme), prospective economic utilisation and physical condition of the assets concerned. Changes to the service lives of assets implemented from 1 April 2013 had no significant impact in aggregate on the results for the year ended 31 March 2014.

BT, Annual Report, 2014, p. 128

In Chapter 8 we take a closer look at depreciation, but at this stage we are simply explaining the amounts shown on the balance sheet for non-current assets. They are the original cost less the estimated residual value shared over the estimated useful economic life of the asset.

The amounts shown on the balance sheet (the carrying amounts) do not show the 'value' of the asset unless it has been revalued or it is impaired. We discussed revaluations earlier in this chapter and we discuss impairment in the next chapter.

Derecognition

After the initial recognition and measurement of the asset, the final stage is derecognition. Either this occurs at the end of the life of the asset, when it is disposed of, or when there are no expected future benefits.

The gain or loss from the sale or disposal of the asset is the difference between the net disposal proceeds, if any, and the carrying amount of the item. When the item is derecognized, the gain or loss arising from the derecognition goes to profit or loss. Although the company may sell the unwanted asset, gains on derecognition cannot be classified as revenue on the income statement.

Worked example 4.5   Gains and losses on derecognition

A company purchases equipment for £12,000. It considers that the equipment has a residual value of £2,000 and a useful economic life of 10 years. At the end of the 10 years, the company is able to sell the equipment for £2,800 but it incurs £300 costs in delivering it to the purchaser. The Production Manager suggests that the £2,800 is shown as revenue and the £300 as additional depreciation.

The accountant explains that **net** disposal proceeds of £500 must be shown on the profit or loss account as a gain on disposal. Because the residual value of the asset is £2,000, the maximum gain could only be the difference between that amount and the selling price of £2,800. The standard states that the **net** disposal proceeds only can be shown as a gain. Thus, the £300 delivery costs must be deducted from the £800 to give the gain of £500. This transaction is not the way we usually generate revenue and therefore cannot be included in that figure, but must be shown separately.

Worked example 4.5 illustrates that transactions that appear similar may need different accounting treatments and will be regulated by different standards. If a company makes equipment and sells it, the transaction is considered as revenue and comes under IFRS 15 (see Chapter 7). However, the sale of an asset it owns is not a revenue transaction, and comes under the regulations of IAS 16.

IAS 23

BORROWING COSTS

borrowing costs

Borrowing costs include the interest and other costs that an entity incurs in connection with the borrowing of funds.

Based on IAS 23, para. 5

Some entities will purchase their non-current assets and others may construct their own. Those entities that construct assets themselves may borrow money to do so. The question arises as to whether the interest on the borrowings is part of constructing the asset, and thus is capitalized on the balance sheet, or, as with other interest payments, it goes to the profit or loss account as an expense.

▼ **Table 4.4** *Timeline of IAS 23*

Date	Comment
1984	Standard first issued
1993	Standard revised
2008	Latest amendment

For several years, there was no guidance on this issue and a company could select its own policy. For the user this could be confusing. Interest treated as an expense decreases profits. Interest considered as part of the asset goes to the balance sheet, and the profit or loss account is not affected.

Scope of the standard

The objective of IAS 23 is to set out the appropriate accounting treatment for **borrowing costs** that are directly attributable to the acquisition, construction or production of a 'qualifying asset'. A non-current asset that takes a substantial time to get ready for its intended use or sale is a qualifying asset. The borrowing costs for a qualifying asset are included in the cost of the asset. Borrowing costs, which do not meet the requirements of the standard, are recognized as an expense in the profit or loss account.

The standard does not apply to:

- qualifying assets measured at fair value, such as biological assets accounted for under IAS 41 *Agriculture*;
- inventories that are manufactured, or otherwise produced, in large quantities on a repetitive basis and that take a substantial period to get ready for sale (for example, maturing whisky).

Examples of qualifying assets include manufacturing plants, power generation facilities and investment properties. In some industries, it can take a long time before such assets are in a saleable condition. The regulation is that such borrowing costs can be capitalized. This does not apply to inventories manufactured on a routine basis or produced in large quantities on a repetitive basis over a short time.

Originally, entities could select whether they expensed the borrowing costs on the balance sheet or expensed them to the profit or loss account. This made it very difficult for users to make comparisons where companies used different accounting treatments for similar transactions. A useful revision to the standard in 2007 resolved this weakness. IAS 23 now states that borrowing costs which are directly attributed to the acquisition, construction or production of a qualifying asset must be capitalized as part of the cost of the asset.

The standard's basis for conclusions explains the use of the term 'borrowing costs' rather than 'interest costs'. The term 'borrowing costs' reflects the broader definition in IAS 23, which encompasses interest and other costs as follows:

- interest on bank overdrafts and borrowings;
- amortization of discounts or premiums on borrowings;
- amortization of ancillary costs incurred in the arrangement of borrowings;
- finance charges on finance leases;
- exchange differences on foreign currency borrowings where they are regarded as an adjustment to interest costs.

Calculating capitalization

There are restrictions on the amount that a company can capitalize. The main rule is that the capitalization is the actual costs incurred less any income earned on the temporary investment of funds. Where the borrowings are one part of a general pool, the capitalization rate is the weighted average of the borrowing costs for the general pool.

In calculating the amount to be capitalized, it is important to identify the date that the project commenced and the date that it finishes. The capitalization of borrowings occurs on major, long-term projects, which can lead to situations where work is temporarily ceased. Capitalization must then be suspended. Diagram 4.5 summarizes the regulations in the standard.

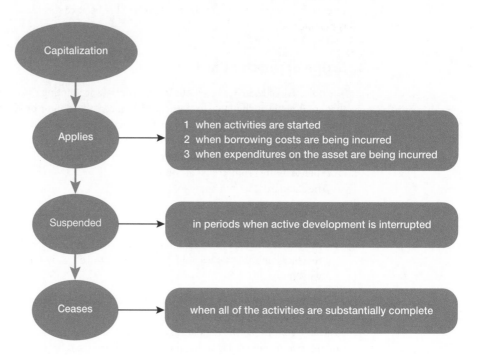

Capitalization

Applies
1 when activities are started
2 when borrowing costs are being incurred
3 when expenditures on the asset are being incurred

Suspended
in periods when active development is interrupted

Ceases
when all of the activities are substantially complete

▲ **Diagram 4.5** *The timing of capitalization of borrowings*

With some projects, work is conducted in stages and there may be a delay before the next stage begins. Capitalization should cease when all of the necessary activities of one stage are substantially complete and work has not yet commenced on the next stage. For example, a company may have cleared the site and put in the major foundations and the supply pipes for water sewage and electricity. For various reasons such as poor weather or late delivery of building materials the project may be delayed. As another example, a Canadian company may have ordered a large machine from Germany. In anticipation of its arrival they have cleared a space in the factory, reinforced the foundations and constructed a conveyor belt system. The German company is late with delivery and, because of extreme winter weather in Canada, it has been decided to delay the delivery of the machine for 3 months, so the project is suspended for that time.

The timing of activities starting and continuing, and the interest to be paid, raises problems. In some circumstances, entities may have to secure a loan and pay interest before construction starts. A project may be suspended part way through but the interest still has to be paid. Finally, the company may not repay the loan until some time after the project has been completed but it will still be required to pay the interest. The rules are:

1 Interest paid prior to the activity commencing is charged as an expense to the profit or loss account. It cannot be capitalized.
2 Where a project is suspended for an extended time, interest cannot be capitalized.
3 If there is a temporary suspension of activity, interest can be capitalized.
4 At the cessation of the project, if the company does not immediately repay the loan, any subsequent interest cannot be capitalized and must be charged as an expense to the profit or loss account.
5 The amount of borrowing costs eligible for capitalization are the actual *borrowing costs* incurred on that borrowing during the period less any investment income on the temporary investment of those borrowings.

Worked examples 4.6 and 4.7 illustrate two treatments of capitalization.

Worked example 4.6   Capitalization and cost of asset

Bedow Co. takes a loan of £3 million at 5% per annum on 1 January 2014 for the construction of a qualifying asset. The work is completed on 31 December 2014. The company is able to repay the loan in full on 30 June 2015.

Construction cost of asset	£3,000,000
Capitalization of interest for one year	£150,000
Total cost of asset on balance sheet	£3,150,000
Interest not capitalized and charged to profit or loss account	£3 million x 5% x 6 months = £75,000

Worked example 4.7   Capitalization and timing

A company arranges a one-year loan for £3 million at 5% per annum on 1 January 2014 when activity commences. Only £2 million is needed immediately and the remaining £1 million is invested for 3 months at 2%. The work is completed on 31 December 2014 and the loan is repaid in full on that date.

Total interest paid on loan for 12 months	£150,000
Deduct interest received for three months	£20,000
Interest to be capitalized	£130,000

It is possible that an entity borrows at a high rate of interest. When the qualifying asset takes a substantial time to be completed, the total cost can be higher than the recoverable amount or written down value. In this case, the carrying amount of the asset must be shown in the balance sheet at the reduced amount.

The standard does not permit a qualifying asset to be shown in the balance sheet at a value higher than its recoverable amount or written-down amount. The recoverable amount is the greater of the price a company could obtain from selling an asset and the value the asset would generate if retained by the company. We provide further explanation of these calculations in Chapter 5 where we discuss impairment of assets.

Company example 4.4 showing the accounting policy for PPE is taken from PAO Severstal, the Russian steel and steel-related mining company.

Company example 4.4

Property plant and equipment

f. Property, plant and equipment

Property, plant and equipment are carried at cost less accumulated depreciation and accumulated impairment losses. Cost includes expenditure that is directly attributable to the acquisition of the asset and, for qualifying assets, borrowing costs capitalized. In the case of assets constructed by the Group, related works and direct project over-heads are included in cost. The cost of replacing part of an item of property, plant and equipment is recognized in the carrying amount of the item if it is probable that the future economic benefits embodied within the part will flow to the Group and its cost can be measured reliably. The carrying amount of the replaced part is derecognized. Repair and maintenance expenses are charged to the income statement as incurred. Gains or losses on disposals of property, plant and equipment are recognized in the income statement.

Depreciation is provided so as to write off property, plant and equipment over its expected useful life. Depreciation is calculated using the straight-line basis, except for depreciation on vehicles and certain metal-rolling equipment, which is calculated on the basis of mileage and units of production, respectively. The estimated useful lives of assets are reviewed regularly and revised when necessary.

The principal periods over which assets are depreciated are as follows:

Buildings and constructions 20–50 years
Plant and machinery 10–20 years
Other productive assets 5–20 years
Infrastructure assets 5–50 years

PAO Severstal, Annual Report and Accounts, 2015, p. 84

Company example 4.4 addresses many of the points in this chapter. It explains that 'qualifying assets' include the capitalization of borrowing costs and that replacements of parts of an asset are incorporated in the cost of the asset. The company also explains its depreciation policies, including the regular review of the value of the assets.

CONCLUSIONS

The accounting equation underpins the balance sheet. All companies have assets, liabilities and cash. Assets can be classified as tangible non-current assets, intangible non-current assets and cash. Although all companies have these components, the nature of the industry determines their comparative importance on the balance sheet.

Standards have been developed over the years to address various aspects of accounting for the different types of assets. In this chapter, we have concentrated on IAS 16 *Property, Plant and Equipment*. This standard applies the historical cost basis for the initial measurement method of the asset and permits, but does not compel, a revaluation upwards for subsequent measurements.

Undoubtedly, the requirement for companies to revalue all assets would be a burden, but a logical progression. Without that requirement, users must be careful in drawing conclusions from the amounts shown on the balance sheet. The carrying amount of an asset on the balance sheet does not necessarily represent its value. It is the original cost of the asset depreciated over its estimated useful life. Sometimes an asset may lose its value (become impaired) so it is less than the calculated carrying amount. In instances where the asset is impaired, the company must adjust the balance sheet amount, and we discuss this in Chapter 5.

The capitalization of borrowing costs under IAS 23 was previously a controversial matter. However, the standard has been revised and all companies must apply IAS 23. The requirement to capitalize borrowing costs is restricted to qualifying assets, and the periods when interest can be capitalized are very specific. Nevertheless, the amount of interest added to the other costs of the qualifying asset depends on a number of factors, including the amount, if any, the company wishes to borrow and the rate of interest charged at that time.

ADDITIONAL RESOURCES

Go online to the companion website for this book to access further teaching and learning materials for this chapter.

www.palgravehighered.com/hussey-cfr

STATEMENT OF FINANCIAL POSITION – INTANGIBLE ASSETS AND IMPAIRMENT

IAS 38 Intangible Assets

IAS 36 Impairment of Assets

LEARNING OBJECTIVES

At the end of this chapter, you should be able to:

- Discuss intangible assets
- Explain the requirements of IAS 38 *Intangible Assets*
- Calculate the amount for goodwill in a corporate acquisition
- Analyze the notion of impairment for both tangible and intangible assets
- Demonstrate the application of the impairment test in IAS 36 *Impairment of Assets*
- Describe a cash-generating unit
- Apply the correct accounting treatment for impairment where there is a cash-generating unit

INTRODUCTION

This chapter is divided into two main sections and links directly with Chapter 4. Although all companies have assets to generate profits, the nature of the assets reflects the industry in which a company operates. Although tangible assets remain the main item on many entities' balance sheets, intangible assets have become very significant for some.

IAS 38 *Intangible Assets* describes the intangible assets that can appear on a balance sheet and their accounting treatment. One issue is the identification of such assets because their definition states that they have no physical substance. Even where the intangible asset is identified, there are questions on the value of the asset.

One intangible asset which has caused much debate over the years is 'goodwill'. We discuss the nature of the arguments and the requirements of the standard.

The second section of this chapter on impairment applies to both tangible and intangible assets. It is possible that a tangible asset held by an entity reduces in value. The property may be in an area that is suffering an economic decline. There could have been market changes

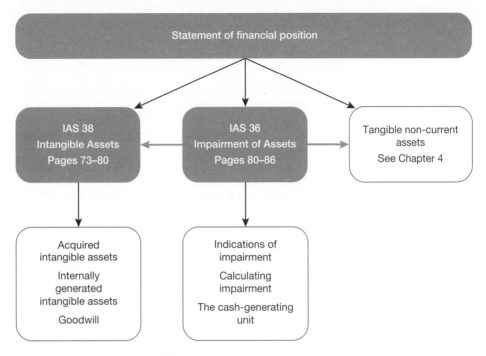

▲ **Diagram 5.1** *Structure of Chapter 5*

and the products or services offered are not in such demand as previously. In these circumstances, the carrying amount of the asset shown in the balance sheet may not reflect the present value.

An intangible asset can also lose value. Brand names may generate sales for products, but what if there is an occurrence that impairs the brand name? We may buy certain food products or medications because the company has a good 'reputation'. A government investigation that casts doubt on the safety of the item could affect negatively on sales.

IAS 36 *Impairment of Assets* was issued in 1998 and revised in 2004. The standard applies to both tangible and intangible assets. Impairment is where the carrying amount of a non-current asset is more than the amount through its use or sale. The standard explains the procedure for identifying impairment of an asset and the proper accounting treatment.

IAS 38

INTANGIBLE ASSETS

intangible asset

An intangible asset is an identifiable non-monetary asset without physical substance.

Based on IAS 38, para. 8

Increasingly, entities have found their most important assets for generating future benefits are not physical assets, such as buildings and machinery, but assets that have no physical substance. For example, every cab in New York City has to purchase a licence in the form of a medallion to display. The city strictly limits the number of licences issued and the cost of a licence in auction can be about $1 million.

▼ **Table 5.1** *Timeline of IAS 38*

Date	Comment
1998	Replaced IAS 9 Research and Development Costs
2014	Latest amendment
Interpretations issued	IFRIC 4 Determining whether an Arrangement contains a Lease
	IFRIC 12 Service Concession Arrangements
	IFRIC 20 Stripping Costs in the Production Phase of a Surface Mine

In 2014, American Airlines paid £18.2 million for a pair of landing slots at Heathrow Airport, UK (*Sunday Times*, 22 June 2014). This gave the airline the right to take off and land at certain times. Other examples of **intangible assets** are:

● broadcast rights
● computer software
● customer lists
● drilling rights
● franchise agreements
● internet domain names
● licensing agreements
● literary works
● motion pictures and television programmes
● musical works
● patented technology
● service contracts
● trademarks

Other items that are not on the list can be a benefit to the entity. Possibly the main one is 'reputation' which may originate from highly trained employees, excellent products and a high degree of customer satisfaction.

The objective of the standard is to set out the accounting requirements for intangible assets. These are defined as assets which are without physical substance and identifiable (either being separable or arising from contractual or other legal rights). There are certain intangible assets that IAS 38 excludes. These are:

● Financial assets such as *bank deposits* and *bonds* (see IAS 32 *Financial Instruments*, Chapter 12).
● Exploration and evaluation assets (see IFRS 6 *Exploration for and Evaluation of Mineral Resources*, Chapter 15).
● Expenditure on the development and extraction of minerals, oil, natural gas, and similar resources.
● Intangible assets arising from insurance contracts issued by insurance companies.
● Intangible assets covered by another IAS or IFRS. The main examples are:
  ○ Intangibles held for sale (see IFRS 5 *Non-current Assets Held for Sale and Discontinued Operations*, Chapter 15).
  ○ Deferred tax assets (see IAS 12 *Income Taxes*, Chapter 14).
  ○ Lease assets (see IAS 17 *Leases*, Chapter 14).
  ○ Assets arising from employee benefits (see IAS 19 *Employee Benefits*, Chapter 9).
  ○ Goodwill (see IFRS 3 *Business Combinations*, Chapter 16).

Intangible assets must satisfy the criteria for any asset to be recognized: future economic benefits must be expected and it must be possible to measure the asset reliably. The requirement of reliable measurement can prevent the recognition of some intangible assets. Reliable measurement means that the asset:

- can be separated from the rest of the company;
- can be sold, licensed, rented or exchanged either individually or together with a related item.

An intangible asset can also be identifiable because it arises from contractual or legal rights even if those rights are not separable from the business.

An entity may generate an intangible asset itself or acquire it from another entity. Because of the necessity for reliable measurement, the standard has different requirements for acquired intangible assets and those that are self-generated. Acquired intangible assets are measured by the price paid on the assumption that the asset was acquired because there are anticipated future benefits. The regulations are more complex for self-generated intangible assets, and we discuss these later in this chapter.

Acquired intangible assets

Recognition

The acquisition of the asset from another party can take place in three ways and this will determine the measurement criteria.

1   The intangible asset is acquired by payment to another party. As the transaction is between willing parties, the purchase price is the fair value.
2   The entity acquires an asset by exchanging another for it. As there is no 'purchase price', the asset is measured at fair value as defined in IFRS 13. Fair value is the price that would be received for selling an asset or paid for transferring a liability in an orderly transaction between market participants at the measurement date. This term is explained at greater length in IFRS 13, which is discussed in Chapter 12. Where it is not possible to ascertain the fair value, the asset is measured at the carrying amount of the asset given up.
3   The intangible asset is acquired in the course of taking over another business: a business combination. In these circumstances, recognition is at fair value.

Measurement

As with tangible assets, an entity has a choice of measurement methods. Disclosure on the balance sheet can be at either:

- Cost less any accumulated amortization and impairment losses; or
- A revalued amount (based on fair value) less any subsequent amortization and any accumulated impairment losses. This method cannot be used at initial recognition.

Cost should be easy to identify from the transaction itself. The standard specifies those components of cost that can be recognized. There are certain items that cannot be included in the original cost:

- administration costs;
- costs of introducing new products or services;
- costs of conducting new business;
- costs incurred whilst waiting to use the asset;
- initial operating losses from operation.

Internally generated intangible assets

Recognition

Entities cannot recognize certain internally generated intangible assets such as goodwill, brands and publishing titles. A company may have several products with well-known brand names but these do not appear on its balance sheet. The reason is that they are internally generated, and it is highly doubtful whether their value can be measured reliably.

Although particular intangibles should not be recognized if they were internally generated, they may meet the general recognition criteria if purchased from another company. This leads to the somewhat bewildering position that the financial statements of some entities do not show their world-renowned brands, which means that users of their financial statements may not realize the value of these brands, whereas, if the brands had been acquired from another entity, they could be shown on the balance sheet.

There is some scope in IAS 38 to recognize on the balance sheet development costs that have been incurred, but not research costs. Expenditure on research must be charged to the income statement of the financial period in which it occurs, and includes such costs as:

- the pursuit of new knowledge;
- the search for, or evaluation, and selection of applications of research;
- the search for such items as alternative materials, products and systems;
- the pursuit of possible alternatives for improved items such as materials, products and systems.

By recognizing development costs on the balance sheet, it must be possible to separate them from the research phase. The expenditure for the development phase can only be capitalized if the following criteria are met:

- It is technically feasible to complete the asset so that it will be ready for sale or use.
- The entity intends to complete the asset and sell it or use it.
- The entity is able to use or sell the asset.
- The asset has the potential to generate future economic benefits for the company.
- There are sufficient technical, financial and other resources available to complete the development of the asset.
- It is possible to measure reliably the costs of development.

The transition from a research phase to a development phase may be difficult to identify, or may not even occur. Many research projects are started but later abandoned because the results do not look promising.

If the research is successful, the project will enter into a development phase. Usually a business plan is required to prove that a project has entered into the development phase. The fact that the project is successful does not allow the company to go back and capitalize the research costs. They must be written off as they are incurred.

Measurement

There are various theoretical methods for measuring an intangible asset. The possible approaches are:

- It remains on the balance sheet unchanged until some event occurs which makes it no longer an asset. In other words, it is unable to generate future benefits.
- It can be depreciated, as with tangible assets, over its useful economic life.
- It can be depreciated over an arbitrary period of time established by the standard setters.

There are different opinions on which is the best method. Some argue that intangible assets rarely lose their value, and point to famous brand names that have been in existence for over 100 years as evidence. Others argue that nothing in this world has an indefinite life. The life span may be unknown, but nothing lasts for ever.

In the absence of an international standard, countries adopted various approaches over the years. Accepting that nothing lasts for ever, the method of depreciation over an arbitrary time has possibly been the most popular method for accounting for intangible assets. The term 'amortization' usually replaces the term 'depreciation'.

Critics of amortization argued that this approach was nonsensical because nobody could predict the life of the intangible asset. If it was depreciated to zero, the company might still be generating sales from the asset – brand names being a good example – and the user would have considerable difficulty in assessing a company if profits were being generated with no assets.

After considerable debate, IAS 38 established an alternative approach that seems to be effective. Two different situations are specified:

1   Intangible assets are treated similarly to tangible assets. The process is the same as we discussed for tangible assets, and companies can select the most appropriate method. As with tangible assets, the IASB does not allow a revenue-based method.
2   An intangible asset cannot have an infinite life, only an indefinite one. If a company is unable to estimate the useful economic life, the standard requires testing of the asset for impairment annually. The requirements of IAS 36 *Impairment of Assets* apply.

Possibly a good example of intangible assets is connected to the film industry.[1] Company example 5.1 shows an extract from Cineworld Group plc's annual report and accounts. The group is one of the UK's leading cinema chains by box office revenues. It operates in nine different countries, including six in Central and Eastern Europe.

Company example 5.1

Intangible assets and goodwill

Identifiable intangibles are those which can be sold separately or which arise from legal rights regardless of whether those rights are separable.
Goodwill is stated at cost less any accumulated impairment losses. Goodwill is allocated to cash-generating units and is not amortised but is tested annually for impairment.

Other intangible assets that are acquired by the Group are stated at cost less accumulated amortisation and impairment losses. Identifiable intangibles are those which can be sold separately or which arise from legal rights regardless of whether those rights are separable.

Distribution rights that are acquired by the Group are stated at cost less accumulated amortisation and impairment losses.

Amortisation is charged to the income statement on a straight-line basis over the estimated useful lives of intangible assets unless such lives are indefinite. Intangible assets with an indefinite useful life and goodwill are systematically tested for impairment at each balance sheet date. Other intangible assets are amortised from the date they are available for use.

continued overleaf

> ## Company example 5.1 *continued*
>
> Distribution rights are amortised by film title from the date of release of the film, at 50% in the first year of release and 25% in each of the two subsequent years. The estimated useful lives are as follows:
>
> - Brands   10 to 20 years
> - Distribution rights   3 years
> - Other intangibles   5 to 10 years
>
> *Cineworld Group plc, Annual Report and Accounts, 2015, p. 92*

The note in Cineworld's accounts explains identifiable intangible assets and states that the method of measurement is at cost less accumulated amortization and impairment losses. The straight line method is used for amortization and the company states the estimated useful lives of the assets.

Goodwill

The intangible asset that best demonstrates the debate on the treatment of intangible assets is **goodwill**, whether purchased or internally generated. The ephemeral nature of goodwill has been the basis of many legal cases, and judges have delighted in drawing zoological comparisons to explain the problems. In the 1934 case of Whiteman Smith Motor Company *v.* Chaplin, four types of customers were identified:

- The dog that stays faithful to the person and not the location.
- The cat that stays faithful to the location and not the person.
- The rabbit who is a customer because the premises are close and for no other reason.
- The rat that is casual and is attracted to neither person nor location.

goodwill

Goodwill is an intangible asset representing the future economic benefits arising from assets that are not capable of being individually identified and separately recognized.

Most acquirers assume they are going to have cat customers who will stay with the business. Unfortunately, the world is full of dogs who follow the owner and leave the business. There are also rat and rabbit customers with little loyalty to the business. Paying for goodwill on the acquisition of a business may not result in a good customer base.

After many years of debate, standard setters decided that acquired goodwill could appear on the balance sheet. Internally generated goodwill cannot be shown on the balance sheet.

If we acquire goodwill and put it on the balance sheet, we need some method to calculate the value. If one company acquires another, the price paid is negotiated. This price, largely, is not based on the possible value of non-current assets but on the future profits that can be expected. In this case, the value of goodwill may be a balancing figure.

This is not to say that the acquiring company does not do its due diligence. It will calculate the physical condition and values of any land, property, plant and equipment. The acquirer will also be interested in any outstanding debts, the products and services the acquiree has, and its reputation in the market place.

However, in the process of acquiring a successful business, the acquirer expects to pay more than the calculated value of the tangible assets. Although simple, Worked examples 5.1 and 5.2 illustrate the process.

Worked example 5.1   Acquired goodwill

A large company acquires a smaller but highly successful company. Because the small company is so successful, the large company agrees to pay £3.5 million. The large company makes the purchase and then calculates the fair value of the tangible assets, the property, plant and machinery, it has acquired. The fair value of the tangible assets it has acquired is calculated to be £3 million.

The large company made the acquisition because the smaller company was successful. It had a good reputation, satisfied customers, trained employees – in other words there was a bundle of attributes to which we give the title 'Goodwill'. As the large company paid for the goodwill it can put it on its balance sheet at a value of £500,000, but it will have to test for any impairment of the goodwill.

Worked example 5.2   Goodwill as a balancing figure

Company A agrees to buy Company B for £1,500,000. After the deal is completed, company A lists the tangible assets it has acquired and the values it will use to put in its own records:

Land	£800,000
Plant and equipment	£400,000
Computers	£50,000
Inventories	£50,000
Total	£1,300,000

Because A paid £1,500,000 and the total value of tangible assets is £1,300,000, the difference of £200,000 is goodwill.

You may not consider that calculating a balancing figure is a 'scientific' method for valuing goodwill. Many would agree and the issue is a subject of constant debate. In Chapters 16 and 17, we consider examples that are more complex and we discuss the problems more fully.

Here, we wish to emphasize the financial importance of goodwill and intangible assets for some industries and some companies. In their annual report for 2015, the beer and soft drinks company, SABMiller, listed its assets on the balance sheet, and the first three were:

	US$m
Goodwill	14,746
Intangible assets	6,878
Property, plant and equipment	7,961

The company gave significant explanations for the method of calculations used. Brands make up a sizable proportion of the intangible assets and these are amortized. The company showed the value of the main brands and the estimated amortization period remaining (see Company example 5.2).

Those unfamiliar with SABMiller may question the values placed on the various brands of beer. As always, the financial results of a company must be considered in their context, so we provide a brief background to SABMiller. The company produces more than 200 beers in over 80 countries. It is a FTSE-100 company, with shares trading on the London Stock Exchange, and a secondary listing on the Johannesburg Stock Exchange. It has around 69,000 employees across the globe, from Australia to Zambia, Colombia to the Czech Republic and South Africa to the USA.

In Chapter 19, we explain how company information is used to construct the context for assessing a company's financial statements. The annual report and accounts and a company's website are excellent sources of that information.

As noted in Worked example 5.1, companies must test for impairment of goodwill, and that leads us to the final section in this chapter.

IAS 36

IMPAIRMENT OF ASSETS

▼ **Table 5.2** *Timeline of IAS 36*

Date	Comment
1998	Standard first issued
2013	Latest amendment
Interpretations issued	IFRIC 10 Interim Financial Reporting and Impairment
	IFRIC 12 Service Concession Arrangements
	SIC 32 Intangible Assets – Web Site Costs

impairment

Impairment of an asset takes place if the carrying amount shown in the organization's financial records is greater than the proceeds the organization considers would be received if the asset was retained in use or sold to an outside party.

IAS 36 applies to both tangible and intangible non-current assets. You may wish to refer to Chapter 4 to ensure that you have a sound base for our explanation of asset **impairment**.

The objective of the standard is to ensure that an entity's assets are not shown on the balance sheet at more than their recoverable amount. Users of financial statements may be misled on the financial strength of the entity and its financial performance if they are not informed of the proper carrying value of assets.

The standard applies to:

- property, plant and equipment;
- intangible assets and goodwill;
- investment property carried at cost;
- subsidiaries, associates and joint ventures.

Assets excluded from the standard are:

- inventories (see IAS 2, Chapter 8);
- assets arising from construction contracts (see IAS 11 and IFRS 15, Chapter 7);
- deferred tax assets (see IAS 12, Chapter 14);
- assets arising from employee benefits (see IAS 19, Chapter 9);
- financial assets (see IAS 39, Chapter 12);
- investment property carried at fair value (see IAS 40, Chapter 15);
- agricultural assets carried at fair value (see IAS 41, Chapter 15);
- insurance contract assets (see IFRS 4);
- non-current assets held for sale (see IFRS 5, Chapter 15).

Where an asset is impaired, the entity must write off the impairment loss in the financial period it occurs. The write-off could have a significant negative effect on earnings and performance ratios.

Indications of impairment

Entities must assess annually whether there has been an indication of impairment of all its assets. This could be a burden but the key words are 'an indication of impairment'. The process for ascertaining whether there has been impairment is in two stages. The first stage is assessing whether there are any indications of possible impairment. The indications can be external or internal.

External indications

- An abnormal fall in the asset's market value.
- A significant change in the technological, market, legal or economic environment of the business in which the assets are used.
- An increase in market interest rates or market rates of return on investments likely to affect the discount rates in calculating the value in use of the assets.
- The carrying value of the net assets being more than its market capitalization.

Internal indications

- Evidence of obsolescence; that is, going out of date or physical damage.
- Adverse changes in the use to which the asset is put.
- The asset's economic performance.

If there are no indications of impairment, no action is required.

In addition to the indication assessment, there are certain assets for which a full impairment assessment is required annually. The assets requiring the full test are:

- Intangible assets with indefinite lives. This is any intangible asset not being amortized over a set time.
- Intangible assets not ready for use.
- Goodwill arising through a business combination. We discuss this fully in Chapter 16.

A company must go to the second stage of the impairment test for these three classes of assets and those assets for which there are indications of impairment.

Calculating impairment

The second stage involves calculating the recoverable amount of the asset and comparing it to its carrying amount in the balance sheet.

Procedure

1   Compare the recoverable amount to the carrying amount of the asset on the balance sheet.
2   If the carrying amount on the balance sheet is higher than the recoverable amount the asset is impaired.
3   The amount of the impairment is a charge to the profit or loss account and the carrying amount on the balance sheet is reduced.

recoverable amount

The recoverable amount is the higher of fair value less costs to sell and value in use.

IAS 36, para. 6

fair value

Fair value is the price that would be received to sell an asset or paid to transfer a liability in an orderly trans-action between market participants at the measurement date.

Based on IFRS 13, Appendix A

value in use

Value in use is the present value of the future cash flows expected to be derived from an asset or cash-generating unit.

IAS 36, para. 6

The **recoverable amount** is the higher of **fair value** and **value in use**. Fair value is the amount expected to be received if the assets were sold. IFRS 13 *Fair Value* provides guidance, and we discuss it in Chapter 12. The fair value of an asset can sometimes be difficult to assess in practice. One must assume that there is a willing buyer for that particular asset.

The two steps required to determine the value in use of an asset are:

1   Estimate the future cash flows anticipated over the remaining life of the asset. This is the cash flow forecast for the one asset. The company has to determine the cash inflows and cash outflows for each asset to find the cash surplus or deficit each year for its remaining years of use.
2   Calculate the present value of those cash surpluses and deficits by applying a discount rate to those cash flows and calculating the present value of those future cash amounts.

Although the amount of work required to identify the various elements is significant, the principles are simple. The recoverable amount is either:

- the estimated amount to be received if the asset is sold (fair value); or
- the discounted future cash flows if the asset is retained (value in use).

The business logic is that you would choose the highest of fair value or value in use.

Worked example 5.3 assumes that there is only one stand-alone asset. Frequently there are several assets operating together to form the production unit and it is impossible to identify the fair value or value in use for any one item. In such circumstances, the calculation for impairment will apply to the cash-generating unit.

Worked example 5.3

You believe you could sell an asset for £16,000 but if you retain it, the total amount of the discounted future cash flows is only £12,000. The rational decision is to sell the asset and the recoverable amount is the fair value.

You can have the situation where you could sell the asset for only £12,000 but if you retain it, the value in use is £16,000. This is the recoverable amount and it would be a sensible decision to retain the asset. The £16,000 is the recoverable amount of the asset and, if this is lower than the carrying amount on the balance sheet, the asset is impaired. In Diagram 5.2, we have assumed that the carrying amount on the balance sheet of the asset is £20,000 and thus the asset value is impaired.

continued

Worked example 5.3 continued

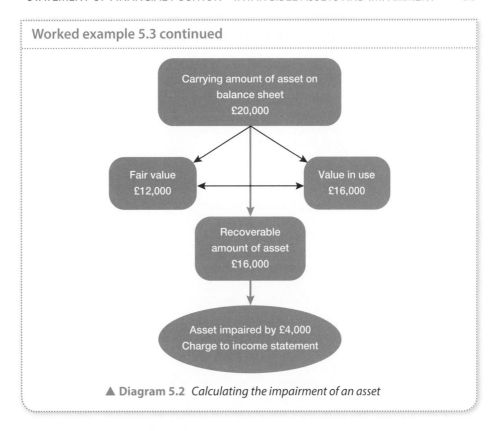

▲ Diagram 5.2 *Calculating the impairment of an asset*

The cash-generating unit

The IASB realized that identifying **CGUs** could present problems in some industries. It has included several illustrative examples in the standard, ranging from retail store chains to single product entities. This provides helpful guidance for specific difficulties.

In most instances, the CGU will consist of tangible non-current assets such as property, plant and equipment. The procedure for the CGU is the same as for individual assets:

cash-generating unit (CGU)

A cash-generating unit is a clearly identifiable group of assets that generates cash inflows that are mostly independent of the cash flows from other assets or groups of assets.

1 Calculate the fair value and value in use.
2 Compare them, and the highest figure is the recoverable amount.
3 If the recoverable amount is lower than the carrying amount shown in the balance sheet, the asset is impaired. This impairment loss is an expense in the profit or loss account and reduces the carrying amount on the balance sheet.

It is possible that the CGU will also consist of acquired goodwill. In this case, the fair value and the value in use are still calculated. If the recoverable amount of the CGU is higher than the carrying amount of the CGU as shown in the balance sheet, the unit and the goodwill allocated to the unit are not impaired and no action is required. However, if there is an impairment, the procedure is:

1 Charge the entire impairment loss to the goodwill if there is sufficient.
2 If the goodwill is insufficient to absorb the entire impairment loss, allocate the balance over the other CGU assets in proportion to the carrying amount of each asset.

See also Worked example 5.4.

Worked example 5.4   Impairment of a CGU

A CGU to which acquired goodwill has been allocated has the following assets at their carrying value in the balance sheet:

	£000
Property	180
Machinery	120
Acquired goodwill	60
Carrying amount of CGU	360

The recoverable amount for the CGU is calculated at £270,000.

Because the CGU is impaired, an amount of £90,000 must be charged to the profit or loss account and the carrying amount of the assets reduced in the balance sheet by the same amount.

The first stage, in compliance with the standard, is to write off the full carrying amount of goodwill. In other words, £60,000 is taken off the balance sheet.

The balance of the impairment loss of £30,000 is deducted from the remaining assets in proportion to their carrying amount. Table 5.3 shows these calculations.

▼ Table 5.3 *Applying impairment loss*

	Pre impairment £000	Amount written off £000	Post impairment £000
Goodwill	60	60	–
Property	180	18	162
Machinery	120	12	108
	360	90	270

Calculations of amount written off

Goodwill	£60,000
Property	$£30,000 \times \dfrac{£180,000}{£300,000} = £18,000$
Machinery	$£30,000 \times \dfrac{£120,000}{£300,000} = £12,000$

The cautious approach of the IASB to accounting for goodwill is apparent where, due to subsequent market improvement, the CGU is no longer impaired. In other words, the new carrying amount shown in the balance sheet is less than the present recoverable amount. The standard allows the company to reverse the impairment but with two restrictions:

1 There can be no reversal of the impairment for goodwill. In other words, it cannot be placed back on the balance sheet.
2 The reversal on other assets is limited to their original carrying value. You cannot increase to the higher recoverable value.

We will use these restrictions to demonstrate the application of these rules in Worked example 5.5.

Worked example 5.5   Impairment and goodwill

The recoverable amount is £350,000

▼ Table 5.4 *Reversing impairment loss*

	Pre impairment £000	Post impairment £000	Reversal £000	Post reversal £000
Goodwill	60	–	–	–
Property	180	162	18	180
Machinery	120	108	12	120
	360	270	30	300

The new recoverable amount of the CGU is £350,000 but we have only increased the carrying amount in the balance sheet to £300,000. There is no reversal of goodwill and the other assets are reversed only to their pre-impairment value. A revaluation has not taken place to provide the users with up-to-date information.

We show an example of impairment and the CGU in Company example 5.3. Siemens (Berlin and Munich) is a large electrical engineering and electronics company. It has 348,000 employees working to develop and manufacture products, design and install complex systems and projects, and tailor a wide range of services for individual requirements. Given the size of the company, the accounting work required to achieve compliance is extensive. The note in Company example 5.3 confirms that the company is following IFRSs and uses CGUs, and that goodwill is not reversed if there are impairment losses.

Company example 5.3

Impairment and CGUs

For the purpose of impairment testing, goodwill acquired in a business combination is allocated to the cash-generating unit or the group of cash-generating units that is expected to benefit from the synergies of the business combination. If the carrying amount of the cash-generating unit or the group of cash-generating units, to which the goodwill is allocated, exceeds its recoverable amount, an impairment loss on goodwill allocated to this cash-generating unit or this group of cash-generating units is recognized. The recoverable amount is the higher of the cash-generating unit's or the group of cash-generating units' fair value less costs to sell and its value in use. If either of these amounts exceeds the carrying amount, it is not always necessary to determine both amounts. These values are generally determined based on discounted cash flow calculations.

Impairment losses on goodwill are not reversed in future periods.

Siemens, Annual Report 2015, p. 66

The non-reversal of goodwill has been a controversial matter. The IASB's opinion was that an entity would need to calculate whether the subsequent increase in the recoverable amount of goodwill was attributable to the recovery of the acquired goodwill or an increase in the internally generated goodwill within the unit. Of course, there is no recognition of internally generated goodwill. The Board, therefore, concluded that it was highly unlikely that such a calculation would be possible and, therefore, there is a prohibition on reversals of goodwill impairment losses.

The standard for impairment is now fully established, although the asset of goodwill is likely to continue to be debated. However, the research indicates that the current regulations provide valuable information to investors. A study based on the top 500 UK listed firms for 2005 and 2006 concluded that 'these impairments are perceived by investors to reliably measure a decline in the value of goodwill and are incorporated in their firm valuation assessments' (AbuGhazaleh et al. 2012: 212).

NOTES

1   Hussey, R. (1994) *The Intangibles of Film and Television*, London: Touche Ross.

CONCLUSIONS

IAS 38 *Intangible Assets* regulates the increasing importance of non-current assets. Goodwill and brands have been, and remain, controversial items. Several companies have developed brands which are household names but they do not appear on their balance sheets. The reluctance of standard setters to allow these items to appear on the balance sheet because of the question of reliability of measurement is understandable. If an entity has purchased an intangible asset, we have evidence of market value. If there is no transaction, we have no credible method of calculating the fair value of internally generated intangible assets. However, the lack of information on internally generated assets does make analysis of an entity difficult for the users.

We return to the subject of goodwill in Chapter 16 where we consider the accounting regulations under IFRS 3 applying to the acquisition of one company by another. This explores the issue of goodwill in greater depth. We also have the opportunity to learn companies' opinions on the matter.

Before IAS 36, there was a need for a standard to address the impairment of both tangible and intangible non-current assets. It was misleading to users of financial statements that companies could keep assets on their balance sheet at a carrying amount higher than their actual value. IAS 36 reduces the burden on companies by having a two-stage process, with the first stage assessing whether there are any indications of possible impairment.

The required accounting treatment for a CGU is debatable. The questions concern the treatment of goodwill. A reduction in value due to impairment is reasonable, but also a reversal is possible. The position taken by the IASB is undoubtedly due to their uncertainties over accounting for goodwill generally.

On a broader basis, if there is an economic downturn the tangible assets can be impaired. If there is an economic recovery, the value of tangible assets cannot increase above their original values. The standards require that any reversal is limited to the original value. Whether the IASB will revisit this requirement is doubtful. If so, it would appear to involve revaluations under IAS 16 that we discussed in Chapter 4.

IN THE PIPELINE

The IASB has on its work plan the topic of goodwill and impairment. At the time of writing, the Board is assessing the issues of identifying and measuring intangible assets acquired in a business combination, accounting for goodwill arising and impairment testing of goodwill and other non-current, non-financial assets. In its work plan dated 20 July 2016, the Board stated that a decision on the direction of the project would not be made within the next six months.

ADDITIONAL RESOURCES

Go online to the companion website for this book to access further teaching and learning materials for this chapter.
www.palgravehighered.com/hussey-cfr

STATEMENT OF FINANCIAL POSITION – EQUITY AND NON-CURRENT LIABILITIES

LEARNING OBJECTIVES

At the end of this chapter, you should be able to:

- Distinguish between equity and non-current liabilities on the balance sheet
- Explain the various components of equity
- Discuss the various forms of reserves
- Describe the concept of capital maintenance and the methods used by entities to achieve capital reduction
- Explain the various components of non-current liabilities

INTRODUCTION

In this chapter, we concentrate on equity and non-current liabilities. The accounting equation equates assets with equity and non-current liabilities. The line items that fall under the heading of 'Equity' are share capital and reserves of various types. Non-current liabilities are items such as long-term borrowings, corporate income tax and provisions. One item that comes under non-current liabilities on most balance sheets is derivative financial instruments. We leave discussion of this item to Chapter 12 where we examine the standards that apply to financial instruments.

As with some other aspects of accounting, the terminology can be fluid. This is particularly true in respect of the words 'capital' and 'equity' that are sometimes used interchangeably. The word 'equity' refers to the share capital and all reserves representing shareholders' total investment held by the entity. In other words, equity comprises the assets minus all liabilities, both current and non-current. The term 'capital' can refer to both the shareholders' investment and any long-term loans. You may see the term 'share capital' to describe the shares purchased by the shareholders.

In discussing equity and non-current liabilities, we refer to the requirements under the Companies Act 2006 and IAS 1 *Presentation of Financial Statements*. IAS 1 introduced a new

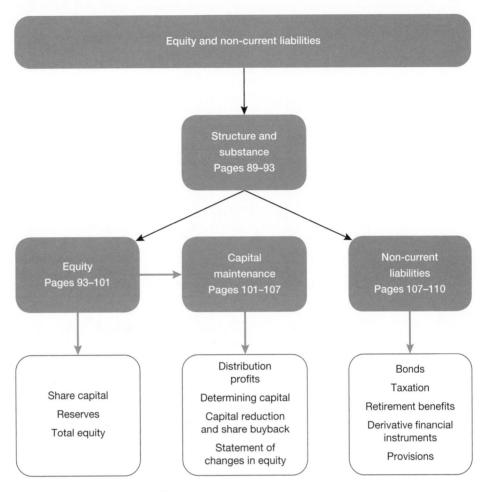

▲ **Diagram 6.1** *Structure of Chapter 6*

financial statement in 2007 that relates to equity. The statement of changes in equity informs the users of financial statements of the factors that cause a change in the owners' equity over the accounting periods. This statement is of particular interest to shareholders wishing to assess the size of their financial interest in the entity.

Non-current liabilities are, in most respects, far simpler to understand than equity. Non-current liabilities describes the money, owed by the entity to various parties, which is not due for payment in the 12 months following the date of the balance sheet. There are some complications with non-current liabilities such as tax and provisions. We introduce these topics in this chapter, but leave the detailed requirements of the accounting standards to later chapters.

STRUCTURE AND SUBSTANCE

Structure

In Chapter 3, we explained the purpose and requirements of IAS 1 *Presentation of Financial Statements*. We explained that the statement of financial position, or balance sheet, shows the economic resources of the entity and the claims on those resources. The recipients of this information use it to assess the entity's financial strength.

The line items relating to capital and long-term liabilities included on the statement of financial position are shown in Table 6.1.

▼ **Table 6.1** *Line items for capital and non-current liabilities*

Line item	Standard	Chapter
Trades and other payables over 12 months	IAS 1	3
Provisions	IAS 8	13
Financial liabilities (excluding the first two items)	IFRS 9	12
Liabilities and assets for deferred tax	IAS 12	14
Liabilities included in disposal groups classified as held for sale	IFRS 5	15
Non-controlling interests, presented within equity	IFRS 3	16

Offsetting is the use of one account to reduce the balance in another, and is generally not permitted. The regulations prohibit the deduction of a liability account from an asset account, or vice versa. There are some exceptions to this rule because a standard may permit offsetting in specific circumstances. It is also possible that the substance of a particular transaction incorporates offsetting.

IAS 1 establishes the minimum information an entity should disclose. In practice, entities provide much fuller information, both in the financial statements and in the accompanying notes. Table 6.2 shows the terms that you are likely to encounter, divided into equity and non-current liabilities.

▼ **Table 6.2** *Components of equity and non-current liabilities*

Equity	Non-current liabilities
Called up share capital	Bonds and bank loans
Capital redemption reserve	Borrowings
Cash flow hedging reserve	Corporate income tax
Currency translation reserve	Derivative financial instruments
Merger reserve	Other payables
Non-controlling interests	Retirement benefit obligations
Other reserves	Provision for liabilities and charges
Own shares	Trade and other payables over 12 months
Retained earnings	
Share premium account	

Substance

Determining which items fall under the heading of 'Equity' is straightforward. When we consider liabilities, the division between current and non-current is less obvious than with assets. Some types of liability can fall into either category. IAS 1 differentiates by stating which liabilities are current. The basic points in identifying current liabilities are as follows.

1 The entity expects to settle the liability in its normal operating cycle. For example, your suppliers would expect payment promptly. In some industries, the normal operating cycle may exceed 12 months and may extend the recognition of current liabilities.
2 The entity holds the liability primarily for the purposes of trading.
3 The liability is due to be settled within 12 months after the reporting period. These liabilities are often related to large, long-term contracts. If the entity is able to defer payment of a liability later than the 12 months, that liability is non-current.

IAS 1 applies the default definition to identify non-current liabilities. If a liability does not meet the criteria as a current liability, it must be non-current. Fortunately, public limited companies are well aware of the detailed requirements of the standard and the classifications on their balance sheets are clear.

In this chapter, our interest focuses on equity and non-current liabilities. The ratio of total equity to non-current liabilities varies considerably, as we show with the example of six entities taken at random. First, Table 6.3 shows the industry and total of equity and non-current liabilities for each company.

▼ **Table 6.3** *Total of equity and non-current liabilities*

Company	Industry	Total equity and non-current liabilities
Burberry Group	Fashion	£1,291 million
Centrica	Energy	£12,746 million
Line Energy (Australia)	Energy	Au$656,661,000 (approx. £380 million)
Mullen (Canada)	Specialized transportation	Can$1,733,436,000 (approx. £1,030 million)
Sainsbury	Supermarkets	£9,773 million
Whitbread	Retail hospitality	£2,862 million

Each entity has its own pattern of non-current liabilities, but usually borrowings are a substantial part. We show in Company example 6.1 (overleaf) the non-current borrowings of the J Sainsbury Group for 2015. This UK company was founded in 1869, operates over 1,200 supermarkets and convenience stores, and has approximately 161,000 employees.

We have extracted only one column from the report that has considerable detail for several years. With all companies, the source and nature of borrowings can change considerably from year to year. The user will be looking at these shifts and seeing how they correspond to the activities of the company. For example, if a company commences a large expansion project lasting 5 years, you could anticipate an increase in the borrowings unless it has its own resources.

Company example 6.1

Non-current borrowings 2015

Secured loans:

	£m
Loan due 2018	778
Loan due 2031	795
Unsecured loans:	
Revolving credit facility due 2017	120
Bank loans due 2016	35
Bank loans due 2019	200
Convertible bonds due 2019	409
Finance lease obligations	169
Total borrowings	**2506**

J Sainsbury Group, Annual Report and Accounts, 2015, Note 20, p. 109

As well as the source of borrowings, the user is interested in what proportion of funding for the entity comes from shareholders and what comes from non-current liabilities. Diagram 6.2 shows the percentage ratios of equity and non-current liabilities.

There are major differences in the ratio of equity to non-current liabilities (as highlighted most dramatically by Burberry and Centrica). For users of financial information, the lesson is to understand the nature of the industry in which the entity operates. It is also important to know what stage of growth the entity has reached and the economics of the markets in which it operates.

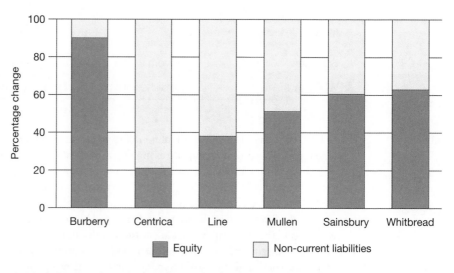

▲ **Diagram 6.2** *Comparison of equity and non-current liabilities*

In looking at the relationship between equity and other forms of funding, such as long-term borrowings, we are considering two groups: the lenders and the shareholders. Both groups are interested in the financial performance of the company, but possibly for different reasons.

Shareholders are interested in the profit the company makes because that is the source of dividends. A healthy profit may also increase the share price, leading to a capital gain for shareholders. Lenders will be looking for evidence that they will receive the interest on the funds that they have lent and that the company will repay the loan when it falls due.

Diagram 6.3 shows the differences between the investments made by both groups and the risks they face.

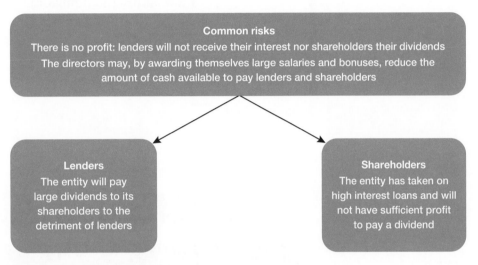

▲ **Diagram 6.3** *Risks facing shareholders and lenders*

Diagram 6.3 simplifies the risks but presents a broad picture of the interests of the users of financial statements. Some of these risks relate to the ratio of liabilities to equity. This is known as leverage or gearing. We explain how to use this method of financial statement analysis in Chapter 19.

In the following sections, we expand our discussions on equity and non-current liabilities. We explain how regulations attempt to reduce these risks, or at least to make them more apparent to the users of financial statements.

EQUITY

equity

Equity is the residual interest in the assets of the entity after deducting all its liabilities.

IASB Exposure Draft, 2015, para. 4.4

Using the word '**equity**' in its broadest sense to mean 'the residual interest', the definition of equity follows the normal accounting equation which is expressed as:

Assets – Liabilities = Capital

This equation works because the value of the equity is on the balance sheet at its par value, that is, the face value of the shares. The balance sheet will balance. The balance sheet does not show the shares at their current market value.

In some respects, the equity section on the balance sheet can be disappointing for readers. You may find one that has unusual items but most will be similar. Of course, the more familiar you are with the information normally published, the easier it is to spot the unusual ones. Company examples 6.2 and 6.3 illustrate the similarities and differences in the items comprising equity.

Company example 6.2

J Sainsbury plc (£million)

Equity	
Called up share capital	548
Share premium account	1,108
Capital redemption reserve	680
Other reserves	146
Retained earnings	3,057
Equity attributable to owners of the parent	5,539
Total equity	**5,539**

J Sainsbury Group, Annual Report and Accounts, 2015, Note 20, p. 84

Company example 6.3

GlaxoSmithKline (£million)

Equity	
Share capital	1,340
Share premium account	2,831
Retained earnings	(1,397)
Other reserves	2,340
Shareholders' equity	5,114
Non-controlling interests	3,764
Total equity	8,878

GlaxoSmithKline, Annual Report and Accounts, 2015, p. 139

In addition to the extract in Company example 6.3 that we have taken from the balance sheet, GlaxoSmithKline's financial statement has a further two pages showing all the movements in equity.

As for all companies, the balance sheets in Company examples 6.2 and 6.3 provide only summary information. You need to refer to the notes to the accounts to understand the separate elements. In this section, we will explain the most typical items coming under the heading of 'Equity'.

Share capital

share capital

Share capital is the amount that shareholders invest by purchasing shares from the issuing entity. The amount of share capital can increase if an entity issues new shares to the public in exchange for cash. Any price differences arising subsequently from price increases or decreases on the stock exchange are not reflected in the balance sheet.

We start this section by giving some background to share ownership. In particular, we consider who are most likely to be the owners of shares.

Essentially, there are two main groups of investors: individual and institutional investors. Individual investors are mostly those who are sufficiently wealthy and knowledgeable to purchase shares directly, although some less rich people speculate in the hope of improving their finances.

Institutional investors are any non-banking organizations or persons that qualify for special treatment and less regulation on their activities. An institutional investor is an investing entity having a very substantial sum for investment. Some examples of institutional investors are endowment funds, mutual funds, brokerages, pension funds and insurance companies. If you are an employee in a pension scheme, there is an institutional investor responsible for making investments for the scheme.

To put some numbers to the above definitions, we show below an overview from the UK Office of National Statistics.[1] These data refer to the position at the end of 2014 and give the estimated ownership of the UK stock market:

- Rest of the world investors owned 54% of the value of the UK stock market, up from 31% in 1998.
- UK individuals owned 12%, up from 10% in 2012.
- Unit trusts held 9%, up from 2% in 1998.
- Other financial institutions held 7%.
- Insurance companies held 6% and pension funds 3%.

The holders of shares are individual and institutional investors from the UK and overseas.

The issuers of shares that interest us are the companies quoted on the London Stock Exchange (LSE). These entities are subject to the regulations of International Financial Reporting Standards (IFRSs). Some entities may have been incorporated in a country that has not adopted IFRSs, but if they have chosen to list on the LSE they must produce financial statements that comply with IFRSs.

Entities, generally, have two main types of shares: ordinary and preference. Ordinary shares are referred to as 'common stock' in the US. The main attributes of ordinary and preference shares are listed in Table 6.4 (overleaf).

You can come across shares that do not have all of these attributes. For example, there may be non-voting shares whose holders cannot vote at annual general meetings. Shares may be divided into Type A shares and Type B shares with differing rights and responsibilities.

There can be a combination of ordinary and preference shares in the form of convertible preference shares which give the holder the option to convert them to ordinary shares. The terms of conversion for such shares specify the date when the conversion takes place and the conversion rate, that is, the number of ordinary shares exchanged for a specific number of convertible preference shares. The option to convert normally belongs to the holder, although some entities may hold the right to compel a conversion.

An entity can issue shares by offering through subscription or placing, or by a rights issue.

Offer by subscription or placing

Subscription is the procedure of issuing the shares directly to the public by way of a sale on the open market. With a placing, the entity offers shares to a small number of select investors such as banks, insurance companies and pension funds.

▼ Table 6.4 *Attributes of shares*

Ordinary equity shares	Preference shares
Carry the main risk	Usually a fixed rate of dividend
If there are no distributable profits, no dividend is paid	Dividend is paid before any dividend to ordinary shareholders
Holders of ordinary shares can vote at annual general meetings	Preference shareholders have no voting powers
Holders receive residual profit in the form of dividends after deduction of any fixed interest, preference dividend and tax	Cumulative preference shares accrue the dividends if there are insufficient profits and pay them in a more successful year
If the entity stops trading, ordinary shareholders receive any net assets after creditors have been paid	Redeemable preference shares allow the entity to redeem the shares at a set future date and price
Entities usually have a dividend policy that determines the share of profit paid to shareholders and the share of profit retained	Convertible preference shares can be converted into ordinary shares at a set date and price

Whichever method is used, the basic bookkeeping entries are the same. If the shares are issued at par value, a debit is made to the cash account and a credit to the capital account. With large public entities, the current market price is likely to be well in excess of the par value and new shares are issued at a premium.

The basic bookkeeping entries for shares at a premium are a debit to the cash account with the full amount received, while the amount of the par value of the issue is credited to the capital account. The amount in excess of the par value is credited to a share premium account. The entity cannot distribute the share premium account. It remains on the balance sheet as part of the entity's permanent capital.

Rights issue

In a rights issue, the entity offers new shares to existing shareholders at a share price lower than the current market price. Usually, this involves a set number of shares in ratio to the shares currently held; for example, the offer could be three new shares for every five held.

The entity may favour this method because existing shareholders are likely to subscribe if they are satisfied with the entity's current performance. The shareholders may favour this method because they can subscribe to shares below the current market price. After such an issue, the market price is likely to drop but the existing shareholders should still benefit.

*   *   *

Although an entity may not be making a rights issue but a general issue of new shares, the rights of existing shareholders must be maintained. Under the law, existing shareholders have pre-emption rights which give them the right to subscribe for their pro rata share of any new shares in that entity that are issued for cash. Pre-emption rights provide existing shareholders with protection against inappropriate dilution of their shareholding in the entity.

An entity is required to provide a considerable amount of information for each class of share capital it has. The details are

(a)   the number of shares authorized;
(b)   the number of shares issued and fully paid, and issued but not fully paid;
(c)   par value per share, or that the shares have no par value;

(d) a reconciliation with the number of shares outstanding at the beginning and at the end of the period;

(e) the rights, preferences and restrictions attaching to that class including restrictions on the distribution of dividends and the repayment of capital;

(f) shares in the entity held by the entity or by its subsidiaries or associates;

(g) shares held for issues under options and contracts for the sale of shares, including terms and amounts;

(h) a description of the nature and purpose of each share reserve with equity.

There are three places you can find this information:

- the statement of financial position, which is not usual;
- the statement of changes in equity;
- the notes to the financial statements, which is the most likely place.

Some companies have very complex notes providing information on their share capital. We have extracted Company example 6.4 from the annual report and accounts of Burberry because it illustrates the core of required disclosures.

Company example 6.4

Burberry

22. Share capital and reserves

Allotted, called up and fully paid share capital	Number	£m
Ordinary shares of 0.05p (2014: 0.05p) each		
As at 31 March 2013	442,160,331	0.2
Allotted on exercise of options during the year	1,481,959	–
As at 31 March 2014	443,642,290	0.2
Allotted on exercise of options during the year	1,101,777	–
As at 31 March 2015	443,744,067	0.2

The Company has a general authority from shareholders, renewed at each Annual General Meeting, to repurchase a maximum of 10% of its issued share capital. During the year to 31 March 2015, no ordinary shares were repurchased by the Company under this authority (2014: nil).

The cost of own shares held by the Group has been offset against retained earnings, as the amounts paid reduce the profits available for distribution by the Company. As at 31 March 2015 the amounts offset against this reserve are £57.0m (2014: £69.7m). As at 31 March 2015, the ESOP trusts held 4.1m shares (2014: 5.2m) in the Company, with a market value of £71.9m (2014: £72.5m). In the year to 31 March 2015 the Burberry Group plc ESOP trust has waived its entitlement to dividends of £1.2m (2014: £1.3m).

During the year profits of £5.3m (2014: £3.0m) have been transferred to capital reserves due to statutory requirements of subsidiaries. The capital reserve consists of non-distributable reserves and the capital redemption reserve arising on the purchase of own shares.

Burberry, Annual Report and Accounts, 2015, p. 147

For the users, the information in Company example 6.4 explains the structure of the share capital. This is the allotted, called up and fully paid share capital. In other words, this is all the shares that have been purchased by shareholders who have paid in full. The note states that the Group did not reacquire any of its own shares during the year. It is not unusual for companies to hold some of their own shares. For various reasons, shares that were once traded in the market may be reacquired by the company.

Reacquired shares, sometimes referred to as 'treasury shares', are not included when calculating dividends or earnings per share. The terms 'treasury shares' and 'treasury stock' can be confusing. In the US, treasury shares are called 'treasury stock'. In the UK, 'treasury stock' usually refers to government bonds.

We have not included in Company example 6.4 the information that Burberry provided on reserves. We explain reserves in the next section.

Reserves

reserves

Reserves are the part of the shareholders' equity excluding the amount of the basic share capital.

Reserves are an important part of equity. There are several types of reserves with their own conditions concerning their use. Company example 6.5 is taken from the annual report and accounts of Intercontinental Hotels Group plc. The Group has more than 5,000 hotels and nearly 742,000 guest rooms in almost 100 countries around the world.

Company example 6.5

Reserves

The nature and purpose of the other reserves shown in the Group statement of changes in equity on pages 89 to 91 of the Financial Statements is as follows:

Capital redemption reserve

This reserve maintains the nominal value of the equity share capital of the Company when shares are repurchased or cancelled.

Shares held by employee share trusts

Comprises $18.3m (2014: $34.5m, 2013: $37.6m) in respect of 0.5m (2014: 0.9m, 2013: 1.2m) InterContinental Hotels Group plc ordinary shares held by employee share trusts, with a market value at 31 December 2015 of $19.8m (2014: $38.2m, 2013: $39.8m).

Other reserves

Comprises the merger and revaluation reserves previously recognised under UK GAAP, together with the reserve arising as a consequence of the Group's capital reorganisation in June 2005. Following the change in presentational currency to the US dollar in 2008, this reserve also includes exchange differences arising on retranslation to period-end exchange rates of equity share capital, the capital redemption reserve and shares held by employee share trusts.

continued

Company example 6.5 *continued*

Unrealised gains and losses reserve

This reserve records movements in the fair value of available-for-sale financial assets and the effective portion of the cumulative net change in the fair value of the cash flow hedging instruments related to hedged transactions that have not yet occurred.

Currency translation reserve

This reserve records the movement in exchange differences arising from the translation of foreign operations and exchange differences on foreign currency borrowings and derivative instruments that provide a hedge against net investments in foreign operations. On adoption of IFRS, cumulative exchange differences were deemed to be $nil as permitted by IFRS 1.

The fair value of derivative instruments designated as hedges of net investments in foreign operations outstanding at 31 December 2015 was a $3m net liability (2014: $2m net asset, 2013: $10m net liability).

Treasury shares

At 31 December 2015, 11.5m shares (2014: 11.5m, 2013: 9.8m) with a nominal value of $2.7m (2014: $2.8m, 2013: $2.4m) were held as treasury shares at cost and deducted from retained earnings.

Intercontinental Hotels Group plc, Annual Report, 2015, p. 137

Given Intercontinental's global position and the complexities of operating in various countries and many currencies, the range of reserves is not surprising. We discuss some of the Group's activities in later chapters. At this stage we concentrate on explaining those reserves most commonly found in financial statements, as shown in Diagram 6.4 overleaf.

The reserves of an entity generally are of two types: distributable and non-distributable. The entity's own memorandum and articles can impose certain restrictions on the reserves that can be distributed to owners in the form of dividends. The main legal requirement is that retained earnings are distributable, but the following reserves are not.

Share premium reserve

As explained above, this reserve arises when shares are issued at a price above their par value.

Capital redemption reserve

An entity can choose to buy back shares from its own shareholders. If it does, the entity must keep a reserve of similar value that cannot be paid to shareholders as dividends.

Merger reserve

This is a complex area.[2] Merger relief, a provision of the Companies Act 2006, permits entities to avoid creating a share premium account.

Retained earnings

These are the accumulated net earnings not paid out as dividends, but kept by the entity. The entity may hold the earnings to reinvest them in assets that generate future profits or to decrease the amount of non-current liabilities, that is, to pay back loans. A continuous growth in

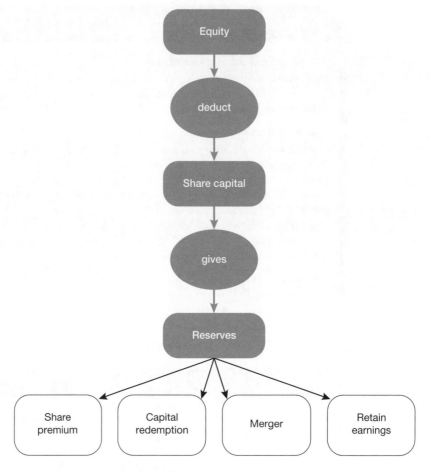

▲ **Diagram 6.4** *The location of reserves*

retained earnings can cause concerns. The shareholder is interested in whether the directors are using the reserves properly to improve the business. If not, an explanation is required from the directors on their intentions.

Any future losses are deducted from the cumulative retained earnings. If this leads to a deficit, the term 'retained losses' is used and there are some very unhappy shareholders.

Total equity

The share capital amount added to the aggregation of all the reserves gives the shareholders equity. Non-controlling interests are added to give the total equity. The basic structure is:

	£
Share capital	XX
Add Reserves	XX
Shareholders' equity	XX
Non-controlling interests	XX
Total equity	XX

The total equity consists of the shareholders' equity (i.e. the sum of the share capital and reserves) *plus* the non-controlling interests. We discuss non-controlling interests in Chapter 16. At this stage, we define them as the equity in a subsidiary that is not attributable, directly or indirectly, to a parent. For example, one entity may own 90% of the shares of another entity. The owners of the other 10% in that entity would have a non-controlling interest because they do not have sufficient power to influence decision making.

CAPITAL MAINTENANCE

Capital maintenance has two aspects: a legal one, as included in the Companies Act 2006, and a conceptual one, as discussed in the Conceptual Framework (CF) in Chapter 3. We have already discussed some parts of the legal requirements, and we expand on them in this section. Our comments are concerned only with public limited companies.

The legal requirements for capital maintenance exist to ensure that all creditors have some protection against shareholders withdrawing from the total shareholders' funds and leaving insufficient to pay creditors. The total shareholders' funds are the share capital, share premium and capital redemption reserve. We have already considered the position of non-distributable reserves.

To pay dividends to shareholders, first an entity must have a distributable profit. Of course, a distribution of profits means paying out cash and an entity may wish to retain cash to maintain and expand the business and to pay creditors when the debt falls due. It is therefore unlikely to pay out all of its distributable profits.

Distributable profits

Unfortunately, the definition of distributable profits is complex. We will summarize the main requirements in this section. First, an entity can only pay a dividend from realized profits. The definition of realized profits depends on the requirements of GAAP when the accounts are prepared. As we have occasional changes in legislation and IFRSs, so the definition of distributable profits may change.

The Companies Act 2006 states that realized profits are in the form of cash or other assets that can be realized with reasonable certainty. This includes profits occurring from a change in fair values because of an accounting standard as long as those profits are convertible into cash. Having identified realizable profits and, using the same criteria for realizable losses, an entity can pay dividends using the calculation illustrated in Diagram 6.5 overleaf.

Determining capital

Financial statements mainly use a financial concept of capital. 'Profit' can be identified by deducting the carrying amount of the net assets at the beginning of the period from the carrying amount of the net assets at the end of the period.

This assumes that there have been no distributions and the calculation uses the historical cost accounting method. The use of the balance sheet for calculation has drawbacks, as Worked example 6.1 demonstrates.

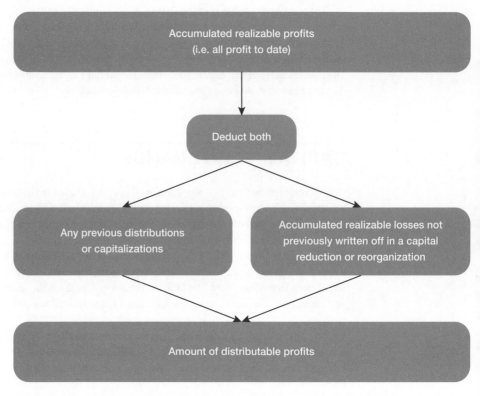

▲ **Diagram 6.5** *Calculating the distributable profits*

Worked example 6.1

An entity purchases a machine that has a life of five years for £50,000. After deducting all the running costs, but not depreciation, the entity makes a profit of £12,000 annually. At the end of the machine's five-year life, the entity has an accumulated profit of £60,000. To purchase a new machine, due to inflation, it will cost £60,000. Did the entity make a profit?

If we had allocated £10,000 to depreciation each year, using historical cost accounting, there would be a profit of £2,000 annually. But one could argue that there is no profit if that 'profit' must be used to replace the machine.

We could take another view of the calculation of profit and capital maintenance. Physical capital maintenance assumes that there is only a profit if the physical productive or operating capacity at the end of the period exceeds that at the beginning of the period. In other words, are you still able to manufacture a greater number of units or offer more hours of service?

The CF does not recommend which concept of capital is best, but argues that the one selected should meet the needs of the users of financial statements. It is reasonable to conclude that users of financial statements are mostly concerned with their capital investment, rather than the protection of operating capacity.

There would be measurement problems in determining operating capacity. Some form of accounting using current cost could be adopted, but the result may be that any increases in the value of assets and liabilities over a financial period would be regarded as capital maintenance adjustments and not profit.

Capital reduction and share buyback

capital reduction

Capital reduction is the process of decreasing an entity's shareholder equity through share cancellations and share repurchases.

Having encouraged entities to maintain the amount of share capital, it is hardly surprising that the standard setters have placed legal restrictions on entities that wish to reduce it. For example, a listed public company may wish to improve the amount of profit that is attributable to each share. It can do this by reducing the number of shares in issue. It may also wish to demonstrate that the amount of net assets attributable to each share is higher.

In these scenarios, the entity wishes to emphasize its financial worth to shareholders. It can do so by reducing the number of shares in issue – the fewer the number of shares, the higher the profit per share and the value of net assets per share. There are two solutions: a **capital reduction** or a **share buyback**.

One reason for a capital reduction is a poor performance by an entity for several years. The entity may have accumulated trading losses. These losses must be deducted from realizable profits to determine distributable profits. Although the entity may be looking forward to a more profitable future, shareholders will not receive any dividends until all the accumulated trading losses have been cleared.

The solution is to write off the accumulated losses to the share capital account. This involves opening a capital reduction account. The debit balance (i.e. loss) on the retained earnings account is transferred to the capital reduction account by a credit to the retained earnings account and a debit to the capital reduction account. The capital reduction account is credited and the share capital account debited.

Capital reduction is more common with private entities than public entities. The latter can only reduce their share capital by special resolution following confirmation by a court.

share buyback or share repurchase

Share buyback or share repurchase occur when an entity purchases its own shares, thus reducing the number of shares on the open market.

Another strategy is share buyback. We discussed the capital redemption reserve that arises from a share buyback in the section on reserves. Share buyback reduces the number of shares in the market place, and the entity may be able to pay a larger dividend on the remaining shares.

The shares purchased by the entity are usually referred to as 'treasury shares' and receive no dividend. (Treasury shares should not be confused with treasury bonds, gilts or stock issued by governments and paying a fixed rate of interest.) Pearson plc gives a comprehensive explanation of its treasury shares in its 2014 annual report and accounts (Company example 6.6 overleaf).

Research indicates that, when entities announce their intention to buy back their shares, the market reacts positively, with an increase in share prices. This occurs although the announcement is not necessarily a firm commitment. One study of UK entities (Andriosopoulos et al. 2013) sought to ascertain the reasons for successful buybacks. The study showed that there were three factors:

1 Providing explicit information on the entity's buyback programme gave it credibility and reassured the market that the programme would be completed.
2 The age, confidence and reputation of the company CEO had a strong impact on the actual completion of the buyback.
3 Entities that started the buyback programme soon after the announcement or had previous programmes were more likely to complete.

In 2015, General Electric Company (GE) announced a buyback of up to $50 billion in GE shares. The company had 10.06 billion shares outstanding at the beginning of 2015. GE expected to reduce that number by as much as 20 per cent. This buyback was a part of GE's strategy to withdraw from the financial business and to generate 90 per cent of profits from industrial operations by 2018.

Company example 6.6

28. Treasury shares

	Number of shares 000s	£m
At 1 January 2013	10,102	103
Purchase of treasury shares	4,111	47
Release of treasury shares	(4,931)	(52)
At 31 December 2013	9,282	98
Purchase of treasury shares	907	9
Release of treasury shares	(2,997)	(32)
At 31 December 2014	7,192	75

The Group holds Pearson plc shares in trust to satisfy its obligations under its restricted share plans (see note 26).

These shares, representing 0.9% (2013: 1.1%) of called-up share capital, are treated as treasury shares for accounting purposes and have a par value of 25p per share.

The nominal value of Pearson plc treasury shares amounts to £1.8m (2013: £2.3m).

At 31 December 2014 the market value of Pearson plc treasury shares was £85.6m (2013: £124.4m).

Pearson plc, Annual Report and Accounts, 2014, p. 186

Statement of changes in equity

The **statement of changes in equity** required by IAS 1 assists users of financial statement in identifying the factors that cause a change in the owners' equity over the accounting periods. The statement discloses information about equity reserves that is helpful in understanding any movements that occur.

A comparison is required with previous years, and Diagram 6.6 shows the flow of detailed information.

▲ Diagram 6.6 *Statement of changes in equity*

The standard requires disclosure of the following information:

- Total comprehensive income for the period, showing separately amounts attributable to owners of the parent and to non-controlling interests.

● The effects of any retrospective application of accounting policies or restatements made in accordance with IAS 8, separately for each component of other comprehensive income. We discuss IAS 8 in Chapter 13.

● Reconciliations between the carrying amounts at the beginning and the end of the period for each component of equity, separately disclosing:

  ○ profit or loss;
  ○ other comprehensive income;
  ○ transactions with owners, showing separately contributions by and distributions to owners and changes in ownership interests in subsidiaries that do not result in a loss of control.

An analysis of other comprehensive income by item must be presented, either in the statement or in the notes.

On the face of the statement of changes in equity or in the notes the amount of dividends recognized as distributions and the related amount per share may be presented.

Entities usually present the information in a grid. Company example 6.7 shows the column headings used in Burberry's annual report and accounts. In the example, the rows describe the numerous components. Below we describe the main ones in a statement of changes in equity.

Company example 6.7

Column headings

Attributable to owners of the entity						
Ordinary share capital	Share premium account	Other reserves	Retained earnings	Total	Non-controlling interest	Total equity

Burberry Group plc, Annual Report and Accounts, 2014, p. 118

Opening balance

This is the balance of shareholders' equity reserves at the start of the comparative reporting period as reflected in the prior period's statement of financial position. There is no adjustment of the opening balance for any correction of prior period errors and the effect of changes in accounting policy implemented during the year. These adjustments appear separately in the statement of changes in equity.

Effect of changes in accounting policies

Under IAS 8, the entity applies changes in accounting policies retrospectively. The reserves at the beginning of the period are adjusted as if the new accounting policy had always been applied

Correction of prior period error

The correction of prior period errors appears separately in the statement of changes in equity.

Restated balance

This is the equity attributable to stockholders at the start of the comparative period after the adjustments in respect of changes in accounting policies and correction of prior period errors.

Share capital

Issues of further share capital during the period are added in the statement of changes in equity, and redemptions of shares are deducted. The issue and redemption of shares appear separately for share capital reserve and share premium reserve.

Dividends

Dividend payments issued or announced during the period are deducted from shareholder equity because they represent a distribution of wealth attributable to shareholders.

Income/Loss for the period

This represents the profit or loss attributable to shareholders during the period as reported in the income statement.

Changes in revaluation reserve

Revaluation gains and losses are recognized during the period to the extent that they are recognized outside the income statement.

Other gains and losses

Any other gains and losses, such as actuarial gains and losses that are not recognized in the income statement, can be shown in the statement of changes in equity.

Closing balance

This is the balance of shareholders' equity reserves at the end of the reporting period as reflected in the statement of financial position.

*   *   *

As you can imagine, the complexity of the statement of changes in equity depends on many factors, including the size of the entity, the type of industry, and the activities in which it engages. It is impossible to comprehend fully the statement without reference to the other financial statements and the notes to the accounts. However, as a guide to the nature of some of the disclosures made we show the row headings for Melrose plc in Company example 6.8. This illustrates the various items that can influence changes in equity.

Company example 6.8

At 1 January 2012

Profit for the year

Other comprehensive income/(expense)

Total comprehensive income/(expense)

Preference C shares redeemed

Dividends paid

continued

Company example 6.8 *continued*

Credit to equity for equity-settled share-based payments

Issue of new shares

Acquisition of Elster

Purchase of non-controlling interests

Capital reduction

At 31 December 2012

Profit for the year

Other comprehensive income/(expense)

Total comprehensive income/(expense)

Dividends paid

Credit to equity for equity-settled share-based payments

Purchase of non-controlling interests

At 31 December 2013

Melrose plc, Annual Report, 2013, p. 96

NON-CURRENT LIABILITIES

liabilities

A liability is a present obligation of the entity to transfer an economic resource as a result of past events.

IASB, Exposure Draft, 2015, para. 4.4

As we stated earlier, similar types of **liabilities** can appear as both non-current liabilities and current liabilities depending on how the entity has decided to classify them in accordance with IAS 1. Company example 6.9 overleaf from Green Dragon Gas Ltd illustrates the classification into the two groups.

Green Dragon Gas Ltd is the largest company involved in the production, distribution and sale of coal bed methane gas in China. It commenced operation in China in 1997 and listed on the LSE's Alternative Investment Market in 2006

The extract from Green Dragon's balance sheet in Company example 6.9 shows a short list of liabilities compared to some other companies. The acronym CUCBM stands for the China United Coal Bed Methane Company Limited. CUBM has exclusive rights to explore, develop and produce *coal bed methane* in cooperation with overseas companies. Green Dragon explains in Note 26 the various arrangements and agreements it has to conduct its operations. In Note 31, it provides the details of the provision. This is an unusual liability and one you are highly unlikely to find in other sets of reports and accounts.

Most non-current liabilities do not warrant a standard of their own. In this section, we will briefly explain some of the terms you may encounter, either on the face of the balance sheet or in the supporting notes. Where there are regulations affecting accounting for that item, we describe these. We provide examples so that you can appreciate the type of information the user is receiving.

Company example 6.9

	Notes	As at 31 December 2015 US$m	As at 31 December 2014 US$m
Liabilities			
Current liabilities			
Trade and other payables	20	15,413	22,103
Current tax liabilities		13	143
		15,426	22,246
Non-current liabilities			
Convertible notes	21	48,398	47,243
Bonds	22	86,807	85,072
CUCBM provision	26, 31	370,217	367,027
Deferred tax liability	16	154,352	163,478
		659,774	662,820
Total liabilities		675,200	685,066

Green Dragon Gas Ltd, Annual Report and Accounts, 2015, p. 34

Bonds

A bond is a debt investment whereby an investor loans money to an entity for a defined time. The entity must repay the loan at the end of the agreed period. There is a fixed interest rate on the bond. As with convertible shares, an entity may choose to issue convertible bonds. These give holders the right to convert the bonds into ordinary shares.

A convertible bond usually gives the holder a lower rate of interest than a non-convertible bond because the holder has the benefit of the right of conversion into shares. The lower rate of interest is of benefit to the entity, but the convertible bond is only attractive to holders if they consider that the entity is going to be profitable in the future.

One disadvantage of convertible bonds is that there will be a dilution for the existing ordinary shareholders. In other words, if the bondholders decide to convert to shares, there will be more shares on the market and more shareholders anticipating a portion of the profits. The impact of share dilution is explained when we discuss IAS 33 *Earnings per Share* in Chapter 19.

In the financial statements of some entities, you may see the term 'debenture'. A debenture is a contract whereby the entity receives a loan for a specified period. It must pay a fixed interest on the debenture and that interest is chargeable against tax. Because the debenture is not secured by physical assets, the entity has to have a solid reputation for creditworthiness.

Large entities issue debentures as a medium- to long-term debt. The terms bonds, notes and debenture are used interchangeably. In Company example 6.10, we can see the movements in borrowings over the course of one year. Kingfisher plc is a home improvement company

Company example 6.10

Note 22 Borrowings

	£ million	
	2015/16	2014/15
Current		
Bank overdrafts	76	91
Bank loans	2	2
Fixed term debt	48	–
Finance leases	12	12
	138	**105**
Non-current		
Bank loans	8	9
Fixed term debt	137	183
Finance leases	34	40
	179	**232**
Borrowings	**317**	**337**

Kingfisher plc, Annual Report and Accounts, 2015/16, p. 113

with over 1,100 stores and growing omnichannel operations across ten countries in Europe. The company employs 74,000 people and weekly nearly six million customers shop in their stores and on their websites.

You can observe from Company example 6.10 that there are significant movements in the types of borrowings over the two periods, with a marked increase in the current borrowings and a marked decrease in the non-current borrowings. The user will be searching the annual report and accounts for explanations of these changes. They may represent a long-term shift in the company's financial strategy, or it may be grasping the advantage of short-term movements. In Note 22, the company describes the borrowings and the movements, and the user will be putting this information into the context of the main financial statements.

Taxation

Entities, like individuals, are subject to taxation on their profits. The publicly declared profits are calculated using accounting rules, and they are then recalculated to comply with the tax rules. The result is that the taxable profits are higher or lower than the accounting profits.

One frequent, major adjustment to the tax profits is for depreciation. Entities will determine their own method of depreciation under IAS 16 for their non-current assets. Understandably, the depreciation charge can vary depending on the policy of the entity. The tax authorities ensure that there is consistency by setting a uniform percentage, known as a capital allowance. Entities apply the capital allowance for the calculation of the corporation tax for the year.

The standard for taxes is IAS 12 *Income Taxes*. This is an important standard because entities usually do not pay taxes on the amount of profit shown on their profit or loss account. The entity must comply with tax legislation that calculates its own version of 'taxable profit'. We discuss this in Chapter 14.

Retirement benefits (Pension liability)

An entity's pension fund may be insufficient to satisfy the demands made upon it. In the event of a shortage, it appears as a liability on the balance sheet. If there is a surplus, it appears as an asset. There is no requirement for entities to put their total pension obligation and pension plan assets on the balance sheet. The standard regulating pensions is IAS 19 that we examine in Chapter 9.

Derivative financial instruments

derivative financial instruments

A derivative financial instrument is a contract wherein the value is established (i.e. derived) from the performance of an underlying asset, index, or interest rate. Derivative financial instruments are widely used in transactions and include options, futures, forwards and swaps.

Entities normally take out insurance on their properties, vehicles and equipment to protect themselves from loss through fire, accidents, and other calamities. Derivatives are also a way of guarding against loss. An entity's financial assets, such as bonds, commodities and cash, change due to volatility in prices and interest rates. Derivatives offer protection.

You are almost certain to find on the balance sheet of major entities a line item for **derivative financial instruments**. In our international economy, entities hold derivatives to minimize the risk of currency exchange rate fluctuations. Oil entities use them to hedge against, or counteract, the prospect of future price changes. Airlines use them to ensure favourable fuel prices. Manufacturers can avoid any sudden hikes in the cost of their inputs.

The advantage of using derivatives is that the capital required up front is minimal and the cost of transactions is low. Instead of having to buy and sell securities, derivatives mimic the performance of the underlying asset.

From an accounting viewpoint, derivatives cause several problems. The question is how to value derivatives to place them on the balance sheet. There have been several years of discussion, but an acceptable solution seems to have been found. This has required a complete overhaul of all the accounting standards that regulate financial instruments, which we discuss in Chapters 11 and 12.

Provisions

provision

A provision is a liability of uncertain timing or amount.

We examine **provisions** more fully in Chapter 13 on standard IAS 37 which regulates provisions. At this stage, we summarize the main points:

- there must be a present obligation (legal or constructive);
- it must have arisen as a result of a past event;
- payment is probable in order to settle the obligation;
- the amount can be estimated reliably.

The importance of provisions is such that they can affect both the profit or loss account and the balance sheet.

NOTES

1 A comprehensive analysis of UK share ownership is the ONS statistical bulletin: *Ownership of UK Quoted Shares*. The 2014 issue is available at *http://www.ons.gov. uk/economy/investmentspensionsandtrusts/bulletins/ ownershipofukquotedshares/2015-09-02* (accessed 30 August 2016).

2 Further guidance on merger reserves can be obtained from: *http://www.icaew.com/en/members/practice-resources/icaew-practice-support-services/practicewire/ news/merger-relief-and-merger-accounting* (accessed 31 August 2016).

CONCLUSIONS

Having discussed assets in the previous chapter, we have completed our explanation of the statement of financial position by considering equity and non-current liabilities. For the student, there is a greater challenge in understanding equity and non-current liabilities because they are less easy than assets to define simply and to give examples of.

With non-current assets, you usually have a significant investment in property, plant and equipment, and these are tangible. The regulations for accounting for these items are somewhat less and do not incur so much variation. Even intangible assets can be discussed using familiar examples such as brands.

Equity and non-current liabilities are, however, where the financing action is likely to be. The entity is using other people's money and there must be safeguards on the management of those funds. Capital maintenance is a key concept and the statement of equity provides information on the components leading to changes in equity.

Non-current liabilities can be difficult for the student because there is a range of such liabilities. Some have their own particular treatments and may be regulated by a specific accounting standard. In later chapters, we discuss the particular standards in detail.

IN THE PIPELINE

The *Exposure Draft Annual Improvements to IFRSs 2010–2012 Cycle* proposed to amend paragraph 73 of IAS 1 regarding the classification of non-current liabilities. The regulation would state that a liability is non-current if an entity expects, and has the discretion, to refinance or roll over an obligation for at least twelve months after the reporting period under an existing loan facility with the same lender, on the same or similar terms. One problem has been that any changes to IAS 1 would involve changes to IAS 39 *Financial Instruments: Recognition and Measurement* and IFRS9 *Financial Instruments*.

The issue remains current and is part of the IASB's Disclosure Initiative (see Chapter 21). At its January 2016 meeting, the Board agreed to consider the application of its proposals when conditions in the lending agreement are tested or reviewed after the end of the reporting period.

ADDITIONAL RESOURCES

Go online to the companion website for this book to access further teaching and learning materials for this chapter.

www.palgravehighered.com/hussey-cfr

7

STATEMENT OF PROFIT OR LOSS – REVENUE

IAS 18 Revenue
IAS 11 Construction Contracts
IFRS 15 Revenue from Contracts with Customers

LEARNING OBJECTIVES

At the end of this chapter, you should be able to:

- Explain the structure and substance of the profit or loss account
- Summarize the requirements of IAS 18 *Revenue* and IAS 11 *Construction Contracts*
- Apply the requirements of IAS 18 and IAS 11
- Explain the five-step model in IFRS 15 *Revenue from Contracts with Customers*
- Apply the requirements of IFRS 15
- Demonstrate the calculation of inventory and the impact on gross profit

INTRODUCTION

The profit or loss account is simply that: an account that is part of the double entry system of bookkeeping. At the end of the financial period, there is a debit entry to close the revenue account, and the corresponding entry is a credit to the profit or loss account. Credit entries close the expense accounts, and the debits go to the profit or loss account.

The great importance of the profit or loss account lies with the final entry. Assuming that the profit or loss account needs a debit entry to close it, that amount is the profit for the financial period that is credited to the retained profit account or distributed to shareholders. One can appreciate that this information is of interest to the user.

The question arises whether the profit or loss account remains appropriate for today's business practices. The issue is how to account the profit attributable for one year for a business that has a continuing existence with a multitude of complex activities.

We start this chapter by examining the 2007 revised requirements of IAS 1 *Presentation of Financial Statements*. The structure and contents of the profit or loss statement are set out in the standard under that heading. In January 2009 a new financial statement was introduced: the statement of comprehensive income. Entities have two choices on how they present this statement. An entity can publish either one single statement of profit or loss and other comprehensive income, or two separate statements.

It would seem that for the entities in our research, and we assume for most listed entities, the term 'income statement' has replaced 'profit or loss statement'.

The first item on the profit or loss account is Revenue. For many years, we have had two international standards: IAS 18 *Revenue* and IAS 11 *Construction Contracts*. One standard, IFRS 15 *Revenue from Contracts with Customers,* will replace these two standards from 1 January 2018. We discuss the three standards in this chapter.

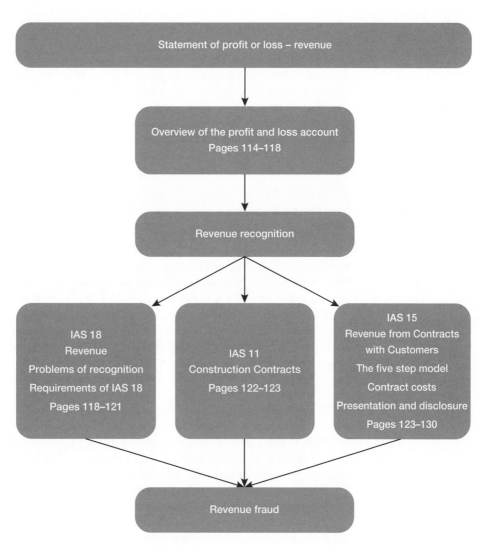

▲ **Diagram 7.1** *Structure of Chapter 7*

OVERVIEW OF THE PROFIT OR LOSS ACCOUNT

Structure

> **profit or loss**
>
> Profit or loss is calculated by deducting the expenses for the financial period from the income. Transactions and events that are classified under the heading of 'Other comprehensive income' are excluded from the calculation.

IAS 1 *Presentation of Financial Statements* requires entities to publish a statement of profit or loss and a statement of comprehensive income. This can be in the form of one statement or two statements. In our survey of annual reports and accounts, the twenty-five UK entities all chose to publish two statements; of the five Australian entities, three chose one statement; and of the five Canadian entities, two chose one combined statement.

The standard requires that, with the two-statement presentation, the separate statement of profit or loss immediately precedes the statement presenting comprehensive income. The comprehensive income statement must begin with the figure of **profit or loss** shown in the separate profit or loss statement.

An entity recognizes all items of income or expense in the profit or loss statement for the financial period. There are some exceptions. IAS 8, which we discuss in Chapter 13, requires entities to recognize some items – the correction of errors and the effects of changes in accounting policies – outside the current period. Some other standards allow or require non-recognition of other components of comprehensive income in the profit or loss account. An entity must recognize these items in the comprehensive income statement.

One clause in the standard may appear confusing to those who are not familiar with the history of the subject. In paragraph 87, the standard has the following note:

> An entity shall not present any items of income or expense as extraordinary items, in the statement(s) presenting profit or loss and other comprehensive income or in the notes.

An extraordinary item is an unusual or unexpected one-time event, such as major employee redundancies or lawsuits. Before the revisions to IAS 1, entities showed these events outside the calculation of profit. The argument was that shareholders were better informed on the continuing trend of profit and, therefore, more able to predict future profits. Extraordinary items, being one-off events, distorted that trend and it was more sensible to exclude them.

The problem was that there was no specific definition of what comprised an extraordinary item. Some entities were continuously omitting expenses, such as redundancy payments, from the main body of their profit or loss statement. Since some of these expenses were occurring reasonably frequently, the suspicion was that it was merely a device for not decreasing the profit. The IASB considered that this procedure was misleading, hence the paragraph forbidding the practice.

However, as we see in Chapter 20, entities are now providing many measures of profit in addition to the requirements of the standard. The financial statements show these under such headings as Key performance indicators, Additional performance measures or Underlying profit. There is no regulation preventing entities from providing more information as long as they also publish that required by the standards.

There are two ways to construct the profit or loss account. The first is the nature of expense method, and the second is the function of expense, or cost of sales, method.

The nature of expense method is exactly that. An entity discloses expenses in the profit or loss account according to their nature; for example, employee benefits, depreciation, material costs.

The function of expense, or cost of sales, method shows the gross profit that many investors find useful.

Company example 7.1

Consolidated Income Statement

	2016	2015
	£m	£m
Continuing operations		
Revenue	40,973	42,227
Cost of sales	(30,435)	(30,882)
Gross profit	**10,538**	**11,345**
Selling and distribution expenses	(3,570)	(3,455)
Administrative expenses	(5,110)	(5,746)
Share of result of equity accounted associates and joint ventures	44	(63)
Impairment losses	(450)	–
Other income and expense	(75)	(114)
Operating profit	**1,377**	**1,967**

Vodafone Group plc, Preliminary Profit Announcement, 2016, p. 23

Company example 7.1 from the financial statements of Vodafone Group plc's preliminary results, issued 17 May 2016, illustrates the function of expense method. The group made its first mobile call in the UK on 1 January 1985. It now operates in around 30 countries and partners with networks in over 50 more.

When you look at the financial statements of major companies, there is a limited amount of detailed information. This is because the information disclosed is complex and the details are in the notes to the accounts.

In addition to items required by other IFRSs, the statement of profit or loss must include line items that give the following amounts for the period:

- Revenue;
- Finance costs;
- Share of the profit or loss of associates and joint ventures using the equity method;
- Tax expense;
- A single amount for the total of discontinued operations, required by IFRS 5.

Substance

There is an understandable temptation for entities to stray beyond the regulatory boundaries to publish a figure of profit that flatters their performance. Directors and senior managers are under pressure to perform. Analysts make profit forecasts and, if management fails to achieve or surpass these, the share price may suffer. Additionally, directors and managers may receive some form of performance bonus, for example on the level of revenue attained – not achieving the target will mean no bonus.[1]

IAS 1 is very specific on the disclosures that entities must make in calculating and disclosing the figure of profit for the financial period. However, entities are increasingly disclosing additional measures of profit using different calculations. There is also evidence that some entities manage their profit figures.

Additional performance measures

There are no regulations preventing entities from providing information additional to that required by the standard. The additional profit measures provided are usually termed underlying or sustainable earnings. This is calculated by taking the profit figure and then adjusting it by any costs that the entity considers are unusual, non-recurring or misleading. The aim is to demonstrate a performance measure that gives the user information on performance in normal conditions.

There is a valid argument that additional information provides the users of financial statements with a better understanding of the performance of the particular entity over a prolonged period. This assists users in making predictions. However, there is the concern that the entity may present biased information that enhances the profit figure and misleads the user. We discuss additional performance measures in Chapter 20.

Profit management

Profit management is defined in two ways, as demonstrated in Diagram 7.2.

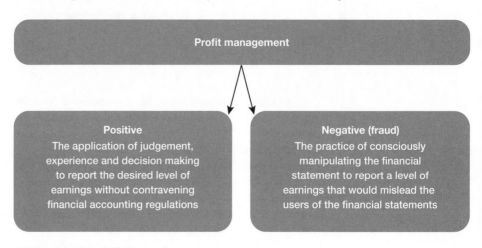

▲ **Diagram 7.2** *Defining profit management*

In spite of the requirements of accounting standards, there is considerable scope for entities to manipulate, without infringing the regulations, the amount of earnings they report. In a country where there is quarterly reporting, such as the US, there are understandable pressures to demonstrate a steady but modest profit increase in the first three quarters, ending with a final flourish in the last quarter. Users make decisions mainly based on their predictions of future company performance. Sound, if modest, profits each quarter might suggest to the owner that the financial results for the entire year will be very good. High profits in the early quarters and a dismal final performance would be a great disappointment.

In addition, entities are aware that, towards the year-end, analysts are publishing their profit expectations. If an entity fails to meet these, the share price will most likely drop. Half-yearly reporting of profit may therefore be cautious so as not to overexcite the expectations of the market.

Even if there is no intent to deceive, the current mood of the economy and that of managers can influence the financial statements. In making their estimates and assumptions, management may be optimistic or they may be cautious. Worked example 7.1 demonstrates that even minor changes to the revenue and costs figures increase the profit.

Worked example 7.1

In Table 7.1, we show the original figures of revenue and costs to arrive at a profit figure of £20,000. Accepting that it is inevitable that estimates and assumptions must be made in constructing the financial statements, we show in column 2 a modest increase in revenue, and in column 3 a modest decrease in costs.

▼ Table 7.1 *The effect of adjustments to revenue and costs*

	Original £000	Revenue increased £000	Costs decreased £000
Revenue	360	370	370
Costs	340	340	330
Profit	20	30	40

By making relatively small increases to the revenue figure and a modest reduction in costs, the profit figure doubles from £20,000 to £40,000. Such 'adjustments' to the figures are, it can be argued, a part of the estimates and assumptions that management must make when preparing financial statements in a complex business world.

Unfortunately, enthusiasm to enhance profit performance may lead to fraud. The division between earnings management and fraud is very fine, and it could be argued that any form of earnings management misleads the user to the true financial performance of the organization.

There are three different approaches to earnings management:

1. Real earnings management

This takes place when managers deviate from optimal business decisions with real business activities. For example, management may cut discretionary expenses such as research and development and training to achieve current earnings targets. Such actions may have adverse effects on future performance.

2. Accrual earnings management

With this technique, managers use discretionary accruals to increase earnings in the current period by shifting anticipated earnings from future periods. Some accruals depend on estimates and assumptions that can be reassessed. Depending on the need, management can also shift earnings from the current period to future periods, thus decreasing current period earnings.

3. Classification shifting

This does not have an impact on net income for the period, but consists of misclassification of items in the financial statement. For example, management may move charges from operating expenses to non-recurring expenses. Although net income is not affected, the user of financial statements may draw different conclusions on the financial performance of the company and its future prospects. If the user believes it is a non-recurring expense they will assume that there will be no impact on profits in future years. A normal operating expense will be a charge against future profits.

Abernathy et al. (2014) conducted a substantial study of classification shifting. They concluded that there is increased use of classification shifting when real earnings management is constrained. This may be because of poor financial performance, high institutional ownership and low industry market share that deny management the flexibility they require for other forms of earnings management. The authors also found a positive relationship between classification shifting and specific costs of accruals earnings management.

Concentrating on negative earnings management may both exaggerate the amount of financial fraud that does take place and ignore the considerable accounting problems that exist in recognizing, measuring and reporting the line items on the profit or loss statement. To remedy this, we explain the legitimate problems in constructing a financial statement that complies with IFRSs. We start our examination by considering both the current existing standards and the new standard IFRS 15 *Revenue from Contracts with Customers*.

IAS 18 REVENUE

Problems of recognition

There is a risk of classifying a revenue transaction as a one-off event conducted between two parties. This can lead to the belief that recognizing and measuring revenue for a financial period is a straightforward undertaking.

Let us take a very simple example. A customer goes into a shop and purchases an item for cash. The shop will record that as revenue. If the customer does not pay immediately, the shop still records the revenue, using the accruals concept. It also records a trade receivable or debtor for the amount outstanding.

Even a minor expansion of this single transaction model raises problems, as shown in Worked example 7.2.

Worked example 7.2   Identifying revenue

Shop Securities, a company supplying, fitting and servicing smoke detectors for commercial premises offers three packages:

Package 1   The supply and delivery only of detectors at a cost of £200 each.
Package 2   The supply, delivery and fitting of detectors at a cost of £450 each.
Package 3   As Package 2 but a three-year service contract is included, with the total cost being £950 per detector.

Customers usually have several premises and purchase a number of packages at the same time. Depending on Shop Securities' opinion of the creditworthiness of the customer, there are three payment methods. The customer can either:

1   pay in full when placing the order;
2   make a deposit with the balance due within one month of completion of the order;
3   defer payment until one month after completion of the order.

continued

Worked example 7.2 *continued*

Shop Securities' year-end is 31 March and it has conducted a review of sales for Package 1.

It has delivered some of the orders or has the goods in store ready to deliver. With other orders, Shop Securities is waiting for the manufacturers to supply the goods before they can make the deliveries, anticipated to be in April.

Table 7.2 summarizes the financial position in the separate categories for Package 1.

▼ **Table 7.2** *Shop Securities' revenue*

	Delivered £000	In store £000	Awaiting supplies £000	Total £000
Paid in full	10	4	2	16
Deposit made	12	8	3	23
Order signed	3	5	7	15
Total	25	17	12	54

What is the revenue to be recognized by Shop Securities? There are numerous possibilities.

1 The most conservative approach is to recognize the £10,000 where the purchaser has paid in full and Shop Securities has made the delivery.
2 It would be reasonable to recognize the total of £16,000 from customers who have paid in full. Whether the detectors are delivered, in store or still awaited from the supplier makes no difference. The customer has paid for them and has ownership.
3 Shop Securities could recognize the £25,000 paid and owing for deliveries made (the total of Column 1). If the customers owe money, Shop Securities can take legal action to recover it.
4 Why not recognize the full £54,000? Some customers may go bankrupt and be unable to pay, and some may cancel their orders. That is part of normal business. Shop Securities can amend its accounting records in the following financial period.

At this stage, we still have not considered the customers for Package 2. It is assumed that some detectors have been supplied and fitted. Others have been supplied and not yet fitted. It is also possible that fitting has commenced but will not be completed until after 31 March.

Package 3 has the same sort of problems as Package 2, but has the additional problem of the service contract of £450 to cover three years. In this instance, the answer is clear. The revenue for the service contract is recognized, one third for each of the three years.

Without an accounting standard, Shop Securities has a dilemma. Whichever approach it takes leads to different measures of performance and different conclusions by the users of the financial statements. An accounting standard provides guidance to the preparer of financial statements and a better understanding of the transactions by the users.

The hypothetical example of Shop Securities highlights some of the recognition issues, but imagine the real-life examples that arise. You could be a member of a consortium that has received an order for 10 aircraft from a foreign government. Without guidance, how do you know the amount of revenue to recognize and when?

Requirements of IAS 18 Revenue

▼ Table 7.3 *Timeline of IAS 18*

Date	Comment
1982	Standard first issued
1993	Revised standard issued
Interpretations issued	IFRIC 18 Transfers of Assets from Customers
	IFRIC 15 Agreements for the Construction of Real Estate
	IFRIC 13 Customer Loyalty Programmes
	IFRIC 12 Service Concession Arrangements
	SIC-27 Evaluating the Substance of Transactions in the Legal Form of a Lease
	SIC-31 Revenue – Barter Transactions Involving Advertising Services

The appropriate allocation of revenue is essential for calculating the correct profit figure for a financial period. IAS 18 identifies the two criteria for the recognition of revenue:

● it is highly likely that future economic benefits will flow to the business; and
● that these benefits can be measured reliably.

The standard defines the circumstances when these two criteria are satisfied, and provides guidance on the practical application of the criteria. Taking the first criterion, which is one of recognition, the standard separates revenue from the sale of goods and revenue from the provision of services.

A seller should only recognize revenue from the sale of goods when:

● the seller has transferred to the buyer the significant risks and rewards of ownership;
● the seller retains neither continuing managerial involvement to the degree usually associated with ownership nor effective control over the goods sold;
● the amount of revenue can be measured reliably;
● it is probable that the economic benefits associated with the transaction will flow to the seller;
● it is possible to measure reliably the costs incurred or to be incurred in respect of the transaction.

An entity should recognize revenue from the provision of services when:

● the amount of revenue can be measured reliably;
● it is probable that the economic benefits will flow to the seller;
● the stage of completion at the balance sheet date can be measured reliably;
● the costs incurred, or to be incurred, in respect of the transaction can be measured reliably.

If there is a failure to satisfy these criteria, the entity should apply a cost-recovery basis. It should only recognize revenue to the extent that the recoverable expenses are recognized.

An entity may receive revenue from interest, royalties and dividends. There are two criteria: there are probable economic benefits and there is reliable measurement of revenue. For the particular sources of revenue, the procedures for recognition are:

- Revenue interest: on a time proportion basis that takes into account the effective yield.
- Royalties: on an accruals basis in accordance with the substance of the relevant agreement.
- Dividends: when the shareholders' rights to receive payment are established.

Revenue is measured at the fair value of the consideration that is received or receivable.

There are examples where entities allow customers to defer payment for one or two years and the company claims that this payment deferral is 'interest free'. In these cases, the fair value of the consideration that is receivable for the goods is actually less than the amount of cash the company will receive in two years' time. The company should separately report the interest element from the cash received for the sale of goods.

Although, in practice, the recognition and measurement of revenue can cause problems, there are two key points you should remember.

- We are using the accruals assumption. In other words, you ignore movements of cash and recognize the transaction when it takes place.
- You are calculating the revenue generated in a specific financial period. This means that sometimes you will have to allocate the revenue over the periods that will benefit from it.

Worked examples 7.3 and 7.4 illustrate some of these problems.

Worked example 7.3   Tuition revenue

Home Tutors has a financial year-end on 30 June. It commenced a new course on 1 March 2015 with ten students undertaking a six-month course in International Accounting. The tuition fee for each student is £3,000 for the six-month course. Students should pay the full amount on 1 March and eight students paid in full. With the two remaining students, one paid half the fee and the other paid one-third of the fee.

For the year ended 30 June 2015, we need to calculate the amount of revenue we should recognize. Remember we are using the accruals assumption so it does not matter whether the students have made payment. There are ten students and the total fees for the six months is 10 x £3,000 = £30,000.

However, by the year-end on 30 June 2015 only four months of the six-month course will have elapsed. The amount of revenue to be recognized is £30,000/6 x 4 = £20,000. The remaining £10,000 will appear on the profit or loss account for the year ended 30 June 2016.

Worked example 7.4   Maintenance contract

Hotflues sells and maintains heating systems for large companies. In the year ended 31 December 2014, it sold a system to a company for £1,000,000. This total included the supply and installation of the system and its maintenance for a three-year period starting on 1 January 2015. The charge for the supply and installation of the equipment alone is £850,000 and the maintenance contract is the balance.

The supply and installation of the equipment took place in the year ended 31 December 2014 and the revenue will be shown as £850,000. The maintenance contract is for a three-year period and £50,000 will be recognized for each of the three years starting in 2015.

IAS 11

CONSTRUCTION CONTRACTS

▼ **Table 7.4** *Timeline of IAS 11*

Date	Comment
1979	Standard first issued
1993	Revised standard issued
Interpretations issued	IFRIC 15 Agreements for the Construction of Real Estate
	IFRIC 12 Service Concession Arrangements

Construction contracts are frequently long-term projects lasting several years. We are not discussing minor home repairs but the construction of large buildings, road networks, bridges and other major projects. Major construction companies undertake these projects for clients such as the government or other large businesses.

The usual procedure is to agree on a total price for the project. There will be an agreement on stage payments, and the client will make these payments on the completion of a specific and identifiable stage of the construction. There will be a final payment on completion of the entire project to the client's satisfaction. For the construction company, the problem is how to determine the allocation of revenue and costs to different financial periods using the accruals basis.

Some countries not using international accounting standards will only accept recognition of the project in the profit or loss account upon completion and not before. The international standard, IAS 11, takes a different approach, recognizing some profit in advance of completion. Two methods of accounting are permitted.

The first approach is the percentage of completion method. An entity applies this method where it can estimate reliably the outcome of the contract. In this case, the entity recognizes revenues and costs by reference to the stage of the completion of the contract activity. The profit for a financial period appears in the income statement for that year.

With the percentage of completion method, the key elements are:

- Contract revenue is the amount agreed in the contract. This will include any variations, claims and incentives that will probably result in revenue that it is possible to measure reliably (see Worked example 7.5).
- Contract costs include costs that are directly attributable, for example, site labour costs, construction materials, and rent of plant and equipment used on the contract. Costs such as insurance, design, and technical assistance can be included in the costs if the entity can identify them with a specific contract.

In calculating contract revenue in Worked example 7.5, the aim is to match contract costs to contract revenues for the stage of completion. This will allow reporting of the profit attributable to the stage of completion at the end of a financial period. The standard does not specify whether the calculation of the percentage of completion is on revenues or costs. It is assumed, therefore, that either method is acceptable.

The second method for recognizing some profit in advance of completion is used when the entity cannot estimate reliably the outcome of a construction contract. In this case, it only recognizes revenue relating to those costs that it has incurred and considers recoverable. The entity must expense all contract costs when incurred. If there is an indication of a probable loss on a contract, it must be expensed immediately.

> ### Worked example 7.5   **Calculating contract revenue**
>
> A construction company has a two-year contract for a price of £15 million. It estimates that its total costs will be £12 million, giving a profit of £3 million. At the end of the first year of the contract, it has incurred costs of £9 million. On a percentage basis, it has completed £9/£12 x100 = 75% of the contract. The profit recognized in the first year of the project is
>
> Revenue for year 1 = £15 million x 75% = £11.25 million
>
> Costs for the year 1 = £12 million x 75% = £ 9.00 million
>
> Profit for the year   £ 2.25 million

IFRS 15

REVENUE FROM CONTRACTS WITH CUSTOMERS

▼ **Table 7.5** *Timeline of IFRS 15*

Date	Comment
2014	Standard first issued, effective for periods beginning on or after 1 January 2018
Standards superseded	IAS 11 Construction Contracts
	IAS 18 Revenue
Interpretations superseded	IFRIC 13 Customer Loyalty Programmes
	IFRIC 18 Transfers of Assets from Customers
	IFRIC 31 Revenue – Barter Transactions Involving Advertising Services

revenue

Revenue arises from the sale of goods, the provision of services, and the use of assets yielding interest, royalties and dividends. It is the gross inflow of economic benefits, for example, cash, receivables, and other assets arising from the ordinary operating activities of an enterprise.

The IASB, working with the US Financial Accounting Standards Board, developed one standard in an attempt to simplify the regulations and to address certain **revenue** transactions that were excluded from the earlier standards.

The outcome of their efforts is IFRS 15 *Revenue from Contracts with Customers*. Entities must comply with this new standard for annual reporting periods starting from 1 January 2018 onwards. The standard allows earlier application.

The objective of the standard is to ensure that entities report useful information to users of financial statements about the nature, amount, timing, and uncertainty of revenue and cash flows. It seeks to achieve this by requiring that revenue calculations recognize the transfer of promised goods or services in an amount that reflects the consideration expected in exchange for the goods or services transferred.

It is important to understand the key definitions of the standard – **contract**, **income**, **performance obligation**, **transaction price** – before discussing the detail of the regulations.

contract

A contract is an agreement between two or more parties that creates enforceable rights and obligations.

Based on IFRS 15, Appendix A

income

Income is defined as increases in economic benefits during the accounting period in the form of inflows or enhancements of assets or decreases of liabilities that result in an increase in equity, other than those relating to contributions from equity participants.

Based on IFRS 15, Appendix A

performance obligation

Performance obligation is a promise in a contract with a customer to transfer to the customer either:
a good or service (or a bundle of goods or services) that is distinct; or
a series of distinct goods or services that are substantially the same and that have the same pattern of transfer to the customer.

Based on IFRS 15, Appendix A

transaction price

The transaction price is the amount of consideration to which an entity expects to be entitled in exchange for transferring promised goods or services to a customer, excluding amounts collected on behalf of third parties.

Based on IFRS 15, Appendix A

customer

A customer is a party that has contracted with an entity to obtain goods or services that are an output of the entity's ordinary activities in exchange for consideration.

Based on IFRS 15, Appendix A

The standard is very specific in what it deems to be contracts with customers. There are contracts that do not come under IFRS 15 but another standard, and these are:

- Leases that come under IAS 17 *Leases* (IFRS 16 from January 2019).
- Financial instruments and other contractual rights or obligations which come under IFRS 9 *Financial Instruments*, IFRS 10 *Consolidated Financial Statements*, IFRS 11 *Joint Arrangements*, IAS 27 *Separate Financial Statements* and IAS 28 *Investments in Associates and Joint Ventures*.
- Insurance contracts which come under IFRS 4 *Insurance Contracts*.

A contract with a customer may be partially within the scope of IFRS 15 and partially within the scope of another standard. In such circumstances:

- Where the other standards direct how to separate one or more parts and/or initially measure them, those separation and measurement requirements are applied first. The transaction price is then reduced by the amounts that are initially measured under the other standards.
- Where no other standard provides guidance on how to separate and/or initially measure one or more parts of the contract, the requirements of IFRS 15 are applied.

Some of the wording in the standard appears straightforward but requires careful attention.

Worked example 7.6 demonstrates the application of the wording of the definition of a **customer**.

Worked example 7.6   Defining a customer for IFRS 15

Mugson manufactures items of kitchen equipment and supplies them to a retailer. After extensive discussions, Mugson agrees to sell some property it owns to the retailer so they can use it as a salesroom.

The kitchen equipment is the normal output of Mugson and falls under IFRS 15. Mugson is not in the business of selling property and that transaction would not come under IFRS 15.

In some cases, there may be non-cash consideration. The customer, with the agreement of the entity, may 'pay' by transferring goods or performing some form of services. The transaction price is equal to the fair value of the non-cash consideration and IFRS 13 *Fair Value Measurement* would apply. If an entity cannot reasonably estimate the fair value of non-cash consideration, it would measure the non-cash consideration indirectly by reference to the estimated selling price of the promised goods or services.

There may also be arrangements between entities in the same line of business to assist in making a sale to a third party. The standard excludes these from its scope.

The five step model

The standard sets out what, somewhat grandly, it calls the five step model framework. The entity must follow a sequence of actions, as demonstrated in Diagram 7.3.

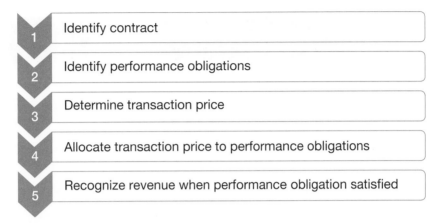

1 Identify contract

2 Identify performance obligations

3 Determine transaction price

4 Allocate transaction price to performance obligations

5 Recognize revenue when performance obligation satisfied

▲ Diagram 7.3 *The five step model*

For each of the five steps, the standard establishes detailed actions.

Step 1: Identify the contract

A contract comes within the scope of IFRS 15 if it meets the following five criteria:

1 the parties to the contract have approved it;
2 each party's rights can be identified;
3 the payment terms for the goods or services can be identified;
4 the contract has commercial substance;
5 it is probable that the entity will collect the consideration in exchange for the goods or services.

The last point seems superfluous as it would seem unwise for an entity to enter into a contract where it is doubtful that it will receive the consideration. A contract, however, may take considerable time to negotiate, with various changes in terms and conditions. The standard requires an entity to continue to reassess the five criteria to determine whether the contract meets all of them. When it does, IFRS 15 will apply to the contract but not before that time.

Contract modifications can be a problem. They occur when there is a change in the scope of the project and/or its price and both parties agree to it. Diagram 7.4 overleaf summarizes the key variations of a modified contract. In practice, this is likely to raise some definitional challenges.

Step 2: Identify the performance obligations in the contract

The contract may require the delivery of a good or service (or bundle of goods and services) that is distinct – a one-off. A good or service is distinct if:

- the customer can benefit from the good or services on its own or in conjunction with other readily available resources; and
- the entity's promise to transfer the good or service to the customer is separately identifiable from other promises in the contract.

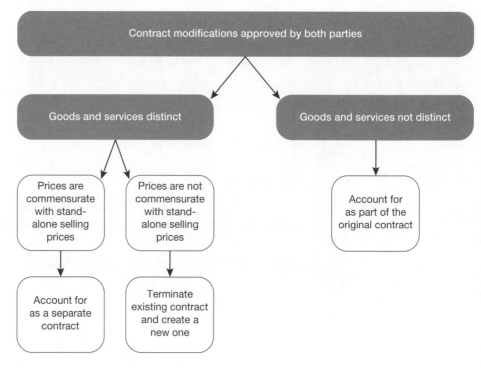

▲ **Diagram 7.4** *Modification of contracts*

An alternative to the distinct contract is a series of distinct goods or services that are substantially the same and have the same pattern of transfer to the customer. The following two criteria identify this type of contract.

● Each distinct good or service in the series that the entity promises to transfer consecutively to the customer would be a performance obligation that is satisfied over time.
● There is a single method of measuring the entity's progress towards complete satisfaction of the performance obligation to transfer each distinct good or service in the series to the customer.

Step 3: Determine the transaction price

The transaction price is the consideration for the goods and services that the entity expects to receive. A contract may have elements of variable consideration which may be determined by the level of business conducted.

These variable considerations arise from such arrangements as discounts, rebates, refunds, credits, price concessions, incentives, performance bonuses and penalties. For example, at the end of a financial year a customer may be entitled to a discount if it has exceeded a certain volume of business. In these circumstances, the entity will estimate the amount of variable consideration to which the customer is entitled under the contract.

Because the final transaction price is uncertain, the standard limits the recognition of the amount of variable consideration in the transaction price. The variable amount must not be so large that, if it is not achieved, the transaction price would suffer a significant revenue reversal.

A further requirement for variable consideration refers to licences of intellectual property. The royalty revenue from such contracts can be based on either sales or usage. In both cases, you can only recognize the revenue when the sale or usage occurs.

Step 4: Allocate the transaction price to the performance obligations in the contracts

A contract could have not one but several performance obligations. The entity will use the stand-alone selling prices to determine the total transaction price. Where stand-alone prices are not available, the entity must estimate them. The standard suggests a number of estimation methods and how to allocate any discounts that are part of the contract.

One section of the standard addresses the situation where consideration is paid in advance or in arrears. In these circumstances, the entity needs to consider whether the contract includes a significant financing arrangement. If it does, the entity should adjust for the time value of money.

Step 5: Recognize revenue when (or as) the entity satisfies a performance obligation

The first decision is determining whether the performance obligation has been satisfied occurs with the passing of control. The standard defines control as the ability to direct the use of and obtain substantially all of the remaining benefits from the asset. This means that other parties cannot use the asset and obtain benefits, which are the potential cash flows. The standard gives the examples of:

- using the asset to produce goods or provide services;
- using the asset to enhance the value of other assets;
- using the asset to settle liabilities or to reduce expenses;
- selling or exchanging the asset;
- pledging the asset to secure a loan; and
- holding the asset.

An entity can satisfy its performance obligation in two ways: over time or at a point in time. The standard describes the recognition criteria for both.

Over time

Examples of the recognition of revenue over time are:

- the customer simultaneously receives and consumes all of the benefits provided by the entity as the entity performs;
- the entity's performance creates or enhances an asset that the customer controls as the asset is created; or
- the entity's performance does not create an asset with an alternative use to the entity and the entity has an enforceable right to payment for performance completed to date.

Point in time

Recognition of revenue occurs with the passage of control at a certain point in time. Examples of when control has passed are:

- the entity has a present right to payment for the asset;
- the customer has legal title to the asset;
- the entity has transferred physical possession of the asset;
- the customer has taken on the significant risks and rewards related to the ownership of the asset; and
- the customer has accepted the asset.

Worked examples 7.7 and 7.8 illustrate the timing issues.

> ### Worked example 7.7   Identifying a transaction under IFRS 15
>
> Jacks Construction orders two separate supplies of material from Concrete Supplies plc. Both companies have a year-end of 31 December. Jacks pays the total for both supplies of £80,000 and requires one delivery to be made in November 2015 and the next delivery to be made in February 2016.
>
> Under IFRS 15, Concrete Supplies must recognize the revenue separately for the two goods or services when they are delivered to the customer. This is the case even if the customer pays the total amount in advance.

> ### Worked example 7.8   Identifying timing under IFRS 15
>
> A company may enter into a contract for the sale and installation of one of its machines. It is confident in its products and guarantees that the machine will operate at a certain speed. The contract states that the buyer will pay £60,000 on delivery and installation. If the machine operates at the guaranteed speed, it will pay a further £10,000. Under IFRS 15, if the seller is confident that the machine will operate at the given speed, it will recognize the full £70,000.

Contract costs

In studying this section it is important to appreciate that the goods and services being negotiated are likely to be extremely large. Sales people, who may be on a high commission, can spend several weeks or months in negotiations. External legal fees may be required. The sales people may incur other legitimate costs in attempting to secure the contract.

The standard allows capitalization of the incremental costs of obtaining a contract if the entity expects to recover these costs. These costs will appear on the entity's balance sheet as an asset.

These costs can only be capitalized if the contract negotiations are successful. For example, sales people may receive a normal salary irrespective of the success of negotiations. If the negotiations do not prove successful, the sales people do not receive a commission. There can be some costs in trying to obtain a contract regardless of whether the contract negotiations are successful. These costs cannot be capitalized unless they can be classified as fulfilment costs.

An entity may incur costs in fulfilling a contract with a customer. There may be costs for the delivery and installation of the equipment over an extended period. There may also be the costs of testing and safety checks. An entity can capitalize these costs if they satisfy the following criteria:

- the costs relate directly to a contract (or a specific anticipated contract);
- the costs generate or enhance resources of the entity that will be used in satisfying performance obligations in the future; and
- the costs are likely to be recoverable.

Of course, as the entity will be showing these costs as an asset on the balance sheet, they must be amortized on a systematic basis. The period of amortization would be consistent with the pattern of transfer of the goods or services to which the asset relates. If the amortization period is less than 12 months, the standard allows the charging of the expenses to the profit or loss statement.

Presentation and disclosure

The aim of the standard is to ensure that entities report useful information to users of financial statements. The financial statements should contain information about the nature, amount, timing, and uncertainty of revenue and cash flows.

An entity is required to present a contract asset, a contract liability, or a receivable in its financial statements once either party to the contract has performed its obligation. With a contract asset, the entity satisfies a performance obligation by delivering the promised good or service. The entity has earned a right to consideration from the customer. Unless the right to consideration is conditional on the passage of time, the entity has a contract asset. If the consideration is only conditional on the passage of time, the entity discloses it as a receivable on the balance sheet and not as an asset. With a contract liability, the customer pays before the entity transfers the promised goods or services.

Qualitative and quantitative disclosures about the revenue and cash flows arising from contracts with customers are required. The objective of the disclosures is to provide users of financial statements with enough information to understand the nature, amount, timing and uncertainty of those revenue and cash amounts.

It is difficult at this stage to assess the impact of the new standard. Some argue that the standard will introduce little change for many transactions, particularly in retail. However, it could bring significant changes for long-term and multi-element contracts. Undoubtedly, there are problems in applying the standard and in April 2016, the IASB issued amendments to the standard.

The amendments clarify some requirements and provide additional transitional relief for companies implementing the standard. The amendments explain how to:

- identify a performance obligation (the promise to transfer a good or a service to a customer) in a contract;
- determine whether a company is a principal (the provider of a good or service) or an agent (responsible for arranging for the good or service to be provided); and
- determine whether the revenue from granting a licence should be recognized at a point in time or over time.

The amendments have the same effective date as the standard: 1 January 2018.

REVENUE FRAUD

For entities wishing to enhance their perceived performance, manipulating the revenue figure is one path to follow. Research on fraudulent financial reporting in the US from 1987 to 1997 (Committee of Sponsoring Organization of the Treadway Commission 1999) revealed that over half of the methods used to perpetuate financial statement frauds were in revenue recognition. Of course, these figures capture the detected frauds. We have no knowledge of those that we have not unearthed.[2]

Examples of financial statement frauds include recording product shipments to entity-owned facilities as sales, re-invoicing past due accounts to improve the age of receivables, pre-billing for future sales and duplicate billings. Some of these frauds are significant and can lead to legal action being taken against the perpetrators. They are not confined to any particular country or industry, and we illustrate the issues with one example from the US and one from the UK.

In 2004, the Securities and Exchange Commission in the US filed an enforcement action against Bristol-Myers Squibb Company, a New York-based company whose largest division, the U.S. Medicines Group, is based in New Jersey. The Commission's complaint alleged that Bristol-Myers perpetrated a fraudulent earnings management scheme by, among other things, selling excessive amounts of pharmaceutical products to its wholesalers ahead of demand, improperly recognizing revenue from 1.5 billion of such sales to its two largest wholesalers and using 'cookie jar' reserves to meet its internal sales and earnings targets and analysts' earnings estimates.

In settling the Commission's action, Bristol-Myers agreed to an order requiring it to pay $150 million and perform numerous remedial undertakings, including the appointment of an independent adviser to review and monitor its accounting practices, financial reporting and internal controls.

Although the Bristol-Myers case has been decided, some examples are not so easy to resolve. At the end of 2014, the UK's Serious Fraud Office (SFO) commenced an investigation into accounting irregularities at UK supermarket giant Tesco. The company had announced the overstatement of its profits by £263 million.

The inflated profit figure was achieved by Tesco bringing forward rebates from suppliers. This was made possible by the accepted business operations in the industry. Supermarkets enter into promotional deals with their suppliers. These agreements reward the supermarkets for achieving certain sales targets for their products, special promotions or placing the suppliers' products in eye-catching places. These agreements are complex, and it is possible to obscure or manipulate the actual figures. It is also possible that the complexity of Tesco's promotional deals led to Tesco making honest mistakes in calculating its profits.

The SFO had not completed its investigation by August 2016. It can take many years to reach a decision. Needless to say, the stock market reacts far more quickly. As soon as the profit correction was publicly announced, Tesco's share price plummeted.

A drop in share price is not necessarily a judgement on the guilt of the company but reflects the sensitivity of the share market to any event that impacts on the reputation of a company and the credibility of its financial reporting.

NOTES

1 Two very readable books that document accounting fraud are:

Jones, M. (2011) *Creative Accounting, Fraud and International Accounting Scandals*, Wiley.

Clikeman, P.M. (2013) *Called to Account: Financial Frauds that Shaped the Accounting Profession*, Routledge.

2 Committee of Sponsoring Organization of the Treadway Commission (1999) Fraudulent Financial Reporting 1987–1997. An analysis of U.S. Public Entities, 1999.

CONCLUSIONS

Investors, whether they are individuals or institutions, are very interested in the financial performance of companies. A healthy profit should mean a dividend and, in all probability, an increase in the share price if the market is pleased with the results.

The profit or loss statement is therefore a key financial statement for users. Given its importance, the history of the statement as part of the double entry system is unremarkable. The contents of the statement are simple, consisting essentially of revenue and costs, but the amount of fraud that it attracts is substantial.

Because of the importance of the profit statement, and to ensure its integrity, standard setters aim to achieve clarity and rigour in their regulations. However, the business transactions can be complex. IFRS 15 attempts to improve the reporting of revenue, but time is needed to see how well it works.

As far as revenues are concerned, we do not anticipate any major amendments in the near future. However, the profit or loss statement receives attention from managers who wish to manipulate earnings for various reasons. It also attracts fraudsters. These practices are outside of the responsibilities of the standard setters.

Whether the profit or loss statement provides all the information the user wants is fiercely debated. In the next chapter, we discuss the accounting treatment of costs. In Chapter 9, we discuss the debate on the concept of comprehensive income.

ADDITIONAL RESOURCES

Go online to the companion website for this book to access further teaching and learning materials for this chapter.

www.palgravehighered.com/hussey-cfr

STATEMENT OF PROFIT OR LOSS – COSTS

IAS 2 Inventories

IAS 16 Property, Plant and Equipment

IFRS 2 Share-based Payments

LEARNING OBJECTIVES

At the end of this chapter, you should be able to:

- Explain the requirements of IAS 2 *Inventories*
- Calculate closing inventory values using both FIFO and weighted average value methods
- Apply the regulation for applying net realizable value
- Discuss the issues in determining the useful life of an asset
- Calculate depreciation using both the straight line and reduced balance methods
- Identify the different methods of share-based payments

INTRODUCTION

In the previous chapter, we examined the standards regulating the recognition and measurement of revenue. In this chapter, we concentrate on those standards that affect the recognition and measurement of costs.

There are no specific standards for many types of cost. Such items as wages, rent, electricity, administration and distribution costs are calculated using normal accounting procedures. The accruals concept applies and the company enters on the profit or loss account those costs that it incurred in generating the revenue for the period.

Some costs do not fit easily into normal accounting procedures. We scrutinize those costs and the standards that regulate them in this chapter. We have already considered two of the standards when we considered the balance sheet. In this chapter, we analyze them from the context of the profit or loss account.

IAS 2 regulates the valuation of the closing inventory at the end of the financial period; in other words, the goods that an entity has not sold. You can only make a profit on the goods actually sold. By calculating the value of goods not sold, we calculate the cost of goods sold and the gross profit.

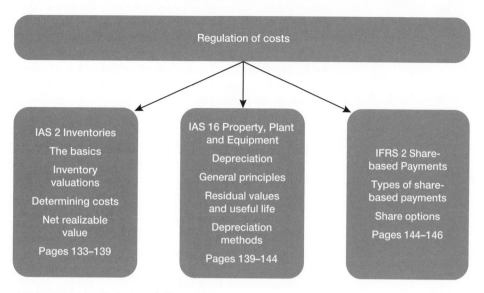

▲ **Diagram 8.1** *Structure of Chapter 8*

The chapter ends with two other standards and their impact on the profit or loss account. The first is IAS 16 *Property, Plant and Equipment*. We discussed this standard in Chapter 4 under non-current assets. In this chapter, we concentrate on the treatment of depreciation as an expense on the profit or loss account.

We complete the chapter with a business practice that has proved controversial in the past. IFRS 2 *Share-based Payments* now regulates these transactions.

IAS 2

INVENTORIES

▼ **Table 8.1** *Timeline of IAS 2*

Date	Comment
1975	Standard first issued
1993	Revised standard issued
2003	Revised standard issued
Interpretations issued	Stripping Costs in the Production Phase of a Surface Mine

The basics

Before we begin to look at the standard, we will recap on the importance of inventory valuation. An entity, using the accruals basis, will record its sales and purchases of goods. At the end of the period there will be some goods unsold – the closing inventory. This is a critical item in arriving at a soundly based figure of gross profit.

An entity can only make a profit on goods that it has sold. Deducting the closing inventory at the end of the period from the opening inventory plus the purchases during the period gives us the value of the goods sold. We say 'goods sold', but some may be stolen, damaged, lost or otherwise 'disappeared'. The entity has to bear these costs. The calculation of inventory values ensures the correct accounting treatment. We provide a simple example (Worked example 8.1) to demonstrate the calculation.

Worked example 8.1   Closing inventory

Hole In plc buys plastic buckets from foreign suppliers. It sells them to the domestic market and its records for the first year show the following:

Sales	5,200 buckets at £10 each = £52,000
Purchases	5,500 buckets at £5 each = £27,500

The Managing Director believes that each bucket makes a profit of £5 so the total profit for the period is 5,200 x £5 = £26,000. The MD also believes that there are 300 buckets that can be sold in the next financial period.

A count of inventory reveals that there are only 200 buckets remaining. The other 100 have been stolen, lost or were damaged and could not be sold. The correct calculation is:

	£	£
Sales for the period		52,000
Purchases	27,500	
Less closing inventory (200 x £5 each)	1,000	26,500
Profit for the period		25,500

The actual profit of £25,500 is lower than the expected profit of £26,000 because of the missing 100 buckets at £5.

---

inventories

Inventories are the assets in the form or finished goods, works in progress or raw materials.

In actual practice, the problems of closing **inventory** can be much greater than illustrated in our simple example. IAS 2 is critical in enabling companies to calculate the correct amount of profit for the period and to show the value of the current asset of inventory on the balance sheet.

Of course, for established companies, the closing inventory at the end of one period is the opening inventory for the next period. Opening inventory plus purchases minus inventory at the end of the period gives the cost of goods sold. It is critical to calculate the correct value of inventory. It can also be very difficult.

The standard provides guidance for determining the cost of these inventories. IAS 2 excludes certain inventories from its scope, the main ones being:

- work in progress arising under construction contracts (see IAS 11 *Construction Contracts*, Chapter 7);
- financial instruments (see IAS 39 *Financial Instruments: Recognition and Measurement*, Chapter 12);
- biological assets related to agricultural activity and agricultural produce at the point of harvest (see IAS 41 *Agriculture*, Chapter 15).

Inventory valuations

The standard has been in force for many years, and there are few problems in its application. However, the practice of inventory valuation raises both practical and conceptual issues, as illustrated in Diagram 8.2.

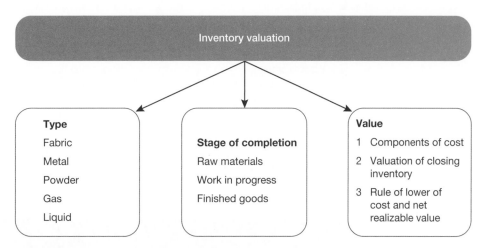

▲ **Diagram 8.2** *Components of inventory valuation*

Given the large amounts for non-current assets in the balance sheet, inventories do not seem important. However, the correct valuation of inventories is critical for arriving at a figure for the cost of goods sold and, therefore, the profit or loss for the financial period.

Auditors take particular care to verify the value of inventory, but they confront two problems. First, is the inventory actually there? Second, is it valued correctly? It would be naïve to believe that auditors can conduct a physical count of inventories in all but the smaller entities. Auditors, therefore, place reliance on the accuracy of the entity's records and statistical sampling.

A physical count resolves one issue, but valuation of inventory can be an even greater problem, particularly for manufacturing organizations. Not only will there be raw materials, but also work in progress and finished goods. Company example 8.1 overleaf from Rolls-Royce illustrates the complexity for managers and auditors in arriving at valuations.

Rolls-Royce grew from the electrical and mechanical business established by Henry Royce in 1884. It now operates in more than 50 countries with 50,000 employees. It provides highly efficient integrated power and propulsion solutions, mainly used in aerospace, marine, energy and off-highway applications. It is one of the world's leading producers of aero engines for large civil aircraft and corporate jets.

We have no knowledge of the types of raw materials that form part of the inventories but we can assume that there is a range of raw materials. The work in progress is extremely challenging, as the company must have a very sound system in place to capture the values of partly finished products. Even finished goods present their own problems. Given the high values of these inventories, correct valuation is essential both for calculating the profit and for disclosing the value of current assets on the balance sheet.

Company example 8.1

Inventory valuation

12 Inventories

	2015	2014
	£m	£m
Raw materials	509	553
Work in progress	882	984
Long-term contracts work in progress	23	22
Finished goods	1,173	1,149
Payments on account	50	60
	2,637	2,768
Inventories stated at net realisable value	221	265
Amount of inventory write-down	64	62
Reversal of inventory write-down	14	1

Rolls-Royce plc, Annual Report and Accounts, 2015, Note 12, p. 138

Determining costs

Inventories must be valued at the lower of cost and net realizable value (NRV). We examine NRV later, but the following list demonstrates what is included in the cost.

- costs of purchase (including taxes, transport, and handling) net of trade discounts received;
- costs of conversion (including fixed and variable manufacturing overheads); and
- other costs incurred in bringing the inventories to their present location and condition.

Although not addressed in the standard, there is an argument that fixed overheads should not be included in inventory costs. These overheads relate to a period and should not be attached to the closing inventory and carried forward to the next financial period.[1]

The phrase 'to their present location and condition' is very important. It establishes the boundaries that prevent further additions of costs to inventory values. You cannot include in cost:

- abnormal waste;
- storage costs;
- administrative overheads unrelated to production;
- selling costs;
- foreign exchange differences arising directly from the recent acquisition of inventories invoiced in a foreign currency;
- interest costs when inventories are purchased with deferred settlement terms.

There are three main methods for valuing inventory. There is a method in the US known as Last In, First Out, but the IASB does not allow this method. The main methods for inventory valuation that are internationally acceptable are shown in Diagram 8.3.

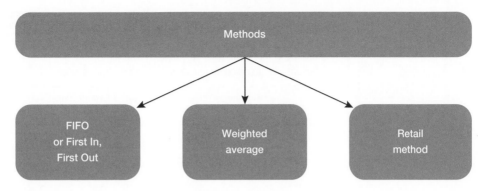

▲ **Diagram 8.3** *Main methods for inventory valuation*

FIFO

The FIFO (First In, First Out) method assumes that the items of *inventory* that were purchased or produced first are sold first. The items remaining in inventory at the end of the period are those most recently purchased or produced and will be valued at that closing figure.

Weighted average

The cost of each item is determined from the weighted average of the cost of similar items at the beginning of a period and the cost of similar items purchased or produced during the period. The company can elect to calculate the inventory on a periodic basis, for example each month, or as each additional shipment is received.

Retail method

This is a technique used to estimate the value of closing inventory using the cost to retail price ratio.

We illustrate the impact of the chosen method on the value of inventory in Worked examples 8.2 and 8.3.

Worked example 8.2   FIFO method

JJ Holdings has the following record of inventory movements.

Date	Received	Issued	Calculation	Total inventory valuation
1 January	5,000 at £1.80 each		5,000 x £1.80 = £9,000	£9,000
15 January	5,000 at £1.90 each		5,000 x £1.90 = £9,500	£18,500
25 January		8,000	5,000 x £1.80 = £9,000	
			3,000 x £1.90 = £5,700	(£14,700)
26 January				£3,800

The issue of inventory of 8,000 units on 25 January, using FIFO, was 5,000 units purchased on 1 January and 3,000 units purchased on 15 January. Closing inventory is 2,000 units purchased on 15 January at £1.90 each.

Worked example 8.3   Weighted average method

We are using the same data as Worked example 8.2 for the number of units received and issued but we are calculating the weighted average values.

Date	Received	Issued	Calculation	Total inventory valuation
1 January	5,000 at £1.80 each		5,000 x £1.80 = £9,000	£9,000
15 January	5,000 at £1.90 each		5,000 x £1.90 = £9,500	
15 January			10,000 x £1.85	£18,500
25 January		8,000	8,000 x £1.85	(£14,800)
			2,000 x £1.85	£3,700

These examples demonstrate that the different methods give different values for the closing inventory. This not only gives a different amount for the balance sheet but, more importantly, gives a different figure in calculating gross profit. It is essential therefore to comply with the following requirements of the standard:

- An entity should apply the same method for all inventories having a similar nature and use to the entity. For inventories with a different nature or use, an entity can apply different methods.
- The entity should use the specific, individual cost of items that are not ordinarily interchangeable and goods or services produced and segregated for specific projects.

The retail method, as its name suggests, is only relevant to certain types of trading activities. The procedure is:

1   Determine the retail value of goods available for sale during the period by adding the retail value of beginning inventory and retail value of goods purchased.
2   Subtract total sales during the period from the retail value of goods available for sale.
3   Calculate the cost to retail price ratio using the formula given below.
4   Multiply the difference obtained in Step 2 and the cost to retail price ratio to obtain the estimated cost of closing inventory.

Cost to retail price ratio is calculated using the following formula:

$$\text{Cost to retail ratio} = \frac{\text{Cost of beginning inventory and purchases during the period}}{\text{Retail value of beginning inventory and purchases during the period}}$$

Net realizable value

An entity must value its closing inventory at the lower of cost or **net realizable value** (NRV). The NRV can be lower than the original cost because:

- the inventories have been damaged whilst in store;
- the inventories have become obsolete;
- the selling prices have declined below the original cost;
- the cost of completing production or making the sale has increased.

Although an entity may purchase or manufacture goods with the intention of selling them at a profit, this may not happen. In some industries, or with certain goods or in certain

net realizable value

The net realizable value is the estimated sales value of the goods minus the additional costs likely to be incurred in completing production, if necessary, and any other costs necessary to make the sale.

Based on IAS 2, para. 6

economic climates, the amount an entity could achieve by selling its inventory is lower than what it cost the entity originally. Examples are fashionable goods, such as certain clothes items, or consumer technology such as mobile phones. If the demand for these items falls, shops will have to lower their prices considerably to sell their goods. The selling price could even be lower than the original cost. In this instance, any closing inventory must be valued at the NRV.

It is important to include the estimated costs of completion or the estimated costs to be incurred to make the sale in the calculations. We illustrate this in Worked example 8.4.

Worked example 8.4   Applying NRV

Pinto Company imports ceramic pots and pans for use in the kitchen. At the year-end it calculates that the closing inventory, using FIFO is:

> 50 saucepans costing £90 each
> 25 baking pans costing £75 each
> 40 boiling pots costing £45 each

The company conducts a physical inspection of its inventory and discovered that some items need repairs before they can be sold. The standard states that the NRV is the estimated sales value of the goods minus the additional costs likely to be incurred in completing production. The company constructs the following table:

Type of pot/pan	Selling price	Repair cost	NRV
Saucepan	£160	£30	£130
Baking pan	£110	None	£110
Boiling pot	£60	£28	£32

Applying the rule of NRV or original cost, the total value of the company's inventory is:

50 saucepans at FIFO valuation £90 each	= £4,500
25 baking pans at FIFO valuation £75 each	= £1,875
40 boiling pots at NRV £32	= £1,280

It is important to note that it is only the additional cost required to sell the inventory, and not the costs that are normally incurred in the business, that is deducted from the selling price.

IAS 16

PROPERTY, PLANT AND EQUIPMENT

Depreciation

The definition of depreciation overleaf requires some further explanation. The depreciable amount of the asset is the original cost of the asset less what can be expected to be received when the entity disposes of it; that is, its residual value, also known as salvage or scrap value.

▼ **Table 8.2** *Timeline of IAS 16*

Date	Comment
1982	Standard first issued
1993	Standard revised
2003	Current version of standard issued
2014	Latest amendment
Interpretations issued	IFRIC 20 Stripping Costs in the Production Phase of a Surface Mine

depreciation

Depreciation is an annual charge to the income statement calculated by dividing the depreciable amount of an asset over its useful economic life. The annual depreciation charge is deducted from the carrying amount of the asset on the balance sheet.

The useful life of an asset has two interpretations:

- the expected period the asset is available for use;
- the expected number of production or similar units the asset will generate.

You can see that **depreciation** is subject to a significant amount of estimation. An entity buying a non-current asset must estimate:

- how long the asset will be used by the entity;
- what amount will be received when the asset is finally sold or scrapped.

Worked example 8.5 demonstrates the calculation of different depreciation amounts based on estimates.

Worked example 8.5   Estimating depreciation

An entity purchases some new machinery for £250,000. One engineer considers the machinery will last for 12 years and is likely to have no value when it is finally disposed of by the entity. The annual depreciation charge is:

$$\frac{£250,000}{12 \text{ years}} = £20,833$$

Another engineer estimates a useful life of 15 years and a residual value of £10,000. The annual depreciation charge is:

$$\frac{£250,000 - £10,000}{15 \text{ years}} = £16,000$$

The value chosen for depreciation impacts directly on the profit. With the scenario in Worked example 8.5, we are looking at a difference of almost £5,000 annually to the net profit. Also, the balance sheets will have differing carrying amounts for the non-current assets. Of course, both engineers may be wrong. They are making estimates and, in one case, predicting a residual value in 15 years' time.

It is essential, therefore, for entities to revisit the calculations and estimates as the machine is used. The standard requires entities to review the *residual value* and the *useful life* of an asset at least at each financial year-end. If there are differences between the previous and current estimates the differences are accounted for as a change in estimate under IAS 8. We discuss this standard in Chapter 13.

Depreciation has an effect both on the balance sheet and the profit or loss account. It has no effect on the cash flow statement. The only cash movement occurs when an entity makes the original payment for the asset. On the balance sheet, the annual depreciation charge reduces the carrying amount of an asset. On the profit or loss account, it is an expense reducing the amount of profit. This is demonstrated in Worked example 8.6.

Worked example 8.6 Depreciation on the balance sheet and profit or loss account

On 1 January 2015, Axles Company purchased equipment for £26,000. It is expected to have a life of 3 years and a residual value of £2,000. Table 8.3 shows the amount of depreciation charged to the profit or loss account and the carrying amount shown on the balance sheet at the end of each of the three years. The annual depreciation charge is:

$$\frac{£26,000 - £2,000}{3 \text{ years}} = £8,000 \text{ each year}$$

▼ **Table 8.3** *Depreciation on the financial statements*

Year	Charge to profit or loss account £	Cost of asset £	Accumulated depreciation £	Carrying amount on balance sheet £
1	8,000	26,000	8,000	18,000
2	8,000	26,000	16,000	10,000
3	8,000	26,000	24,000	2,000

General principles

Throughout IAS 16 and its Basis for Conclusions are various paragraphs that, essentially, establish the general principles. We have extracted these, and the following list establishes the regulations for the depreciation of property, plant and equipment (PPE).

- Once there is recognition of an item of PPE, an entity should disclose it at its cost less any accumulated depreciation and accumulated impairment losses.
- The depreciation charge commences when the asset is available for use. It continues until derecognition of the asset. This is regardless of periods of idleness. However, in some instances the depreciation charge constitutes part of the cost of another asset and is included in its *carrying amount*. For example, under IAS 2 the depreciation of manufacturing plant and equipment is included in the costs of conversion of inventories.
- If an item of property plant and equipment has separate parts with differing useful lives, the entity should depreciate each part separately. The standard gives the example of an aircraft and the separate depreciation of the airframe and the engine. A building can have parts such as the heating system, windows and security system. These have differing economic lives and are depreciated separately.
- Land and buildings are separable items. Land usually has an unlimited useful life. Buildings have a limited useful life and are depreciated.
- An entity can choose to depreciate a separate part, although the cost may not be significant.
- Where there are different parts of an item, it is possible that some of them will have similar useful lives and depreciation methods. In this case, the parts can be grouped together to determine the depreciation charge.

Residual values and useful life

The residual value of an asset is the estimated amount that an entity would currently obtain from disposal of the asset, after deducting the estimated costs of disposal, if the asset were already of the age and in the condition expected at the end of its *useful life*.

Entities can determine that the amount of residual value will be zero. Even if the entity decides an amount for residual value, it is usually insignificant and has little impact on the calculation of the depreciable amount.

There has been debate on the determination of the residual value. The calculation of the depreciable amount is the net cost of the asset – that is, the purchase price less the residual value. In times of rising prices, it is reasonably certain that the residual value will have increased. Some argue that this 'economic value' or future price is most informative as the estimated residual value.

The Board considered the arguments and changed the original definition of residual value to clarify its meaning. The residual value is the amount which could be received for the asset currently (at the financial reporting date) if the asset were *already* as old and worn as it will be at the end of its future useful life. Using this explanation, the expected residual value of an asset is based on past events. Estimations of changes in residual value are due to the effects of expected wear and tear, and no other reasons.

The useful life of an asset may be determined in three ways. First, the entity may have a policy; for example, all cars will have a useful life of three years. Second, the manufacturers may also suggest what the useful life will be. Third, the useful life is an estimate of the:

- expected usage of the asset;
- expected physical wear and tear;
- technical or commercial obsolescence;
- legal or similar limits on the use of the asset.

The estimations required and the stipulation in the standard for the annual review of these estimations lead to changes in estimations and the annual depreciation charge. This is particularly so if the useful life is changed. Worked example 8.7 illustrates the accounting procedure.

Worked example 8.7   Change in useful life

A company acquires a non-current asset with a useful life of 10 years and no residual value for £200,000. The annual depreciation charge is £20,000 and at the end of Year 4, the carrying value is £120,000. The remaining useful life is revised from 6 years to 4 years.

Original cost of asset	£200,000
Cumulative depreciation charge at end of year 4 (£20,000 x 4)	£80,000
Carrying amount at end of Year 4	£120,000

$$\text{New depreciation charge} = \frac{£120,000}{4 \text{ years}} = £30,000 \text{ each year}$$

This revision of the useful life of the asset increases the depreciation charge in the income statement by £10,000.

Depreciation methods

There are a variety of depreciation methods and the standard identifies three:

1 Straight line method.
2 Diminishing balance.
3 Units of production method.

Depreciation starts when the asset is available for use. It continues until the sale or derecognition of the asset. Depreciation does not stop when the asset becomes idle or retired from active use unless it is fully depreciated. If the units of production method is used, the depreciation charge may be zero when there is no production.

The straight line method is the simplest and the following formula is used:

$$\text{Annual depreciation charge} = \frac{\text{Cost of asset} - \text{Residual value}}{\text{Useful life of asset}}$$

The diminishing balance method calculates the annual depreciation charge by applying a set percentage rate to the cost of the asset in the first year. In subsequent years, the depreciation rate is applied to the carrying amount of the asset in the preceding year. This results in a decreasing annual charge for depreciation. There are tables that show the percentage rate to be charged.

Some prefer the diminishing balance method and argue that as the asset ages it becomes less productive and costs more in repairs. The depreciation charge is decreasing as the charge for repairs is increasing thus, one hopes, resulting in the total of the two charges to the profit or loss account being similar over the years.

Worked example 8.8 illustrates the diminishing balance method and the straight line method.

Worked example 8.8   Comparison of depreciation methods

The asset cost is £10,000, has a life of four years and an estimated scrap value of £2,000 at the end of its useful economic life. For the diminishing balance method, the approximate rate of depreciation required to give a value of £2,000 after four years is 33%. We have rounded the amounts to the nearest £10.

▼ Table 8.4 *Comparison of diminishing balance and straight line depreciation methods*

Depreciation method	Diminishing balance method (33%)		Straight line method	
	Annual depreciation charge to income statement £	Written-down amount shown on balance sheet £	Annual depreciation charge £ 163	Written-down amount £
Original cost 1 January 2012		10,000		10,000
Depreciation to 31 December 2012	3,300	6,700	2,000	8,000
Depreciation to 31 December 2013	2,210	4,490	2,000	6,000
Depreciation to 31 December 2014	1,480	3,010	2,000	4,000
Depreciation to 31 December 2015	990	2,020	2,000	2,000

continued overleaf

> **Worked example 8.8** *continued*
>
> The diminishing balance method leads to a substantial charge for depreciation in the early years and a lower charge in later years compared to the straight line method. Similarly, the written-down amounts on the balance sheets vary. The method of depreciation will result in different profits for the year. To comply with the consistency concept, once chosen the same method of depreciation should be used every year unless there is good reason to change it.

A further method of depreciation is revenue based depreciation. This has been used for both tangible and intangible assets. The principle is that the asset should generate over its useful economic life a specific amount of revenue.

In 2014, the IASB issued an amendment to IAS 16 and IAS 38 explicitly prohibiting revenue as a method for depreciating PPE. The reason was that a revenue-based depreciation method is inappropriate because factors other than consumption of an asset affect the level of revenue in a financial period.

The depreciation charge and the revenue generated share some common attributes, but the IASB did not consider them intrinsically linked. They are not the same. Depreciation is an estimate of the economic benefits of the asset consumed in the period, whereas revenue is the output of the asset.

Revenue changes because of other factors that do not affect depreciation, such as changes in sales volumes and selling prices, the effects of selling activities and changes to inputs and processes. The IASB concluded that revenue is an inappropriate basis for measuring depreciation expense.

The amendment to IAS 38 is very similar to that for IAS 16, but the Board recognized that there could be 'limited circumstances' that would permit such a depreciation method.

The standard accepts the use of the revenue generated to amortize an intangible asset when either:

- the rights embodied in that intangible asset are expressed as a measure of revenue; or
- there is evidence that revenue and the consumption of economic benefits are 'highly correlated'.

A 'highly correlated' outcome only occurs where a revenue based method of amortization is expected to give the same answer as one of the other methods permitted by IAS 38. One example is where revenue is earned evenly over the expected life of the asset which results in a similar depreciation charge to that by the straight line method.

IFRS 2
SHARE-BASED PAYMENTS

▼ Table 8.5 *Timeline of IFRS 2*

Date	Comment
2004	Standard first issued
2013	Latest amendment

share-based payments

A share-based payment is a transaction where the entity transfers equity instruments (e.g. shares or share options) in exchange for goods or services supplied by employees or third parties.

Based on IFRS 2, Appendix A

Share-based payments are often associated with schemes for rewarding employees with share-based options, but the standard covers more than that one transaction. Other transactions included in the scope of IFRS 2 are share appreciation rights, employee share purchase plans, employee share ownership plans, share option plans and plans where the issuance of shares (or rights to shares) may depend on market or non-market related conditions.

IFRS 2 does not apply to share-based payment transactions other than for the acquisition of goods and services. Share dividends, the purchase of treasury shares, and the issuance of additional shares are therefore outside its scope.

Although IFRS 2 is broad in its scope, there are some exemptions. The issuance of shares in a business combination comes under IFRS 3 *Business Combinations*. Share-based payments for commodity-based derivative contracts that may be settled in shares or rights to shares come under IAS 32 *Financial Instruments: Presentation*, or IAS 39 *Financial Instruments: Recognition and Measurement*.

Types of share-based payments

There are three types of share-based payments:

Share-based payment transactions where payment may be made in cash on a value based on the entity's share price or in shares.

Equity settled share-based payment transactions where the entity issues shares in exchange for goods or services.

Cash-settled share-based payment transactions where the entity pays cash to a value based on the entity's share price.

The basic principle for accounting for share-based payments is the recognition of an expense in the income statement in the period in which a share-based transaction takes place. The corresponding entry will be either a liability or an increase in equity depending on whether payment is by cash or shares to settle the transaction.

Where there is a choice in payment, the entity will recognize a liability if it determines that it will pay in cash. If the entity finally settles by issuing shares rather than paying cash, the value of the liability is transferred to equity.

Several entities have a policy of rewarding some employees with shares or share options. This is particularly applicable for senior managers and directors. The reason is the belief that the share option will motivate the employee to perform better.

The question arises on how best to account for the share option. IFRS 2 provides the answer: a share option is recognized in the profit or loss account.

The need for a standard arose mainly because of the accounting treatment in the US for stock options. A review of the experiences in that country underlines the need for a standard to protect shareholders and illustrates the practices that may occur without strong accounting regulations.

Share (Stock) options

A simple example of a share option is an entity giving a director the option to purchase shares at a future date at the price when the option was first granted. Let us say that the director pays £5 for the option and the price of the share at that time is £40. If in six months' time the share price drops to £30, the director does not exercise the option and loses the £5. Alternatively, if

share options (US – stock options)

A share option is a benefit, given or sold by one party to another (in this case the employee), that gives the recipient the right, but not the obligation, to buy (call) or sell (put) a share at an agreed-upon price within a certain period or on a specific date.

in six months' time the share price is £60 the director purchases the share for £40 and makes a profit; a clear incentive for the director to ensure that the share price increases.

When employees receive **share options**, they usually do not gain control over the share or options for a period. This period is the vesting period and is usually three to five years. During the vesting period, the employee cannot sell or transfer the share or options. Thus, the employee is obliged to continue working for the entity to get the benefit of the share options. The use of share options led to highly questionable practices in the US. In 1972, a revision in US GAAP meant that entities did not have to report executive incomes as an expense to their shareholders where the income resulted from an issuance of 'at the money' share options; that is, the share option's strike price was *identical* to the prevailing market price. The result was that organizations reported higher profits and directors benefitted without the full knowledge of shareholders.

As demonstrated by the history of share options, this is an area where directors may conduct questionable (or even fraudulent) activities if the accounting regulations are not appropriate. One study (Persons 2012) took a sample of 111 fraudulent entities and 111 matched non-fraudulent entities. The results indicated a significantly positive association between director stock-option compensation and the likelihood of fraud. On the other hand, there is no association between the likelihood of fraud, and independent directors' cash compensation and stock ownership.

Possibly the most publicized case of the abuse of stock options is that of Greg Reyes in 2007 in the US, as detailed in Company example 8.2.

Company example 8.2

Greg Reyes was the former CEO of Brocade Communications Systems Inc. Bloomberg (BRCD). In a broad government crackdown on options backdating, Reyes was the first chief executive convicted by a jury. He lost his bid to reverse his conviction for backdating employee stock-option grants and hiding the practice from auditors and investors.

Reyes received an 18-month prison sentence and $15 million fine imposed after his second criminal trial. Brocade investors lost as much as $197.8 million in 2005 when they sold shares that had fallen in value after the practice was uncovered and the entity restated financial results, prosecutors said in court filings.

In December 2004, the FASB published FASB Statement 123 (Revised 2004): *Share-Based Payment*. This required the recognition of the compensation cost relating to share-based payment transactions in financial statements. It took the Board two years to develop a revised standard that provided investors and other users of financial information with more complete and neutral financial information.[2]

NOTES

1 A study that investigates these issues in the US is Alexander Brüggen, Ranjani Krishnan, Karen L Sedatole (2010) 'Drivers and Consequences of Short-Term Production Decisions: Evidence from the Auto Industry', *Contemporary Accounting Research*, 28(1), pp. 83–123.

2 A fuller account of the issues regarding US stock options can be found in Hussey and Ong (2014).

CONCLUSIONS

The correct identification of the costs for a financial period is critical. To a large extent, the normal accounting procedures are sufficient. The cost is recognized for the financial period on an accruals basis. Measurement does not usually cause a problem and the transaction is entered in the accounting records. Two items of cost that can cause difficulties are closing inventory and depreciation of non-current assets.

Closing inventory shown as a deduction on the profit or loss account enables an entity to identify the cost of goods sold. The adjustment ensures that any losses, for any reason, of inventory are properly accounted for on the profit or loss account.

IAS 2 *Inventories* is a well-established standard. The regulations are clear and easy to understand. Most companies use either FIFO or weighted average. Different methods could arrive at different answers, but the requirement for consistency ensures that is not an issue. The requirement to calculate the net realizable value is also a safeguard against profit alterations.

IAS 16 contains the regulations for depreciation. It is another well-established standard. Some conceptual issues can sometimes erode the usefulness of the information. Depreciation is the allocation of the original cost of the non-current asset over a period. The carrying amount of the depreciated asset, in all probability, has little relationship to its current value. The depreciation charge on a long-held asset, in all probability, has little relationship to the depreciation charge on a new asset. Despite these deficiencies, there are no indications that the IASB intends to make any amendments to IAS 16.

In the UK, IFRS 2 did not have the same impact as in the US where fraud was taking place. At the time of writing, the standard has been in force for over 10 years with no criticisms of its application.

IN THE PIPELINE

Preparers of financial statements have complained that IFRS 2 *Share-based Payments* is a complex standard and that there are difficulties in determining its requirements. The IASB commenced a research project to identify the main reasons for complexity. In May 2016 the IASB considered the findings of the research and the feedback from constituents, but decided not to perform further research on this project. We do not consider any changes will be made to the standard for several years.

ADDITIONAL RESOURCES

Go online to the companion website for this book to access further teaching and learning materials for this chapter.
www.palgravehighered.com/hussey-cfr

STATEMENT OF COMPREHENSIVE INCOME

IAS 1 Presentation of Financial Statements
IAS 21 The Effects of Changes in Foreign Exchange Rates
IAS 19 Employee Benefits

LEARNING OBJECTIVES

At the end of this chapter, you should be able to:

- Discuss the theoretical debate associated with the statement of comprehensive income
- Explain the purpose of a statement of comprehensive income
- Discuss the issues regarding changes in exchange rates
- Demonstrate the accounting for transactions in a foreign currency and translations to a presentation currency
- Identify the different types of employee benefits
- Describe and explain the accounting issues for the two main types of pension plans

INTRODUCTION

The International Accounting Standards Board (IASB) made a significant amendment to IAS 1 in 2011, introducing a completely new statement of comprehensive income. The format of the existing profit or loss account or income statement remains and links to the new statement. Comprehensive income recognizes both realized and unrealized gains and losses that have increased or decreased the owners' equity in the business.

The items that are in a comprehensive income statement but not reported in the traditional profit or loss account are such transactions as revaluations of non-current assets under IAS 16. Two other items are gains and losses from translating the financial statements of a foreign operation (IAS 21) and remeasurement of defined benefit plans (IAS 19). We explain the requirements of both these standards in this chapter.

There has been considerable debate on the purpose of the statement of comprehensive income and its conceptual basis. Some argue that it is difficult to understand and provides little information of value to users. Others claim that it has information value and that preparers and users of financial data need time to become accustomed to it.

The two standards (IAS 21 and IAS 19) discussed in this chapter are connected to the comprehensive income statement because transactions covered by these two standards can appear on the comprehensive income statement. The two standards also have a broader agenda. IAS 21 has gained greater importance with the growing internationalization of business. It is increasingly common for entities to engage in various forms of relationships with entities in different countries; for example, conducting transactions with foreign buyers or sellers, or participating in foreign operations which involve foreign currencies. Entities therefore require guidance to account for these currency transactions in a consistent manner.

The main requirements of IAS 21 are as follows:

- transactions in foreign currencies must be expressed in the entity's reporting currency;
- the financial statements of foreign operations must be translated into the entity's reporting currency.

We examine these two requirements in depth and explain the appropriate selection of the exchange rate and the recognition of the financial effects of changes in exchange rates.

IAS 19 is concerned with the entire spectrum of employee benefits. This might initially seem to involve only wages and salaries. There are, however, different types of benefits from company to company and country to country.

Possibly the most complex, from an accounting viewpoint, is the payment of pensions and other benefits such as health care. Depending on the nature of the scheme and the assumptions concerning the payment of future benefits, the standard requires disclosure of certain gains and losses in other comprehensive income.

There are other standards with a connection to the statement of comprehensive income. We list those standards and the relevant chapters in this book in Diagram 9.1 overleaf.

PROFIT AND INCOME

Defining profit

IAS 1 does not define profit as a concept but as the result of a calculation. It is the total of income less expenses excluding comprehensive income. This explains the mechanics of arriving at a figure of profit or loss but does not describe the nature of profit. Barker observes that a 'curious anomaly exists in the Framework, whereby income and expenses are explicitly defined yet profit is not' (2010: 147).

Unfortunately, the terms 'profit' and 'income' are used somewhat loosely in both IAS 1 and elsewhere. As the calculation of profit excludes other comprehensive income, the conclusion is that profit does not tell the complete story.

It is possible to calculate profit in two ways. We can take our revenues, deduct the expenses and the result will be a 'profit' as defined above. This calculation uses the accruals method and relies on conventions that have developed over many years. It is the definitions and the identification of income and expenses that determine what profit is.

An alternative method is to take the difference in the entity's wealth at the beginning and the end of the financial period. The owners' equity is the measure of wealth. A decline in equity indicates a decrease in wealth, an increase in equity indicates an increase in wealth. This analysis assumes that there have been no direct transactions with shareholders, such as payments of dividends during the financial period.

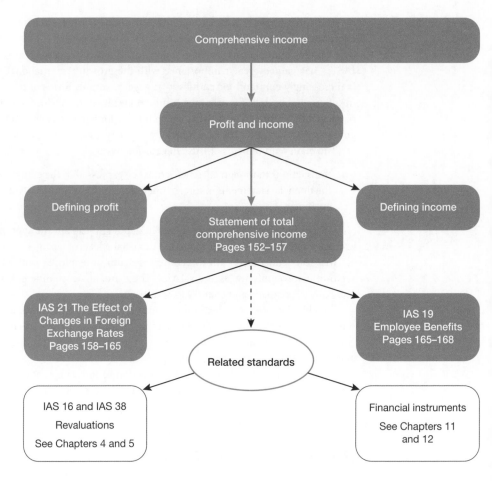

▲ **Diagram 9.1** *Structure of Chapter 9*

The statement of comprehensive income gives a fuller picture than profit because it captures the gains and losses, both realized and unrealized, that increases or decreases the owners' equity. One example of a non-realized gain leading to a gain in equity is a revaluation of non-current assets. We discussed this issue in Chapter 4 where we examined IAS 16 *Property, Plant and Equipment*.

Worked example 9.1 prompts the question of what information should be given to shareholders and how it should be given.

Worked example 9.1

An entity owns property it purchased for £1 million. Due to its location and a buoyant property market, the entity revalues the property at £1.25 million. The entity is wealthier and, using the accounting equation of Assets – Liabilities = Capital, the shareholders are wealthier. If we have increased the assets by a quarter of a million pounds, equity must have increased by the same amount.

This increase may be good news for the shareholders but the gain has not been realized. The entity has not sold the property and, until it does, the gain will not be realized in the form of cash.

In Chapter 5, we explained that the profit or loss account is essentially the output of the double entry system. Disclosure of the profit or loss account has been legally required since 1929 yet users' criticisms have been several and long-standing, identifying many deficiencies in the statement from their point of view.

The main weaknesses for users are:

- It is transaction based. It only records profits that have been realized. An entity may own land or buildings that have increased in value, and there is no recognition of that increase until the sale of the asset.
- It is historical and does not reflect the impacts of inflation. Even over the period of 12 months, if inflation is high, the financial statements do not reflect this. The closing inventory an entity holds may have increased in price. As explained in Chapter 4, the amounts for non-current assets on the balance sheet, in all probability, have little resemblance to their present value.
- It is not possible to compare the actual profit for the period with the predictions of managers, making it difficult to judge whether the entity has been as successful as managers anticipated originally.
- Depreciation is only an allocation, on an estimated basis, of the original historic cost of an asset. We explained in Chapter 4 how the estimates of the expected useful life of the asset and its estimated scrap value formed the annual depreciation charge.
- The definition from IAS 1 emphasizes that the profit or loss excludes comprehensive income; in other words, the income statement does not capture all transactions that may affect shareholder equity.
- It is not based on concepts and applies accounting conventions that do not have a clear foundation.

Despite the criticisms of the profit or loss account, it has been an important source of information for users for many years. It could be that it is familiar and most users are aware of its deficiencies. It could also be that it is difficult to design an alternative that better captures the financial performance of a company. It is still too early to judge whether the subject of this chapter – the statement of comprehensive income – meets the challenge

Defining income

income

The definition of income encompasses both revenue and gains. Revenue arises in the course of the ordinary activities of an entity and is referred to by a variety of different names including sales, fees, interest, dividends, royalties and rent.

IASB, Conceptual Framework for Financial Reporting 2010, para. 4.29

The important aspect of the definition from the Conceptual Framework (CF) is that it includes both revenue and gains. Revenue is part of the calculation of profit but gains are different. The CF states that gains meet the definition of **income** and may, or may not, arise in the course of the ordinary activities of an entity. They include realized gains, such as the disposal of a non-current asset. They also include unrealized gains such as gains on the revaluation of marketable securities and increases in the carrying amount of long-term assets.

The argument put forward in the CF is that profit is not a sufficient measure of the financial progress of an entity. A much fuller picture is obtained by including gains to arrive at an amount for comprehensive income.

Economists, most notably Irving Fisher and Sir John Hicks, have derived theories of income that remedy the deficiencies of the profit or loss account. Hicks considered income as 'the amount an individual can consume and expect to be as well off at the end of a week as he was at its beginning' (1946: 175). The thinking for the IASB and FASB requiring a statement of comprehensive income comes from the work of Hicks. The

Boards claim that, based on economic theory, 'income is a measure of the increase in net resources of an enterprise during a period, defined primarily in terms of increases in assets and decreases in liabilities' (FASB/IASB 2005: 7).

The decision of the IASB to apply Hicks' theory as the basis for the comprehensive income statement has caused fierce controversy. Bromwich et al. argue that the IASB and the FASB 'have selectively picked from, misquoted, misunderstood and misapplied Hicksian concepts of income' (2010: 348).

The Boards' argument for a statement of comprehensive income is that it adopts an asset/liability view (the accounting equation) rather than the revenue and expense (matching) perspective in measuring an entity's income.[1]

Despite the criticisms, the FASB and the IASB introduced the statement of comprehensive income. However, as we explain in the next section, they were unable to restrict the regulations to one statement. If they wish, entities can continue to publish a profit or loss statement separately from the statement of comprehensive income or they can publish one combined statement.

Clean and dirty surpluses

Many users of financial information support the statement of comprehensive income because it allows for clean surplus accounting. Clean surplus accounting means that all changes in shareholder equity that do not result from transactions with shareholders (such as dividends, share repurchases or share offerings) are reflected in the comprehensive income statement.

Clean surplus allows investors to determine the companies that show the best financial performance. According to the clean surplus theory, accountants can determine the value of a company based solely on information found on balance sheets and income statements. A handful of factors, including net income, go into determining the value of a firm under clean surplus theory.[2]

Dirty surplus accounting occurs when some items affect the shareholders' equity but do not appear in the traditional profit or loss account. In other words, the entity has become wealthier but there is no disclosure of the source of this increase. Two activities that we discuss later in this chapter are foreign currency translation adjustments and certain pension liability adjustments.

Whatever the merits of the different opinions on dirty surplus items, we now have the comprehensive income statement. In the following section, we examine the requirements and, not surprisingly, the continuing debate on the concept and value of comprehensive income.

STATEMENT OF TOTAL COMPREHENSIVE INCOME

statement of total comprehensive income

Total comprehensive income is all components of 'profit or loss' and of 'other comprehensive income'. It is reflected in the change of an entity's equity during a period due to transactions and other events. Changes as a consequence from transactions with owners in their capacity as owners are not included.

IAS 1, para. 7

The IASB introduced the **statement of total comprehensive income** in 2011 with an amendment to IAS 1 *Presentation of Financial Statements*. Entitled 'Presentation of Items of Other Comprehensive Income', the amendment became effective for annual periods beginning on or after 1 July 2012.

The amendment raised several issues and there remains uncertainty on the proper treatment of certain items. Questions have also been asked regarding users' needs and understanding of comprehensive income. Nevertheless, entities are required to present this information, as illustrated in Diagram 9.2 and explained in this section.

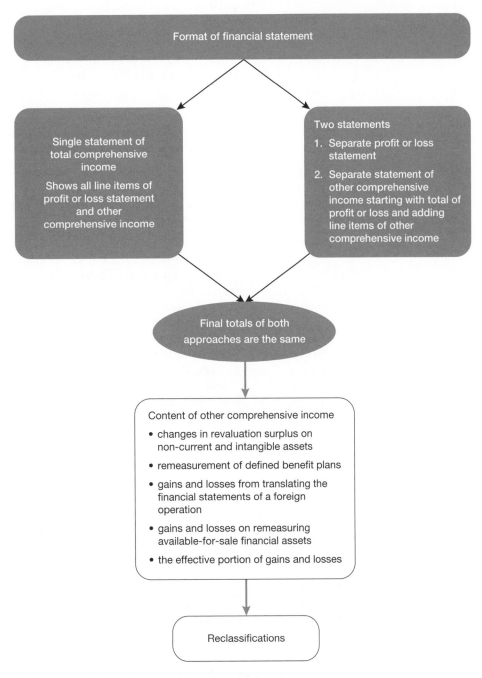

▲ Diagram 9.2 *The statement of total comprehensive income*

Format

The standard requires the disclosure of all non-owner changes in equity either in a single statement or in two statements. A single-statement presentation incorporates all items of income and expense; in other words, it is a statement of total comprehensive income.

With a two-statement presentation:

- The first statement discloses income and expenses recognized in profit or loss.
- The second statement begins with the amount of profit or loss from the first statement. It then shows all items of income and expense where IFRSs require or permit recognition outside profit or loss. In other words **other** comprehensive income.

The IASB preference would have been for a single statement of total comprehensive income, incorporating all the information given in the profit or loss account, in alignment with the position and perspective laid out in the CF. The Board's opinion was that the Framework:

- contains definitions of income and expenses that cover all items of non-owner changes in equity;
- does not define profit or loss and therefore does not clarify what those terms express;
- does not provide criteria for distinguishing the characteristics of items that should be included in profit or loss from those items that should be excluded.

In its Basis for Conclusions the Board argued that it was conceptually correct for an entity to present all non-owner changes in equity (i.e. all income and expenses recognized in a period) in a single statement. It argued that there are no clear principles or common characteristics to separate income and expenses into two statements.

However, the Board accepted that there was a strong lobby for the retention of a separate profit or loss account. Accordingly, companies have the option. In our sample of twenty-five UK companies, all used the two-statement approach. The ten Australian and Canadian companies show a mixed approach, with five using two statements.

As the separate statement of other comprehensive income must, under the requirements, commence with the figure of profit from the separate statement of profit or loss the final figure is the total comprehensive income. Companies will, therefore, produce either a single statement of total comprehensive income or, more frequently, two separate statements: the profit or loss statement and the statement of other comprehensive income that starts with the figure of profit shown on the profit or loss account.

This section concentrates on the two-statement approach of a profit or loss statement and a statement of other comprehensive income. At its simplest, the profit or loss account shows the revenue for the period (Chapter 7) less the expenses incurred in generating that revenue (Chapter 8).

To ensure that the financial statements provide all necessary information the Board requires that the other comprehensive income statement shows:

- the profit or loss amount for the financial period;
- the line items of other comprehensive income for the period;
- a total of the comprehensive income for the period being the total of profit or loss and the other income for the period.

Company example 9.1 comes from Royal Dutch Shell. This company was formed in 1907 and its headquarters are in The Hague, the Netherlands. The company is a leader in the oil and gas industry, operating in over 70 countries with 93,000 employees. We have extracted only the main information and omitted many of the amounts so that we can concentrate on the structure.

The disclosure commences with the heading 'Consolidated Income Statement'. This is the profit or loss account. It gives the total revenue, deducts the total expenses and makes adjustments for tax, and finishes with the income for the period of $2,200 million. This is essentially the standard format for the profit or loss account and many companies would use the term 'profit' instead of income. The standard does not compel companies to use a specific term.

Company example 9.1

CONSOLIDATED STATEMENT OF INCOME	$ million 2015
Revenue	
Share of profit of joint ventures and associates	
Interest and other income	
Total revenue and other income	**272,156**
Purchases	
Production and manufacturing expenses	
Selling, distribution and administrative expenses	
Research and development	
Exploration	
Depreciation, depletion and amortisation	
Interest expense	
Total expenditure	**270,109**
Income before taxation	
Taxation (credit)/charge	
Income for the period	**2,200**

CONSOLIDATED STATEMENT OF COMPREHENSIVE INCOME	$ million 2015
Income for the period	**2,200**
Other comprehensive income, net of tax	
Items that may be reclassified to income in later periods:	
Currency translation differences	
Unrealised losses on securities	
Cash flow hedging gains	
Share of other comprehensive loss of joint ventures and associates	
Total	**(7,807)**
Items that are not reclassified to income in later periods:	
Retirement benefits remeasurements	
Other comprehensive (loss)/income for the period	
Comprehensive (loss)/income for the period	
Comprehensive income/(loss) attributable to non-controlling interest	
Comprehensive (loss)/income attributable to Royal Dutch Shell plc shareholders	**(811)**

Royal Dutch Shell plc, Annual Report, 2015, p. 116

Following is the statement of comprehensive income, headed 'Consolidated Statement of Comprehensive Income'. This starts with the income figure of $2,200 million, as required by the standard. It continues by giving details of other gains and losses divided into those that may be reclassified as income in later periods and those that will not be reclassified.

We proceed in this chapter to explain the requirements of the standard for other comprehensive income and an explanation of reclassifications.

Content – other comprehensive income

The components of **other comprehensive income** include:

- changes in revaluation surplus on non-current and intangible assets;
- remeasurement of defined benefit plans;
- gains and losses from translating the financial statements of a foreign operation;
- gains and losses on remeasuring available-for-sale financial assets;
- the effective portion of gains and losses on a cash flow hedge.

In Chapter 4, we discussed changes in revaluation surplus on non-current and intangible assets. In this chapter, we explain IAS 19 *Employee Benefits* and IAS 21 *The Effects of Changes in Foreign Exchange Rates*. In Chapters 11 and 12, we explain financial assets and cash flow hedge.

The line items in the other comprehensive income statement are either:

(a) net of related tax effects; or
(b) before related tax effects with one amount shown for the aggregate amount of income tax relating to those items.

If an entity selects alternative (b) it allocates the tax between the items that might be reclassified subsequently to the profit or loss section and those that will not be reclassified subsequently to the profit or loss section.

The information disclosed must show separately the share of the other comprehensive income statements of associates and joint ventures accounted for using the equity method. Chapter 17 discusses in detail accounting for associates and joint ventures.

To assist the users' understanding, the statement of comprehensive income should separately disclose every material expense. These can be included in the notes to the financial statements. The kind of material items that may require separate disclosure may include the following, although this is not an exhaustive list:

- write-down of inventories to net realizable value;
- write-down of property, plant and equipment;
- disposals of investments;
- restructuring costs;
- discontinued operations;
- litigation settlements.

The standard requires the line items to be grouped into those that:

- will not be reclassified subsequently to profit or loss; and
- will be reclassified subsequently to profit or loss.

This classification was exemplified by Royal Dutch Shell in Company example 9.1.

There have been criticisms over the lack of guidance from the IASB on what items should be included in profit or loss and in other comprehensive income. Holt (2014b) claims that some users' confusion between the choice of including items in the profit or loss or other consolidated income revolves around the question of realized versus unrealized gains. However, the reality is even more complex, particularly concerning the concept of reclassifications.

Reclassifications

Not all items of other comprehensive income can be recycled and the regulations state that:

1   **Reclassification** adjustments are permissible for such items as the disposal of a foreign operation (see IAS 21) and when some hedged forecast cash flow affects profit or loss (see IFRS 9 in relation to cash flow hedges in Chapter 12).

2   There are no reclassification adjustments in revaluation surplus recognized in accordance with IAS 16 or IAS 38 or on remeasurements of defined benefit plans recognized in accordance with IAS 19. These components are recognized in other comprehensive income and are not reclassified to profit or loss in subsequent periods.

Changes in revaluation surplus may be transferred to retained earnings in subsequent periods as the asset is used or when it is derecognized (see IAS 16 and IAS 38).

Other IFRSs specify whether and when the reclassification of amounts previously recognized in other comprehensive income to profit or loss can be made. A reclassification adjustment is included with the related component of other comprehensive income in the period that the adjustment is reclassified to profit or loss.

> **reclassifications**
>
> Reclassification is the recycling of an item by moving it from the other comprehensive income section to the profit or loss statement, thus affecting the profit for that financial period.
>
> *IAS 1*

These amounts may have been recognized in other comprehensive income as unrealized gains in the current or previous periods. The standard requires unrealized gains to be deducted from other comprehensive income in the period in which the realized gains are reclassified to profit or loss. This prevents their inclusion in total comprehensive income twice.

KPMG has published an illustrative example of the other comprehensive income statement (Company example 9.2). We have extracted the details of the line items and segregated them into items that will not be reclassified and those that may be reclassified.

Company example 9.2

Other comprehensive income

Items that will not be reclassified to profit or loss:

Revaluations of property, plant and equipment
Defined benefit plan actuarial gains (losses)
Income tax on items that will not be reclassified to profit or loss

Items that may be reclassified subsequently to profit or loss:

Foreign currency translation differences for foreign operations
Share of foreign currency translation differences of associates
Net loss on hedge of net investments in foreign operations
Cash flow hedges
Available for sale financial assets
Income tax on items that may be reclassified to profit or loss

Other comprehensive income, net of tax

KPMG, 'In the Headlines', 2011, Issue 2011/19, June

IAS 21

THE EFFECTS OF CHANGES IN FOREIGN EXCHANGE RATES

▼ **Table 9.1** *Timeline of IAS 21*

Date	Comment
1983	Standard first issued
1993	Revised standard issued
2003	Revised standard issued
2008	Further revisions issued
Interpretations issued	IFRIC 16 Hedge of a Net Investment in a Foreign Operation

Definitions and key principles

IAS 21 has two objectives (see Diagram 9.3):

1   To set out how to include foreign currency transactions in an entity's financial statements.
2   To explain how to translate the financial statements of foreign operations into a presentation currency.

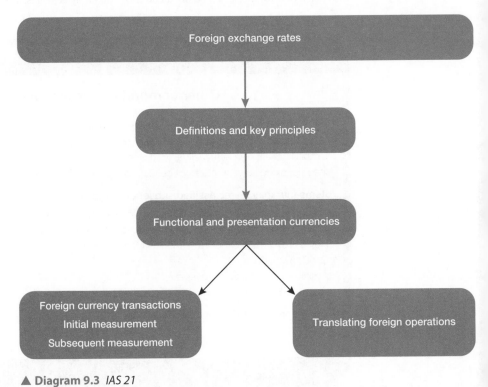

▲ **Diagram 9.3** *IAS 21*

Functional currency and presentation currency

Functional currency

> **functional currency**
>
> The functional currency is the currency of the primary economic environment in which the company operates.

Every individual entity must measure its results and financial position in its **functional currency**. This is the currency of the primary economic environment in which the entity operates. The functional currency must be determined at the lowest foreign operational level; for example, a subsidiary, associate, branch or joint venture.

An entity's functional currency is the basis for determining whether the entity has any foreign exchange transactions. By identifying its functional currency, the entity is identifying the treatment of exchange gains and losses from the currency translation process and its reported results.

If we are considering consolidated financial statements, each individual entity in the group, wherever it operates in the world, must prepare its financial statements in its functional currency.

The standard offers guidance on identifying the functional currency. One important characteristic is the currency in which transactions are normally conducted. The standard expands on this characteristic by identifying the indicators of the functional currency.

Indicators of the functional currency

Primary indicators

- The currency that mainly influences sales prices for an entity's goods and services. This is normally the currency in which sales prices for goods and services are denominated and settled. For example, the entity may operate in an active local sales market. It prices its products in the local currency and makes payments primarily in that local currency.
- The currency of the country whose competitive forces and regulations mainly determine the sales prices of an entity's goods and services.
- The currency that mainly influences the costs of labour, materials, goods and services. If such costs are incurred and settled in the local currency this will be the functional currency.

Secondary indicators

- The currency in which finance is generated. If this is arranged within the country, it may indicate that this is the functional currency.
- The currency in which the receipts from operating activities are normally retained.

Where the entity is a foreign operation such as a subsidiary, branch, associate or joint venture, there are five additional indicators.

1 The foreign operation, regardless of size, operates with significant autonomy and not as an extension of the reporting entity. In this situation, the foreign entity would use the local currency as the functional currency.
2 A foreign operation that only sells the goods and sends the proceeds to the reporting company in another country would not normally use the local currency as the functional currency to prepare its financial statements.
3 A foreign operation that has few transactions with the reporting entity would normally use the local currency as the functional currency.
4 If the cash flows of the foreign operation do not affect the cash flows of the reporting company and are mainly in the local currency that will be the functional currency.
5 If the foreign operation can maintain its activities from its own cash flows in the local currency that will be the functional currency.

In some instances, it is difficult to determine the functional currency. The operation may be diverse, with cash flows, financing and transactions occurring in more than one currency. Management may have to decide the relative importance of each of the indicators in the particular circumstances.

The standard states that, in making its judgement, management must give priority to the primary indicators before considering the secondary indicators. If a decision is possible with the primary indicators, there is no need to consider the secondary indicators.

Usually, the functional currency will be the currency of the country whose economy drives the business and reflects the economic effects of the underlying transactions, events and conditions. There are variations however, and one example is where an entity may have several operations in one foreign country. It is possible that these have different functional currencies. One may be operating in the local currency whereas another may meet the characteristics of the primary indicators.

An entity does not have a choice of functional currency. All currencies, other than the functional one, are foreign currencies. An entity does have a choice in its presentation currency.

Presentation currency

presentation currency

The presentation currency is the currency in which the financial statements are presented.

An entity's management may choose a different **presentation currency** in which to present financial statements.

At the group level, various entities within a multinational group will often have different functional currencies, identified at entity level for each group entity. Each group entity translates its results and financial position into the presentation currency of the reporting entity. For example, an Australian subsidiary would prepare its accounts in Australian dollars (the functional currency) but the Canadian holding company would present its group results in Canadian dollars (the presentation currency).

Companies usually state clearly their policy on currencies. Company example 9.3 is taken from an Indian company that complies with IFRSs. Great Eastern Energy Corporation Limited is a coal-bed methane (CBM) production company, which is located in Asansol district of West Bengal. It has its primary listing on the London Stock Exchange.

Company example 9.3

Functional and presentation currency

Items included in the financial statements of the Company are measured using the currency of the primary economic environment in which the entity operates ('the functional currency'). The functional currency of the Company is Indian Rupees ('Rs.' or 'INR'). The financial statements are presented in US Dollar (US$), which is the Company's presentation currency, which the Company considers most appropriate for its investors being an overseas listed Company.

Great Eastern Energy Corporation Limited, Annual Financial Report, 2015, p. 13

Foreign currency transactions

An entity may well conduct transactions denominated in a currency other than the local (domestic) currency of the country in which it is located. Purchases, sales and other services may be conducted with entities in other countries and their currency used for the transaction. This leads to the need to translate those currencies into the functional currency.

Initial recognition

spot exchange rate

The spot exchange rate is the exchange rate for immediate delivery.

An entity initially records a foreign currency transaction in the functional currency. It does this by applying to the foreign currency amount, the **spot exchange rate** between the functional currency and the foreign currency at the date of the transaction. For revenues, expenses, gains and losses, the entity applies the spot exchange rate at the dates on which those elements are recognized.

An entity that has few transactions or large, one-off transactions can apply the actual spot exchange rate.

For an entity of any size, it is usually impracticable to apply the spot rate on the dates that all the transactions are taking place. It is usual in these cases to use a rate that approximates the actual rate, such as an average rate for the period in which the transactions are conducted. The standard allows this as long as there are no significant changes in rates during the period.

Worked example 9.2   **Conversion of foreign currency**

A Canadian entity purchases 10,000 kilos of materials at £12 per kilo from a UK entity. The total agreed price is £120,000. The rate of foreign exchange at the date of the transaction is £1.00 to $1.80.

The Canadian entity records in its purchases account:

£120,000 x $1.80 = $216,000

The same amount is shown in accounts payable.

The Canadian company settles the debt before the end of the year but the exchange rate is £1.00 to $1.70. The cost in dollars of this is

£120,000 x $1.70 = $204,000

The amount of profit on conversion ($12,000) is shown on the income statement at the year-end.

---

exchange differences

Exchange differences are the differences resulting from translating a given number of units in one currency into another currency at a different exchange rate.

The settlement of transactions completely within the financial period is usually referred to as 'conversion' (see Worked Example 9.2). It is only exchanging the amount of one foreign currency to another in the financial period. Any profits or losses on conversion are included in the profit or loss account for the year in which the conversion is made. The difficulty arises where amounts are outstanding at the year-end. At this stage, the assets or liabilities obtained or incurred in a foreign company have to be shown on the balance sheet.

Subsequent measurement

Currency translation is required at the end of an accounting period when a company still holds assets or liabilities in its statement of financial position that were obtained or incurred in a foreign currency.

At the end of the financial period when the balance sheet is being prepared, items fall into three classifications:

- Monetary items, e.g. accounts receivable/payment;
- Non-monetary items measured at historic cost;
- Non-monetary items measured at fair value.

Non-monetary items are items such as intangible assets, plant and equipment, and inventories (see Chapters 4 and 5).

Exchange differences arising on the settlement of monetary items, or on translating monetary items at rates different from those at which they were translated on initial recognition during the period or in previous financial statements, should be recognized in profit or loss in the period in which they are settled.

Monetary items arising from a foreign currency transaction that remains outstanding at the statement of financial position date should be translated using the **closing rate** and should be reported as part of the profit or loss for the year.

Non-monetary items measured at historical cost are translated at the date of the transaction.

For non-monetary items remeasured at fair value, for example, where property is revalued, any gain or loss should be recognized in comprehensive income. In addition, any related differences are recognized in other comprehensive income.

closing rate

The closing rate is the spot exchange rate at the balance sheet date.

The exception to the above rules is exchange differences arising on monetary items that form part of the reporting entity's net investment in a foreign operation. The reporting entity recognizes these differences in the consolidated financial statements that include the foreign operation in other comprehensive income. When the reporting entity disposes of the net investment, the results of the transaction will be recognized in profit or loss and not in other comprehensive income.

In Worked example 9.2, the Canadian company had completed all its transactions by the year-end. The goods had been sold and the supplier paid. There are three other year-end scenarios for that company that we demonstrate in Worked examples 9.3 to 9.5. We assume a closing rate of $1.90.

Worked example 9.3   The goods not sold and the supplier not paid

The purchases are now part of the closing inventory, and remain at the initial rate not the closing rate. Inventory appears in the accounting records at $216,000 (£120,000 x $1.80), assuming that the net realizable value is not lower than cost.

The amount owing to the supplier is £120,000 x $1.90 = $228,000. The liability to the UK supplier was originally $216,000. The original accounts payable would be changed to $228,000 and the difference of $12,000 would be shown as an exchange loss in the statement of income (profit or loss statement).

Worked example 9.4   The goods sold and the supplier paid

There is no inventory at the year-end because the goods have been sold. The entity restates the accounts payable at the new exchange rate of $228,000. The loss shown in the statement of income is as in Worked example 9.2.

> ### Worked example 9.5   The goods not sold and the supplier paid
>
> As long as the inventory is valued at cost, no change is required. If the net realizable value is lower than cost, the entity shows the difference between the cost of $216,000 and the net realizable value as a loss on the statement of income.

Translating foreign operations

A foreign operation is an entity that is a subsidiary, associate, joint venture or branch of a reporting entity, the activities of which are based in or conducted in a country or currency other than those of the reporting entity.

As mentioned earlier, with consolidated financial statements, each individual entity in the group, wherever it is in the world, must prepare its financial statements in its functional currency.

- Foreign currency items and transactions should be translated into the entity's functional currency.
- The spot exchange rate between the functional currency and the foreign currency at the *date of the transactions* should be used.
- Average rates can be used but care must be exercised. If exchange rates fluctuate significantly over time or if there are a small number of irregular transactions, the average can be distorted.

In preparing group accounts, the financial statements of foreign subsidiaries are translated into the presentation currency of the reporting entity. If the presentation currency differs from the functional currency, the financial statements are retranslated into the presentation currency. If the financial statements of the entity are not in the functional currency of a hyperinflationary economy,[3] then they are translated into the presentation currency as follows.

- Assets and liabilities (including any goodwill arising on the acquisition and any fair value adjustment) are translated at the closing spot rate at the date of that balance sheet.
- Income and expenses for each statement of comprehensive income are translated at the spot rate at the date of the transactions. (Average rates are allowed if there is no great fluctuation in the exchange rates.)
- All exchange differences are recognized in other comprehensive income.

Any goodwill and fair value adjustments are treated as assets and liabilities of the foreign entity, and therefore retranslated at each balance sheet date at the closing spot rate.

Exchange differences on intra-group items are recognized in profit or loss, unless they are a result of the retranslation of an entity's net investment in a foreign operation when it is classified as equity. We discuss intergroup transactions in Chapter 16. In the financial statements that include the foreign operation and the reporting entity (e.g. consolidated financial statements when the foreign operation is a subsidiary), such exchange differences are recognized initially in other comprehensive income and reclassified from equity to profit or loss on disposal of the net investment.

Dividends paid in a foreign currency by a subsidiary to its parent firm may lead to exchange differences in the parent's financial statements. They are not eliminated on consolidation, but recognized in profit or loss.

It is possible that an entity will dispose of a foreign operation. In these circumstances, the cumulative amount of the exchange differences recognized in other comprehensive income, and accumulated in the separate components of equity, are reclassified from equity to profit or loss (as a reclassification adjustment) when the gain or loss on disposal is recognized.

If there is a gain or loss on a non-monetary item, an entity recognizes it in other comprehensive income. The entity recognizes any exchange component of that gain or loss in other comprehensive income. The alternative is where an entity recognizes a gain or loss on a non-monetary item in the profit or loss account. It recognizes any exchange component of that gain or loss in the profit or loss account.

There are separate regulations if the functional currency is the currency of a hyperinflationary economy. In such a case the entity's financial statements are restated in accordance with IAS 29 *Financial Reporting in Hyperinflationary Economies*. The entity uses the following procedure to translate the results and financial position into a different presentation currency.

(a) All amounts (i.e. assets, liabilities, equity items, income and expenses, including comparatives) are translated at the closing rate at the date of the most recent statement of financial position, except that

(b) When amounts are translated into the currency of a non-hyperinflationary economy, comparative amounts are those that were presented as current year amounts in the relevant prior year financial statements (i.e. not adjusted for subsequent changes in the price level or subsequent changes in exchange rates).

Company example 9.4 illustrates the treatment of foreign exchange.

Company example 9.4

Treatment of foreign exchange

Foreign currencies

Foreign currency transactions are translated into the functional currency using the exchange rates prevailing at the date of the transaction. Foreign exchange gains and losses resulting from the settlement of transactions and the translation of monetary assets and liabilities denominated in foreign currencies at period end exchange rates are recognised in the income statement line which most appropriately reflects the nature of the item or transaction.

On consolidation, assets and liabilities of foreign undertakings are translated into Sterling at year end exchange rates. The results of foreign undertakings are translated into Sterling at average rates of exchange for the year (unless this average is not a reasonable approximation of the cumulative effects of the rates prevailing on the transaction dates, in which case income and expenses are translated at the dates of the transactions). Foreign exchange differences arising on retranslation are recognised directly in a separate component of equity, the translation reserve. In the event of the disposal of an undertaking with assets and liabilities denominated in a foreign currency, the cumulative translation difference associated with the undertaking in the translation reserve is charged or credited to the gain or loss on disposal recognised in the income statement.

BT Group, Annual Report and Accounts, 2016, p. 178

Multinational groups can find the process of translating foreign operations time-consuming and challenging. The assessment of functional currency is a key step when considering any change in the group structure or when implementing any new hedging or tax strategies.

IAS 21 does not apply to:

- Hedge accounting for foreign currency items, including the hedging of a net investment in a foreign operation. We discuss hedge accounting in Chapter 12.
- The presentation in a statement of cash flows of the cash flows arising from transactions in a foreign currency, or to the translation of cash flows of a foreign operation.

IAS 19
EMPLOYEE BENEFITS

▼ Table 9.2 *Timeline of IAS 19*

Date	Comment
1983	Standard 'Accounting for Retirement Benefits in Financial Statements of Employers' issued
1993	Employee benefits standard issued
2013	Amendment issued: 'Defined Benefit Plans: Employee Contributions'
Interpretations issued	IFRIC 14 The Limit on a Defined Benefit Asset, Minimum Funding Requirements and their Interaction

When studying this standard we are considering *all* forms of consideration given by a business in exchange for services provided by its employees in a financial period. These include:

employee benefits

Employee benefits include all forms of consideration given to an employee in exchange for their services. Examples are cash bonuses, retirement benefits and private health care.

- Short-term benefits that fall due within 12 months of services being given, e.g. wages, salaries, bonuses, non-monetary benefits.
- Post-employment benefits, e.g. pensions and continued private medical health care.
- Other long-term benefits, e.g. long-term disability benefits and paid sabbaticals.
- Termination benefits, i.e. when employee leaves.

The standard identifies the various types of benefits to which it applies. These are:

- wages and salaries;
- compensated absences (paid vacation and sick leave);
- profit sharing plans;
- bonuses;
- medical and life insurance benefits during employment;
- housing benefits;
- free or subsidized goods or services given to employees;
- pension benefits;
- post-employment medical and life insurance benefits;

- long-service or sabbatical leave;
- 'jubilee' benefits that are paid to employees upon completion of a certain number of years of service;
- deferred compensation programmes;
- termination benefits.

The standard does not apply to employee benefits within the scope of IFRS 2 *Share-based Payment* or reporting by employee benefit plans (see IAS 26 *Accounting and Reporting by Retirement Benefit Plans*).

In this section, we discuss short-term benefits and post-employment benefits. The benefit that raises the most difficult accounting issues is post-employment benefits and therefore requires concentrated attention.

The aim of the standard is to establish whether entities should recognize specific employee benefits as a liability or an expense. With all types of benefits the general principle is that the cost of providing employee benefits should be recognized as an expense in the period when the employee earns the benefit, rather than when it is paid or payable.

With pensions, the employer receives the benefits of the employee's service now, but does not pay the pension until the employee retires. The employer must pay the future pension and will classify it as a liability.

Short-term benefits

Short-term employee benefits are those payable within 12 months after service is provided. This includes vacations, paid sick leave, and other acceptable absences where the benefits are still payable. The cost is an expense in the period that service is provided.

The benefit is a charge to the income statement. If the benefit remains unpaid at the end of the financial period, it is a current liability on the balance sheet. When the company finally pays the benefit, the amount of cash held by the company declines. The company removes the amount of the payment and the liability from the balance sheet. Worked example 9.6 illustrates the process.

Worked example 9.6   Recognizing short-term benefits

A company has 200 employees who are all paid the same rate of £100 per day. Each employee is entitled to 10 days' holiday on full pay. The expense to the company in its income statement for 2015 for vacation pay is 200 x £100 x 10 days = £200,000. Five employees decide to take only 5 days' holiday in 2015, carrying over the remaining 5 days into 2016. The company agrees to this plan. The amount of £200,000 in the income statement is correct. The company will show a current liability on the balance sheet of £2,500 to represent the wages to be paid.

Post-employment benefits

Post-employment benefits, also known as retirement benefits, cause the greatest accounting problems. There are two main types of retirement schemes: the defined contribution plan and the defined benefit plan.

Defined contribution plan

For defined contribution plans, the employing entity recognizes contributions as an expense in the period that the employee provides service. In many schemes, the employee and the employer both agree to contribute specific amounts to the plan.

The amount paid into the defined contribution plan is fixed and the payments invested to build up a 'fund' for the particular employee. The amount of the contributions and the income that the investment has generated should be a substantial amount by the date the employee retires. This fund provides regular payments to the pensioner.

The disadvantage of the defined contribution plan is that the amount of the final fund relies heavily on the success of the investments. If there is a very poor economic period, the fund will be much smaller than the employee hoped and the pension is correspondingly less. With the defined contribution plan, the risk lies with the employees: they may not receive the pension they anticipated. There is no risk to the employer and the only commitment is the agreed amount of contribution.

Defined benefit plan

Defined benefit plans are not calculated on contributions but the amount of pension an employee is guaranteed to receive on retirement. The pension is usually calculated by using a formula that takes into account the employee's length of service and salary. For example, an employee may be in a scheme that pays one-sixtieth for each year of service multiplied by the employee's average salary for the last three years of their employment. An employee with 30 years' service and an average salary of £60,000 per annum will receive a pension of 30/60 × £60,000 = £30,000.

To operate the scheme an employer needs to know now the amount of contribution that they must make each year to pay for the final pension. Imagine that a company has an employee starting on 1 January 2015 who will retire in 2055. To determine the contribution that must be invested annually until the employee retires, the employer must assess:

- Is the employee likely to leave or die before they are due to retire?
- How many years' service will they actually have?
- What will their final salary be?
- What will be the investment return on the contributions made each year?
- How long will the employee live after retirement, because the pension will have to be paid until the employee dies?

As these questions cannot be answered, and there are many other variations and possibilities that the entity has to resolve, it is normal practice to rely on the expert judgement of actuaries when calculating the contribution payments required.

The main issue for companies is that, with defined benefit plans, they have an obligation to make up any shortfall if there are insufficient funds to pay out the promised benefits. The risk lies with the employer and not the employee.

The above is only a brief description, and companies often have several types of pension schemes for different groups of employees. There are also hybrid plans that are part defined benefit and part defined contribution. Pension plans is really a task for actuaries, and accounting for them relies on their professional opinions.

Our discussion on pension plans has been concentrated on the accounting issues. It is the laws of a country that determine the nature, operation and regulation of pension plans. Companies must comply with the national laws.

In 2011, the IASB issued important amendments to IAS 19 *Employee Benefits*. Employers with a defined benefit scheme must ensure that the contributions they make to the fund are sufficient to ensure that there is enough to pay the pensions to employees when they retire. Their calculations are based on the market value of the assets into which the contributions are invested until they are needed to pay retirement pensions.

Actuaries work with long-term forecasts and, understandably, their assessment of the market value of the assets is likely to change. This can lead to a surplus in the scheme or, more worryingly, a deficit. This deficit must appear on the balance sheet as a liability. As there are likely to be movements in the balance sheet figure, these must be recorded. Under IAS 19, actuarial gains or losses are referred to as remeasurements. These remeasurement movements must be shown in the statement of other comprehensive income.

In 2011, the IASB also made amendments to IAS 19, announcing that it would examine closely schemes known as contribution-based promises (CBPs).

A CBP scheme is a hybrid scheme that involves both contribution and benefit aspects. The employee receives a pension based on the performance of the assets in the pension plan (the contribution basis) and the employer provides a guarantee of the minimum performance of those assets (the benefit basis). The employee accordingly receives a benefit that is the higher of the contributions plus the actual return on the assets in the plan and the guaranteed amount. Alternatively, the employee may receive a guaranteed benefit based on a specified return on 'notional' plan contributions by the employer.

Holt (2015a) has identified the difficulties of accounting for CBPs. Some schemes have features that match the defined benefit category of IAS 19. However, an examination suggests that the scheme more closely resembles a standard defined contribution plan and full defined benefit accounting does not seem applicable. Other schemes may have attributes of a defined benefit scheme, but have risk-sharing provisions that reduce the employer's liability. Where a pension scheme apparently is insufficient to meet its obligation to employees, the scheme has a deficit. The employer must classify this as a liability. It appears that some companies have attempted to enter into arrangements that turned pension obligations into equity instruments in their accounts.

The Financial Reporting Review Panel (FRRP) investigated these cases and the companies concerned have revised these arrangements. However, the FRRP have stated that they will investigate any company that reclassifies material pension liabilities into equity (FRC 2014a).

This discussion on pension plans has explained the two main schemes and the accounting issues, based on UK practices. The actual operation and regulation of pension plans for employees must comply with the laws of the countries in which they operate. This may add another complication to the application of IFRS 19.

NOTES

1   A useful book that expounds the economists' views but argues for strong accounting standards is R.A. Rayman (2006) *Accounting Standards True or False?*, Routledge.

2   The claims for the use of clean surplus accounting can be found on *http://www.buffettandbeyond.com/what-is-clean-surplus.html* (accessed 2 September 2016).

3   IAS 29 *Financial Reporting in Hyperinflationary Economies* sets out the regulations for such a position. The standard does not define a hyperinflationary economy but offers guidelines to assist in identifying one.

CONCLUSIONS

The debate on the nature and definition of profit has encouraged the IASB to require a statement of total comprehensive income. Their reasons for doing so have not received overwhelming agreement. Undoubtedly, there is confusion over the rationale for the contents of the statement and the mixture of realized and unrealized gains. Reclassifications are also likely to require considerable thought by both the preparers and the users.

It is too early to assess the value of the statement of total comprehensive income to the user. As familiarity with the statement increases, doubts and uncertainties may be dispelled. It is also possible that the IASB will decide to revisit the requirements and produce a stronger conceptual basis.

The changes to IAS 1 have involved other standards and this chapter has examined IAS 21 *The Effects of Changes in Foreign Exchange Rates* and IAS 19 *Employee Benefits*. Both of these standards deal with complex accounting issues but have been in force for several years without any major changes.

The growth of international trade has made IAS 21 a necessity. Entities require guidance on including foreign currency transactions in their financial statements, particularly regarding issues of the correct treatment when transactions are completed within the financial year and when they are not. The standard provides guidance that is clear and comprehensive.

Addressing the translation of the functional currency of foreign operations into a presentation currency is more problematic. This is less to do with the requirements of the standard and more due to the complexity of international business.

It could similarly be argued that any apparent deficiencies in IAS 19 is less to do with the standard than with the difficulties in recognition and measurement of employee benefits, particularly with defined benefit plans. Understandably, companies are reluctant to show large liabilities on their balance sheets. Users could interpret this as a financial weakness that the company may have considerable difficulty in rectifying.

The practice that arose with a few entities reclassifying pension liabilities as equity instruments has been promptly corrected by the Financial Reporting Council. Although this does not relieve entities of the problem of resolving the liabilities, it does ensure that users of financial statements are informed.

IN THE PIPELINE

The Board had a research project on foreign currency translation. It announced in 2016 that it will remove this project from the research programme.

ADDITIONAL RESOURCES

Go online to the companion website for this book to access further teaching and learning materials for this chapter.

www.palgravehighered.com/hussey-cfr

10

STATEMENT OF CASH FLOWS

IAS 7 Statement of Cash Flows

LEARNING OBJECTIVES

At the end of this chapter, you should be able to:

- Summarize the requirements of IAS 7 *Statement of Cash Flows*
- Differentiate between the direct and indirect methods of presenting operating cash flows
- Prepare a statement of cash flows using the indirect method for operating cash flows
- Identify the items appearing on the financing and investing sections of the statement of cash flows
- Discuss some of the definitional difficulties when examining a statement of cash flows

INTRODUCTION

The use of the accruals concept (discussed in Chapters 3 and 7) establishes the figure of profit for a financial period but tells us little about the cash the entity has. Experience has shown that apparently profitable entities can become insolvent for the simple reason that they have run out of cash.

Although the statement of cash flows will not prevent insolvency, it alerts the users of financial statements to potential cash problems. It also reveals the decisions entities make with financing and investing activities that support their operating activities. In this chapter, we first explain the purpose and main requirements of IAS 7 *Statement of Cash Flows* and then examine the three separate sections of the statement of cash flows: operating activities, financing activities and investing activities.

Users want to know how much cash the company generated from its operating activities and what it did with its cash. They expect to see a surplus of cash from operating activities, and will investigate carefully if there is a deficit the company has not explained.

Both the financing and investing activities sections disclose movements of cash. The financing activities section shows whether the company invested in non-current assets that

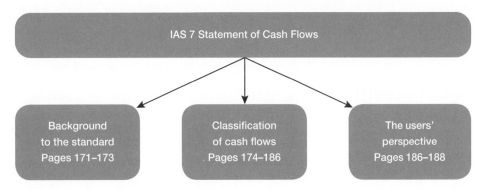

▲ **Diagram 10.1** *Structure of Chapter 10*

would help the company grow or whether it sold non-current assets. The investing section shows whether the company has issued shares or debentures or repaid amounts of borrowings.

Entities can show the cash flows for operating activities by using the direct or the indirect method. We demonstrate the disclosure of operating cash flow using both approaches, as permitted by the standard. We also show the calculation when entities use the indirect method.

Commentators have criticized the use of the indirect method and some of the weaknesses of the definitions in the standard. The IASB is responding to these and we conclude the chapter by discussing the amendments to IAS 7 issued by the IASB in 2016.

▼ **Table 10.1** *Timeline of IAS 7*

Date	Comment
1992	First issued as a statement of cash flows
2007	Name of standard changed to Statement of Cash Flows as a consequential amendment to IAS 1
2010	Amended
2016 – 29 January	Amended by Disclosure Initiative with effect from 1 January 2017

BACKGROUND TO THE STANDARD

The accruals concept is the foundation of the income statement. Its application results in the calculation of profit for the financial period but does not give any guide to the cash activities of an entity.

In the late twentieth century, some apparently profitable companies became insolvent. These events dismayed stakeholders who had relied solely on the profit figure to assess a company's performance. Their dismay arose because the entity appeared to be making a profit, but was unable to turn it into cash. One frequent reason was that the entity had long-term projects with up-front expenditure but would not receive the payments until the project was completed.

The situation encouraged debate on the need for a statement of cash flows. There were persuasive arguments for the disclosure of cash flows, including:

- Cash is crucial for survival. Companies can become insolvent even when they are making a profit.

- Cash may be easier to understand than profit by users unfamiliar with the accruals concept applied in the calculation of profit.
- Cash is less subjective than profit for forecasting because income statements contain non-cash entries such as depreciation and provisions. The entity decides the amounts for these items.
- Loan repayments depend on cash availability so lenders can assess whether the entity is likely to repay its loans.
- Cash satisfies the stewardship function (Chapter 2) because managers are responsible for safeguarding the assets of the entity.
- Independent auditors can physically count the cash or request a bank to confirm the amounts held in the name of the entity, thus objectively verifying cash.
- Inter-entity comparison is improved because cash is a definite figure regardless of the accounting regulations and practices an entity uses.

If the users of financial reports are to understand fully an entity's financial performance, they need information on cash. They require disclosures about an entity's operating, investing and financing activities. Such disclosures help users of financial statements to understand the liquidity of an entity.

Disclosure of a balance sheet and a profit and loss account had been a requirement for many decades. By comparison, the statement of cash flows is a new and major financial disclosure.

At the national level, Canada issued a standard in 1985, the US in 1987 and Australia, the UK and the Republic of Ireland in 1991. Although the International Standards Committee (IASC) had issued a standard in 1978, this had not influenced national practices in the above countries.

The introduction of a robust standard, IAS 7, in 1992 was a major innovation. The objective of the standard is to require the presentation of information about the historical changes, for a financial period, in cash and cash equivalents of an entity.

cash equivalents

A cash equivalent is a highly liquid investment having a maturity of three months or less. It must be unrestricted so that it is available for immediate use and there should be a minimal risk of change in value.

'**Cash equivalent**' is a term introduced by the standard to resolve a practical issue. It does not make financial sense for entities to hold large amounts of cash. Businesses, if they have a cash surplus, invest it to earn interest. They can do this through a long-term investment where they commit to leave their funds, without making any withdrawals, for an extended period. A business may also decide to put part or all of its surplus funds in a short-term investment, possibly something that will mature in less than three months.

For example, if you had deposited money in an account with a bank that had to stay there for six months or longer, this would not be a cash equivalent. Deposits tied up for a specific period are known as time deposits or fixed deposits. Generally, three months from the date of making the investment is regarded as short term. Usually fixed deposits earn a better interest rate than short-term deposits. The standard considers short-term investments as the equivalent of cash.

The terms 'cash' and 'cash equivalents' require some further description. We give below the types of cash and cash equivalents that you may come across:

- cash on hand and deposits that can be withdrawn immediately in cash without suffering any penalties;
- short-term, highly liquid investments that are readily convertible to a known amount of cash and that are subject to an insignificant risk of changes in value;
- bank overdrafts that are repayable on demand and are an integral part of cash;
- equity investments if they are in substance a cash equivalent (e.g. preferred shares acquired within three months of their specified redemption date).

The standard distinguishes between cash equivalents and equity investments because of the variability of the amount of equity investments. There is no certainty about the value of the investment at any one time due to the volatility of share prices. This means that you cannot convert with certainty the number of shares into known amounts of cash.

Cash is obviously an important asset to an entity, but how far does it differ from the profit for the same financial period? In Diagram 10.2, we use four UK examples taken at random from our sample:

Burberry Group – fashion industry
Diageo – beverages industry
Rolls-Royce – manufacturing industry
Whitbread – retail hospitality

We have used the figures for cash and cash equivalents from the balance sheets and the profit is the profit before tax on the income statement.

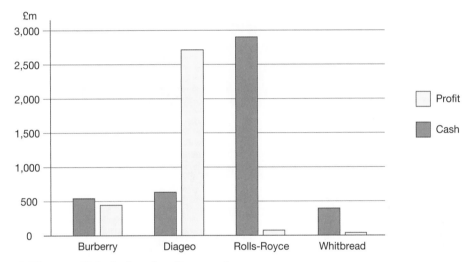

▲ Diagram 10.2 *Cash and profit comparisons*

We have two large entities, Diageo and Rolls-Royce, and two smaller entities, Burberry and Whitbread. In three of the cases, the difference between the profit and cash amounts is substantial. Only Burberry's figures are close, with their cash and cash equivalent total being £545.5 million and their profit before tax being £444.4 million.

Even with Burberry, the gap between profit and cash is sufficiently wide to demonstrate the importance of users receiving a statement of cash flows. The differences between the large companies are considerable. Diageo has a relatively small amount of cash amounting to £622 million but a large profit of £2,711 million. Rolls-Royce has a substantial cash and cash equivalent holding of £2,862 million but a much more modest profit of £67 million.

With this very small sample of entities from very different industries, we cannot make any overarching conclusions on performance. We would need to compare companies in the same industry over a number of years. Guidance to analyzing corporate reports is given in Chapter 19.

Diagram 10.2 however, emphasizes that users require information on cash as well as profit if they are going to make a sensible analysis of an entity's performance. At this stage, we concentrate on explaining the format and contents of the statement of cash flows.

CLASSIFICATION OF CASH FLOWS

The statement of cash flows is now one of the main financial statements entities publish. The standard sets out a structured approach to disclosing the amounts of cash coming into and going out of the entity in a financial period.

The statement of cash flows classifies the cash flows under three main activities: operating, investing and financing. Diagram 10.3 shows these headings with examples of typical cash flows.

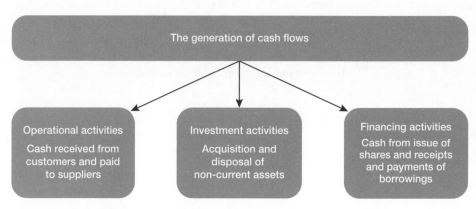

▲ **Diagram 10.3** *Classification of cash flows*

We now consider those three headings in detail. Not surprisingly, the main cash flow amount usually falls under operating activities.

Operating activities

Examples of cash flows from operating activities are:

- cash receipts from sale of goods and services;
- cash receipts from royalties, commissions;
- cash payments to employees;
- cash payments to suppliers of goods and services.

The standard permits entities to choose one of two methods for disclosing operating activities: the direct or the indirect method. The direct method discloses the amount of cash generated by operating activities. The indirect method starts with the profit for the financial year and this is adjusted by non-cash transactions to arrive at the calculated amount of cash.

A statement of cash flows using the direct method for operating activities normally has the headings shown in Worked example 10.1. We have inserted amounts so that you can see what the deductions and additions are.

Worked example 10.1 is a simplified example. In practice, you will encounter more items disclosed. The type of headings and the detail provided depends on the cash activities of the entity. There are some definitional problems associated with some items, such as interest which some entities may classify as a financing activity, while others consider it as an operating activity. We discuss these issues at the end of this section where we consider possible changes to the standard.

Worked example 10.1   Cash flows from operating activities

	£000
Cash collected from customers	1,100
Interest and dividends received	150
Cash paid for operating expenses, such as employee salaries and wages	(250)
Cash paid to suppliers	(250)
Cash for other operating expenses	(150)
Interest paid	(100)
Taxes paid	(150)
Net cash flow from operating activities	350

Company example 10.1 shows part of a statement of cash flows using the direct method. Incitec Pivot Ltd (IPL), an Australian company, is a global manufacturer and marketer of commercial explosives and fertilisers. IPL owns and operates 20 plants in the US, Canada, Australia, Mexico, Indonesia and Turkey. It also has joint venture operations in South Africa, Malaysia, China and Australia.

Company example 10.1

Consolidated Statement of Cash Flows

For the year ended 30 September 2014

	Notes	Consolidated 2014 $mill Inflows/ (outflows)	2013 $mill Inflows/ (outflows)
Cash flows from operating activities			
Receipts from customers		3,820.8	3,791.5
Payments to suppliers and employees		(3,254.1)	(3,069.2)
Interest received		18.1	18.5
Financial expenses paid		(75.8)	(89.4)
Other revenue received		24.7	30.2
Income taxes refunded/(paid)		1.5	(67.1)
Net cash flows from operating activities	(29)	535.2	614.5

Incitec Pivot Limited, Annual Report and Accounts, 2014, p. 45

The statement in Company example 10.1 shows actual cash paid by customers and the amounts of cash that the company has paid out.

There is a considerable amount of evidence (Goyal 2004; Farshadfar and Monem 2013) that all types of users prefer the direct method because it is far more useful for forecasting future cash flows. The users of the information are not only interested in the present cash position but in using that information to predict the future cash position. This is also the method recommended in the standard because it shows each major class of gross cash receipt and gross cash payment.

However, the IASB also permits, and many companies use, the indirect method which adjusts the net profit or loss for the effects of non-cash transactions. All the companies in our sample of 25 UK companies used the indirect method. One reason put forward for this company preference is that the information needed to use the direct method is not available in the accounting records. Critics argue that this is not a credible reason and it is merely that companies are reluctant to release the information.

Instead of the detailed cash movements, the indirect method starts with the net profit figure from the income statement and adjusts this with non-cash movements (adding back depreciation and other non-cash transactions). We can explain the basis of these adjustments with a few simple Worked and Company examples.

Worked example 10.2   Indirect method – first year

NB: Ignore taxation

Sam Jones commenced a very simple business on 1 January 2015. At the end of the period the income statement was as follows.

Revenue		£100,000
Purchases of goods	£40,000	
All other costs	£25,000	£65,000
Profit		£35,000

At the end of the year, customers owed £10,000 and Sam owed £5,000 to the suppliers of goods. We know the profit figure but not the amount of cash at the year-end.

We will calculate the cash by starting with the profit figure and adjusting this by the cash movement for each transaction.

Profit for the year (this is not cash)	£35,000
As Sam is still owed money, the profit must be reduced by this amount	£10,000
	£25,000
Sam has not paid his suppliers in full so he still has this cash	£5,000
Cash in hand at the end of the year	£30,000

As a reminder: money owed to Sam appears on the statement of financial position as accounts receivable. The money owed by Sam appears on the statement of financial position as accounts payable.

It is easy to confirm this cash in hand amount by a simple calculation:

Cash received from revenue	(£100,000 – £10,000)		£90,000
Cash paid to suppliers	(£40,000 – £5,000)	£35,000	
Other costs paid in full		£25,000	£60,000
Cash balance at year-end			£30,000

At this stage, you may consider that the calculation of cash is very simple. In practice, and in the examination room, the task becomes more complex. We show an entity example (Company example 10.2) before working through less complicated calculations.

We have extracted the data in Company example 10.2 from the financial statements of Halfords plc. We have not copied the amounts for the prior year as we are demonstrating the types of adjustments.

Halfords is the UK's leading retailer of motoring and cycling products and a leading independent operator in garage servicing and auto repair. It owns over 460 stores selling both motoring and cycling products.

Company example 10.2

Statement of cash flows – indirect method

CONSOLIDATED STATEMENT OF CASH FLOWS

	52 weeks to 28 March 2014 £m
Cash flows from operating activities	
Profit after tax for the period, before non-recurring items	55.8
Non-recurring items	(0.3)
Profit after tax for the period	55.5
Depreciation – property, plant and equipment	18.0
Impairment charge	0.4
Amortisation – intangible assets	5.3
Net finance costs	5.0
Loss on disposal of property, plant and equipment	2.1
Equity-settled share based payment transactions	1.0
Fair value loss/(gain) on derivative financial instruments	1.4
Income tax expense	17.1
(Increase)/decrease in inventories	(17.0)
Decrease/(increase) in trade and other receivables	1.0
Increase in trade and other payables	10.7
Increase in provisions	6.7
Finance income received	0.2
Finance costs paid	(4.6)
Income tax paid	(35.3)
Net cash from operating activities	**67.5**

Halfords plc, Annual Report and Accounts, 2014, p. 121

The statement issued by Halfords is for a group of companies and thus the term 'consolidated' (see Chapter 16).

Halfords is using the indirect method and starts with the figure of profit. That figure is adjusted by all the non-cash transactions to arrive at the amount of net cash from operating activities. We see items such as adding back depreciation, amortization and adjustments for trades receivable and payable.

As well as transactions and events that are normally disclosed, Halfords has some items that are not found so frequently. We discuss later in the book items such as tax (Chapter 14), financial instruments (Chapters 11 and 12), and provisions (Chapter 13).

In Halfords, we are also dealing with a continuing business, and this introduces some complications. With Worked example 10.2, it was Sam's first year of business. We can add some complications by looking at Year 2.

Worked example 10.3   Indirect method – continuing basis

In Year 2, Sam has the same revenue and costs on his income statement, as shown below.

Revenue		£100,000
Purchases of goods	£40,000	
All other costs	£25,000	£65,000
Profit		£35,000

At the end of the second year, customers owe Sam £15,000 and he owes £8,000 to the suppliers of goods. We calculate the Year 2 closing cash by starting with the profit figure and adjusting this by the cash movement. However, we must take the cash position in Year 1 for each transaction.

Profit for the year (this is not cash)		£35,000
Amount owed by customers end of Year 2	£15,000	
Deduct amount owed by customers Year 1	£10,000	£5,000
		£30,000
Amount owed to suppliers end of Year 2	£8,000	
Deduct amount owed to suppliers Year 1	£5,000	£3,000
Cash increase in Year 2		£33,000
Add cash at end of Year 1		£30,000
Total cash at end of Year 2		£63,000

This example poses more problems as we have Year 1 to bring into our calculations. Later in this chapter, we give you the rules for calculating increases and decreases in accounts receivable and accounts payable. At this stage, we examine the movements of cash to demonstrate where the figures came from.

Customers	
Accounts receivable at end of Year 1	£10,000
Value of goods sold in Year 2	£100,000
Total	£110,000
Less accounts receivable at end of Year 2	£15,000
Cash received	£95,000
Sam's payments	
Accounts payable at end of Year 1	£5,000
Value of goods purchased	£40,000
Total	£45,000
Less accounts payable at end of Year 2	£8,000
Cash paid	£37,000

continued

Worked example 10.3 *continued*

Opening cash at beginning of Year 2		£30,000
Cash received from customers		£95,000
		£125,000
Deduct		
Cash paid to suppliers	£37,000	
Other costs	£25,000	£62,000
Closing balance Year 2		£63,000

If you are still uncertain of the calculations, you can use double entry bookkeeping to re-assure yourself. If you are not confident of your double entry knowledge, you can find an explanatory chapter and examples on the book's website (*www.palgravehighered.com/hussey-cfr*).

In the simplified Worked example 10.4, we reinforce your understanding of the adjustments by showing you the movements in accounts receivable and accounts payable.

Worked example 10.4   **Summary of main adjustments**

Statement of cash flows

Information available at the year-end

	£000
Net profit as shown on the income statement	600
Depreciation charged in income statement	100
Accounts receivable at beginning of year	250
Accounts receivable at end of year	350
Accounts payable at beginning of year	200
Accounts payable at end of year	320

Explanation of adjustments to Worked example 10.4

We have used the accruals basis to calculate the net profit of £600,000. This figure does not represent cash. To determine the total cash flows from operating activities we must adjust the net profit figure as follows.

Depreciation

This item appears as an expense on the income statement but it is not a cash movement. The cash movement was when the entity paid for the asset. As the depreciation is a non-cash movement, it must be added back to the net profit for the year to arrive at the cash received.

Accounts receivable

The revenue figure on the profit or loss statement would have been on an accruals basis. The accounts receivable has increased in the year by £100,000. This represents cash we did not receive from revenue. The profit must be reduced by £100,000 to calculate the cash amount.

Accounts payable

The purchase of goods is a deduction on the profit statement on an accruals basis. However, the accounts payable has increased by £120,000. In other words, the company has not paid for all the goods it has received. We therefore increase the net profit by £120,000 to calculate the cash figure.

Once we have made these adjustments, the statement of cash flows appears as in Worked example 10.5.

Worked example 10.5   Cash flow from operating activities – indirect method

	£000
Net profit as shown on the income statement	600
Adjustments for	
Add depreciation	100
Increase in accounts receivable	(100)
Increase in accounts payable	120
Net cash flow from operating activities	720

We have started with the net profit figure. Depreciation was charged in the profit or loss account to arrive at that figure. Depreciation is not a movement of cash so we add it back to the profit. The revenue figure shown in the profit or loss account used the accruals concept.

The increase in the accounts receivable is payments we did not receive. We need to deduct this figure back to profit as the revenue on the profit or loss account is on the accruals basis and we did not receive £100,000 cash. The increase in accounts payable of £120,000 cash represents cash we should have paid but we did not. We are holding more cash than we should, so this is added to the profit figure.

We provide the rules for making these adjustments in Table 10.3 at the end of the chapter.

You will find that some entities do not show all the details of the adjustments on the main statement of cash flows but provide them in the notes, as illustrated in Company example 10.3

Company example 10.3

Consolidated statement of cash flows
Year ended 31 December 2014

All figures in £ millions	Notes	2014	2013
Cash flows from operating activities			
Net cash generated from operations	34	704	684
Interest paid		(86)	(82)
Tax paid		(163)	(246)
Net cash generated from operating activities		455	356

Pearson plc, Annual Report and Accounts, 2014, p. 127

from Pearson. This company can trace its origins to 1724 when Thomas Longman founded a publishing house. There have been several transitions over the years and Pearson is now a multinational publishing and education company headquartered in London. It is the largest education company and book publisher in the world.

The net cash figure is not based on actual cash as shown by the direct method, but by adjusting profit as permitted under the indirect method. In Note 34, Pearson provides a comprehensive explanation of their adjustments, as do other companies. Users, however, have more confidence in the figure of actual cash rather than an amount that has been generated through a series of adjustments.

Investing activities

Operating activities generate cash. These activities must have resources such as buildings, machinery and equipment to manufacture products or provide services. During the year an entity may invest in new assets or sell some of those it already has. This represents movements of cash. We have condensed the list given in IAS 7 to extract the following examples of investing activities cash flows:

- payments to acquire property, plant and equipment, intangibles and other long-term assets;
- receipts from sales of property, plant and equipment, intangibles and other long-term assets;
- payments to acquire equity or debt instruments of other entities and interests in joint ventures;
- receipts from sales of equity or debt instruments of other entities and interests in joint ventures;
- advances and loans made to other parties;
- receipts from the repayment of advances and loans made to other parties;
- payments for futures contracts, forward contracts, option contracts and swap contracts.

The investing activities section reflects an entity's strategies in its management of wealth creating resources. If this strategy is successful, the financial performance of the entity will improve. Company example 10.4 overleaf is from the financial statements of Lynas Corporation Limited, an Australian mining entity. The cash flows show a significant increase in the acquisition of property, plant and equipment that reflects the nature of the industry.

Not surprisingly in a mining entity, the major investing amount is for the payment of property, plant and equipment. One would expect other types of industries to have investing activities that reflect their major operations. The statement in Company example 10.4 overleaf, as the standard requires, shows not only cash flows from the statements made but also cash flows from the divestments made by the entity.

The user may derive insights from the information on investing activities into the entity's strategy. A substantial investment in non-current assets suggests that the entity is optimistic about the future of the entity. If the entity is disposing of non-current assets, it suggests that there could be a cash problem. In Chapter 19 we explain the accounting ratios used to analyze the entity.

Before moving on to the final section of the statement of cash flows, financing activities, we explain the calculations required using the indirect method to ascertain the net cash flows from operating and investing activities.

Company example 10.4

Cash from investing example

	June (AUS$000)	
	2014	2013
Cash flows from investing activities		
Payment for property, plant and equipment	(17,241)	(111,351)
Payment for deferred exploration, evaluation and development expenditure	–	(102)
Payment for intangible assets	(135)	(90)
Security bonds paid	(6,845)	(3,053)
Security bonds refunded	12,819	349
Receipt from sale of available for sale financial assets	2,703	–
Proceeds from sale of property, plant and equipment	105	–
Net cash from (used in) investing activities	(8,594)	(114,247)

Lynas Corporation Ltd., Annual Report and Accounts, 2014, p. 39

We provide the general rules for calculating cash movements from changes in the balance sheets. We reinforce the process, by constructing a simple example of a small start-up company in Worked example 10.6. This will require the comparison of balance sheets at the beginning and end of the financial period and the profit or loss account for the financial period.

The general rules for the balance sheet changes reflect the accounting equation:

Assets = Liabilities + Capital

As the balance sheet must always balance, any change in one of the three classifications must bring about a change in another. We demonstrate these movements in Table 10.2, assuming at this stage that the changes are cash based; for example, a non-current asset is either bought or sold in a cash transaction.

▼ Table 10.2 *Cash movements and the accounting equation*

ITEM	CASH	
Non-current asset increases		Decreases
Non-current asset decreases	Increases	
Current asset increases (other than cash)		Decreases
Current asset decreases	Increases	
Non-current liabilities increase	Increases	
Non-current liabilities decrease		Decreases
Current liabilities increase	Increases	
Current liabilities decreases		Decreases
Equity increases	Increases	
Equity decreases		Decreases

In real life a company would not conduct all transactions on a cash basis. An asset may be purchased with long-term borrowings. The asset would increase on the balance sheet and so would the liabilities by the same amount. We can explain these transactions with Worked example 10.6.

Worked example 10.6

A business starts up at the beginning of Year 1 with £120,000 in cash comprising £80,000 from the owners and £40,000 from the bank as a long-term loan.

The opening balance sheet is:

Balance sheet at beginning of year

	£		£
Cash	120,000	Equity	80,000
		Loan	40,000
	120,000		120,000

The profit or loss account for the first year of trading is:

Profit or loss account Year 1

	£	£
Revenue		250,000
Purchase of goods	200,000	
Less closing inventory	30,000	170,000
Gross profit		80,000
Expenses		60,000
Net profit		20,000

During the year, the company acquired equipment for £15,000 cash.

At the year-end it owed £10,000 to its suppliers and was owed £32,000 by its customers.

Balance sheet at end of year

	£		£
Equipment	15,000	Equity	80,000
Inventory	30,000	Retained earnings	20,000
Accounts receivable	32,000	Loan	40,000
Cash	73,000	Accounts payable	10,000
	150,000		150,000

The cash movements are

	£	£
Opening cash		120,000
Net cash from operating activities		
Add receipts from customers	250,000	
less amount owed	32,000	218,000
Deduct purchase of goods	200,000	
less amount owed	10,000	(190,000)
Expenses paid		(60,000)
		88,000
Net cash flow from investing activities		
Purchase of equipment		(15,000)
Closing cash		73,000

Financing activities

Although this tends to be the shortest section of the statement of cash flows for most entities, this does not detract from its importance to the user of the information. Entities may be securing finance to make acquisitions or may be repaying amounts borrowed. Financing activities show how the entity is funding its activities and reveals possible claims on future cash flows. We have condensed the list given in IAS 7 to give the following examples of financing activities cash flows:

- proceeds from issuing shares or other equity instruments;
- payments to owners to acquire or redeem the entity's shares;
- proceeds from issuing debentures, loans, notes, bonds, mortgages and other short-term or long-term borrowings;
- repayments of amounts borrowed;
- payments by a lessee for the reduction of the outstanding liability relating to a finance lease.

In preparing a statement of cash flows from the profit or loss statement and the statement of financial position, we are trying to adjust our profit, which is a non-cash figure, into a cash figure.

You should remember that the statement of cash flows relates to the other main financial statements. Although we demonstrated that the indirect method for operating activities requires data from the income statement, the statement of cash flows links to the balance sheet. Worked example 10.7 demonstrates these relationships.

Worked example 10.7

The following is the summarized income statement and balance sheet of a hypothetical company, Clubhouse plc, in the UK.

Income statement for the year ended 31 December 2015

	£000	£000
Revenue		650
Purchases	70	
Employee costs	100	
Depreciation	110	280
		370
Interest payable		30
Profit before tax		340

Balance sheets at year-ends

	2015		2014	
	£000	£000	£000	£000
Non-current assets				
Cost	1650		1450	
Depreciation	334	1316	224	1226
Current assets				
Inventory	20		20	
Accounts receivable	76		60	
Cash	368	464	94	174
		1780		1400

continued

Worked example 10.7 *continued*

Share capital	600	600
Retained earnings	640	300
Long-term loans	400	380
Accounts payable	140	120
	1780	1400

Calculation of statement of cash flows

Calculations

1 The operating profit of £370 is not a cash figure and we need to adjust it.
2 Depreciation of £110 is not a cash movement. It is added back to the net profit.
3 Accounts receivable increased by £16. We did not receive this cash and must deduct it from the profit figure.
4 Accounts payable increased by £20. This must be added to the profit figure.
5 The balance sheet shows the cost of non-current assets increased by £200 so that is cash going out.
6 With financing activities, we received £20 from an increase in the loan as shown on the balance sheet and we paid out £30 for interest.

Statement of cash flows for the year ended 31 December 2015

	£000	£000
Net cash flow from operating activities		
Operating profit	370	
Depreciation	110	
Increase in accounts receivable	(16)	
Increase in accounts payable	20	484
Cash flows from investing activities		
Acquisition of non-current assets		(200)
Cash flows from financing activities		
Increase in loans	20	
Interest	(30)	(10)
Increase in cash and cash equivalents		274
Cash and cash equivalents at 1 January 2015		94
Cash and cash equivalents at 31 December 2015		368

Table 10.3 overleaf demonstrates the main calculations made in converting a profit figure to cash. It is also a useful summary of the various transactions we have discussed in this chapter.

▼ **Table 10.3** *Calculations made in converting a profit figure to cash*

Additions to net earnings

Movement	Reason
Depreciation	It is deducted in the income statement to calculate profit but it is not cash
Decrease in inventory	Inventory has been sold that was acquired in a previous period so we have more cash than profit
Decrease in accounts receivable	Customers have paid from sales made in a previous period so we have more cash
Increase in accounts payable	We have not paid suppliers fully for this financial period so we have more cash

Deductions from net earnings

Movement	Reason
Increase in inventory	We have purchased more inventory so we have less cash
Increase in accounts receivable	Not all customers have paid for the sales shown on the income statement
Decrease in accounts payable	We have paid more to suppliers than for the period's receipts of goods so we have less cash

THE USERS' PERSPECTIVE

Most would agree that IFRS 7 has enhanced corporate reporting. The statement of cash flows provides information of value for the users. The separation of cash flows into three separate activities offers an analysis of the cash flows for operations, investing and finance.

If we consider the history of the standard, including national requirements, there have been few changes over the years. There are some perceived weaknesses. A long-standing complaint from users is that entities can use either the direct or the indirect method.

Numerous surveys over the years have confirmed that users prefer the direct approach. By late 2016, the IASB had given no indication that it intends to make the direct method compulsory.

The argument is that the complicated adjustments required by the indirect method are difficult to understand. The indirect method also provides entities with more leeway for manipulation of cash flows. In previous chapters, we have commented on examples of companies manipulating their financial statements. This is mostly where the company is trying to enhance the profit figure, and this is the very figure that is used in the indirect method to calculate the net cash from operating activities.

An issue for users is the abuse or confusions regarding the classifications of specific cash flows. Classification can occur within different sections of the statement. Cash outflows that could have been reported in the operating section may be classified as investing cash outflows to enhance operating cash flows.

The IASB allows some flexibility in classifications to reflect specific industry and entity practices. An entity can classify interest and dividends received and paid as operating, investing or financing cash flows. Even a single transaction may include cash flows that are classified differently. For example, the cash repayment of a loan can include both interest and capital. An entity may classify the interest element as an operating activity and the capital element as a financing activity.

Some preparers and users welcome this flexibility as it permits entities to select the most appropriate activity for a transaction. Others find it disquieting and would prefer more rigid regulation. They argue that an entity may select the activity that presents the information in the most favourable light. Critics also argue that the flexibility makes it more difficult to make comparisons.

The complexity of the adjustments to net profit before tax can lead to the manipulation of cash flow reporting. Cash flow information should help users to understand the operations of the entity, evaluate its financing activities, assess its liquidity or solvency and interpret earnings information. A problem for users is that entities can choose the method, and there is not enough guidance on the classification of cash flows in the operating, investing and financing sections of the indirect method used in IAS 7.

Tax cash flows can also cause a problem. The regulations require entities to classify tax flows as operating unless the entity can specifically identify them under another heading. There are variations. The Financial Reporting Council (FRC) has reported that many investors reclassify amounts of 'tax and interest from investing and financing cash flows into operating cash flows' (Financial Reporting Lab 2012).

The adjustments made to reconcile net profit before tax to cash from operations are confusing to some users. In many cases, it is difficult to reconcile these to observed changes in the statement of financial position. Thus, users will only be able to understand the size of the difference between net profit before tax and cash from operations.

A report from the Financial Reporting Lab (2012) discussed the views of five companies and over thirty individuals from investment organizations on the statement of cash flows. Some of the main points were as follows.

Operating cash flows

- report the indirect method of reconciling a profit or loss amount to operating cash flows as part of the main cash flow statement, rather than in a note;
- start the cash flow statement with operating income or loss;
- list separately adjustments between the starting profit or loss figure and operating cash flows
- list separately on the cash flow statement the cash amounts paid for income taxes and interest, and interest income received.

Investment cash flows

- separately disclose capital expenditure for tangible and intangible components, indicating through disclosure the company's view on the portion attributable to maintenance and growth where this is significant to the business.

General comments

- describe each item on the cash flow statement so that its relationship to any corresponding item on the balance sheet or in the income statement can be understood;
- regularly disclose the cash amounts related to any profit or loss amounts that are highlighted as being 'unusual', 'exceptional' or referred to by a similar term.

The International Accounting Standards Board (IASB) has been aware of these, and other, issues and is considering potential changes to the standard to remedy weaknesses. The IASB published in December 2014 an Exposure Draft (ED) of proposed amendments to IAS 7 *Statement of Cash Flows*.

The IASB analyzed the comments to the ED and identified users' interest in knowing changes in net debt. The Board concluded that users required a net debt reconciliation to conduct a financial analysis of an entity. They wished to:

(a) check their understanding of the entity's cash flows to reconcile the statement of financial position and the statement of cash flows;
(b) improve their confidence in forecasting the entity's future cash flows;
(c) be provided with information about the entity's sources of finance;
(d) use them to help understand the entity's exposure to risks associated with financing.

Unfortunately, net debt is not defined or required to be disclosed in current IFRSs. The IASB also considered that formulating a definition would not achieve wide agreement.

It therefore decided that it could use the definition of financing activities in IAS 7. This defines financing activities as activities that result in changes in the size and composition of the contributed equity and borrowings of the entity.

This conclusion led to the requirement for reconciliation between the amounts in the opening and the closing statements of financial position for liabilities. This referred specifically to present cash flows or future cash flows classified as financing activities in the statement of cash flows.

The Board considered that a reconciliation of liabilities arising from financing activities would provide the information about debt that users were requesting.

Although some respondents broadly welcomed the proposals, notwithstanding some reservations, others have been less encouraging. Holt (2015b) claims that there is no general agreement about the need for the ED.

However, in January 2016 the IASB issued amendments to IAS 7 with effect from 1 January 2017. The requirements are intended to address investors' concerns that financial statements do not currently enable them to understand the entity's cash flows; particularly with respect to the management of financing activities. The amendments are brief and require an entity to disclose the following changes in liabilities arising from financing activities:

(a) changes from financing cash flows;
(b) changes arising from obtaining or losing control of subsidiaries or other businesses;
(c) the effect of changes in foreign exchange rates;
(d) changes in fair values; and
(e) other changes.

The FRC (2016) welcomed the improved debt disclosures. They considered that the new requirements would assist in transparency on changes in debt. The FRC also encouraged the IASB to examine the potential disclosure of cash and cash equivalent balances. It would seem that the IASB might have to revisit IAS 7.

CONCLUSIONS

Users wished to understand the cash movements undertaken by an entity. The introduction of the statement of cash flows greatly improved the financial information entities disclosed. Although the standard has been a positive addition, there are criticisms.

Many commentators have called for the standard to allow only the direct method for disclosing cash from operating activities. Entities argue that their accounting systems do not allow them to capture cash information that would meet the needs of IAS 7. They also contend that it is more efficient to adjust net income to net cash flow from operating activities than to ascertain gross operating cash receipts and payments.

The critics are sceptical about this claim. They argue that the indirect method could lead to manipulation of the figures or confusion as to the actual cash movements. Our research shows that UK entities overwhelmingly use the indirect method.

The principal advantage of the indirect method is that it focuses on the differences between net income and net cash flow from operating activities. That is, it provides a useful link between the statement of cash flows and the income statement and *balance sheet*.

IN THE PIPELINE

The 2016 amendments have gone some way to providing the information that users require. However, they are pressing for greater disclosures. At the very least one might predict that there will be some further disclosure requirements for cash and cash equivalents.

ADDITIONAL RESOURCES

Go online to the companion website for this book to access further teaching and learning materials for this chapter.
www.palgravehighered.com/hussey-cfr

LEARNING OBJECTIVES

At the end of this chapter, you should be able to:

- Identify the methods used by entities to obtain finance
- Describe the financial risks that entities face
- Explain the types of financial instruments
- Describe the different types of financial contracts an entity can enter into

INTRODUCTION

financial instruments

Financial instruments are created by a contract between two parties. The contract gives one party a financial asset and the other party has a financial liability or equity.

Based on IAS 32, para. 11

We look more closely at the definition of **financial instruments** as we work through this chapter. The simple definition does not reflect the complexity of accounting for financial instruments. Neither does it hint at the corporate practices that have evolved over the years and the several financial crises that have occurred. This chapter is an introduction to the subject of financial instruments. We explain the relevant accounting standards in the following chapter.

The catalyst in bringing us to the present regulations was the global financial crisis of 2007/8. Before we consider the impact of this crisis, we discuss the financial environment, the use of financial instruments and the different types of financial instruments.

As we work through this chapter, we explain some of the terms used and the requirements of IAS 39 and the other accounting standards that regulate all financial assets and financial liabilities.

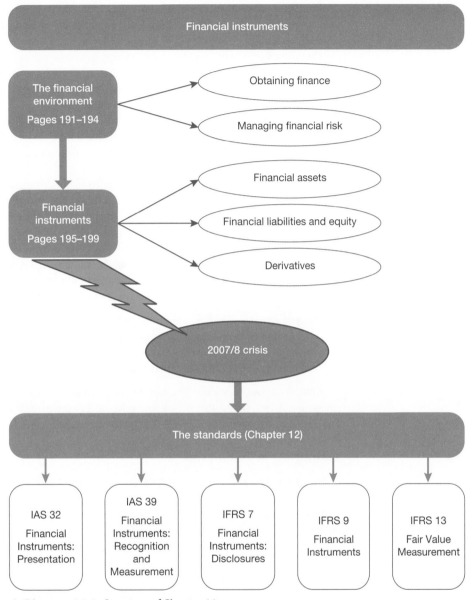

▲ **Diagram 11.1** *Structure of Chapter 11*

THE FINANCIAL ENVIRONMENT

Obtaining finance

Entities need finance to operate. They may raise finance internally by their own activities or externally by transactions in various financial markets. External finance is either short term or long term. Short-term financial markets, usually less than a year, are often called money markets. Long-term financial markets are capital markets, and include the equity market, the debt market that includes borrowing from other firms, and the bank market.

Multinational companies that used to raise equity capital solely from sources within their own country now look to other countries for potential shareholders by listing their shares on a foreign exchange.

Companies engage in cross-border financing for a variety of reasons. Financial reasons include the fact that an entity might be able to obtain cheaper financing outside its own borders, lowering its overall cost of capital. In addition, it might find it convenient to obtain external financing in countries where it has significant operations.

Non-financial reasons to engage in cross-border financing include the objective of being a world-class enterprise maintaining financial relationships in many countries. An entity might wish to broaden its shareholder base to include citizens and other institutions from many countries in addition to its home base.

An entity could find it politically expedient to maintain financial relationships inside a particular country. The relationship could lead to additional business contacts both inside and outside of a foreign government, or favourable recognition by the national government. In any case, cross-border financial activity is increasingly compatible with the cross-border movement of goods and services.

The problems of borrowing and lending substantial amounts in foreign countries can result in exposure to risks of various types, ranging from political instability to economic fluctuations. From a financial instrument perspective, there are two main risks:

- *Interest rate risk*. The fair values or cash flows of interest-sensitive assets or liabilities will change if interest rates increase or decrease.
- *Exchange rate risk*. Changes in foreign currency exchange rates may negatively affect the profitability of an entity's international operations.

Entities can use derivatives to offset the risks that these market forces will negatively affect fair values or cash flows. This use of derivatives to minimize these risks is known as *hedging*. The next section covers this important aspect of the use of financial instruments.

Managing financial risk

Companies and investors face many types of risk, both nationally and internationally. There are those risks that are associated with the conduct of the business itself and the manufacturing, trading and retailing operations. Other types of risk arise because of the financial transactions that take place in the normal course of business.

> **hedging**
>
> Hedging is reducing risk by taking action now to reduce the possibility of future losses, usually with the possibility of not enjoying any future gains.

It is impossible to eliminate financial risk completely but management must find ways to handle the risk. One method used to reduce risk is by **hedging**.

An example of hedging is as follows. An entity decides that it must purchase supplies of materials in three months' time. The materials, such as agricultural crops, may not be ready to purchase right away, or the entity may not wish to hold the materials for three months. There is a risk that the price of materials will increase before the end of the three months.

The entity can enter into an agreement (contract) now to purchase the goods in three months' time, but at the current price. The entity avoids the risk of the prices increasing in three months' time when it requires the materials. It also loses the opportunity to make a gain if the price decreases in three months' time. To avoid the potential loss if there is a significant increase in price, an entity can hedge this risk.

To demonstrate the importance that entities and users give to the management of financial risk, Company examples 11.1 and 11.2 show extracts from annual reports and accounts. The first example is from Diageo, which is still a relatively young company, having been in its current form since 1997. It is a global leader in alcoholic beverages, with brands such as Johnnie Walker, Smirnoff, Captain Morgan and Guinness. The company has a presence in over 180 countries and employs more than 33,000 people.

Because of the importance of risk, companies usually have five or more pages of notes in their annual report and accounts explaining how they manage their risks. The following extract is a good example of the explanations you should be able to find in companies that you are investigating.

Company example 11.1

Management of risk

The group's funding, liquidity and exposure to foreign currency and interest rate risks are managed by the group's treasury department. The treasury department uses a range of financial instruments to manage these underlying risks.

Treasury operations are conducted within a framework of board-approved policies and guidelines, which are recommended and monitored by the finance committee, chaired by the chief financial officer. The policies and guidelines include benchmark exposure and/or hedge cover levels for key areas of treasury risk which are periodically reviewed by the board following, for example, significant business strategic or accounting changes. The framework provides for limited defined levels of flexibility in execution to allow for the optimal application of the board-approved strategies. Transactions arising from the application of this flexibility may give rise to exposures different from the defined benchmark levels that are separately monitored on a daily basis using Value at Risk analysis. These transactions are carried at fair value and gains or losses are taken to the income statement as they arise. In the year ended 30 June 2014 and 30 June 2013 gains and losses on these transactions were not material. The group does not use derivatives for speculative purposes. All transactions in derivative financial instruments are initially undertaken to manage the risks arising from underlying business activities.

The group purchases insurance for commercial or, where required, for legal or contractual reasons. In addition, the group retains insurable risk where external insurance is not considered an economic means of mitigating these risks.

The finance committee receives monthly reports on the activities of the treasury department, including any exposures different from the defined benchmarks.

Diageo, Annual Report and Accounts, 2014, pp. 119–120

The extract in Company example 11.1 demonstrates important procedural and management practices:

1   There is a group treasury department responsible for managing the risks.
2   The policies and guidelines are set at the board level.
3   On a daily basis, the company monitors transactions giving rise to exposures that are different from the benchmark levels.
4   The group does not use derivatives for speculative purposes. The finance committee, chaired by the chief financial officer, receives monthly reports on the activities of the treasury department.

Point number 4 is important because some entities use financial instruments for speculative purposes. We explain this when we look at the financial crisis of 2007/8.

Our second example is from GSK, a British pharmaceutical company formed in 2000 by a merger of Glaxo Wellcome and SmithKline Beecham. It is a global health company manufacturing products for major disease areas such as asthma, cancer, infections, diabetes and mental health. It employs 59,000 people, including over 13,000 in the UK. It has 76 operating companies and 50 manufacturing facilities worldwide. We have omitted much of the detail from their Note 41 to emphasize the financial assets, financial liabilities, and the amounts for the year 2014.

Company example 11.2

Financial instruments and related disclosures

	2014 £m
Cash and cash equivalents	4,338
Available-for-sale investments:	
Liquid investments:	
– Government bonds	69
Other investments	1,114
Loans and receivables:	
Trade and other receivables and certain other non-current assets in scope of IAS 39	4,232
Financial assets at fair value through profit or loss:	
Other non-current assets in scope of IAS 39	269
Derivatives designated as at fair value through profit or loss	76
Derivatives classified as held for trading under IAS 39	70
Total financial assets	10,168
Financial liabilities measured at amortised cost:	
Borrowings excluding obligations under finance leases:	
– bonds in a designated hedging relationship	(4,124)
– other bonds	(13,540)
– bank loans and overdrafts	(379)
– commercial paper	(656)
Total borrowings excluding obligations under finance leases	(18,699)
Obligations under finance leases	(85)
Total borrowings	(18,784)
Trade and other payables, Other provisions and certain other non-current liabilities in scope of IAS 39	(7,566)
Financial liabilities at fair value through profit or loss:	
Trade and other payables, Other provisions and certain other non-current liabilities in scope of IAS 39	(1,724)
Derivatives designated as at fair value through profit or loss	(3)
Derivatives classified as held for trading under IAS 39	(410)
Total financial liabilities	(28,487)
Net financial assets and financial liabilities	(18,319)

GlaxoSmithKline, Annual Report and Accounts, 2014, Note 41, p. 193

Company example 11.2 shows the importance of financial assets and financial liabilities to the company.

If you examine the accounts and reports of other companies, you will find a considerable amount of information on managing risk and financial instruments. The use of these instruments has been expanding and their complexity increasing. In the next section, we examine the topic in detail.

FINANCIAL INSTRUMENTS

We started this chapter by defining a financial instrument as any contract that gives rise to a **financial asset** of one entity and a **financial liability** or equity instrument of another entity. We can illustrate the relationship of financial instruments to the balance sheet of the entity by the accounting equation: Assets = Liabilities + Equity.

financial asset

A financial asset is cash, an equity instrument in another entity, a contract or a contractual claim.

Based on IAS 32, para. 11

financial liability

A financial liability is a contractual obligation to deliver cash or another financial asset to another entity or to exchange financial assets or financial liabilities under potentially unfavourable conditions. It can also be a contract that will or may be settled in the entity's own equity.

Based on IAS 32, para. 11

In the following sections, we explain financial assets and financial liabilities in detail. The important concept to note at this stage is both financial assets and liabilities are based on contracts.

A simple example of the use of financial instruments is the sale of goods on credit by one entity to another. The entity doing the selling will raise an invoice and it therefore has a financial asset that appears as accounts receivable on its balance sheet. The purchaser has to pay for the goods and, until it does so, it has a financial liability on its balance sheet.

An entity may be seeking additional finance. If it issues shares, it has increased its equity and the holders of the shares have a financial asset. If the entity raises a long-term loan, it has a financial liability and the lender has a financial asset. The financial liability of the borrower is the regular payment of interest on the loan and the repayment of the principal. The financial asset of the lender is the regular receipt of interest on the loan and the contractual agreement for the loan to be repaid.

In the following sections we explain financial assets and financial liabilities and give examples of both.

For transactions to take place there must be formal agreements in the form of contracts. The contracts are usually in paper form but they do give rise to assets, liabilities and equity. These financial instruments appear on the balance sheets of the entities that are party to the contracts.

The examples we have given are of contracts between two parties. The objectives of the parties determine the nature of the contract. As such, these contracts are illiquid because they cannot easily be bought or sold to other parties.

To overcome the hurdle of illiquidity, financial instruments based on standard contracts with standard conditions have been created. These financial instruments are called 'securities'. They are based on real assets, and can be traded in the financial markets.

Other standardized contracts are known as 'financial derivatives'. These are not based on real assets but on some underlying asset or another benchmark. Derivatives have become extremely important and their use is contentious. We explain these fully in the section on types of financial instruments.

Agreement on an acceptable method for accounting for financial instruments has proved elusive. The issues that have to be resolved fall under three headings: classification, initial measurement and subsequent measurement. We consider the measurement issues in Chapter 12 when we examine the standards in detail. At this stage, we concentrate on correctly classifying debt (financial liability) and equity (see Worked example 11.1) because they have a significant impact on our financial statements. We look at this more closely when we discuss leverage in Chapter 19.

In Worked example 11.1, the entity is making the decision but others are involved. In the financial markets, are their financiers willing to give a loan to the entity? Are their prospective shareholders wishing to acquire shares? Although the entity is making the decision, there are other parties to the contract and they will have their own views.

Worked example 11.1   Classifying debt and equity summary

An entity wishes to raise £5 million. It can do so by either issuing shares or taking a loan. The consequences of the decision are as follows.

- Debt, being a financial liability, appears on the balance sheet. Interest on the loan is a charge to the income statement.
- Equity appears in its own category on the balance sheet. Any dividends paid are taken from profits in the statement of changes in equity and are not a charge against profits.

The decision made by the entity has an impact on the future profits it will report and various ratios such as the gearing ratio and the return on capital employed. These are discussed in Chapter 12.

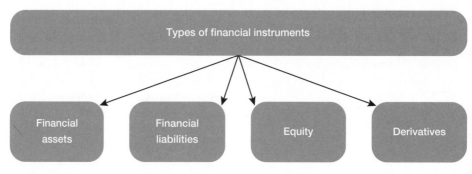

▲ Diagram 11.2 *Types of financial instruments*

In this section, we concentrate on financial assets, financial liabilities and equity (see Diagram 11.2). We then proceed to explain derivatives as a separate topic.

Financial assets

This is possibly the easiest of the financial instruments to understand and we can explain financial assets by listing some examples:

- cash;
- equity instrument of another entity (e.g. investment in another entity's shares);
- accounts receivable;
- investments in bonds and other debt instruments issued by other entity;
- derivative financial assets.

The example of cash can give problems as it seems 'valuable'. Cash is a financial asset because its value is derived from what it represents. You can buy something with cash but the paper it is printed on has little value. Compare this to gold, which is not a financial asset because it has an inherent value based on its use in electronics, jewellery and dentistry.

The following assets are not financial assets but either tangible or intangible assets:

- inventories;
- property plant and equipment;
- leased assets;
- intangible assets;
- prepaid expenses.

We have examined these types of asset and the particular standards that set out their accounting treatment in earlier chapters.

Financial liabilities

Financial liabilities are slightly more complex and include:

- a contractual obligation to deliver cash or another financial asset to another entity or to exchange financial assets or financial liabilities with another entity under conditions that are potentially unfavourable to the entity; or
- a contract that will or may be settled in the entity's own equity instruments and not classified as an equity instrument of the entity.

Examples of financial liabilities are:

- trades payable;
- loans from other entities;
- bonds and other debt instruments issued by the entity;
- derivative financial liabilities;
- preference shares that must be redeemed at a specified date and for a specified amount;
- obligations to issue a variable number of its own shares worth a fixed amount of cash.

The last example refers to shares with a fixed amount in value. Normally shares fluctuate in price. With a contract that specifies the number of shares, the price is not known until the contract is completed. You can enter into a contract where the amount is known but not the number of shares. For example, an entity enters into a contract in 2010 that entails issuing its own shares in January 2015 to the value of £500,000. This is a financial liability because the number of shares is variable but the amount is fixed.

The following examples are NOT financial liabilities:

- warranty obligations;
- income tax liabilities;
- constructive obligations.

Equity

The main examples of **equity** are:

- ordinary shares;
- preference shares (non-redeemable and discretionary dividend).

equity

In accounting, equity refers to an ownership interest in a business. It is a contract that evidences a residual interest in the assets of an entity after deducting all of its liabilities.

A company may decide to raise finance by issuing new shares. If the current share price on the market is high, this is an attractive option. The new shares it issues have the face value of existing shares but the market price of the new shares will be higher. The difference between the face value of the existing shares and the market price of the new shares is the share premium. This appears on the company's balance sheet. We discussed the premium in Chapter 6.

The company is permitted to deduct the costs it incurs in issuing shares from the share premium (see Worked example 11.2).

Worked example 11.2   Accounting for the issue of equity

Rebore issues 20,000 £1 ordinary shares for a cash consideration of £2.50 each. Issue costs are £1,000. The entity has raised finance (received cash) by issuing financial instruments (equity). Rebore has issued ordinary shares and has no obligation to repay the monies received but it has increased the ownership interest in its net assets. The issue costs are written off against share premium.

Equity instruments are not remeasured. An entity does not recognize a change in the fair value of its share. The investor who has purchased the shares enjoys any gain and suffers any loss.

The entity makes the decision whether to pay dividends in the reporting period. This has no effect on the carrying value of the equity instruments shown in its balance sheet. The dividends are a reduction in the entity's retained earnings.

An entity may issue redeemable shares where it has a contractual obligation to buy back the shares at some future date. It therefore has incurred a debt. As the entity has to repay the investor, it will classify the redeemable shares as a financial liability.

Derivatives

A derivative has the following characteristics:

1   The value of the derivative changes in response to changes in a specified interest rate, financial instrument price, commodity price, foreign exchange rate, index of prices or rates, credit rating or credit index, or other variable.
2   It requires no initial investment or an initial investment less than that required for other types of contracts expected to have a similar response to changes in market factors.
3   It is settled at a future date.

Entities, understandably, wish to reduce risk in their transactions to minimize the possibility of not being paid with sales on credit. They may also have the risk that they are party to a contract to purchase goods at a certain price in the future but the market price may fall. A common risk many entities grapple with is changes in foreign exchange rates.

Entities can use derivatives for risk management by hedging. This technique provides offsetting compensation in case of an undesired event. In this case, it is a type of insurance. Like insurance, derivatives are a way of guarding against loss. In a similar way to insuring plant and equipment, an entity is limiting the exposure to risk of financial assets to volatility in prices and interest rates by using derivatives.

Derivatives are also used for speculation (i.e. making a financial 'bet'). The use of derivatives for speculation offers entities and investors a risky opportunity to increase profit. As we saw in the example of Diageo in Company example 11.1, few companies would embrace this strategy. However, stakeholders in the entity may not properly understand the risk even where an entity makes it clear that the purpose of using derivatives is a speculative one.

The four main types of derivatives we discuss in this section are forward contracts, futures contracts, options and swaps.

Forward contract

A forward contract is an agreement to buy or sell an asset at a certain future time for a certain price. These are the simplest form of derivative and are traded in the over-the-counter market. One of the parties in a forward contract agrees to buy the underlying asset on a future specified date for a certain specified price. The other party agrees to sell the asset on the agreed date for the agreed price. The price at which the parties agree to transact in the future is the delivery price. No money changes hands at the time the parties enter into a forward contract.

Futures contract

A futures contract is very similar to a forward contract. The main difference is that futures contracts are traded on an exchange that sets rules for trading. This simplifies the process and helps the market achieve higher liquidity. Futures contracts are traded on a variety of commodities, including live cattle, sugar, wool, timber, copper, gold, tin and aluminum. They are also used on a wide array of financial assets, including stock indices, currencies, and Treasury bonds.

Options

In contrast to forwards and futures, options give the owner the right, but not the obligation, to transact. As there is only the right, the cost of the option is much less than the complete transaction. The owner of the option will only transact if it is profitable to do so. The price at which the parties transact in the future is the strike price. When the transaction takes place, the owner of the option exercises the option.

There are two types of option. A call option can give the holder the right to buy shares at a predetermined price. For example, an investor has the option to buy 5,000 shares in Exton Company at £25 per share. If the share price on the open market rises from £25 to £28 per share, it is worthwhile for the investor to exercise the option and purchase the shares at the agreed price of £25. A profit has been made. If the share does not increase above £25, the investor does not exercise the option and makes a small loss on the cost of the derivative.

A put option gives the holder the right to sell the shares at a pre-set price. If the investor believes the shares will decline in price, he will enter into an agreement to sell the shares at a pre-set price. If the share price falls then the holder will exercise the put option.

The general rule is that a call option increases in value when the underlying asset increases in value; a put option increases in value when the underlying asset decreases in value.

Swaps

A swap is simply an agreement between two parties to exchange cash flows in the future. The agreement defines the dates when they will exchange the cash flows and the calculation of the amounts. Swaps typically lead to cash flow exchanges on several future dates.

In an interest rate swap, the parties agree to exchange a floating-rate loan for a fixed-rate loan by paying a fixed amount in return for a variable amount. Similarly, currency swaps can be used to transform borrowings in one currency to borrowings in another currency, by agreeing to make a payment in one currency in return for a payment in another currency.

For example, an entity holds a bond with a fixed interest rate of 5%. It predicts that interest rates generally will increase in the future. If interest rates go up, a 5% return is not attractive and the bond will consequently lose value. Management can enter into an interest rate swap arrangement in which they pay a fixed interest payment in exchange for a payment based on a variable interest rate.

Having had a brief review of the financial environment, you can imagine that there are difficulties in accounting for these complex financial instruments. The situation is made even more difficult for the standard setters because new derivatives are being designed that are not dealt with adequately in the existing regulations.

Embedded derivatives

These are sometimes referred to as 'hybrid instruments' because they have characteristics of both debt and equity. For example, a convertible bond, which we examine at length in our explanation of IAS 32 (see Chapter 12), is a hybrid instrument because it is a debt security with an option to convert the bond to shares, which is the embedded derivative.

The accounting treatment for such hybrid securities is to separate the values of the debt security and the embedded derivative. The entity then accounts for the embedded derivative in the same way as all other forms of derivatives.

*   *   *

The above explanation of the use of financial instruments has demonstrated their attractiveness but also their complexity. Financial instruments can make money for speculators and also help companies that are financially distressed. Unfortunately, financial instruments can also be misunderstood and misused. The next section records the consequences of one such episode.

THE 2007/8 CRISIS

A crisis frequently commences with a single, spectacular event. Most commentators would identify the collapse of Lehman Brothers as that event in the 2007/8 global financial crisis. The company had reported record revenue and earnings for 2007, but, in September 2008, it became the largest company in US history to file for bankruptcy.[1] On the day that Lehman Brothers Holdings Inc. (LBHI) filed for bankruptcy, its affiliates had over 930,000 derivative contracts outstanding. It is claimed that: 'The fate of these contracts illustrates the challenges facing those who work with derivatives' (Barkhausen 2010: 7).

The failure of Lehman was part of the global financial crisis of 2007/8[2] which caused considerable panic. Understandably, people wanted to know the cause of the crisis, and accounting for financial instruments became the focus. The reasons offered for financial instruments being the culprit fell into two main camps.

There were those who argued that speculators and investment houses used complex financial instruments inappropriately. They entered into contracts that were too speculative and with no safeguards. To put it bluntly, the players did not know the game they were playing.[3]

Others, particularly the banks, argued that it was not the financial instruments that were to blame but the way that they had to be accounted for – in other words, the accounting regulations.

Critics castigated the accounting standards because of the requirement for fair value accounting instead of historical cost. There are two main methods for fair value accounting. Marking 'to market' is the valuation of financial assets at the price found for identical assets traded in active markets. Marking 'to model' refers to valuing financial assets based on analytically derived expectations of future cash flows.

Meder et al. (2011) examined the nature and calculations of both models. They do not advance a strong recommendation for either method. They do recommend, however, that users and preparers should understand how underlying economic fundamentals affect expectations of future cash flows.

Their advice is valuable but in 2007/8 the accounting regulation for fair value accounting forced companies to write down financial asset values where a decrease had occurred. This weakened balance sheets and, in turn, affected banks' lending practices.

The defenders of fair value accounting argued that the method was not the cause of the crisis. They claimed that fair value only revealed the effects of poor decisions by the banks. Whatever the merits of this argument, the accounting focus on financial instruments had started early in 2006 as part of the project to converge all international and US accounting standards.

The FASB and the IASB declared their intentions to work together to improve and converge financial reporting standards by issuing a Memorandum of Understanding (MoU), A Roadmap for Convergence between IFRSs and U.S. GAAP—2006–2008. As part of the MoU, the Boards worked jointly on a research project to reduce the complexity of the accounting for financial instruments.

The 2007/8 crisis may have accelerated their efforts but, as with all efforts to develop a new or revised standard, progress was slow. Considerable pressure and lobbying took place and the Boards were strongly encouraged to speed up their deliberations. The Boards were aware of the need for short-term responses to the worldwide credit crisis, and emphasized their commitment to developing common solutions aimed at providing greater transparency and reducing complexity in the accounting of financial instruments.

The Boards' work resulted in the IASB's issuance of the March 2008 discussion paper, Reducing Complexity in Reporting Financial Instruments, which the FASB also published for comment by its constituents. Focusing on the measurement of financial instruments and hedge accounting, the discussion paper identified several possible approaches for improving and simplifying accounting for financial instruments.

The Financial Instruments Project made very slow progress, despite the many meetings and documents issued. It would appear that the FASB and the IASB could not agree which approach they should adopt. In 2014, we reached the stage where the FASB had decided its own approach and the IASB had issued its own standards.

Whatever happened behind the scenes, the FASB has gone its own way and, at the international level, we now have a constellation of standards. In the following chapter, we discuss the requirements of these standards.

NOTES

1 See D.H. Caplan, S.K. Dutta and D.J. Marcinko (2012) 'Lehman on the Brink of Bankruptcy: A Case about Aggressive Application of Accounting Standards', *Issues in Accounting Education*, 27(2) pp. 441–459.

2 A useful case study for students examining the collapse is in the American Accounting Association's *Issues in Accounting Education*, 27(2), pp. 441–459. DOI: 10.2308/iace-50126 2012.

3 Although the financial crisis of 2007/8 hit the headlines, there were warning signs before then. An interesting book that investigates these is L.L. Jacque (2015) *Global Derivative Debacles from Theory to Malpractice*, 2nd edn, World Scientific.

4 An excellent award winning documentary which investigates the collapse in depth is *An Inside Job* (Sony Classics), produced and written by Charles Ferguson.

CONCLUSIONS

At one level, financial instruments are easy to understand. Entities have numerous financial assets and liabilities on their balance sheets that cause relatively few problems. Cash, investments in bonds, loans from other entities and redeemable preference shares must be properly accounted for, but do not introduce major problems.

When we look at derivatives and the practices of some entities, however, complications arise.[4] The financial crisis of 2007/8 exemplified these issues, but it did not suggest any quick and easy answers. The IASB, initially in partnership with FASB, has spent years attempting to achieve a sensible regime.

The FASB has decided to issue its own regulations for financial instruments, and these are not a subject for this book. The IASB has revised and issued its regulations and, in the following chapter, we look at the standards in force in August 2016.

ADDITIONAL RESOURCES

Go online to the companion website for this book to access further teaching and learning materials for this chapter.
www.palgravehighered.com/hussey-cfr

CHAPTER 1

FINANCIAL INSTRUMENTS – THE STANDARDS

IAS 32 Financial Instruments: Presentation

IAS 39 Recognition and Measurement

IFRS 7 Financial Instruments: Disclosures

IFRS 9 Financial Instruments

IFRS 13 Fair Value Measurement

LEARNING OBJECTIVES

At the end of this chapter, you should be able to:

- Classify and describe the financial instruments under IAS 32
- Differentiate the types of hedging and the accounting treatment under IAS 39
- Discuss the disclosure of various aspects of financial assets under IFRS 7
- Identify and explain classification and measurement, impairment and hedge accounting under IFRS 9
- Describe the application of IFRS 13 and explain the three level hierarchy.

INTRODUCTION

Deciding the appropriate accounting treatment for financial instruments has proved to be a major headache for the International Accounting Standards Board (IASB). A brief summary of standards issued illustrates the tortuous route that standard setters have followed to arrive at the present stage.

1986 IAS 25 *Accounting for Investments* – withdrawn in 2000 and replaced with IAS 40 *Investment Property*

1995 IAS 32 *Financial Instruments: Presentation*

1998 IAS 39 *Financial Instruments: Recognition and Measurement*

2003 IAS 39 *Financial Instruments: Recognition and Measurement*. Revised version reissued

2004–2009 During this period 10 separate amendments were made to IAS 39

2005 IFRS 7 *Financial Instruments: Disclosures*

2009 IFRS 9 *Financial Instruments*. Replaces the classification and measurement of financial asset provisions in IAS 39

2010 IFRS 9 Reissued with new requirements on accounting for financial liabilities

2013 Two further amendments to IFRS 9

2014 IFRS 9 *Financial Instruments* issued and effective for annual periods beginning on or after 1 January 2018 with early adoption possible

IFRS 9 *Financial Instruments* issued on 24 July 2014 is the IASB's replacement for IAS 39 *Financial Instruments: Recognition and Measurement*. The standard includes requirements for recognition and measurement, impairment, derecognition and general hedge accounting. The IASB completed its project to replace IAS 39 in phases, adding to the standard as it completed each phase.

The financial crisis of 2007/8 raised many concerns about the complexity of the standards and their application when accounting for financial instruments. As the previous chapter discussed, some argued that the standards at that time contributed to the crisis because they forced some entities to record substantial losses that were not representative of what was actually happening.

There are significant difficulties in establishing an acceptable method for accounting for financial instruments. Not only are the transactions complex, but also any proposals on the appropriate accounting treatment are debatable. Diagram 12.1 shows the position in respect of accounting standards in force in 2016, which is reflected in the chapter structure.

IAS 32
FINANCIAL INSTRUMENTS: PRESENTATION

▼ Table 12.1 *Timeline of IAS 32*

Date	Comment
1995	Standard first issued, effective date 1 January 1996
1998	Revised standard issued
2003	Revised standard issued
2005	Disclosure provisions removed and covered by IFRS 7
2014	Effective date of previous amendments
Interpretations issued	IFRIC 2 Members' Shares in Co-operative Entities and Similar Instruments
	IFRIC 12 Service Concession Arrangements
	IFRIC 19 Extinguishing Financial Liabilities with Equity

IAS 32 establishes principles for presenting financial instruments as liabilities or equity and for offsetting financial assets and financial liabilities. The stance that it adopts for the classification is that of the issuer of the financial instruments. The standard links with IFRS 9, that deals with the recognition of financial assets and financial liabilities, and with IFRS 7, that deals with the disclosure of financial instruments.

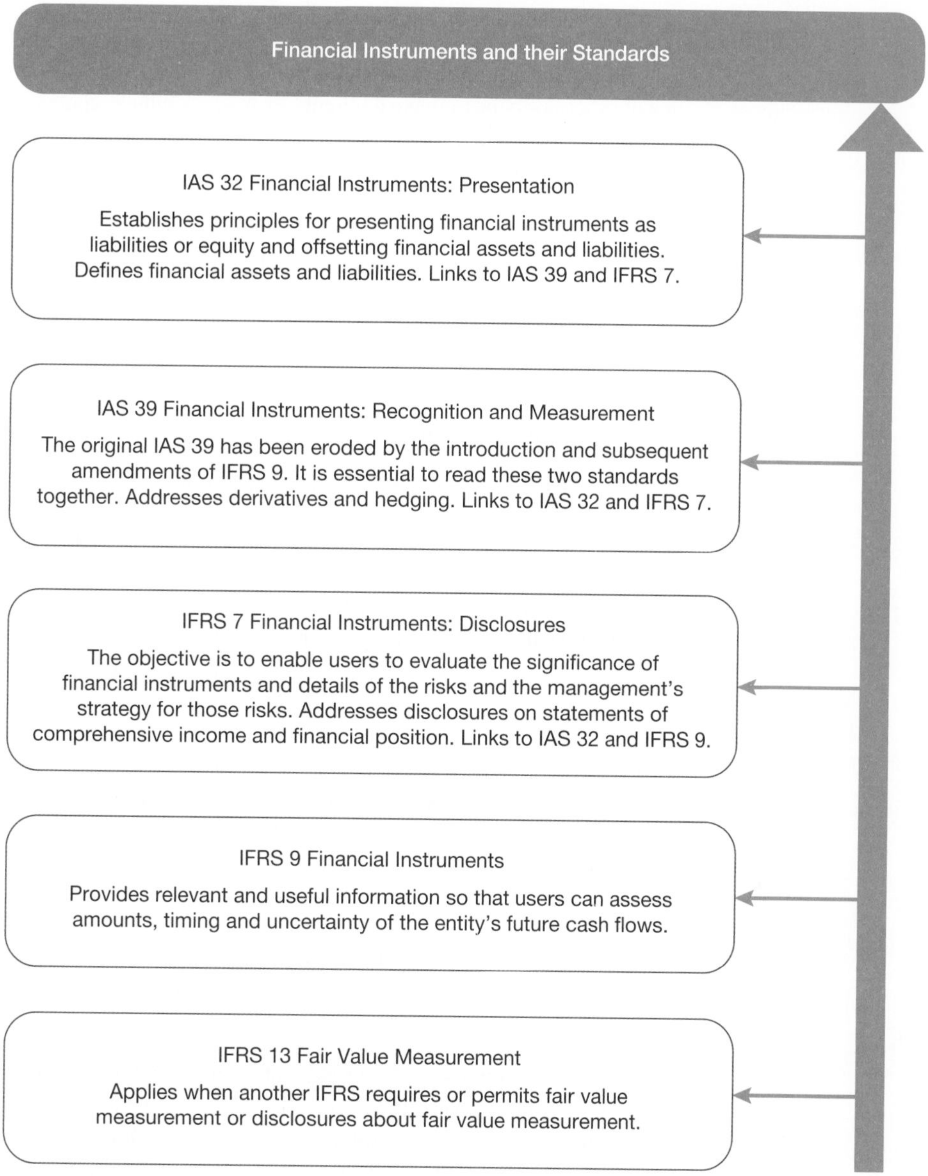

Financial Instruments and their Standards

IAS 32 Financial Instruments: Presentation

Establishes principles for presenting financial instruments as
liabilities or equity and offsetting financial assets and liabilities.
Defines financial assets and liabilities. Links to IAS 39 and IFRS 7.

IAS 39 Financial Instruments: Recognition and Measurement

The original IAS 39 has been eroded by the introduction and subsequent
amendments of IFRS 9. It is essential to read these two standards
together. Addresses derivatives and hedging. Links to IAS 32 and IFRS 7.

IFRS 7 Financial Instruments: Disclosures

The objective is to enable users to evaluate the significance of
financial instruments and details of the risks and the management's
strategy for those risks. Addresses disclosures on statements of
comprehensive income and financial position. Links to IAS 32 and IFRS 9.

IFRS 9 Financial Instruments

Provides relevant and useful information so that users can assess
amounts, timing and uncertainty of the entity's future cash flows.

IFRS 13 Fair Value Measurement

Applies when another IFRS requires or permits fair value
measurement or disclosures about fair value measurement.

▲ Diagram 12.1 *Structure of Chapter 12: the constellation of standards*

The standard uses the term 'entity' to include individuals, partnerships, incorporated bodies, trusts and government agencies. It contains a long list of circumstances where the regulations do not apply. This is usually because other standards regulate certain entities and types of financial instruments.

The main thrust of IAS 32 is ensuring that, on initial recognition, the entity correctly classifies a financial instrument as a financial liability, a financial asset, or an equity instrument. Classification of financial assets usually presents no problems. The major difficulty addressed by the standard is determining whether the instrument is an equity instrument or a financial liability.

To be classified as an equity instrument, there are two conditions:

1 The instrument must not include an obligation to deliver cash or another financial asset to another entity or to make a potentially unfavourable exchange of financial assets or liabilities with another entity.
2 If the instrument can be settled by the issuer's own equity it must either be a non-derivative that does not require the issuer to deliver a variable number of its own equity instruments or a derivative that can only be settled by the issuer exchanging a fixed amount of cash or another financial asset for a fixed number of its own equity instruments.

There are two types of instruments that cause particular problems: puttable instruments and compound instruments.

Puttable instruments

Puttable instruments come in two forms that either:

1 Give the holders the right to put the financial instrument back to the issuer for cash or another financial asset; or
2 Automatically puts back the instrument to the issuer on the occurrence of an uncertain future event or the death or retirement of the holder of the puttable instrument.

Worked example 12.1

A partnership has a requirement that any new partners that are admitted subscribe capital into the business. When a partner leaves or retires from the partnership, the capital that he or she initially paid is repayable at fair value.

Under IAS 32, the partners' capital meets the definition of a puttable instrument.

Puttable instruments can be a financial liability or an equity instrument. To meet the second classification the instrument must contain certain features. We summarize these as follows:

(a) If an entity is liquidated the holder of the puttable instrument is entitled to a pro rata share of the entity's net assets.
(b) It must be in the class of instruments that is subordinate to all other classes of instruments. This subordinate class of instruments must have identical features.
(c) The only condition the contract must have is the obligation for the purchaser to purchase or redeem the asset for cash or another financial asset.
(d) The total cash flows from the instrument are based on the profit or loss and changes in the recognized net assets or in the fair value of recognized and unrecognized net assets.

Compound financial instruments

An entity may issue a compound financial instrument that has both liability and equity components. In such cases, the entity must classify the components separately. Convertible bonds are one example of compound financial instruments. These usually require the issuer to deliver cash or another financial asset (a liability) but also grant the holder the right to convert the bond into a fixed number of ordinary shares (the equity).

To be classified as compound financial instruments the main requirements are that:

- They are non-derivative instruments that possess both equity and liability characteristics.
- The equity and liability components must be separated on initial recognition. This is a process sometimes referred to as 'split accounting'. This involves first calculating the fair value of the liability component. The equity component is then determined by deducting the fair value of the financial liability from the fair value of the compound financial instrument as a whole.
- The split and the amount of the liability and equity components is determined on initial recognition and not altered subsequently.

Many convertible bonds are classified as compound instruments. The procedure for split accounting is as follows:

1. Calculate the carrying amount of the liability component. The method involves calculating the net present value of the discounted cash flows of interest and principal without including the possibility of exercise of the conversion option.
2. Determine the carrying amount of the equity instrument represented by the conversion option by deducting the fair value of the financial liability calculated in Step 1 from the fair value of the compound financial instrument as a whole.

Worked example 12.2   Convertible bonds – split accounting

Year 1. An entity issues 5,000 convertible bonds with a face value of £5,000 per bond and annual interest at 5%. Each bond is convertible into 200 shares and has a three-year term.

Calculation of liability component

The present value of the principal and the interest of 5% for 3 years is calculated using the present discount rate. This would usually be the market interest rate for similar bonds having no conversion rights. The result gives the financial liability component. In this example, we assume that the calculations give a result of £18,000,000. This is deducted from the proceeds of the issue to give the equity component.

Proceeds of issue (5,000 x £5,000)	£25,000,000
Liability component	£18,000,000
Equity component	£7,000,000

For the above method to be applied, the bond must satisfy a 'fixed for fixed' test. For example, with a convertible denominated in a foreign currency the conversion component may fail the fixed for fixed test. This is because the fixed amount of foreign currency does not represent a fixed amount of cash. The solution is to scrutinize the terms of each financial instrument to determine whether separate equity and liability components exist.

Offsetting

The standard, under certain conditions, permits the offsetting of financial assets and liabilities. This is a process in which the holder of financial assets and financial liabilities can set the amount of one against the other and only show the net amount on the statement of financial position.

An entity can only make this type of transaction where it has a current legal enforceable right to set off recognized amounts and intends either to settle on a net basis or to realize the asset and liability at the same time.

IAS 39

FINANCIAL INSTRUMENTS: RECOGNITION AND MEASUREMENT

▼ Table 12.2 *Timeline of IAS 39*

Date	Comment
1998	Standard issued with effective date 1 January 2001
2003	Revised standard issued with effective date 1 January 2005
2004	Revision to reflect macro hedging
2009	Classification and measurements requirements removed by issue of IFRS 9
2013	IFRS 9 issued allowing entities to continue to use hedge accounting requirements in IAS 39
2014	IFRS 9 Financial Instruments issued replacing IAS 39 requirements for classification and measurement, impairment, hedge accounting and derecognition. Effective for annual periods beginning on or after 1 January 2018
Interpretations issued	IFRIC 16 Hedge of a Net Investment in a Foreign Operation
	IFRIC 12 Service Concession Arrangements
	IFRIC 9 Reassessment of Embedded Derivatives

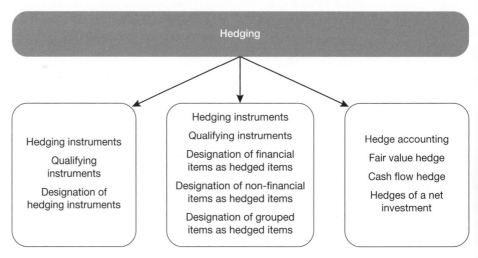

▲ Diagram 12.2 *Main contents of IAS 39*

This standard is about hedge accounting. An entity may have purchased a financial asset and its value on the balance sheet is established by marking to market. The entity is concerned about adverse price movements. It can avoid these by acquiring an offsetting position in a related security. If the value of the asset declines, this decrease is balanced by an increase in the value of the hedge.

The difficulty lies in deciding the accounting treatment. The regulation as it stands in 2016 is that the ownership of the security and the opposing hedge are accounted for as one item. Table 12.2, listing some of the events in the life of IAS 39, illustrates the problems that the IASB has had with accounting for financial instruments.

Examples of the type of financial instruments that remain in the scope of IAS 39 are:

- cash;
- demand and time deposits;
- commercial paper;
- accounts, notes, and loans receivable and payable;
- debt and equity securities: these are financial instruments from the perspectives of both the holder and the issuer, and include investments in subsidiaries, associates, and joint ventures;
- asset backed securities such as collateralized mortgage obligations, repurchase agreements, and securitized packages of receivables;
- derivatives, including options, rights, warrants, futures contracts, forward contracts, and swaps.

IAS 39 does not include accounting for equity instruments and entity issues. It sets the requirements for accounting for financial liabilities, and IAS 32 determines the classification of financial instruments as either equity or liability.

The purpose of IAS 39 is to ensure that all entities apply the regulations to all financial instruments within the scope of IFRS 9 *Financial Instruments* if, and to the extent that:

1. IFRS 9 permits the application of the hedge accounting requirements of IAS 39.
2. The financial instruments are part of a hedging relationship that qualifies for hedge accounting in accordance with this standard.

The standard defines the various terms connected to the process of hedging as follows.

Firm commitment

This is a binding agreement for the exchange of a specified quantity of resources at a specified price on a specified future date or dates.

Forecast transaction

This is an uncommitted but anticipated future transaction.

The activities of hedging and using hedging instruments have many specific terms. The standard defines and explains these. We summarize the key points in the following section.

Hedging instruments

A hedging instrument is a designated derivative (applies to foreign exchange hedges only) or a designated non-derivative financial asset or non-derivative financial liability whose fair value or cash flows are expected to offset changes in the fair value of a designated hedged item.

Hedged item

A hedged item is an asset, liability, firm commitment, highly probable forecast transaction or net investment in a foreign operation that (a) exposes the entity to risk in changes of fair value or future cash flows, and (b) is designated as being hedged.

Hedged effectiveness

This is the degree to which changes in fair value or cash flows of the hedged item that are attributable to a hedged risk are offset by changes in the fair value or cash flows of the hedging instrument.

The above terms are not easy to understand immediately. The meaning of the terms becomes clear as we draw from the requirements of the standard to demonstrate their application.

Hedge accounting

Hedging is a technically complex transaction and new developments occur from time to time. Entities are attempting to reduce their exposure to financial risk and several different methods are used. Establishing the accounting for these hedging transactions has proved difficult for the standard setters. We present an outline of the present regulations below.

Hedging relationships

There are three types of hedging relationship.

1 Fair value hedge

This is a hedge relating to a recognized financial asset, liability or firm commitment where there is the risk of changes in fair value.

2 Cash flow hedge

This is a hedge where there is the risk of variability in cash flow that is associated with a recognized asset or liability

3 The hedge of net investment in a foreign operation.

IAS 21 defines a foreign operation as an entity that is a subsidiary, associate, joint arrangement or branch of a reporting entity, the activities of which are based or conducted in a country or currency other than those of the reporting entity.

Derivatives as hedging instruments

There are five conditions under which an entity can determine a derivative is a hedging instrument. These conditions have some technical details, so we have extracted the main requirements below.

1   When the hedging relationship commences there must be a formal designation and document of the relationship. This includes the entity's risk management and the objective and strategy for undertaking the hedge.
2   The entity expects the hedge to be highly effective in achieving offsetting changes in fair value or cash flows attributable to the hedged risk.
3   For cash flow hedges, a forecast transaction that is the subject of the hedge must be highly probable and must present an exposure to variations in cash flows that could ultimately affect profit or loss.
4   The effectiveness of the hedge can be reliably measured.
5   The hedge is assessed on an ongoing basis and determined actually to have been highly effective throughout the financial reporting periods for which the hedge was designated.

Accounting for fair value hedges

1 Any gain or loss from remeasuring the hedging instrument at fair value is recognized in profit or loss.

2 Any gain or loss on the hedged item attributable to the hedged risk adjusts the carrying amount of the hedged item and is recognized in profit or loss.

3 Fair value hedge accounting is discontinued prospectively if:

   o The hedging instrument expires or is sold, terminated or exercised.
   o The hedge no longer meets the five conditions for being a hedging instrument.
   o The entity revokes the designation.

4 Where hedge accounting is discontinued, adjustments to the carrying amount of a hedged financial asset for which the effective interest rate is used are amortized to profit or loss.

Accounting for cash flow hedges

1 The part of the gain or loss on the hedging instrument that is determined to be an effective hedge is recognized in the statement of other comprehensive income (see Chapter 9). The ineffective part of the gain or loss on the hedging instrument is recognized in profit or loss.

2 The hedge may result in the recognition of a financial asset or a financial liability. In this case, the associated gains or losses that were recognized in other comprehensive income are reclassified from equity to profit or loss as a reclassification adjustment.

3 Where the hedge results in the recognition of a non-financial asset or a non-financial liability, the standard permits the entity to select from a choice of accounting policies.

4 Cash flow hedge accounting is discontinued prospectively if:

   o The hedging instrument expires or is sold, terminated or exercised.
   o The hedge no longer meets the five conditions for being a hedging instrument.
   o The forecast transaction is no longer expected to occur.
   o The entity revokes the designation.

Accounting for hedges of a net investment in a foreign operation

Hedges of a net investment in a foreign operation are accounted for similarly to cash flow hedges. This includes a hedge of a monetary item that is accounted for as part of the net investment.

The part of the gain or loss on the hedging instrument that is determined to be an effective hedge is recognized in equity and the ineffective part is recognized in profit or loss.

The gain or loss on the hedging instrument relating to the effective portion of the hedge that has been recognized in the statement of other comprehensive income is reclassified from equity to profit or loss as a reclassification adjustment on the disposal of the foreign operation.

IFRS 7

FINANCIAL INSTRUMENTS: DISCLOSURES

The IASB issued IFRS 7 to bring disclosure requirements up to date with what had been happening in practice. The techniques entities adopt for managing exposure to risks arising from financial instruments had developed over the years. It recognized that users need information about risk exposure and how the entity manages it.

▼ **Table 12.3** *Timeline of IFRS 7*

Date	Comment
2005	Standard first issued, effective on or after 1 January 2007
2008–14	Numerous amendments
2014	Amendment effective on or after 1 January 2016
Interpretations issued	None

As with the other standards on accounting for financial instruments, there have been some movements. In 2003, all disclosure requirements were transferred to IAS 32. This resulted in that standard being renamed Financial Instruments: Disclosure and Presentation. In 2005, the IASB issued IFRS 7 *Financial Instruments: Disclosures* to replace the disclosure requirements in IAS 32. This became effective on 1 January 2007.

Two amendments in the standard regulate the transfers of financial assets (applicable for financial years beginning on or after 1 July 2011) and offsetting financial assets and financial liabilities (applicable for financial years beginning on or after 1 January 2013). In addition, some disclosure requirements previously included in IFRS 7 were transferred to IFRS 13.

The objectives of IFRS 7 are to require disclosures regarding financial instruments that enable users to evaluate:

1　Their significance for the entity's financial position and performance.
2　The nature and extent of risk to which the entity is exposed during and at the end of the reporting period, and how the entity manages those risks.

The entity must group its financial instruments into classes that are appropriate to the nature of the information disclosed and reflect the characteristics of the financial instruments. An example of a statement of accounting policy is given in Company example 12.1.

Company example 12.1

Derivative financial instruments and hedge accounting

Initial recognition and subsequent measurement

We use derivative financial instruments, such as forward currency contracts, interest rate swaps and forward commodity contracts, to hedge our foreign currency risks, interest rate risks and commodity price risks, respectively. Such derivative financial instruments are initially recognised at fair value on the date on which a derivative contract is entered into and are subsequently remeasured at fair value. Derivatives are carried as financial assets when the fair value is positive and as financial liabilities when the fair value is negative.

Any gains or losses arising from changes in the fair value of derivatives are taken directly to the income statement, except for the effective portion of cash flow hedges, which is recognised in other comprehensive income.

continued

Company example 12.1 *continued*

For the purpose of hedge accounting, hedges are classified as:

(a) Fair value hedges when hedging the exposure to changes in the fair value of a recognised asset or liability or an unrecognised firm commitment.

(b) Cash flow hedges when hedging the exposure to variability in cash flows that is either attributable to a particular risk associated with a recognised asset or liability or a highly probable forecast transaction or the foreign currency risk in an unrecognised firm commitment.

Australian Agricultural Company Limited, Annual Report, 2015, p. 75

The extract in Company example 12.1 is concerned with the initial recognition and measurement of derivatives and hedge accounting. As one would expect with a company complying with IFRSs, its disclosures satisfy the regulations. We emphasize that Company example 12.1 is an extract from an entire page of the report providing a summary of the accounting policy. Later in the document, Note 4 explains in detail the company's financial risk policy (Australian Agricultural Company Limited, Annual Report, 2015, pages 83–87).

The standard is wide in scope and includes a list of the financial instruments in its remit. The standard applies to all entities: those with only a few financial instruments and those with many. The amount of disclosure required depends on the range and number of financial instruments held.

IFRS 7 is divided into two distinct sections. The first section covers quantitative disclosures about the numbers in the balance sheet and the income statement. The second section deals with qualitative risk disclosures. These are the management's objectives, policies and processes for managing those risks.

The quantitative disclosures provide information about the extent to which the entity is exposed to risk, based on information provided internally to the entity's key management personnel. The standard identifies the different types of risk to which the entity may be exposed as credit risk, liquidity risk and market risk. We examine risk management disclosures in Chapter 20.

IFRS 9

FINANCIAL INSTRUMENTS

IFRS 9 *Financial Instruments*, issued on 24 July 2014, replaced IAS 39 *Financial Instruments: Recognition and Measurement*. The standard includes requirements for recognition and measurement, impairment, derecognition and general hedge accounting.

The version of IFRS 9 issued in 2014 supersedes all previous versions and is mandatorily effective for periods beginning on or after 1 January 2018 with early adoption permitted. For a limited period, previous versions of IFRS 9 could be adopted early if not already done so, provided the relevant date of initial application was before 1 February 2015.

▼ Table 12.4 *Timeline of IFRS 9*

Date	Comment
2009	Standard issued, effective 1 January 2013
2010	Revised standard issued, effective 1 January 2013
2014	Revised standard issued incorporating all previous amendments and revisions. Effective 1 January 2018
Interpretations issued	None

IFRS 9 is a lengthy standard. It addresses the weaknesses of accounting for financial instruments revealed by the 2007/8 financial crisis. It also incorporates in one standard the three major activities of accounting for financial instruments: classification and measurement, impairment and hedge accounting.[1]

The standard establishes requirements for reporting financial assets and financial liabilities so that users are better able to determine the amounts, timing and uncertainty of an entity's future cash flows. An article (Lloyd 2014) by a member of the IASB identifies the main differences from previous regulation as follows.

Accounting for financial assets

A major change is that the standard requires entities to estimate and account for expected credit losses for all relevant financial assets from the date they first lend money or invest in a financial instrument. This provides the users of financial statements with information on an entity's exposure to credit risk.

Accounting for financial liabilities

Although there are no substantial changes in accounting for financial liabilities, where an entity chooses to measure liabilities at fair value, it must include them on the statement of financial position at full fair value. This involves consideration of the entity's own credit risk that we discuss later in the chapter.

Hedge accounting

The standard contains a new hedge accounting model that brings risk management and accounting closer together. This provides the users of financial statements with a link between accounting transactions and the risk management policies of an entity. It also reveals the impact of hedge accounting on the financial statements.

*   *   *

IFRS 9 is structured into four main accounting issues: recognition and derecognition, classification, measurement, and hedge accounting. In each of the first parts of the standard, the treatment of both financial assets and liabilities is set out. We discuss first the accounting treatment of financial assets, then the treatment of financial liabilities and finally hedge accounting.

Financial assets

In considering financial assets, we are considering the acquirer of the financial instrument; that is, it is an asset and appears as such on the balance sheet. Financial assets can include debt instruments where the entity expects to be repaid the loan it has made and equity instruments (shares) where the entity has ownership interest in the residual net assets of another entity. This division is important as we look at classification and measurement of financial assets.

The recognition and derecognition of financial assets has certain conditions, but the main requirements are logical. An entity recognizes a financial asset in its statement of financial position when, and only when, the entity becomes party to the contractual provisions of the instrument.

amortized cost

The amortized cost is the amount at which the financial asset or financial liability is measured at initial recognition minus the principal repayments, plus or minus the cumulative amortization.

The effective interest method is used on any difference between that initial measurement and the maturity amount and, for financial assets, adjusted for any loss allowance.

Based on IFRS 9, Appendix A

effective rate method

The effective rate method is the application of the rate that exactly discounts estimated future cash payments or receipts through the expected life of the financial asset or financial liability to the gross carrying amount of a financial asset.

Based on IFRS 9, Appendix A

fair value through profit or loss (FVTPL)

Financial assets at fair value through profit and loss are carried in the consolidated balance sheet at fair value with gains or losses recognized in the consolidated statement of income.

IFRS 9, Appendix A

fair value other comprehensive income (FVOCI)

Fair value other comprehensive income recognizes all gains and losses in the other comprehensive income statement (see Chapter 9).

Based on IFRS 9, Appendix A

An entity derecognizes a financial asset when either the cash flows from the financial asset cease or it transfers the financial asset. What constitutes a transfer has many conditions, but the essence is that the transfer must involve either transferring the right to receive the cash flows or the entity has to pay the cash flows to one or more recipients.

There are several technical terms that are defined in Appendix A of IFRS 9.

Accounting requirements

Classification and measurement of the debt instrument are linked. An entity can classify its debt instruments either at **amortized cost** or at **fair value through profit or loss** (FVTPL). If the debt instrument meets two simple tests it is subsequently accounted for using amortized cost.

The two tests are the business model (hold to collect model) and the cash flow test (hold to collect and sell model). The business model test is satisfied where the entity holds the asset for the contractual cash flows rather than selling it before maturity. The cash flow test is satisfied where the contractual terms result in receipts of cash flows on specified dates of either the principal or interest.

If a debt instrument satisfies these two tests, the initial measurement is at fair value plus transaction costs. Subsequent measurement is at amortized cost. If a debt instrument does not satisfy these two tests the default requirement is that initial and subsequent measurement is at FVTPL with any gains and losses shown in the income statement.

Equity investments must be measured at fair value in the statement of financial position. An entity can decide at inception that equity investments are irrevocably classified and accounted as **fair value other comprehensive income** (FVOCI). Any gains and losses are recognized in other comprehensive income, but dividend income is still recognized in income. Such an election cannot be made if the equity investment is acquired for trading.

Reclassification

It is possible that an entity decides to change its business model for financial assets. Instead of holding the asset for the contractual cash flows until maturity, it could decide to sell it before maturity. If the business model objective for its financial assets changes so its previous model no longer applies, then other financial assets can be reclassified between FVTPL and amortized cost, and vice versa. The entity cannot restate any recognized gains, losses, or interest. In other words, it is a prospective action. However, once an equity investment has been classified as FVOCI it cannot then be reclassified.

▼ **Table 12.5** *Reclassification of financial assets*

Category		Measurement consequences
Original	**New**	
Amortized cost	FVPL	Fair value is measured at reclassification date.
FVPL	Amortized cost	Fair value at the reclassification date becomes its new gross carrying amount.
Amortized cost	FVOCI	Fair value is measured at reclassification date.
FVOCI	Amortized cost	Fair value at the reclassification date becomes its new amortized cost carrying amount.
FVPL	FVOCI	Fair value at reclassification date becomes its new carrying amount.
FVOCI	FVPL	Fair value at reclassification date becomes its carrying amount.

Impairment of financial assets

The impairment of financial assets is a new requirement and the regulations are lengthy and complex. In this section, we concentrate on the basic principles and the definitions of specific terms. The objective of requiring the impairment to financial assets stems from the concept of recognizing expected **losses** in the financial statements.

The standard is wide in its scope and the same impairment model applies to all types of financial assets covered by the standard. There are exceptions for purchased or originated credit-impaired financial assets. We explain these at the end of this section.

An entity holding a financial asset expects to receive future cash flows as set out in the contractual agreement. The standard setters assume that the expected life of a financial instrument can be estimated reliably but, if this is not possible because the future is uncertain, the entity uses the remaining contractual term of the financial instrument.

The measurement of the **loss allowance** depends on the level of credit risk. If the credit risk of a financial instrument has increased significantly since initial recognition, it is measured at an amount equal to lifetime expected losses. If the credit risk is low at the reporting, the entity can assume that credit risk on the financial instrument has not increased significantly since initial recognition.

The assessment of the level of credit risk is important. Credit risk is considered to be low if:

- there is a low risk of default;
- the borrower has a strong capacity to meet its contractual cash flow obligations in the near term;
- the ability of the borrower to fulfil its obligations will not necessarily be reduced by adverse economic and business conditions in the longer term.

credit losses

A credit loss is the difference between all contractual cash flows that are due to an entity in accordance with the contract and all the cash flows that the entity expects to receive (i.e. all cash shortfalls), discounted at the original effective interest rate (or credit-adjusted effective interest rate for purchased or originated credit-impaired financial assets).

Based on IFRS 9, Appendix A

loss allowance

A loss allowance is the allowance for expected credit losses on financial assets measured according to the regulations in the standard.

Credit risk is high where the entity holding the financial asset observes one or more of the following events that will have a significant impact on the expected future cash flows.

- Significant financial difficulty of the issuer or borrower.
- A breach of contract, such as a default or past-due event.
- The lenders for economic or contractual reasons relating to the borrower's financial difficulty granted the borrower a concession that would not otherwise be considered.
- It becomes probable that the borrower will enter bankruptcy or other financial reorganization.
- The disappearance of an active market for the financial asset because of financial difficulties.
- The purchase or origination of a financial asset at a deep discount that reflects incurred credit losses.

Purchased or originated credit-impaired financial assets

Purchased or originated credit-impaired financial assets are treated differently because the asset is credit-impaired at initial recognition.

A financial asset is identified as credit-impaired if one or more of the following events occur that have a detrimental impact on the estimated future cash flows.

> **active markets**
>
> An active market is one in which transactions for the asset or liability take place with sufficient frequency and volume to provide pricing information on an ongoing basis
>
> *Based on IFRS 13, Appendix A*

- Significant financial difficulty of the issuer or borrower.
- A breach of contract.
- It becomes necessary for the holder of the financial asset to grant concessions because of the borrower's financial difficulties.
- It is probable that the borrower will enter bankruptcy.
- An **active market** for the financial asset disappears because of financial difficulties.

An entity must recognize changes in lifetime expected losses since initial recognition as a loss allowance with such changes recognized in profit or loss. Under the requirements, any favourable changes for such assets are an impairment gain even if the resulting expected cash flows of a financial asset exceed the estimated cash flows on initial recognition.

Financial liabilities and equity

In considering financial liabilities, we are considering an entity attempting to raise finance. Financial liabilities can include debt instruments where the issuing entity has to pay regular interest and repay the principal. Equity instruments entail an issue of shares. In both instances, the financial instruments appear on the balance sheet and the standard sets out the requirements.

Financial liabilities are divided into either amortized cost or FVTPL. If financial liabilities are classified as amortized cost, the initial measurement is at fair value less the issue costs. Subsequent measurement is at amortized cost.

Hedge accounting

Earlier in this chapter, we discussed hedge accounting. As of 2016, the hedge accounting requirements in IFRS 9 are optional and IAS 39 remains. The hedge accounting model in IFRS 9 is not designed to accommodate hedging of open, dynamic portfolios. For a fair value hedge of interest rate risk of a portfolio of financial assets or liabilities, an entity can apply the hedge accounting requirements in IAS 39 instead of those in IFRS 9.

In addition, when an entity first applies IFRS 9, it may choose as its accounting policy to continue to apply the hedge accounting requirements of IAS 39 instead of the requirements of IFRS 9.

Hedging relationship

A hedging relationship qualifies for hedge accounting only if all of the following criteria are met.

1   The hedging relationship consists only of eligible hedging instruments and eligible hedged items.
2   At the inception of the hedging relationship, there is formal designation and documentation of the hedging relationship and the entity's risk management objective and strategy for undertaking the hedge.
3   The hedging relationship meets all of the hedge effectiveness requirements.

Hedging instruments

The reporting entity can only designate contracts with an external party as hedging instruments.

Hedged items

A hedged item must be reliably measurable and can be:

- a recognized asset or liability;
- an unrecognized firm commitment;
- a highly probable forecast transaction;
- a net investment in a foreign operation.

Accounting for qualifying hedging relationships

There are three types of hedging relationships:

1 Fair value hedge

A hedge of the exposure to changes in fair value of a recognized asset or liability or an unrecognized firm commitment, or a component of any such item, that is attributable to a particular risk and could affect profit or loss (or OCI in the case of an equity instrument designated as at FVOCI).

2 Cash flow hedge

The cash flow hedge reserve in equity is adjusted to the lower of the following (in absolute amounts):

- the cumulative gain or loss on the hedging instrument from inception of the hedge; and
- the cumulative change in fair value of the hedged item from inception of the hedge.

3 Hedge of a net investment in a foreign operation

This type of hedge includes a monetary item that is accounted for as part of the net investment. As specified in IFRS 9, para. 6.5.13, the accounting is similar to cash flow hedges:

- the portion of the gain or loss on the hedging instrument that is determined to be an effective hedge is recognized in OCI; and
- the ineffective portion is recognized in profit or loss.

The cumulative gain or loss on the hedging instrument relating to the effective portion of the hedge is reclassified to profit or loss on the disposal or partial disposal of the foreign operation.

Hedge effectiveness requirements

A hedging relationship must be effective to qualify for hedge accounting. To verify this, the relationship must satisfy the effectiveness criteria, stated in IFRS 9, para 6.4.1, at the beginning of each hedged period.

- There is an economic relationship between the hedged item and the hedging instrument.
- The effect of credit risk does not dominate the value changes that result from that economic relationship.
- The hedge ratio of the hedging relationship is the same as that actually used in the economic hedge.

IFRS 13

FAIR VALUE MEASUREMENT

▼ Table 12.6 *Timeline of IFRS 13*

Date	Comment
2011	Standard issued, effective for annual periods beginning on or after 1 January 2013
2013	Amendment
Interpretations issued	None

The standard is applied when another standard either requires or permits fair value measurements or disclosures about such measurements apart from:

- share-based payment transactions under IFRS 2 *Share-based Payments* (see Chapter 8);
- leasing transactions under IAS 17 *Leases* (see Chapter 15).

Some methods of measurement have the attributes of fair value but do not satisfy the accounting requirements. Examples are the use of net realizable value (IAS 2 *Inventories* – see Chapter 8) and value in use (IAS 36 *Impairment* – see Chapter 5).

fair value

Fair value is the price that would be received to sell an asset or paid to transfer a liability in an orderly transaction between market participants at the measurement date.

Based on IFRS 13, Appendix A

The aim of the standard is to improve the consistency and comparability in **fair value** measurements contained in some standards. To achieve this aim, the standard has developed a three level fair value hierarchy. This is based on the inputs that entitles users to estimate the fair value.

Diagram 12.3 illustrates the levels of input, but we need to add further explanation.

An entity attempting to make a fair value measurement must estimate the price for an orderly transaction to sell the asset or to transfer the liability. It is assumed that the transaction would take place between market

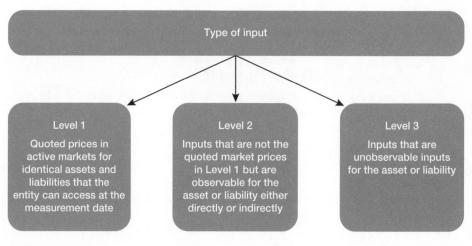

▲ **Diagram 12.3** *Fair value hierarchy*

highest and best use

Highest and best use is the use of a non-financial asset by market participants that would maximize the value of the asset or the group of assets and liabilities (e.g. a business) within which the asset would be used.

Based on IFRS 13, Appendix A

most advantageous market

The most advantageous market is one that maximizes the amount that would be received to sell the asset or minimizes the amount that would be paid to transfer the liability, after taking into account transaction costs and transport costs.

Based on IFRS 13, Appendix A

principal market

The principal market is the one with the greatest volume and level of activity for the asset or liability.

Based on IFRS 13, Appendix A

participants at the measurement date under current market conditions. In making the fair value measurement, an entity must decide:

- the particular asset or liability that is the subject of the measurement (consistently with its unit of account);
- for a non-financial asset, the valuation premise that is appropriate for the measurement (consistently with its **highest and best use**);
- the **principal (or most advantageous) market** for the asset or liability;
- the valuation technique(s) appropriate for the measurement, considering the availability of data with which to develop inputs that represent the assumptions that market participants would use when pricing the asset or liability and the level of the *fair value hierarchy* within which the inputs are categorized.

A critical criterion for the hierarchy is the separation of observable and unobservable inputs. Observable inputs consist of publicly available information about actual events or transactions; for example, securities traded on stock exchanges. Unobservable inputs consist of management's assumptions that cannot be corroborated with observable market data; for example, an internal forecast of cash flows from intangible assets.

Both Level 1 and Level 2 of the fair value hierarchy consider the use of observable inputs.

Level 1 inputs are quoted prices (unadjusted) in active markets for identical assets or liabilities that the entity can access at the measurement date. One example is when the asset is a share actively traded on a stock exchange – the quoted price is for an identical asset, so it would be categorized as Level 1.

Level 2 inputs are defined as inputs other than quoted prices included within Level 1 that are observable for the asset or liability, either directly or indirectly. If the price for an identical asset or liability is not available, an entity can use a quoted price for an asset or liability that is similar to the asset or liability being measured.

Level 3 is concerned only with unobservable inputs. There is no market data available for these inputs. These inputs must be developed by the entity using the best information available about the assumptions that market participants would use when pricing the asset or liability. The measurements therefore depend on the reporting entity's own view on the assumptions that market participants would use.

IFRS 13 requires extensive disclosures related to fair value measurements. We emphasize that IFRS 13 does not only apply to financial instruments but to all assets and liabilities where the relevant standards either require or allow fair value measurements.

There are a few instances where the standard requires entities to comply with the measurement requirements but not have to make disclosures. These exceptions are:

- defined benefit plan assets measured at fair value under IAS 19;
- retirement benefit plan investments measured at fair value under IAS 26;
- assets tested for impairment using fair value less costs to sell under IAS 36.
  Where an entity must make a disclosure, examples of key items are:
- fair value at end of reporting period;
- the level within hierarchy;
- a description of valuation technique;
- quantitative information about significant unobservable inputs.

Where an entity is using valuation, IFRS 13 requires extensive disclosures related to fair value measurements. The volume of disclosures entities make can be considerable. In Company example 12.2, we show a small extract from the disclosures made by Randgold Resources which reports using IFRS.

Company example 12.2

Fair value hierarchy

The table above [not reproduced here] shows the level of the fair value valuation hierarchy applied to financial instruments carried at fair value. The total financial assets valued using level 1 is $1.5 million (2013: $1.8 million) – company: $1.5 million (2013: $1.8 million). There have been no transfers between the levels of fair value hierarchy during the current or prior year. Randgold does not hold any financial instruments that are fair valued using a level 2 or level 3 valuation. No derivative financial instruments currently exist. All other financial instrument carrying values approximate fair value.

Estimation of fair values

Trade and other receivables, trade and other payables, cash and cash equivalents, loans to and from subsidiaries and joint ventures

The carrying amounts are a reasonable estimate of the fair values because of the short maturity of such instruments or their interest bearing nature.

Gold price contracts

The group is fully exposed to the spot gold price on gold sales.

Randgold Resources Ltd, Annual Report, 2014, p. 238

Randgold Resources Limited is an Africa focused gold mining and exploration company. The company is listed on the London Stock Exchange and on NASDAQ. The company shows the detailed information in a table which is not reproduced here.

The company in Company example 12.2 uses fair value but has no financial instruments in the Level 2 or 3 hierarchies. In addition, it states that it does not have any derivatives. It does have trade and other receivables, payables, cash and loans. The company correctly points out that these have a short maturity time. IFRS requires an entity to use the best information available when pricing the asset or liability and the carrying amounts are a reasonable estimate of fair value. Financial instruments with a long maturity time would require further calculations.

NOTES

1 The IFRS's *Project Summary: IFRS Financial Instruments* (IFRS Foundation 2014) explains the rationale for the development of the requirements in the standard.

CONCLUSIONS

Although the IASB has made considerable efforts to answer the criticisms of accounting for financial instruments, we suspect that we have not reached the final stage. In 2015, there were several standards in issue dealing with various aspects of accounting requirements. We summarize the position by listing the standards, their issue date, the date of the latest amendment and the date that the standard became (or becomes) effective in Table 12.7.

For preparers, users and auditors, the mix of standards regulating differing aspects of financial instruments, with various effective dates and a significant number of amendments and revisions over the years, makes the regulatory framework difficult to understand.

In defence of the IASB, one can argue that the complexity of the accounting regime is a result of the complexity and rapid changes in the use, and abuse, of financial instruments. The convergence project with the FASB also involved considerable discussions that did not achieve agreement.

The IASB, with the issue of IFRS 9, claims that it has 'completed the final element of its comprehensive response to the financial crisis' (IFRS Foundation 2014). Undoubtedly, it has met many of the challenges and, as more entities apply IFRS 9, so the relationship of the various standards will become clearer.

Unfortunately, we suspect that accounting for financial instruments will remain a major topic for the IASB. The complete solution may not rest in the power of the standard setters but in the strength of the legal requirements established by various governments. The 2007/8 financial crisis was not only due to defects in accounting regulations but also to the methods that some entities adopted in the use of financial instruments.

▼ Table 12.7 *Summary of standards*

Standard	Issue date	Date effective	Most recent amendment
IAS 32	1995	2014	1996
IAS 39	1998	2001	2014
IFRS 7	2005	2007	2014, effective 2016
IFRS 9	2009	2018	–
IFRS 13	2011	2013	–

IN THE PIPELINE

Not surprisingly, with so many new standards, changes are taking place. We list below the changes that were taking place as of 30 June 2016. We anticipate other changes will occur in the future.

IFRS 9 Financial Instruments

The Board has commenced a research project to address the temporary accounting consequences of the different effective dates of IFRS 9 and the new insurance contracts standard, IFRS 4 *Insurance Contracts*.

IFRS 13 Fair Value Measurement

The Board has commenced a research project concerning financial assets that are investments in subsidiaries, joint ventures and associates measured at fair value. The project also addresses questions received on the interaction between the use of Level 1 inputs and the measurement of quoted investments at fair value and the portfolio exception in IFRS 13 *Fair Value Measurement*.

IAS 32 Financial Instruments: Presentation

The Board is assessing:

(a) the classification of liabilities and equity in IAS 32 *Financial Instruments: Presentation*, including investigating potential amendments to the definitions of liabilities and equity in the *Conceptual Framework*; and

(b) the presentation and disclosure requirements for financial instruments with characteristics of equity, irrespective of whether they are classified as liabilities or equity.

The next stage is likely to be a discussion paper

Financial instruments with characteristics of both liabilities and equity

The Board is assessing whether there can be improvements to the classification of these financial instruments and the requirements for presentation and disclosure.

Proposed amendments to IFRS 3 and IFRS 11

Exposure Draft: Definition of a business and accounting for previously held interests was issued in June 2016 (ED/2016/1 Definition of a Business and Accounting for Previously Held Interests).

ADDITIONAL RESOURCES

Go online to the companion website for this book to access further teaching and learning materials for this chapter.
www.palgravehighered.com/hussey-cfr

13

ACCOUNTING POLICIES AND PROVISIONS

IAS 8 Accounting Policies, Changes in Accounting Estimates and Errors

IAS 37 Provisions, Contingent Assets and Contingent Liabilities

LEARNING OBJECTIVES

At the end of this chapter, you should be able to:

- Differentiate between accounting policies, changes in accounting estimates and prior period errors
- Explain the criteria for determining a provision
- Identify those circumstances where a provision cannot be made
- Identify the criteria for contingent liabilities
- Differentiate between provisions and current liabilities
- Explain contingent assets

INTRODUCTION

Some standards do not address a specific financial statement or items but are more general in their coverage. These standards help provide a context in which to place the entity's activities. They also ensure that users receive relevant information that other specific standards do not include. In this chapter, we deal with two standards that help to frame the context in which users can better understand financial statements.

IAS 8 *Accounting Policies, Changes in Accounting Estimates and Errors* is the key to understanding the financial statements of an entity. The standard covers three aspects: policies, estimates and errors.

The disclosure of accounting policies assists users in understanding how an entity accounts for its transactions and events. Annual financial statements include many pages explaining the entity's policies used in constructing the financial statements.

In preparing its financial statements, entities must make some estimates because not all of the information will be available. The entity must therefore make estimates based on the most recent information it has. In Chapter 8, we discussed depreciation and the need for management to determine the useful economic life of an asset and its future disposal value.

As the years pass so management may revise its estimates. IAS 8 explains the procedure for making changes in the financial statements. A change in an estimate will affect an entity's expected future benefits and obligations and therefore it must adjust its financial statements.

In addition to policies and estimates, IAS 8 also addresses prior period errors. It is possible that there was a mistake in past financial statements but the entity has only now realized it. Errors can be due to occurrences such as computer malfunctions, fraud, or mistakes in applying accounting policies. These errors are not changes in accounting policies or in accounting estimates.

If the entity, unknowingly, published information that was misleading, it can now correct the error. The error may be so minor as to have no material effect on the financial statements. Where the error is material the entity must correct it retrospectively. The standard explains the procedure.

The second standard we discuss, IAS 37 *Provisions, Contingent Liabilities and Contingent Assets*, has the objective of preventing accounting abuses. At one time entities had considerable latitude in making provisions for future events. It is reasonable for entities to make a provision for some future occurrence it anticipates. However, they should not use these provisions as a method for managing earnings or misdirecting shareholders. The standard requires that there is a future obligation arising from a past event, payment is probable and a reliable estimate can be made of the amount.

Although an entity may wish to make a provision, the circumstances may not satisfy the above criteria. In particular, there may be a level of uncertainty. The standard sets out the treatment of these uncertainties under the topics of contingent liabilities and contingent assets.

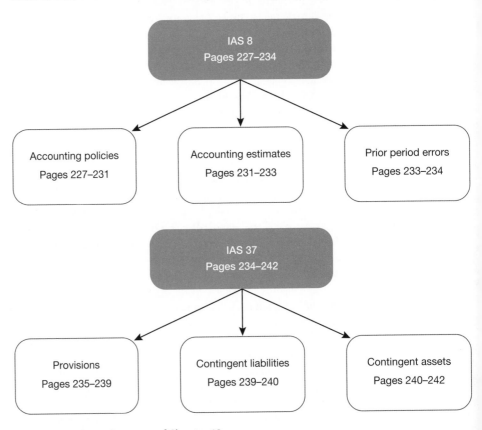

▲ **Diagram 13.1** *Structure of Chapter 13*

IAS 8

ACCOUNTING POLICIES, CHANGES IN ACCOUNTING ESTIMATES AND ERRORS

▼ Table 13.1 *Timeline of IAS 8*

Date	Comment
1978	Standard first issued
2003	Latest revision
2005	Effective date for revised standard

Accounting policies

accounting policies

Accounting policies are the specific principles, bases, conventions, rules and practices applied by an entity in preparing and presenting financial statements

Based on IAS 8, para. 5

As can be seen from the definition of **accounting policies**, the standard includes all the financial statements and the decisions or choices the board makes when it is selecting the way it accounts for and discloses financial transactions and events.

The standard sets out the criteria for selecting and applying accounting policies, and accounting for changes in accounting policies. IAS 1 *Presentation of Financial Statements* requires the disclosure of these policies, the judgements used in applying them, and assumptions and other sources of estimation uncertainty.

The purpose of accounting policies

The purpose of disclosing the accounting policies is to assist users in better understanding the treatment of transactions, other events and conditions in the financial report. The following arguments support the disclosure of accounting policies:

- The users of the financial statements would expect the entity to disclose certain policies because of the nature of its operations.
- A policy may be significant in the present financial period because of the nature of the entity's operations even if amounts for current and prior periods are not material.
- An entity has selected a particular policy from alternatives allowed in IFRSs.

Usually the statement on accounting policies precedes the financial statements. Company example 13.1 overleaf demonstrates the importance that directors attach to the disclosures.

The company identifies the following three 'critical' accounting policies:

- Revenue and profit recognition;
- Carrying value of intangible assets;
- Value of retirement benefit obligations.

In addition to these three, BAE notes that there have been changes in disclosure requirements (Company example 13.2 overleaf).

Accounting policy disclosures of companies applying IFRS often fill many pages in the notes accompanying the financial statements because companies usually disclose more than just the significant accounting policies. There has been discussion and experiments by companies in determining the most effective way to make the disclosures.

Company example 13.1

BAE Systems

Principal accounting policies, judgements and estimates

The principal accounting policies applied in the preparation of these consolidated financial statements are set out in the relevant notes. These policies have been applied consistently to all the years presented, unless otherwise stated.

Certain of the Group's principal accounting policies are considered by the directors to be critical because of the level of complexity, judgement or estimation involved in their application and their impact on the consolidated financial statements. The critical accounting policies are listed below and explained in more detail in the relevant notes to the Group accounts...

BAE Systems, Annual Report and Accounts, 2014, p. 102

Company example 13.2

BAE Systems

Changes in accounting policies

With effect from 1 January 2014, the Group has adopted the following new standards and amendments to existing standards:

– IFRS 10, Consolidated Financial Statements
– IFRS 11, Joint Arrangements
– IFRS 12, Disclosure of Interests in Other Entities
– IAS 27, Separate Financial Statements (revised 2011)
– IAS 28, Investments in Associates and Joint Ventures (revised 2011)

With the exception of new disclosure requirements, none of these have impacted the consolidated financial statements of the Group.

There are no other EU-endorsed IFRSs or IFRIC interpretations that are not yet effective that are expected to have a material impact on the Group.

IFRS 15, Revenue from Contracts with Customers, issued in May 2014, is not yet EU endorsed. Management is in the process of reviewing the impact that this will have on the Group.

IFRS 9, Financial Instruments, issued in July 2014, is not yet EU endorsed. It is not expected to have a material impact on the Group.

BAE Systems, Annual Report and Accounts, 2014, p. 103

The FRC's Financial Reporting Lab (2014) has conducted research into the possible needs of users. It concluded that investors apply their knowledge and experience to determine which accounting policies are significant for an entity's specific business and transactions. However, their report identified several attributes that make policies significant and we summarize these below.

Material transaction classes and amounts

Not every material balance indicates a significant policy but the policy on revenue is always significant. Investors are particularly interested in policies that are important or unique to the business' operations.

Accounting policy choices

The number of explicit choices of accounting policy allowed in IFRS is decreasing. Where a choice is allowed, that policy should be considered significant unless it is clearly immaterial.

Judgement and/or estimation

Accounting policies that require significant levels of estimation and/or judgement in their application are significant. Investors want insight into the sensitivity of balances and earnings amounts stemming from elements of estimation and judgement.

*   *   *

Investors in the FRC study wanted accounting policy disclosure to be entity-specific, and it should enable a user to understand:

- the relevance of the policy to the entity and its business transactions;
- where the entity has made a policy choice and why that choice is most appropriate for the business;
- how the entity applies its policies;
- the impact of judgement and estimation required in the application; and
- consequences for the reported amounts.

Selecting and applying accounting policies

Users cannot understand the financial statements unless they know the policies the entity selects in compiling the financial information. They can analyze an entity's results over several years with confidence if there have been no changes in policies. If there have been changes, users are interested in the reasons for the change and the possible impact on the financial results. If the IASB has revised a standard, users have less concern because the entity is complying with the regulations.

An entity should follow the requirements of standards or interpretations in selecting and applying its accounting policies and introducing any subsequent changes. Where the regulations do not address specific issues, the management must use its own judgement in setting its policy by referring to the following sources:

- any other IASB standard or interpretation dealing with relevant matters;
- definitions, recognition criteria and measurement concepts for assets, liabilities, income and expenses contained in the IASB's Framework for the Preparation and Presentation of Financial Statements;
- recent pronouncements by other standard-setting bodies that do not conflict with IFRSs and Framework.

The listing of an entity's accounting policies in its annual report and accounts is critical, but may present the user with some difficulty in understanding their application. Volvo is one company that has addressed this weakness in disclosure (see Company example 13.3).

The Volvo Group is one of the world's leading manufacturers of trucks, buses, construction equipment and marine and industrial engines. Its headquarters in Gothenburg employs about 100,000 people, and Volvo has production facilities in 18 countries and sells its products in more than 190 markets. We show the note on accounting policies from its annual report and accounts in Company example 13.3.

Company example 13.3

Accounting policies

The Volvo Group describes the accounting policies in conjunction with each note in the aim of providing enhanced understanding of each accounting area. The Volvo Group focuses on describing the accounting choices made within the framework of the prevailing IFRS policy and avoids repeating the actual text of the standard, unless the Volvo Group considers it particularly important to the understanding of the note's content. The following symbols **I/S** and **B/S** show which amounts in the notes that can be found in the income statement or balance sheet. The total amount in tables and statements might not always summarize as there are rounding differences. The aim is to have each line item corresponding to the source and it might therefore be rounding differences in the total. Refer to the table below [not reproduced here] to see the note in which each accounting policy is listed and for the relevant and material IFRS standard.

Volvo Group plc, Annual and Sustainability Report, 2015, p. 111

This note is followed by a very helpful linking of the policy, the accounting standard and the application of the policy. The user can trace the establishment of the policy to the relevant standard. The link can then be made with the application of the policy in the financial statements.

Although an entity should be consistent in applying its policies, there are two circumstances in which it can make a change.

- The issue by the IASB of a standard or interpretation that requires companies to make the change. In this case the new standard will provide transitional arrangements to assist the entity in introducing the change.
- The entity is of the opinion that a change is required to improve the reliability and relevance of information in the financial statements.

Company example 13.4 from Wolseley plc illustrates a change involving a retrospective adjustment. This is in respect to amendments made to IAS 19. The company is the world's leading specialist distributor of plumbing and heating products. It has 38,000 employees in over 2,700 locations.

Entities undertake a substantial amount of work to ensure that their financial statements comply with existing standards. As Company example 13.4 illustrates, they must also be familiar with new standards, amendments to existing standards and any interpretations.

Where there are amendments, the entity must apply the change retrospectively to all periods presented in the financial statements as if the new accounting policy had always been applied. In other words, the financial statements of the current period and each prior period presented in the current annual report are adjusted so that it appears as if the new accounting policy had always been the one used.

Retrospective application can create a substantial amount of work for an entity. The standard setters recognize this and an entity need not make retrospective application where it is impracticable and the entity has made every reasonable effort to do so.

> ### Company example 13.4
>
> ## Accounting developments and changes
>
> IAS 19 (as revised in June 2011) 'Employee Benefits' has been adopted by the Group in the current financial year and has been applied retrospectively. The interest cost and expected return on defined benefit pension scheme assets used in the previous version of IAS 19 are replaced with a 'net interest' amount, which is calculated by applying a single discount rate to the net defined benefit liability or asset.
>
> Furthermore, IAS 19 (Revised) also introduces more extensive disclosures in the presentation of the defined benefit cost, including the clarification on treatment of the schemes' administrative expenses. To aid comparison, the consolidated financial statements and affected notes for the year ended 31 July 2013 have been restated, with the following effects on the previous year's consolidated financial statement…
>
> *Wolseley plc, Annual Report and Accounts, 2014, p. 110*

There is some potential for scope in judgement regarding terms such as 'impracticable' and 'reasonable effort'. The standard aims to ensure that entities do not overstretch the notion of impracticability and requires that entities meet the following criteria:

- The effects of the retrospective application cannot be determined, or require assumptions about what would have been management's intent at that time.
- Significant estimates of amounts are required and it is impossible to distinguish objectively information about those estimates that:
  o provides evidence of circumstances that existed on the dates at which those amounts are to be recognized, measured and disclosed, and
  o would have been available when the financial statements for that prior period were authorized for issue from other information.

The ability of management to change accounting policies is severely restricted and should not be confused with accounting estimates that we discuss in the next section.

Accounting estimates

At the year-end, when an entity is preparing its financial statements, not all the information that is required will be available. The entity must therefore make estimates. Examples of activities where estimates may be required include:

- Doubtful debts – this is the amount customers owe but the entity believes it may not be able to collect for various reasons. An estimate must be made on the amount which is not collectable.
- Depreciation – companies have to estimate both the useful economic life of the asset and the future scrap value of the asset. These estimates may change for many reasons. Machinery and equipment may last longer than anticipated, possibly because there has not been significant usage.
- Inventory obsolescence. At the year-end an entity may have closing inventory. It has to place a value on the inventory, and we discussed the approach in Chapter 8.

- The carrying value of assets that may be subject to impairment. For example, machinery may have become technologically impaired. We discussed IAS 36 *Impairment of Assets* in Chapter 5.

Understandably, as time progresses, entities receive new information and this may cause them to change their estimates. The standard explains how these changes are actioned in the financial statements. A change in an estimate affects the expected future benefits and obligations of the entity. The entity, therefore, must adjust the financial statements.

The standard emphasizes that changes in accounting estimates are not corrections of errors but estimates resulting from new information or new developments. The estimates involve the carrying amount on the balance sheet of an asset or a liability or the amount of the periodic consumption of an asset, in other words, the asset's expected life.

There is no need to change the financial statements for previous years because the entity issued these based on the best information available at that time. When there is a change in estimates, an entity should change the financial statements in the present period and in future periods if appropriate. We show two hypothetical examples in Scenario 13.1 and Worked example 13.1 of appropriate changes in accounting estimates.

Scenario 13.1   Change in doubtful debts estimate

An entity knows from experience that it will not be able to collect all the money from its customers. In the past, at the year-end it has always estimated these 'bad debts' at 2%. There has been a rapid economic decline and the entity is contemplating increasing the amount for doubtful debts from 2% to 3% of the accounts receivable. It is concerned, however, that if it changes the estimate it will have to revise the financial statements in previous years.

Under IAS 8, this is a change in the accounting estimate. The entity does not have to revise previous financial statements because they were constructed on the best information at that time, that is, when the economy was healthier.

Note that sometimes entities will refer to a provision for doubtful debts or credit losses. These terms are misleading. Doubtful debts are an **estimate** and IAS 8 sets out the accounting treatment. IAS 37 defines **provisions** and sets out their accounting treatment.

Worked example 13.1   Change of asset life estimate

A company purchases machinery on 1 January 2012 for £100,000. The company considers that the machinery has a useful life of 10 years and no residual value. The annual depreciation charge using the straight line method is:

$$\text{Annual depreciation charge} = \frac{£100,000}{10 \text{ years}} = £10,000$$

Three years later, on 31 December 2014 the carrying amount of the machinery is £70,000.

On 1 January 2015, the company decides that the remaining useful life of the machinery is only 5 years and not 7 years. The annual depreciation charge from 1 January 2015 and for the following years will be:

$$\text{Annual depreciation charge} = \frac{£70,000}{5 \text{ years}} = £14,000$$

We discussed depreciation in Chapter 4 and at greater length in Chapter 8. Depreciation is calculated by an entity estimating the economic life of an asset and the residual value, if any, at the end of that life.

As with doubtful debts, an entity should not apply any change in accounting estimates retrospectively. The original depreciation amount was estimated on the best information at that time. In Worked example 13.1, it was 10 years.

The entity has now received new information that persuades it to change its estimates of the life of the asset. This could be due to greater usage of the asset, technological changes, poor maintenance or other factors. The depreciation charge has to be changed in the current and future years.

Prior period errors

> **prior period errors**
>
> Prior period errors are omissions from, and misstatements in, the entity's financial statements for one or more prior periods arising from a failure to use, or misuse of, reliable information.
>
> *IAS 8, para. 5*

We all make mistakes and entities are no exception. If we know we have made a mistake then we have the opportunity to correct it. The standard refers to **prior period errors**. These arise where there was a mistake in past financial statements but the entity has now realized it. Examples of prior period errors are:

- mathematical errors;
- fraud;
- mistakes in applying accounting policies;
- misinterpretations or failure to observe facts.

Such errors are not changes in accounting policies or changes in accounting estimates. The entity has made a mistake in its financial statements. Errors will frequently be so insignificant they have no impact on the financial statements. In this case, the error can be corrected through net profit or loss for the current period.

To determine whether an error is insignificant, an entity has to apply the concept of materiality. This can be difficult to determine. The standard explains that an error is material if it could influence the economic decisions of users. For example, if fraud had occurred or the entity had incorrectly arrived at a higher figure for closing inventory and this led to a very favourable profit, investors may be enthusiastic to purchase shares.

The standard adds that materiality depends on the size and nature of the omission or misstatement judged in the surrounding circumstances. This leaves it to the entity to determine materiality and whether users will make different economic decisions. This is a difficult task and you may consider that the accounting requirements are not rigorous. The IASB are reconsidering the concept of materiality, as we explained in Chapter 3.

Where the error is material the entity must correct it retrospectively. There are two possibilities:

- Restating the comparative amounts for the prior periods in which the error occurred.
- Where the error occurred before the earliest prior period presented, restating the opening balances of assets, liabilities and equity for that period.

For example, if a prior period error has occurred the entity must adjust the financial statements for when it occurred and not the present financial statements. Thus, an entity preparing its financial statements for 2014 may find a previous error in the 2013 financial statements. The correction should not be made in the 2014 financial statements but in the year when the error took place. To do otherwise would make the 2013 financial statements incorrect.

Prior period errors are fundamental in nature because they have a direct effect on the information reported in the financial statements. An entity should recognize them only if it is clear that they should not have issued the original financial statements because of these errors.

The error could have arisen due to a fault in an accounting estimate. However, it was the best estimate that the entity could make at that time with the information available. In this situation, the error is a change in accounting estimates.

As with accounting policies, the standard permits companies not to make the changes if it would be impracticable, but various disclosures are required.

IAS 37

PROVISIONS, CONTINGENT LIABILITIES AND CONTINGENT ASSETS

▼ Table 13.2 *Timeline of IAS 37*

Date	Comment
1998	Standard first issued
2005	Proposal for change but none made
Latest interpretation	IFRIC 21 Levies

This standard attempts to regulate the way that companies account for future uncertainties. It deals with three related topics: provisions, contingent liabilities and contingent assets, as shown in Diagram 13.2.

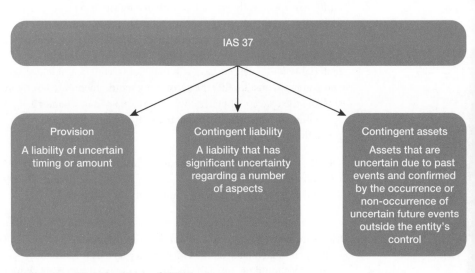

▲ **Diagram 13.2** *Structure of IAS 37*

Provisions

Some people refer to 'provision for depreciation' and 'provision for doubtful debts'. Neither of these items are provisions under IAS 37. As we stated earlier in the chapter, they are accounting estimates and IAS 8 sets out the requirements for accounting estimates. We discussed that standard in the previous section.

IAS 37 was introduced to prevent dubious accounting practices that were being exploited by some entities. For example, an entity could use a provision to manage the amount of profit reported. If the entity had a very profitable year, it could reduce the profit by creating a provision: a type of fund to deal with future uncertainties. If in future years, profits declined for some reason, the entity could reverse these provisions to boost their profits.

Some types of provisions were known as 'big bath provisions' or 'cookie jar provisions'. Entities were using them to sweeten their profits and clean up any financial messes they did not like. The result was that the financial statements for any particular financial period could mislead users.

The standard introduces the criteria that an entity must fulfil to make a provision. Essentially a provision is a liability of uncertain timing or amount. Diagram 13.3 illustrates the four key criteria for determining whether the entity can make a provision.

We will break down the steps and explain each stage.

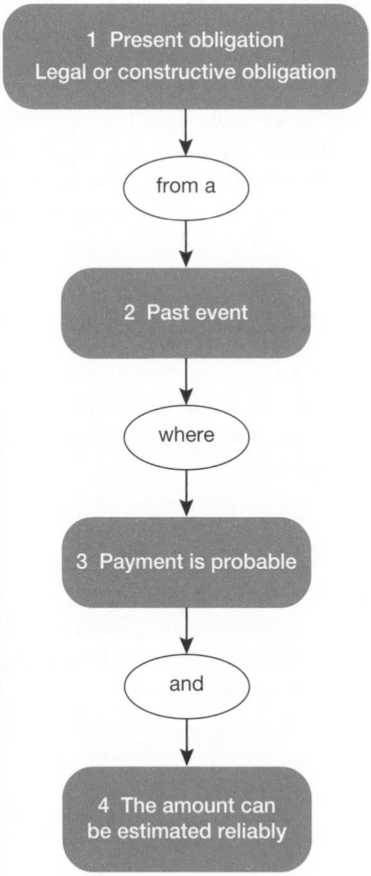

Step 1   Present obligation

There must be a present obligation; in other words, a present liability. The standard defines two types of obligations: legal and constructive. A legal obligation is possibly the easiest to identify and could be:

- a contract entered into by the parties;
- due to legislation;
- a result from some other operation of law.

If an entity is embroiled in a court case, there will be some uncertainty as to whether the entity has a present obligation. It needs to know whether it is likely to win or lose the case. In such an event, the entity would seek legal advice as to the likely outcome. If the advice is that the entity is probably going to lose the case, the entity makes a provision for the estimated amount of damages.

When we are considering court cases for international companies, the time span can be many years and the levels of uncertainty complex. Company example 13.5 overleaf from the 2014 annual report and accounts of Diageo plc exemplifies the problems facing accountants in determining the appropriate level of disclosure. The key words in the extract are 'meaningfully quantify'.

This note illustrates the problems of the time such cases can take and the levels of uncertainty. The action was first launched in 2004. It was not dismissed until eight years later. Even at that stage in 2012, the plaintiffs still have the right to take similar legal action in the future. Understandably, Diageo cannot meaningfully quantify the potential losses of any future legal action. It does not even know whether such legal action will be taken.

Constructive obligation

This is an obligation arising from an entity's own practices or policies in that it has led others to believe that it will act in a certain way. This includes those

▲ Diagram 13.3
Criteria for a provision

> ### Company example 13.5
>
> **(b) Colombian litigation**
>
> An action was filed on 8 October 2004 in the United States District Court for the Eastern District of New York by the Republic of Colombia and a number of its local government entities against Diageo and other spirits companies, alleging several causes of action, including violations of the Federal RICO Act. This claim was dismissed in November 2012. The dismissal was without prejudice and as such, plaintiffs are not barred from bringing a similar action in future. Diageo cannot meaningfully quantify the possible loss or range of loss in the event of any future litigation. Diageo remains committed to continued dialogue with the Colombian governmental entities to address the underlying issues.
>
> *Diageo plc, Annual Report and Accounts, 2014, p. 130*

circumstances where past practice leads third parties to assume that the entity will settle the obligation. For example, a retailer may have a favourable return policy on goods purchased by customers. A constructive obligation is established.

Step 2   Past event

The standard refers to the past event as an obligating event. The entity has taken or not taken some action in the past that results in it having a present obligation now. It is very important under the standard that companies do not make provisions for something they consider may happen in the future. For example, businesses cannot make provisions for future operating losses.

Step 3   Payment is probable

The payment will involve an outflow of economic resources and it is more likely than not that the entity will have to make this payment. This is a challenging judgement that management has to make. Probable is explained by the phrase 'more likely than not' but this could be construed in several ways, particularly where the issues are complex. Management will disclose their reasoning and their policy in the annual report and accounts.

Step 4   Amount can be estimated reliably

Reliably does not mean exactly. If you refer to the definition, it states that a provision is uncertain in amount. The amount recognized as a provision should be the best estimate of the expenditure required to settle the present obligation at the balance sheet date. A business should assess the risks and uncertainties that may operate in reaching their best estimate. If there are any material future cash flows, the entity should discount these to present values.

If the entity considers that it can estimate the amount reliably, this could be an indication that payment is probable.

*   *   *

Examples of provisions include warranty obligations, a retailer's policy on refunds to customers, obligation to clean up contaminated land, and restructuring and onerous contracts.

The regulations on the requirement to make a provision are unambiguous and the hypothetical Scenario 13.2 demonstrates the position.

> ### Scenario 13.2   Legal obligation
>
> Incomp plc operates in the UK where there is legislation compelling the entity to clean up environmental damage it may cause. In the month of December 2015, the company causes environmental damage and estimates that it will cost approximately £750,000 to remedy. It intends to carry out this work in June 2016. Its year-end is 31 December. What action should Incomp plc take?
>
> Some may argue that the cost has not been incurred and should not appear on the financial statements. Even if one accepts the company caused environmental damage, some unforeseen events may occur and the company does not have to remedy the damage. Notwithstanding these arguments, IAS 37 is clear that Incomp should make a provision for the full amount in the financial statements for the year ended 31 December 2015.

There are occasions where an entity might consider making a provision but the situation does not meet the requirement of the standard. Essentially, there is not a present obligation because of a past event. The most common examples are where the entity is confronting a future problem or opportunity and is making the decision in the current financial year but will not take action until the following year.

For example, an entity may be aware that a competitor is launching a new product next year that will affect its own sales. It decides to launch its own version of the product next year with a massive advertising campaign. However, the entity cannot make a provision this year for the campaign it plans for next year.

Exceptions to accounting for provisions requirements

The standard refers specifically to some events that do not meet the conditions of the standard but where an entity can make a provision. The first we discuss is where some form of entity restructuring is taking place. The second is where there are onerous contracts.

Corporate restructuring

It is not unusual for entities to decide that they need to make some form of organizational restructure. This could be the closure of parts of the business or some form of amalgamations or reorganization. The entity may have determined in the present financial year on the action it will take but have decided not to implement it until the following year.

As this is a future and not a past event, it does not meet the main requirements of the standard. However, if the entity complies with the criteria laid down in the standard for restructuring it may make a provision. The events recognized in the standard as entity restructuring are:

- Sale or termination of a line of business.
- The closure of a business location in a country or region or the relocation of business activities from one country.
- Changes in management structure, for example, eliminating a layer of management.
- Fundamental reorganizations that have a material effect on the nature and focus of the business operations.

Where the above events are going to occur, the restructuring may be identified as a constructive obligation. The standard defines this as an obligation arising from an entity's own practices or policies in that it has led others to believe that the entity will act in a certain way. To demonstrate there is a constructive obligation, the entity must fulfil two criteria.

1   There must be a detailed formal plan.
2   The entity communicates the plan to those affected by the restructuring.

The main contents of a formal plan are shown in Table 13.3.

▼ **Table 13.3** *Outline of a formal restructuring plan*

- The business or part of a business concerned
- The principal locations affected
- The location, function and approximate number of employees who will be compensated for terminating their services.
- Suppliers and customers who will be affected
- The expenditure that will be undertaken
- The date the plan will be implemented.

The critical element in the plan is the communication to those likely to be most affected: the employees who will lose their jobs. It is normal for an entity to make a public announcement and discuss the details of the plan with those affected. Frequently, the trade unions will be closely involved if there are any in the organization. We demonstrate the importance of the timing in the Scenarios 13.3 and 13.4.

Scenario 13.3   Provisions for restructuring

Martino plc makes up its annual financial statements to 30 April. The Board approves on 20 March 2016 the permanent closure of one of its factories on 31 July in that year. The Board is unable to communicate its decision to any of those affected before 30 April.

Should the Board make a provision for the intended closure?

In these circumstances no provision for the costs to be incurred in 2016 can be made in the financial statements.

Scenario 13.4

The details are similar to Scenario 13.3, but by 12 April the company has informed the affected employees at a meeting and has written to all its suppliers and customers. In this case, a provision can be made in its financial statements for the year ended 30 April 2016 for the costs it can reliably estimate that it will incur.

Onerous contracts

During the course of business, an entity will enter into many contracts. Some will have terms that allow it to cancel the contract without incurring any financial penalties. There are others containing terms that compel the entity to pay some form of damages on cancellation of the contract. This falls under the concept of onerous contracts and the entity is able to make a provision.

An example of an onerous contract is a non-cancellable lease. An entity may enter into a non-cancellable lease to occupy office premises. With two years of the lease remaining, the entity decides to move to another location. The lease is non-cancellable so the entity still has to make the lease payments for the office it is vacating until the end of the contract. The accepted accounting method is to make a provision for the outstanding amounts that the lessee still has to pay to the lessor under the lease agreement. There are changes to accounting for leases which will be effective in 2018. We discuss these fully in Chapter 14.

Reversing provisions

An entity may have made a provision that complies fully with the standard. For example, there may be a planned restructuring and all the various parties affected have been informed. However, circumstances may have changed and the restructuring will not take place. As the provision is no longer required, the entity should reverse the provision by a credit to the profit or loss account.

The standard requires entities to make an annual review of provisions. If the provisions are no longer required, they should be reversed. The entity cannot use a provision it made for one eventuality that did not occur for another eventuality that was not predicted.

Contingent liabilities

contingent liability

A contingent liability is where there is significant uncertainty with a number of aspects regarding the liability.

IAS 37, para. 10

The criteria for identifying a provision are clear. There is a present obligation because of a past event and there is a probable outflow of resources. If the past event does not give rise to a provision, the next stage is a **contingent liability**.

IAS 37 contains guidance to its implementation, including the requirements for a past event to be classified as a contingent liability instead of a provision. The difference between the two is the level of certainty.

The key term in the definition of contingent liability is 'significant uncertainty' and this can take one of two forms:

1 There is a possible obligation, arising from past events, but more information is required to determine whether it is a present obligation. Note that the term 'present obligation' refers to provisions that we discussed earlier in the chapter.
2 There is a present obligation but it is uncertain whether it will be settled or it cannot be measured reliably.

The standard requires contingent liabilities to be disclosed in the notes in the annual report and accounts whereas provisions appear as a charge in the profit or loss account.

There is a relationship between provisions and contingent liabilities. Differentiating between the two is a matter of the level of certainty and this may take a considerable time to determine. For example, an entity may recognize a particular event as a contingent liability. However, as time passes, the nature of the event changes. It may change to such an extent that the entity can define it as a provision, as shown in Diagram 13.4 overleaf.

Scenario 13.5 overleaf illustrates the 'certainty' relationship between a contingent liability and a provision.

In specific cases, it may be very difficult to differentiate between provisions and contingent liabilities. It is most prudent for entities to make some form of disclosure. However, where the possibility of an outflow of resources embodying economic benefits is remote, the standard does not require disclosure.

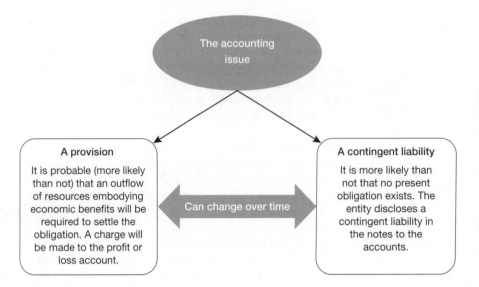

▲ **Diagram 13.4** *Provisions and contingent liabilities*

Scenario 13.5   Contingent liability to provision

Pitfalls plc is being sued for damages by one of its major customers who commences legal action in 2014. When preparing the year-end 2014 financial statements the directors' opinion was that the likelihood of their making any payments to the claimant was **remote**. In accordance with IAS 37, they did not adjust their financial statements or make any disclosures.

In 2015 the court case was still proceeding. The company's lawyers informed the directors that they considered that it was **possible** that the customer would win the case. The directors therefore disclosed a contingent liability in Pitfall's financial statements for 2015.

In 2016, the lawyers advised Pitfalls that it was **probable** that the customer would win the case, and their best estimate was that the damages would be £2.5 million. Accordingly, the directors made a provision in the financial statements for that amount.

This example illustrates the potential difficulty in deciding what is probable, possible or remote. Pitfalls is depending on legal advice but that may not be reliable. The standard does not define these three terms and directors must make their own judgement.

You will find that most disclosures on contingent liabilities refer to court cases. As these cases can take many years to resolve, an entity may disclose a court case as a contingent liability. As the case proceeds and it becomes probable that the entity will lose the case, it will make a provision based on the best estimate of the costs it will suffer.

Contingent assets

The definition of a contingent asset, taken from the standard, is not easy to follow. They are usually related to court cases. An example is a legal claim that an entity is pursuing but is uncertain whether it will be successful. Contingent assets should not be recognized in the financial statements themselves but are disclosed when an inflow of economic benefits is probable.

contingent asset

A contingent asset is a possible asset that arises from past events and whose existence will be confirmed only by the occurrence or non-occurrence of one or more uncertain future events not wholly within the control of the entity.

IAS 37, para. 10

In a court case, an entity is dependent on legal advice. If this states that it is probable that the entity will win the case, it should disclose a **contingent asset** in the notes to the accounts. If the legal advice states that it is virtually certain that the entity will win the case, it is no longer regarded as 'contingent' and would appear in the balance sheet as an asset.

If it is only possible that the entity will win then nothing will appear in the annual report regarding the matter.

IAS 37 is a standard that causes some difficulties for entities in its application. The concepts of probable, possible and remote are matters of judgement and opinions may differ. Additionally, we are dealing with uncertainties and our ability in predicting future events and measuring them in monetary terms is not foolproof.

We illustrate the complexity of the transactions and events that may fall under IAS 37 in Company example 13.6, which is taken from the Annual Report and Accounts, 2014 of GSK. This is a lengthy note but demonstrates the problems of conducting international business, particularly in certain industries. The note also demonstrates the various stages of complying with IAS 37.

Company example 13.6

Contingent liabilities

Legal and other disputes

The Group is involved in a substantial number of legal and other disputes, including notification of possible claims, as set out in Note 45 'Legal proceedings'. Provisions for legal and other disputes include amounts relating to product liability (principally relating to *Avandia*, and *Paxil*), anti-trust (principally relating to *Wellbutrin XL* and *Lamictal*), government investigations (principally relating to the China settlement and SEC/DOJ and SFO related investigations), contract terminations, self insurance, environmental clean-up and property rental.

The charge for the year of £549 million (£547 million net of reversals and estimated insurance recoveries) included a £301 million fine paid to the Chinese government and provisions for product liability cases regarding *Paxil* and other products, commercial disputes and various other government investigations.

The discount on the provisions decreased by £nil in 2014 (2013 – £nil) and was calculated using risk-adjusted projected cash flows and risk-free rates of return. The movement in 2014 includes an increase of £1 million (2013 – £nil) arising from a change in the discount rate in the year. In respect of product liability claims related to certain products, there is sufficient history of claims made and settlements to enable management to make a reliable estimate of the provision required to cover unasserted claims. The ultimate liability for such matters may vary from the amounts provided and is dependent upon the outcome of litigation proceedings, investigations and possible settlement negotiations.

It is in the nature of the Group's business that a number of these matters may be the subject of negotiation and litigation over many years. Litigation proceedings, including the various appeal procedures, often take many years to reach resolution, and out-of-court settlement discussions can also often be protracted.

continued overleaf

Company example 13.6 *continued*

The Group is in potential settlement discussions in a number of the disputes for which amounts have been provided and, based on its current assessment of the progress of these disputes, estimates that £0.5 billion of the amount provided at 31 December 2014 will be settled within one year. At 31 December 2014, it was expected that £nil (2013 – £1 million) of the provision made for legal and other disputes will be reimbursed by third party insurers.

This amount is included within the Other receivables balances in Note 22 'Other non-current assets' and Note 24, 'Trade and other receivables'. For a discussion of legal issues, see Note 45, 'Legal proceedings'.

GSK, Annual Report and Accounts, 2014, p. 175

Users should be aware, as GSK states, that events giving rise to provisions or contingent liabilities are subject to negotiation and litigation over several years. The notes to the account inform users of probable or possible payments that a company may have to make in the future. The main difficulty lies with contingent liabilities because the uncertainties do not indicate whether there will be an impact on profits in the future.

CONCLUSIONS

IAS 8, *Accounting Policies, Changes in Accounting Estimates and Errors* and IAS 37, *Provisions, Contingent Liabilities and Contingent Assets* are key standards. They ensure that the user of financial statements can assess the context in which the financial statements are constructed.

The nature of the accounting policies that an entity decides to adopt determines the information in the financial statements. It is argued that too many entities merely repeat the wording of various standards without demonstrating the effect on their activities. The Financial Reporting Council has offered advice and guidance on how entities can improve their disclosures.

In May 2015, the IASB discussed a proposal about possible amendments to IAS 8. The proposal suggested amendments to the existing definitions of accounting policies and changes in accounting estimates. These amendments would clarify:

(a) changes in the measurement bases that are specified in relevant standards are changes in accounting policies;

(b) changes in the measurement bases include changes in cost measures and, therefore, changes in the methods used to determine different cost measures are changes in accounting policies; and

(c) changes in inputs, assumptions and methods for making an accounting estimate are changes in accounting estimates.

Although no decision was made, we can expect that the revised Conceptual Framework (see Chapter 2) may lead to changes in IAS 8, particularly the definition of a liability.

IAS 37 is future orientated in that it gives users of financial reports information on what might happen. We have given examples in this chapter from company annual reports and accounts. These emphasize the uncertainty and complexity of the business world.

Critics argue that the standard includes definitions and guides that are vague. This is to be expected because we are dealing with future events. The IASB is considering amendments to IAS 37, some of which are related to the final version of a new conceptual framework. Entities have difficulty in identifying the transactions and events that fall under the standard. Despite these deficiencies, the standard has been effective and we do not anticipate there being any major changes.

IN THE PIPELINE

As part of the IASB's Disclosure Initiative, there is a proposed amendment to clarify the existing distinction between a change in accounting policy and a change in accounting estimate. The proposal is that:

- changes in the measurement bases that are specified in relevant standards are changes in accounting policies; and
- changes in inputs, assumptions and methods that are used to make an accounting estimate are changes in accounting estimates.

The IASB is considering amendments to IAS 37. This is because of past difficulties in interpreting guidance on identifying liabilities, the inconsistency between IAS 37 criteria for recognition and those of other standards and evidence of diversity by companies in the application of the standard. The IASB is unlikely to issue a Discussion Paper until the Conceptual Framework project is completed.

ADDITIONAL RESOURCES

Go online to the companion website for this book to access further teaching and learning materials for this chapter.
www.palgravehighered.com/hussey-cfr

CHAPTER

14

INCOME
TAXES AND
LEASES

IAS 12 Income Taxes
IAS 17 Leases
IFRS 16 Leases

LEARNING OBJECTIVES

At the end of this chapter, you should be able to:

- Summarize the basic procedures for accounting for taxes in IAS 12
- Calculate the amount of deferred tax liability
- Explain the issues surrounding accounting for leases
- Compare the requirements of IFRS 16 and IAS 17
- Explain the treatment of leases under IFRS 16

INTRODUCTION

In this chapter, we cover two standards. Each standard is complete in its own right, with no strong links to other standards. If we are to understand the effect of tax and lease transactions and events on an entity's financial statements, we need to understand the requirements of the standards.

The first standard we discuss, IAS 12 *Income Taxes* applies to all entities. Profit as calculated on an income statement is not necessarily the profit that the tax authorities will use. The standard explains the accounting treatment the entity should follow. It also allows an early introduction to some of the issues that we discuss in later chapters of this book.

IAS 17 *Leases* sets out the requirements for a particular activity. Leasing is a common business transaction undertaken by many entities. There has been considerable debate for many years on how a lease should be recognized and measured. The IASB has issued IFRS 16, which takes effect in January 2019, that we discuss in this chapter.

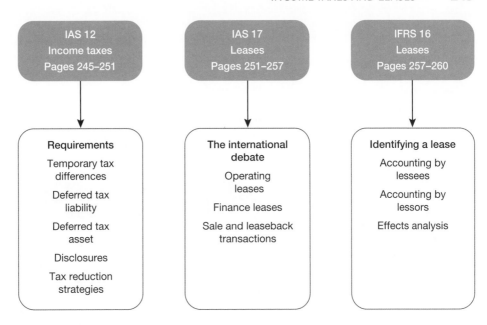

▲ Diagram 14.1 *Structure of Chapter 14*

IAS 12
INCOME TAXES

▼ Table 14.1 *Timeline of IAS 12*

Date	Comment
1979	Standard issued
2010	Latest amendment
Latest interpretation	SIC 25 Income Taxes – Changes in the Tax Status of an Enterprise or its Shareholders

Requirements of the standard

Entities usually do not pay taxes on the amount of profit shown on their profit or loss account. The entity calculates the profit shown on its financial statements using accounting regulations. The tax authorities use tax legislation to calculate the actual tax charge.

If an entity calculated its tax solely on **accounting profit**, there could be an inducement for entities to make their profit the smallest amount possible, although shareholders may not be happy. Tax authorities are not enthusiastic about entities using accounting standards to calculate profit, and use their own rules to calculate **taxable profit**. This means that we need a standard to reconcile the differences between the accounting and tax methods for calculating taxable profits.

accounting profit

The accounting profit is the profit or loss for a period before deducting the tax expense.

Based on IAS 12, para. 5

taxable profit (taxable loss)

The taxable profit (loss) is the profit (loss) for a period, determined in accordance with the rules established by the taxation authorities, upon which income taxes are payable (recoverable).

Based on IAS 12, para. 5

tax expense (tax income)

The tax expense (income) is the aggregate amount included in the determination of profit or loss for the period in respect of current tax and deferred tax.

Based on IAS 12, para. 5

current tax

The current tax is the amount of income taxes payable (recoverable) in respect of the taxable profit (tax loss) for a period.

Based on IAS 12, para. 5

Each country has its own tax laws even if entities are using international standards. Tax legislation therefore determines what the entity's **current tax expense** will be in a particular country. Adjustments are made to the current tax expense so that the reported tax charge is consistent with the reported profit for the period.

Tax legislation will vary from country to country. This can raise difficulties in the interpretation of the legislation within that country and compliance with IAS 12. Company example 14.1 emphasizes some of the problems confronting companies.

> ### Company example 14.1
>
> ### Tax legislation
>
> The taxation system and regulatory environment of the Russian Federation are characterized by numerous taxes and frequently changing legislation, which is often unclear, contradictory and subject to varying interpretations between the differing regulatory authorities and jurisdictions, who are empowered to impose significant fines, penalties and interest charges.
>
> *PAO Severstal, Annual Report, 2015, p. 131*

PAO Severstal ('Severstal', 'the Company', or 'the Group') is a vertically integrated steel and steel-related mining company with major assets in Russia, as well as investments in other regions. The auditors report that Severstal's financial statements comply with IFRSs. The company's opinions on tax legislation probably are shared by companies in some other countries. Compliance with IAS 12 is therefore challenging.

The objective of IAS 12 is to set the accounting treatment for income taxes for entities using IFRSs. This includes all domestic and foreign taxes calculated on taxable profits. The standard also deals with transactions and other events of the current period that are recognized in the financial statements. These are:

- recognition of deferred tax assets arising from unused tax losses or unused tax credits;
- the presentation of income taxes in the financial statements;
- the disclosure of information relating to income taxes.

Temporary tax differences

temporary difference

Temporary difference is the difference between the carrying amount of an asset or liability and its tax base.

Based on IAS 12, para. 6

Temporary differences give rise to deferred tax and this section concentrates on that issue (see Diagram 14.2).

Deferred tax is the difference between the current tax expense and the adjusted figure. The main differences between the taxable 'profit' and the entity's reported profits are:

- The depreciation calculated under IAS 16 for reporting purposes differs from the allowances accepted by the tax authorities.

taxable temporary difference

A taxable temporary difference is a temporary difference that will result in taxable amounts in the future when the carrying amount of the asset is recovered or the liability is settled.

Based on IAS 12, para. 6

deductible temporary difference

A deductible temporary difference is a temporary difference that will result in amounts that are tax deductible in the future when the carrying amount of the asset is recovered or the liability is settled.

Based on IAS 12, para. 6

permanent difference

A permanent difference is a one-off difference due to certain transactions not being taxable.

Based on IAS 12, para. 6

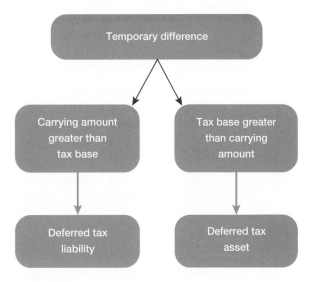

▲ Diagram 14.2 *Basis of temporary tax differences*

- Employee expenditure is recognized when incurred for accounting purposes and when paid for tax purposes.
- Costs of research and development are charged in the income statement in one period for accounting purposes but allowed for tax purposes in another period.

Deferred tax liability

> **Worked example 14.1   Calculation of deferred tax liability**
>
> An entity purchases machinery for £120,000. The life of the machinery is estimated at three years with a nil scrap value. The depreciation charge in Year 1 to the profit or loss account is £40,000. The carrying value shown in the balance sheet at the year-end is £80,000.
>
> The tax legislation allows the full cost of the asset in Year 1 of £120,000. There is a 'temporary' difference of £80,000. The tax expense shown in the profit or loss account is £40,000 in the first year. However, under tax legislation the entity received tax relief of £120,000.
>
> The actual current tax expense the company bears is lower than that calculated on the reported profits in the profit or loss account. The deferred tax liability shows the liability of the company in future years. Of course, if the entity is growing and each year is acquiring non-current assets it could be several years before the entity has to pay the full tax charge.

Users may misinterpret the reported profit without knowing that the entity has enjoyed significant tax relief. To remedy this, the entity must inform the user of the deferred tax as a deferred tax liability because this amount becomes an actual tax liability in future periods. An entity should recognize a deferred tax liability in full for all tax differences unless it arises from:

- goodwill for which amortization is not deductible for tax purposes;
- the initial recognition of an asset/liability that is not part of a business combination and affects neither the accounting or the taxable profit at the time of the transaction;

- investments where the enterprise is able to control the timing of reversal of the tax difference and it is probable that the reversal will not occur in the foreseeable future.

The accounting requirements and the tax legislation in the UK make it highly likely that the profit shown in the profit or loss account for one particular year is different from the amount of profit on which tax is calculated. These differences are only temporary and there will be a reversal adjustment at some future stage.

The entity must make a provision for the deferred tax using the liability method, which is also known as the statement of financial position liability method or simply as the balance sheet liability method. We illustrate the calculations in Worked example 14.2.

Worked example 14.2   The balance sheet liability method

An entity purchases machinery for £4,000 in 2014. The asset has a life of two years with no residual value. Tax legislation makes an allowance of 100% in the year of purchase of machinery. The current tax rate is 25%. The entity has a profit before tax of £50,000 in 2014 and 2015.

The steps in calculating the taxable income in both years are:

1 The entity has charged depreciation in arriving at its profit before tax. This must be added back.
2 The tax allowance of 100% in 2014 must be deducted. There is no tax allowance in 2015.
3 The tax payable is based on the taxable profit calculated in Step 2.

	2014 £	2015 £
Accounting profit for year	50,000	50,000
Add back depreciation	2,000	2,000
Total	52,000	52,000
Deduct tax allowance	4,000	0
Taxable income	48,000	52,000
Tax charge 25%	12,000	13,000

The accounting profit reported in the financial statements is £50,000. If tax had been paid on this amount, the tax would have been £12,500 each year. The calculations are therefore

	2014 £	2015 £
Calculated tax expense	12,500	12,500
Actual tax charge	12,000	13,000
Deferred tax	500	(500)

Deferred tax asset

A deferred tax asset is likely to cause less anxiety to users than a tax liability. The deferred tax asset arises from a temporary difference as explained above, and recognizes an overpayment of tax in one period. This overpayment can be set against tax charges in future periods.

An entity must assess the carrying amount of its deferred tax assets at the end of each reporting period. If it is not probable that there will be sufficient taxable profit to benefit partly or completely from the deferred tax asset, an appropriate reduction must be made in the tax asset. An entity can reverse this deduction if future tax profits are more favourable than originally anticipated.

Disclosures

An expert in taxation usually deals with the application of the tax regulations and the requirements of IAS 12. The basic procedure followed and the one we have explained in this section is:

- Determine the tax base of the assets and liabilities in the balance sheet. Normally this tax base will be the amount that is allowed for tax purposes.
- Compare the carrying amounts in the balance sheet with the tax base. Any differences will normally affect the deferred taxation calculation.
- Identify the temporary differences not recognized due to exceptions in IAS 12.
- Apply the tax rates to the temporary differences.

Entities operating at the international level can have very complex arrangements, but the amount of deferred tax shown on the balance sheet can be important to users assessing the assets or liabilities of an entity.

The standard satisfies the users' needs by requiring an entity to disclose the tax from ordinary activities on the face of the statement of comprehensive income. The standard also requires the disclosure of the separate components of tax. This includes the current tax expense and any tax expense recognized in the financial period.

In the context of our examination of temporary differences, an entity should disclose the amount of any benefit arising from a previously unrecognized tax loss, tax credit or a temporary difference of a prior period used to reduce the current tax expense.

Tax reduction strategies

There are two basic national philosophies of taxation – the territorial principle and the worldwide principle – which determine the tax an entity should pay.

The territorial principle implies that income earned outside a home country's territory is not taxable. The worldwide principle implies that a country has the right to collect taxes on income earned outside the home country by an entity domiciled in the home country. The worldwide principle results in double taxation because the income an entity earns outside a country is taxed by the foreign tax authorities and taxed by the home tax authorities.

Understandably, multinational organizations wish to minimize the taxes they pay worldwide and to avoid double taxation. Entities adopt various strategies, but in this section we discuss two legally acceptable ones: transfer prices and tax inversion.

Transfer prices

One method for reducing worldwide taxes is through the judicious use of transfer prices. This is the pricing used by entities with units in different countries. Internationally, the transfer price is the price paid for the transfer of goods and/or services between two subsidiaries of the same multinational corporation. These transfer prices can occur for both goods and services.

Many multinationals produce a product in one country and sell it in a second country, or charge a subsidiary for some type of service the multinational may provide. Thus, transfer prices occur even if no actual goods cross borders. Since there are different tax rates from one country to another, the issue of transfer prices gives multinationals an incentive to shift taxable profit to low tax rate jurisdictions using transfer prices as a mechanism.

In 2014/2015, the UK had a spate of accusations on tax avoidance by large corporates with operations in the UK. There were allegations that some large name entities were syphoning large parts of their profits to countries with a much lower tax rate. Although some of the practices may have been questionable, they were not necessarily illegal.

Tax inversion

In 2015/2016, a strategy of lowering tax charges, known as tax inversion, made the headlines, particularly with US corporates. The US has one of the highest corporate income tax rates in the world at 35%. Foreign profits returned to the US less any foreign taxes that the entity has already paid on them are also subject to US tax. Tax inversion is a strategy used by US corporates to buy a foreign competitor, relocate their headquarters to that jurisdiction and evade the 35% tax rate in the US.

We emphasize that these practices are not illegal, but they have collected significant press coverage. Not surprisingly, the US government is not enamoured by these practices and has taken steps to prevent them.[1]

* * *

IAS 12 sets out how to account for taxation. Despite the complexities of tax legislation and the accusations of corporate abuses, the standard serves its purpose on the disclosure of tax issues. It is not the role of the IASB to determine tax laws; that is the responsibility of national governments.

The attention paid to some doubtful practices used to reduce the corporate tax burden has resulted in an understandable backlash. Corporates have become willing and able to demonstrate that they contribute substantial sums to the countries in which they operate.

In 2014, the Canadian Council of Chief Executives and PricewaterhouseCoopers LLP (PwC) conducted a survey of 63 leading corporations (Kingston and Schreiner 2014). The survey revealed that the firms taking part in the survey collectively paid £6 billion in federal corporate income tax in 2012. The companies are subject to 50 different types of taxes and, on average, pay a total tax rate of 33.4%.

Many annual reports and accounts contain substantial information on their tax activities and disclose their strategies and practices regarding taxation. We show in Company example 14.2 a very brief extract from the annual report and accounts of Kingfisher plc explaining the tax contribution that the entity makes.

Company example 14.2

Corporate tax contributions

Kingfisher makes a significant economic contribution to the countries in which it operates. In 2013/14, it contributed £1.71 billion in taxes it both pays and collects for these governments.

The Group pays tax on its profits, its properties, in employing 79,000 people, in environmental levies, in customs duties and levies as well as other local taxes. The most significant taxes it collects for governments are the sales taxes charged to its customers

continued

Company example 14.2 *continued*

on their purchases (VAT) and employee payroll related taxes. Taxes paid and collected together represent Kingfisher's total tax contribution which is shown below:

	2013/14	2012/13
Total taxes paid as a result of Group operations	£bn	£bn
Taxes borne	0.74	0.70
Taxes collected	0.97	0.90
Total tax contribution	1.71	1.60

Kingfisher participates in the Total Tax Contribution survey that PwC perform for the Hundred Group of Finance Directors. The 2013 survey ranked Kingfisher 31st for its Total Tax Contribution in the UK. In 2013, 101 companies contributed to the survey.

Kingfisher plc, Annual Report and Accounts, 2013/2014, p. 23

Kingfisher is a retail conglomerate formed in 1982. It operates over 1,100 stores and growing omnichannel operations across 10 countries in Europe. It employs 74,000 people and nearly six million customers shop in their stores and through their websites every week.

In this chapter, we explain the requirements of IAS 12 *Income Taxes*. It is not our intention to discuss corporate ethics and the application of tax regulations. However, in later chapters where we discuss other aspects of corporate reporting, we return to aspects of corporate activities.

IAS 17
LEASES

▼ Table 14.2 *Timeline of IAS 17*

Date	Comment
1982	First issued
2009	Latest amendment, effective 2010
Latest interpretation	SIC Evaluating the Substance of Transactions in the Legal Form of a Lease

The international debate

This standard is possibly one of the most written about in the history of accounting. It exemplifies the differences between the US rules approach to standards setting and the IASB principles based approach. In this section, we compare the US and IASB approaches, and explain the requirements of the current international standard, IAS 17. We also explain the international standard, IFRS 16, that is effective from January 2019.

The international standard (IAS 17 *Accounting for Leases*) identifies two classes of leases: finance leases that appear on the statement of financial position, and operating leases that appear only on the income statement. The classification of a lease depends on the substance of the transaction rather than the form. The standard describes situations that would normally result in an entity classifying a lease as a finance lease. This includes such considerations as whether:

- the lease transfers ownership of the asset to the lessee by the end of the lease term;
- the lease term is for the major part of the economic life of the asset, even if title is not transferred;
- at the inception of the lease, the present value of the minimum lease payments amounts to at least substantially all of the fair value of the leased asset.

The US standard (SFAS 13) uses the term 'capital' instead of 'finance' and applies different criteria to classify a lease. The standard defines a capital lease as one that meets any one of the following four conditions:

(i) the present value at the beginning of the lease term of the payments not representing executory costs paid by the lessor equals or exceeds 90% of the fair value of the leased asset;

(ii) the lease transfers ownership of the asset to the lessee by the end of the lease term;

(iii) the lease contains a bargain purchase price;

(iv) the lease is equal to 75% or more of the estimated economic life of the leased asset. (FASB 1976)

Some commentators argue that the US's so-called 'bright-line rules' in the form of quantitative thresholds lead to illusory compliance. By carefully structuring agreements, entities can avoid the thresholds to define the lease that best meets their purposes. For example, the US standard identifies a capital (finance) lease is where the leased asset is equal to 75% or more of the estimated economic life of the leased asset. It is relatively easy to adjust the economic life of the asset slightly so that it falls below the 75% threshold.

The FASB's rules are therefore establishing narrow and specified control limits whereas principles based standards encourage the examination of the economic substance of the transaction (McBarnet and Whelan 1991). If you compare the IASB and US sets of criteria, you can understand the two different approaches.

It is obviously difficult for standard setters to reconcile these two positions. In the following part of this section, we explain the motivation for leasing and the requirements of IAS 17. At the end of the section, we discuss the IASB's proposals for a new leasing standard, IFRS 16.

Worked example 14.3   Example of leasing

A hypothetical company, Peapod plc, seeks to acquire machinery with a life of ten years costing £500,000. The company requires finance and has arrived at two options for raising the finance

Option 1

Borrow £500,000 from the bank. The bank will want repayment of the loan and interest.

The important point with Option 1 is that Peapod will show a large loan on its balance sheet. It may not wish users of the financial statements to conclude from the financial statements that it is financially weak because it has a large loan.

Option 2

Lease the asset because, under IAS 17, it may be possible to avoid showing a loan on the balance sheet.

In Worked example 14.3, some entities may find Option 2 attractive. This depends on whether the entity can keep the loan off the balance sheet, and the answer to this is in the requirements of the standard. IAS 17 attempts to ensure proper accounting for these transactions and identifies two situations.

1   A financier acquires an asset and transfers it to the entity that intends to use it. This is a finance or capital lease transaction. The asset and the loan appear on the entity's balance sheet.

2   Where the lessee rents the asset from the lessor (the owner of the asset) it is an operating lease. In this instance, the entity only shows the rental payment on its income statement.

In Chapter 19, we explain accounting ratios which analyze the performance of an entity. To show a loan on the balance sheet affects the ratios and the users may interpret the result as a poor performance by the entity. The regulations of IAS 17, by identifying two types of leases, finance and operating, enable some options in the treatment of the asset. Essentially, if the entity does not wish to show a large loan on its balance sheet, it will seek to identify the transaction as an operating lease.

Operating leases

operating lease

An operating lease is an agreement that permits one party (the lessee) the use of an asset, but not the ownership. This remains with the owner (lessor) of the asset. An operating lease does not appear on the balance sheet as an asset. The rental expense appears on the income statement.

An **operating lease** is easiest to define because it is any lease agreement that is not a finance lease. In these cases, the lessee charges the lease payments as a rental to its income statement. The standard contains comprehensive guidance on how to identify a finance lease.

Some operating leases may be short term, possibly for one or two years. Others can be for longer periods and it is helpful for the users of the financial statements to be aware of the obligations of the entity. We show in Company example 14.3 an extract from the annual report of Rolls-Royce. The company provides highly-efficient integrated power and propulsion solutions. Their power systems are used in aerospace, marine, energy and off-highway applications. It currently employs over 50,000 people in more than 40 countries around the world.

Company example 14.3

Operating leases

Leases as lessee

	2015 £m	2014 £m
Rentals paid – hire of plant and machinery	122	123
– hire of other assets	124	75
Non-cancellable operating lease rentals are payable as follows:		
Within one year	190	182
Between one and five years	488	542
After five years	496	438
	1,174	1,162

Rolls-Royce Holdings plc, Annual Report, 2015, Note 22, p. 154

Rolls-Royce not only provides information on the leases it has but it also acts as lessee and lessor for both land and buildings and gas turbine engines, and as lessee for some plant and equipment. In addition to disclosures on operating leases, the Group provides details of finance leases.

Finance leases

> **finance lease**
>
> A finance lease is an agreement between two parties that transfers substantially all risks and rewards of ownership from the lessor to the lessee.

The definition of **finance leases** specifies risks and rewards. Remember it is the lessee, the entity using the asset, that bears substantially all the risks. It also has the rewards of using the asset to generate profits which are identified in Diagram 14.3.

Lease agreements can be very complex and lengthy documents. They are legal agreements and cover all aspects of the relationship between the lessor and lessee. In Diagram 14.3, we include the costs of maintaining and repairing the asset as a risk. Lease agreements will normally include a specific requirement relating to this risk. Failure to comply may make the lease agreement void. The asset being idle or becoming technologically impaired are risks that must be borne by the lessee.

The standard identifies various events and arrangements to identify a finance lease. Not all of these need to be present in the one transaction.

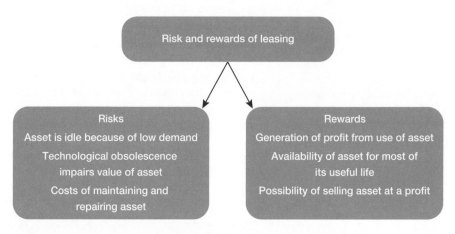

▲ **Diagram 14.3** *Leasing risks and rewards*

Characteristics of a finance lease

- The ownership of the asset transfers to the lessee at the end of the lease term.
- The lessee can purchase the asset at a bargain price at the end of the lease term.
- The asset is so specialized that only the lessee could use it.
- The present value of the minimum lease payments is substantially equal to the fair value of the asset.
- Any losses to the lessor due to the lessee cancelling the agreement are borne by the lessee.
- Fluctuations in fair value at the end of the lease term are borne by the lessee.
- The lessee can extend the term of the lease for a second term at a rate below the current market rate.

The items on this list are all self-explanatory, apart from the reference to minimum lease payments. These can affect several aspects of the agreement and require further explanation.

The minimum lease payment is the amount that the lessee must pay over the term of the lease. The lessee may have an option to purchase the asset outright at some future date at below market price. In that case, the minimum lease payments are the payments to the date of the option plus the amount of payment required to purchase the asset at that date.

The minimum lease payment includes not only rental payments but there will also be certain costs incurred in negotiating and arranging the lease. These costs incurred by the lessee are initial direct costs and can be added to the cost of the asset. There are other costs paid by the lessees that should be included, and one of these is contingent rent. This is the portion of the lease payment that fluctuates due to movements in another factor. For example, a lessee may have to pay a percentage of the sales they achieve or an amount based on the actual usage of an asset.

Having established that an entity, the lessee, has entered into a finance lease, the question arises as to the amount that the entity should show on the balance sheet as a non-current asset (i.e. capitalized). The standard states that it is the lower of the fair value of the asset and the present value of the minimum lease payments. Diagram 14.4 illustrates the comparison.

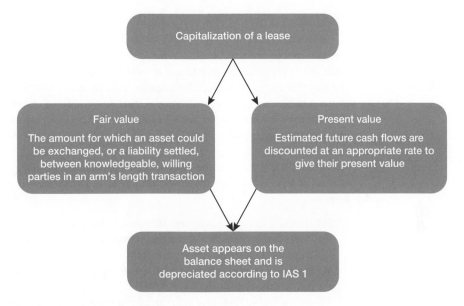

▲ Diagram 14.4 *Lease amount on the balance sheet*

Here, we regard fair value as the equivalent of the current market value. We show, in Worked example 14.4 of a finance lease, the amount to be entered on the balance sheet and the calculation of the depreciation.

Worked example 14.4   **Finance lease**

Nopence plc entered into a lease agreement for equipment on 1 January 2015. The lease agreement is for 5 years and Nopence is responsible for all maintenance and repair charges. At the end of the lease, ownership of the asset becomes Nopence's. The company must pay an annual rental charge of £53,000. The market value of the equipment on 1 January 2015 is £200,000. The present value of the lease payments is £199,000. It is estimated that the equipment has a useful life of 7 years.

continued overleaf

> ### Worked example 14.4 *continued*
>
> **Answer:**
>
> 1 The amount of the non-current asset to be shown on the balance sheet is the lower of the fair value of the asset and the present minimum lease payments. In the case of Nopence this is £199,000.
> 2 The standard states that the depreciation policy for assets held under finance leases should be consistent with that for owned assets. Where there is no reasonable certainty that the lessee will obtain ownership at the end of the lease it should depreciate the asset over the shorter of the lease term or the life of the asset. Since Nopence obtains ownership at the end of the lease term, it will depreciate the asset over 7 years.
> 3 Assuming there is no residual value, the annual depreciation charge is £199,000/7 years = £28,429

Sale and leaseback transactions

Sometimes a business may enter into a sale and leaseback transaction. Usually, this transaction arises where the entity owns an asset but is short of cash. The owner of the asset sells it to another party (a finance institution) and immediately leases it back. For example, an entity owns and occupies a large office block but requires cash. The entity sells the office block to a financial institution. The asset is immediately leased back to the entity that continues to occupy it.

Such transactions have formal agreements but there is no actual break in the use of the entity. The agreement entered into may be an operating or finance lease and certain regulations apply.

Where there is a sale of the asset under an operating lease, any profit is immediately recognized as long as the transaction was conducted at fair value. If it was not at fair value, the rules are:

1 Where the sale price is lower than fair value, recognize the profit or loss immediately unless the loss is compensated by a rental below market rates. In this case, defer and amortize the loss in proportion to the rental payments over the period the asset is used.
2 Where the sale price is above fair value, defer and amortize the excess above fair value over the period the asset is used.
3 Where the fair value is less than the carrying amount, the loss should be recognized immediately.

If it is a finance lease, any apparent profit on the sale is not recognized as income. Instead, it should be deferred and amortized over the lease term. Essentially, the transaction is one where the lessee is raising finance secured on an asset that it continues to hold. The sale is not a disposal of the asset because it is leased back to the owner.

One particular situation occurs when an entity enters into a lease for land and buildings. Land has an indefinite life and, usually, the title for the land will not pass at the end of the lease so the lessor retains ownership. In these circumstances, the land is treated as an operating lease.

Any buildings on the land may be a finance lease and the minimum lease payment is apportioned between the land and buildings to their relative fair values. The land will not appear on the lessees' balance sheet because it is an operating lease but the buildings will be capitalized if they are on a finance lease. The sale and leaseback of land is a normal business transaction.

The following example describes a sale and leaseback agreement by a Canadian company. Gemini provides multi-disciplined engineering, field and environmental solutions for energy and industrial facilities. Started in 1982, Gemini is a public company headquartered in Calgary, Canada. In 2015 it announced that it had agreed a sale and leaseback arrangement for its land and buildings with the purpose of improving its working capital.

The strategy used by Gemini is not unusual and it is the responsibility of the investor to determine its significance when interpreting the financial statements. It is because of the potential importance of such information to decision making by users that companies must disclose these activities.

In Chapter 1, we illustrated the many communication channels used by companies to keep their investors informed. Annual and half-yearly financial statements need to be analyzed in the context of current events. In Chapter 19 we explain how to construct the context in which financial statements are analyzed and interpreted by those interested in a company's financial performance and position.

IAS 17 is a complex standard and we have only considered the main requirements. Lease agreements are very lengthy and contain many specific conditions and responsibilities of the parties. Remember that the lease agreement is a legal document. The agreement may be written in such a way that it appears as an operating lease although in substance it is really a finance lease.

In Chapter 3 we explained that international accounting standards are concerned with principles not rules so the economic reality of the transaction must be accounted for, and not the legal form. It is important that the accountant considers the examples in the standard of finance leases and does not rely solely on the legal agreement.

IFRS 16
LEASES – A NEW STANDARD

The IASB added a new project to its agenda in 2006 when it declared its intention to develop a new international accounting standard that remedied the deficiencies in existing regulations for accounting for leases. The FASB was involved because there was a commitment to converge US standards with international standards.

The aim of the project was to develop a new single approach to lease accounting. The new standard would ensure the recognition of all assets and liabilities arising under lease contracts in the statement of financial position. The project was lengthy and the two boards were unable to agree on a joint standard. Table 14.3 shows the progress from 2006 to the present.

▼ Table 14.3 *Timeline of IFRS 16*

Date	Issuer(s)	Output
May 2009	IASB	Discussion paper
August 2010	FASB/IASB	Exposure draft
May 2013	FASB	Standards update
August 2014	IASB	Project update
February 2015	IASB	Definition of a lease
January 2016	IASB	Standard IFRS 16 Leases

Possibly, the key stage in all these deliberations was the February 2015 document that defined a lease. This definition rules out the use of operating **leases** and it also applies to subleases. There are, however, certain agreements to which IFRS 16 does not apply. We list them below, with the chapter where we discuss the particular item:

> **lease**
>
> A lease is a contract that conveys to the customer the right-to-use an asset for a period of time in exchange for consideration.
>
> *Based on IASB, Project Update: Definition of a Lease, February 2015*

- leases to explore for or use minerals, oil, natural gas and similar non-regenerative resources (IAS 41, Chapter 15);
- leases of biological assets held by a lessee (IAS 40, Chapter 15);
- service concession arrangements;
- licences of intellectual property granted by a lessor (IFRS 15, Chapter 7);
- rights held by a lessee under licensing agreements for items such as films, videos, plays, manuscripts, patents and copyrights within the scope of IAS 38 *Intangible Assets* (Chapter 5).

The operating lease, or at least the concept, is not totally abandoned. An entity can elect to treat lease payments as an expense where:

- The lease has a lease term of 12 months or less and the lessee does not have the option to purchase the asset. This election is made by class of underlying asset.
- The lease is for an underlying asset with a low value when new; for example, personal computers. The entity can elect to do this for individual leases.

Identifying a lease

There is a lease agreement if there is payment to secure the right to control the use of an asset for a period of time. The customer has control where they:

- have the right to control the use of the asset;
- obtain substantially all the economic benefits from the use of the asset.

The standard has several clauses in establishing the identity of the asset. This is critical to establishing whether there is a lease. The standard discusses several specific scenarios:

- It is explicitly specified in the contract.
- It is implicitly specified at the time it is made available to the customer.
- If the supplier has the right to substitute the asset in the lease period, the user does not have the right-to-use an identified asset.
- Where the user has the right to a capacity portion of an asset that is physically distinct, e.g. the floor of a building, that is an identified asset.
- Where the user has the right-to-use the capacity portion of an asset that is not physically distinct, e.g. capacity portion of a fibre optics cable, this is not an identified asset unless it is the customer that receives substantially all the benefits from its use.

In addition to the above, there are situations where a contract is for an identifiable asset but there is a non-lease component. For example, the customer may have leased the use of a floor in the building but the contract also includes maintenance and servicing. In this scenario, the lessee allocates the payments based on the stand-alone prices, either observed or estimated. The lessee can elect not to separate the non-lease components and treat them as part of the lease.

The issues of identifying and accounting for a lease relate to the lessee. As far as the lessor is concerned, all consideration from lease agreements comes under IFRS 15 *Revenue from Contracts with Customers*.

Accounting by lessees

We described above accounting for lessors to which IFRS 16 applies. Accounting by lessees is somewhat more difficult. Diagram 14.5 shows the general framework.

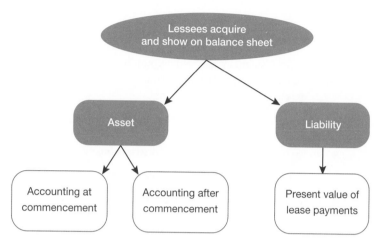

▲ **Diagram 14.5** *Overview of IFRS 16*

Lease commencement

The lessee recognizes a right-of-use asset and a lease liability on the balance sheet. The lessee measures the asset at the amount of the lease liability plus any initial direct costs it incurs. Other adjustments may be made for lease incentives and payments made in conjunction with the contract.

After lease commencement

The lessee measures using a cost model. This involves measuring the asset at cost less accumulated depreciation and impairment.

This does not apply if it is an investment property and the lessee uses the fair value model (see Chapter 15) or the lessee uses the revaluation model to that class of assets (see Chapter 4).

Lease liability

The lessee measures the liability at the present value of the lease payments payable over the lease term. The payments are discounted at the rate implicit in the lease payments. If that cannot be determined the lessee should use their incremental borrowing rate.

Of course, it may be that the contract specifies variable lease payments. Payments linked to an index or rate, are initially measured using the index or the rate at the commencement date of the lease. They are included in the lease liability. Other variable lease payments that are not included in the lease liability are shown in profit or loss.

The standard sets out four situations where the lease liability is remeasured:

- a change in the lease term (using a revised discount rate);
- a change in the assessment of a purchase option (using a revised discount rate);
- a change in the amounts expected to be payable under residual value guarantees (using an unchanged discount rate but revised lease payments); or

- a change in the future lease payments resulting from a change in an index or a rate used to determine those payments (using an unchanged discount rate but revised lease payments assuming a change in cash flows).

Where the liability is remeasured there is an adjustment to the right-to-use asset.

Accounting by lessors

IFRS 16 has substantially changed accounting for leases by lessees. There is little change for lessors and we summarize the main requirements.

Lessors classify each lease as either:

- a finance lease if it transfers substantially all the risks and rewards incidental to ownership of an underlying asset; or
- an operating lease if it is not classified as a finance lease.

For finance leases, the lessor recognizes:

- the lease as a receivable: the calculation of the amount is the net investment in the lease;
- the income over the lease term at a constant periodic on the net investment rate of return;
- selling profit or loss in line with its accounting policy under IFRS 15.

A lessor can recognize operating lease payments either as:

- income on a straight line basis; or
- any systematic basis that represents the pattern of the benefits from the use of the underlying asset.

Effects analysis

The IASB reported on its effect analysis that examined the likely impact of the new standard in January 2016 (IASB 2016). The most significant effect for lessees is an increase in lease assets and financial liabilities. Both appear on the balance sheet. Users of financial statements of entities with substantial off balance leases under IAS 17 will find changes to key financial ratios. We discuss these in Chapter 19.

Under IAS 17, operating leases were an expense appearing on the profit or loss account. Under the new standard, the right-to-use asset is depreciated. The interest expense on the lease liability is shown under operating costs.

The IASB considers that the new standard provides more faithful representation of an entity's assets and liabilities. By the disclosures on the balance sheet, users will not need to adjust the balance sheet and income statement to compare entities that buy assets with those that lease them. The new disclosures will better demonstrate total assets and liabilities than the numbers previously estimated by users.

NOTES

1   Sources that give brief but interesting insights into tax inversion by US corporates are:
- *http://www.bloombergview.com/quicktake/tax-inversion*
- *http://finance.yahoo.com/news/investing-tax-inversions-25-stock-151127107.html*
- *http://www.forbes.com/sites/jeremybogaisky/2014/09/22/obama-administration-moves-to-crack-down-on-tax-inversions/*

(All sources accessed 8 September 2016.)

CONCLUSIONS

In this chapter, we have examined standards that the IASB has issued to address accounting for income tax and leases. Perhaps it is because these situations are unusual, or differ from the majority of transactions, that the standards are technical. This does not detract from their importance.

If an entity publishes a profit figure that does not immediately correspond to the taxable amount, the user requires an explanation. IAS 12 is designed to provide that explanation. The standard was issued in 1979 with the IASB making very few changes. We cannot foresee the standard setters making any changes in the future. The important aspects are differentiating between deferred tax liabilities and deferred tax assets. The process for calculating deferred tax liabilities is also important.

IAS 17 is also a standard that was issued many years ago, but it has caused significant controversy. At its simplest, the question is where an entity which claims to be 'renting' an asset should place it on its balance sheet. IAS 17 attempted to provide a solution by classifying leases as either financial or operating leases. The latter did not appear on the balance sheet. It was argued that this could mislead users and also give entities an opportunity to massage their financial statements.

The standard setters have moved away from this dual classification by issuing IFRS 16 that becomes effective on 1 January 2019. Most leases should appear on the balance sheet because an entity has control of the asset and the future economic benefits it generates. This is a significant change to the balance sheet but it should assist users.

ADDITIONAL RESOURCES

Go online to the companion website for this book to access further teaching and learning materials for this chapter.

www.palgravehighered.com/hussey-cfr

SPECIFIC BUSINESS ACTIVITIES

IAS 40 Investment Property
IAS 41 Agriculture
IFRS 6 Exploration for and Evaluation of Mineral Resources
IFRS 5 Non-current Assets Held for Sale and Discontinued Operations
IFRS 8 Operating Segments

LEARNING OBJECTIVES

At the end of this chapter, you should be able to:

- Differentiate between the accounting treatment for investment property and owner occupied property under IAS 40
- Identify the two measurement models that an entity can use for investment property
- Explain the criteria for identifying biological assets and agricultural produce under IAS 41
- Summarize the recognition and measurement requirements under IFRS 6
- Discuss the main requirements of IFRS 6
- Describe when IFRS 6 requires an impairment test and give examples of how the asset's carrying amount may exceed its recoverable amount
- Explain the purpose of IFRS 5 and identify the criteria to identify non-current assets held for sale and discontinued operations
- Summarize the disclosures IFRS 5 requires
- Discuss the method for identifying operating segments under IFRS 8 and the required disclosures

INTRODUCTION

Every standard contains a section where it describes the scope of the transactions and events to which the standard applies. This section also identifies those types of businesses and activities to which the standard does not apply. This 'scoping out' results in some specialized types of businesses and activities that need their own standard.

In this chapter, we concentrate on the specific standards that address those special needs. There is no unifying theme to these standards so we discuss them in the order they were first issued.

IAS 40 *Investment Property* adds a new dimension to non-current assets. We discussed in Chapter 3 that entities owning and occupying a property would apply IAS 16. However, there are entities that own a property for investment purposes, to either sell at a profit or rent. The standard explains the accounting requirements in this situation.

IAS 41 *Agriculture* is concerned with a large industry that affects all of us and yet attracts little attention. Accounting for agriculture involves some particular issues. For example, there is a difference between trees grown for the timber they provide and those grown for the fruit they produce. Raising of livestock can be a period of years rather than months. IAS 41 provides guidance on profit measurement and valuations of agricultural assets.

IFRS 6 *Exploration for an Evaluation of Mineral Resources* is of particular interest to those citizens who believe they have 'struck oil' in their back garden. The standard establishes the accounting differences between hoping that you will strike it rich compared to how you calculate your wealth when you do. Two countries with substantial mining activity that comply with IFRSs are Australia and Canada. We use examples from companies in mineral exploration industries to illustrate the application of the standard.

Entities may have non-current assets that they intend to sell for various reasons. Until they achieve the disposal, these assets could be on the balance sheet at their carrying amount. However, the value of the assets may be less than the carrying amount. There is also the issue that the assets, if sold, will not generate future profits. IFRS 5 *Non-current Assets Held for Sale and Discontinued Operations* addresses these issues.

The final standard in this chapter, IFRS 8 *Operating Segments*, establishes disclosure requirements for those identifiable segments of a business that contribute to profit. Users find this information useful in assessing the future prospects of the business. The standard defines the meaning of operating segment.

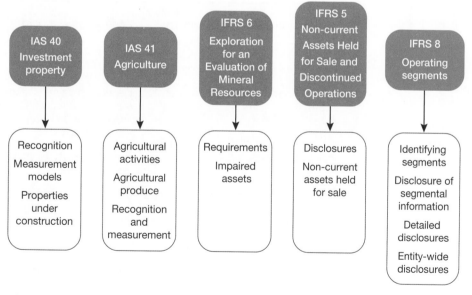

▲ **Diagram 15.1** *Structure of Chapter 15*

IAS 40
INVESTMENT PROPERTY

investment property

Investment property comprises land, a building, part of a building held by the owner or, if there is a finance lease, by the lessee to earn rentals or for capital appreciation or both.

▼ **Table 15.1** *Timeline of IAS 40*

Date	Comment
2000	Standard issued
2003	Latest revision
2008	Amendment, effective January 2009
2013	Latest amendment

The standard makes a clear distinction between property that an entity acquires for its own use (owner occupied property) and one the entity acquires for investment purposes. The standard sets out the appropriate accounting treatment and disclosures are required so that the user can gain a better understanding of the financial statements. IAS 40 addresses these issues and this is the first standard the IASB has issued that incorporates a fair value model for non-financial assets. We have given an explanation in Chapter 12 of 'fair value' under IFRS 13.

If you refer to previous chapters, you will see that we have referred to various types of properties. The one that you may immediately recall is property, plant and equipment that comes under IAS 16 (Chapter 4). In that case, the owner occupies the property.

To explain better the types of properties that are covered by IAS 40 we show in Table 15.2 properties that are NOT investment property. Other standards regulate their accounting treatment.

▼ **Table 15.2** *Non-investment properties*

Type of non-investment property	Accounting standard	Chapter
Intended for sale in ordinary course of business by a construction company	IAS 2 Inventories	8
Property being constructed on behalf of others	Depending on the date of transaction IAS 11 Construction Contracts IFRS 15 Revenue from Contracts with Customers	7
Owner occupied property	IAS 16 Property, Plant and Equipment	4
Property being constructed/developed as an investment property	IAS 40 since 1 January 2009	15

Recognition

There are two criteria for the recognition of investment property. They are that:

- the property should be recognized as an asset when it is probable that the future economic benefits that are associated with the property will flow to the business;
- a reliable measurement can be made of the cost of the property.

The owner of the investment property may provide ancillary services. This may only be cleaning but could also cover maintenance and security. If those services are a relatively insignificant component of the arrangement as a whole, then the entity may treat the property as an investment property.

There are circumstances in which the identification is not so clear. This is particularly so with hotels which not only involve a building, but also extensive services for running the hotel. Where the services are significant, as in the case of an owner-managed hotel, the entity classifies the property as owner occupied property and accounts for it under IAS 16 *Property, Plant and Equipment*.

Measurement models

When an entity initially recognizes the investment property, it measures the acquired property at cost. Cost is the purchase price and any directly attributable expenditure such as legal fees and property transfer taxes.

After the initial recognition, an entity can record investment property either at:

● fair value: this is the amount at which the property could be exchanged between knowledgeable and willing parties in an arm's length transaction; or
● cost less accumulated depreciation and any accumulated impairment losses as prescribed by IAS 16.

An arm's length transaction is one in which the buyer and seller are considered to be independent in the negotiations. They have no significant, prior relationship that might influence them to act against their own interest.

If an entity selects the cost model, it must also disclose the fair value of the properties, usually in the Notes to the accounts. If the entity cannot determine the fair value then it must give:

1 A description of the investment property.
2 An explanation of why fair value cannot be determined reliably.
3 If possible, a range of estimates for fair value.

Certain conditions are in force if an investment entity selects fair value, and these are:

● All investment property held must be at fair value.
● A gain or loss arising from a change in fair value is recognized in the income statement.
● Fair value must reflect market conditions at balance sheet date.
● Transfers to and from the designation of investment property only when there is a change in use.

An entity may choose the cost model but there are some connections with other standards. Although IAS 40 allows the cost model, it requires disclosure of the fair value. This means that an entity must apply IFRS 13 *Fair Value* to measure the fair value.

Although an entity initially chooses the cost model, IAS 40 allows the entity to change its policy and use the fair value model. IAS 8 permits this policy change if the change in model provides more relevant and useful information. It is highly unlikely that an entity using the fair value model could change to the cost model, as the information would not be relevant and reliable.

It is possible that the fair value of the investment property changes over time. The entity must recognize these changes in the fair value in the profit or loss for the period in which they arise. IAS 40 requires the disclosure of rental income and direct operating expenses separately.

Of course, an entity may have an investment property but then decide to use the premises itself. Alternatively, it may own and use a property then decide to vacate it and rent it out. If such a change in use takes place, a different standard applies. Scenarios 15.1 and 15.2 are two common cases demonstrating the change of use and the change in standard.

Scenario 15.1

Bigroom Co. is the owner of an office block. It has been renting the space to a third party from January 2013. It has decided to occupy the office block itself from January 2017. What accounting standards apply?

From January 2013 Bigroom would have been using IAS 40 because the property was for investment purposes. As from January 2017, it will apply IAS 16, because Bigblock is the owner occupier.

Scenario 15.2

Butterfly Co. is remodelling a building it owns with the intention of selling it. Unfortunately, when the conversions are complete, Butterfly finds that the market is very poor and there are no buyers. Butterfly decides to re-occupy the building itself. What accounting standards apply?

Butterfly's intention was to sell the building and therefore it was accounted for under IAS 40. Because Butterfly is going to re-occupy the building itself, it now comes under IAS 16.

On disposal or permanent withdrawal from use, a property should be derecognized. The gain or loss on derecognition should be calculated as the difference between the net disposal proceeds and the carrying amount of the asset. The gain or losses should be recognized in the income statement.

The distinction between owner property under IAS 16 and investment property under IAS 40 introduces certain accounting differences which are shown in Table 15.3.

▼ Table 15.3 *Comparison of investment and owner occupied properties*

Investment property	Owner occupied
Comes under IAS 40	Comes under IAS 16
Measured at fair value	Measured at cost
No depreciation charge	Depreciation charge over useful life of asset
No revaluations	Revaluation permitted
Changes in fair value to profit or loss	Revaluation differences to Statement of other comprehensive income

Properties under construction

In 2008, as part of its annual improvement process, the IASB included property under construction or development for future use as investment property. The result is that property under construction is now subject to the same recognition, presentation and disclosure requirements as completed investment property. Valuing properties under construction is problematical.

An entity may decide that it is impossible to measure the fair value of an investment property under construction. In these circumstances, the entity can measure the property at cost until it can either measure reliably the fair value or the construction is complete. When the construction is complete, the entity can use fair value. If that is not possible, the entity can use the cost model under IAS 16.

In this section, we have concentrated mainly on examples of owner occupied properties as if there were only one owner with one property. In fact, there is substantial activity through Real Estate Investment Trusts (REITs). These receive funds from investors and purchase or build investment properties. The evidence available suggests that these companies may not comply fully with the amended regulations.

Ciartano (2012) extracted 21 REITs listed on the London Stock Exchange as at 31 December 2011. Among those REITs, 10 had investment property under construction and they comprise the final sample.

The results show that only 30% of the REITs presented the investment properties under construction separately from completed investment properties on the face of the balance sheet. Only 20% of the REITs gave a more detailed disclosure of the assumptions they made in valuing investment property under construction.

IAS 41
AGRICULTURE

▼ Table 15.4 *Timeline of IAS 41*

Date	Comment
2000	Standard first issued
2014	Latest amendment effective from 2016

Agricultural activities

agricultural activity

Agricultural activity comprises the management by an entity of the biological transformation and harvest of biological assets for sale or for conversion, into agricultural produce, or into additional biological assets.

Based on IAS 41, para. 5

Agricultural activity, particularly in some countries and regions, is a significant part of the economy. There is a range of activities that come under the heading of 'Agriculture' but IAS 41 establishes the accounting treatment, financial statement presentation, and disclosures only for specific agricultural activities. Diagram 15.2 illustrates the scope of the standard.

The standard applies to biological assets except for bearer plants, agricultural produce at the point of harvest, and government grants. The standard only applies when these three items relate to agricultural activity. We omit government grants from our discussion and concentrate on explaining the other two items.

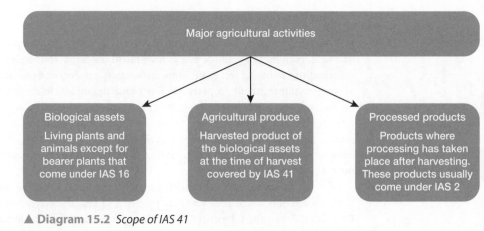

▲ **Diagram 15.2** *Scope of IAS 41*

Biological assets except bearer plants

Biological assets are items such as dairy cattle that provide milk, fruit trees that provide fruit, and grape vines that provide grapes. These three examples all provide an agricultural product that can be harvested – the milk, fruit and grapes. However, after harvesting another product can be created: the milk turned into cheese, the fruit into processed fruit and the grapes into wine. The standard does not apply to products that are processed after harvesting.

An amendment to the standard scoped out bearer plants from annual periods beginning on or after 1 January 2016. Bearer plants are living plants that:

● are used in the production or supply of agricultural produce;
● are expected to bear produce for more than one period; and
● have a remote likelihood of being sold as agricultural produce, except for incidental scrap sales.

Examples of bearer plants are grape vines and oil palms. If the plant meets the definition of a bearer plant it comes under IAS 16 *Property, Plant and Equipment* (see Chapter 4). Although the plant comes under IAS 16, the produce from the plant comes under IAS 41.

Agricultural produce

Agricultural produce is the harvested produce from the biological assets. In other words, it is the milk from the cows, the apples from the trees and the grapes from the vines.

We can put the formal definition of agricultural produce into an everyday perspective by looking at the products we eat and drink. Calves, cows, pigs, sheep, vines and fruit trees are all examples of biological assets because they are living animals and plants. The agricultural produce is the wool from the sheep, the milk from the cows and the fruit from the trees. Some produce will need processing after the harvest, and examples are cheese from the milk, clothes from the wool and wine from the grape.

Recognition and measurement

The standard has the following criteria for recognition of biological assets or agricultural produce:

● the entity controls the asset because of past events;
● it is probable that future economic benefits associated with the asset will flow to the entity;
● the fair value or cost of the asset can be measured reliably.

The standard accepts that cost can be used since it may approximate the fair value. This could be because little transformation has taken place in the period. For example, the seeds have not yet germinated.

The standard assumes that the most frequently used method is fair value because it is a reliable method for measuring a biological asset. On initial recognition and subsequently, an entity should recognize biological assets at fair value less costs to sell, if it can measure fair value reliably. Point-of-sales costs include commissions, levies and transfer duties and taxes.

Agricultural produce harvested from the biological asset is also measured at fair value less costs to sell at the point of harvest.

If there is a gain or loss on initial recognition of biological assets or agricultural produce at fair value, and changes in fair value of biological assets during a period, the entity shows this in the profit or loss for that period.

It is easier to understand the regulations and the issues in applying by looking at the size of some agricultural entities and the problems that arise with recognition and measurement. First, we show an extract in Company example 15.1 from the annual report and accounts of the Australian Agricultural Company Ltd. Established in 1824, AAC is the oldest continuously operating company in Australia. It owns and operates a strategic balance of properties, feed-lots and farms comprising around 7 million hectares of land in Queensland and the Northern Territory. This equates to roughly 1% of Australia's land mass. The financial statements comply with Australian International Accounting Standards that have the same requirements as IAS 41.

Company example 15.1

Biological assets

15. Biological Assets – Livestock

	31 March 2015 Au$000	31 March 2014 Au$000
Current		
Cattle at net market value – trading cattle	200,077	144,765
Total current livestock	200,077	144,765
Non-Current		
Cattle at net market value		
– commercial and stud breeding herd	265,109	238,282
Total non-current livestock	265,109	238,282
Total livestock	465,186	383,047

Note 3

(g) Biological assets

Biological assets comprise cattle, other livestock, crops not yet harvested, and harvested crops. Biological assets are measured at fair value less costs to sell, with any change recognised in the income statement. Costs to sell include all costs that would be necessary to sell the assets, including freight and direct selling costs.

The fair value of a biological asset is based on its present location and condition. If an active or other effective market exists for a biological asset or agricultural produce in its

continued overleaf

> ## Company example 15.1 *continued*
>
> present location and condition, the quoted price in that market is the appropriate basis for determining the fair value of that asset. Where we have access to different markets then we use the most relevant one. The relevant one is defined as the market 'that access is available to the entity' to be used at the time the fair value is established.
>
> If an active market does not exist then we use one of the following, when available, in determining fair value:
>
> >> the most recent market transaction price, provided that there has not been a significant change in economic circumstances between the date of that transaction and the end of the reporting period; or
>
> >> market prices, in markets accessible to the entity, for similar assets with adjustments to reflect differences; or
>
> >> sector benchmarks.
>
> In the event that market determined prices or values are not available for a biological asset in its present condition we may use the present value of the expected net cashflows from the asset discounted at a current market determined rate in determining fair value.
>
> *Australian Agricultural Company Ltd, Annual Report, 2015, pp. 96 and 74*

Company example 15.1 is very clear on the methods used to determine fair value. If there is no active market the company explains the methods it uses to determine fair value. One can appreciate the time and effort expended to obtain and apply the data. Nevertheless, fair value may not be as reliable as we may think, and commentators have pointed to some of the difficulties.

The standard is clear on what biological assets and agricultural produce come under its remit. The reasons for the distinctions are not always understandable to those unfamiliar with agriculture practices.

A light-hearted approach serves as a platform to appreciate some possibly debatable parts of the regulations. Waine (2009) has identified some of the practical difficulties in recognizing and measuring biological assets (see Scenario 15.3). Although he writes from a New Zealand perspective, his opinions have a widespread application.

> ## Scenario 15.3
>
> Waine gives the example of an egg. If the management of the poultry farm decide to fertilize the egg and hatch it, the egg is a biological asset. If the management decide to sell the egg, it comes under IFRS 2 *Inventory*. It is the same egg.
>
> Waine then uses the dairy industry to extend his argument. A dairy cow is recognized as a biological asset under IAS 41 because it meets all the criteria:
>
> - the farmer controls the cow (has ownership rights);
> - probable economic benefits will flow (milk);
> - fair value or cost can be measured (market comparisons from sale days).
>
> *continued*

> ### Scenario 15.3 *continued*
>
> He then poses the question of whether grass is a biological asset under IAS 41. Taking the three criteria above he argues:
>
> - the farmer controls the grass as he owns the field;
> - the cow eats the grass and turns it into milk – the economic benefit;
> - as for measurement, grass is a feed supplement and market transactions for feed supplements would provide a value.
>
> Whilst Waine accepts that his arguments are open to dispute, he adds a final thought. A farmer can grow grass and convert it into hay and silage for sale. This hay or silage is a biological asset under IAS 41, but the grass that the cows eat is not.

We do not want to extend Waine's argument, but it sounds a warning note. Even if you are familiar with the industry and know the relevant accounting standards, there can still be accounting uncertainties and oddities.

IFRS 6

EXPLORATION FOR AND EVALUATION OF MINERAL RESOURCES

▼ **Table 15.5** *Timeline of IFRS 6*

Date	Comment
2004	Standard first issued
2005	Latest amendment

The oil and gas industry is large and complex. Looking at the entire process, we have entities involved in finding, extracting, refining and selling oil and gas. There are also the refined products and related products. The operations require substantial capital investment and have long lead times. A critical issue is which costs the entity should capitalize and show on the balance sheet and which costs it should expense on the income statement.

Previously, entities used a wide variety of accounting policies in the exploration for and evaluation of **mineral resources**. Standard setters wished to regulate these practices but a completely new standard may have been too disruptive.

With all standards, some levels of lobbying of the standard setters takes place. A survey (dos Santos and dos Santos 2014) of the comment letters to the IASB showed that large oil companies were more likely to submit comment letters on IFRS 6, and that these were predominately opposed to the IASB proposals.

Another focused study reached the same conclusion and argued for 'the web of relationships that is characteristic of standard setting process and that arguably contributed to the final outcome, IFRS 6, being a codification of the existing practices' (Cortese 2013: 55).

mineral resources

The exploration and evaluation of mineral resources includes the search for mineral resources, including minerals, oil, natural gas and similar non-regenerative resources after the entity has obtained legal rights to explore in a specific area, as well as the determination of the technical feasibility and commercial viability of extracting the mineral resource.

Based on IFRS 6, Appendix A

Requirements

Given the circumstances of diverse industrial practices and the opinions of industry, it is not surprising that IFRS 6 permits entities to continue to use their existing accounting policies. There is an additional factor. Accounting policies must comply with IAS 8, as we discussed in Chapter 13.

The requirement to comply with IAS 8 means that accounting policies must provide information that is relevant to the economic decision-making needs of users, and that is reliable. Entities, if they choose, can change their accounting policies for exploration and evaluation expenditures if the change makes the financial statements more relevant and reliable.

Under the standard, we have two occasions for measurement of assets: the initial measurement and the subsequent measurement. At first recognition in the balance sheet, the standard requires entities to measure exploration and evaluation assets at cost. Entities can set their own consistent policies on what should be included in cost and IFRS 6 lists the following as examples of expenditures that might be included in the initial measurement of exploration and evaluation assets (the list is not exhaustive):

- Acquisition of rights to explore; topographical, geological, geochemical and geophysical studies.
- Exploratory drilling; trenching; sampling; and activities in relation to evaluating the technical feasibility and commercial viability of extracting a mineral resource.
- Obligations for removal and restoration through the exploration for and evaluation of mineral resources. These obligations come under IAS 37 *Provisions, Contingent Liabilities and Contingent Assets* that we examined in Chapter 13.

After the initial recognition, entities can apply either the cost model or the revaluation model to exploration and evaluation assets. As there is likely to be both tangible and intangible assets, entities will apply the requirements of IAS 16 *Property Plant and Equipment* and IAS 38 *Intangible Assets*.

Impaired assets

Identifying impaired assets (see Chapter 5) can cause problems because of the difficulty in obtaining the information necessary to estimate future cash flows from exploration and evaluation assets. IFRS 6 modifies the rules of IAS 36 to make it more practicable to identify where impairment has taken place. A detailed impairment test is required in two circumstances:

1   When the technical feasibility and commercial viability of extracting a mineral resource become demonstrable, at which point the asset falls outside the scope of IFRS 6 and is reclassified in the financial statements.
2   When facts and circumstances suggest that the asset's carrying amount may exceed its recoverable amount.

The reference to facts and circumstances seems vague but the standard offers some examples.

1   The right the entity has to explore in the specific area has expired during the agreed period or will expire in the near future. It is not expected that the right will be renewed.
2   The entity has not budgeted or planned more substantive expenditure on further exploration for and evaluation of mineral resources in the specific area.
3   The entity has not discovered commercially viable quantities of mineral resources and has decided to discontinue exploration in the specific area.
4   Analysis indicates that the development or sale of the site is unlikely to recover the carrying amount of the exploration and evaluation asset.

Although oil and gas mining may dominate the headlines, IFRS 6's scope is far wider than that. The UK may not be one of the foremost countries for gold mining, but other countries adopting IFRSs are. Australia is the second highest gold producing country in the world and Canada is eighth.

To complete this section, Company example 15.2 includes an extract from Goldcorp's annual report for the year ending 31 December 2014. Goldcorp is a Canadian company engaged in the mining and exploration of silver, copper and gold throughout North and South America. It is one of the world's top gold producers.

Company example 15.2

Mining

The costs of acquiring rights to explore, exploratory drilling and related costs incurred on sites without an existing mine and on areas outside the boundary of a known mineral deposit which contain proven and probable reserves are exploration and evaluation expenditures and are expensed as incurred to the date of establishing that costs incurred are economically recoverable. Exploration and evaluation expenditures incurred subsequent to the establishment of economic recoverability are capitalized and included in the carrying amount of the related mining property.

Management uses the following criteria in its assessments of economic recoverability and probability of future economic benefit:

(i) Geology: there is sufficient geologic certainty of converting a mineral deposit into a proven and probable reserve. There is a history of conversion to reserves at operating mines;

(ii) Scoping or feasibility: there is a scoping study or preliminary feasibility study that demonstrates the additional reserves and resources will generate a positive commercial outcome. Known metallurgy provides a basis for concluding there is a significant likelihood of being able to recover the incremental costs of extraction and production;

(iii) Accessible facilities: the mineral deposit can be processed economically at accessible mining and processing facilities where applicable;

(iv) Life of mine plans: an overall life of mine plan and economic model to support the economic extraction of reserves and resources exists. A long-term life of mine plan and supporting geological model identifies the drilling and related development work required to expand or further define the existing ore body; and

(v) Authorizations: operating permits and feasible environmental programs exist or are obtainable.

Prior to capitalizing exploratory drilling, evaluation, development and related costs, management determines that the following conditions have been met:

(i) It is probable that a future economic benefit will flow to the Company;

(ii) The Company can obtain the benefit and controls access to it;

(iii) The transaction or event giving rise to the future economic benefit has already occurred; and

(iv) Costs incurred can be measured reliably.

Goldcorp, Annual Report and Accounts, 2015, p. 87

This exemplifies the information required by IFRS 6. The extract from its report is a good guide to the criteria it uses in its assessments of economic recoverability and probability of future economic benefit of mines. It also ends with a clear explanation of the information it uses when deciding to capitalize various costs.

IFRS 5

NON-CURRENT ASSETS HELD FOR SALE AND DISCONTINUED OPERATIONS

▼ **Table 15.6** *Timeline of IFRS 5*

Date	Comment
2004	Standard first issued
2014	Latest amendment

The objective of the standard is to require disclosure of non-current assets held for sale and discontinued operations so that the user of financial statements can evaluate their effects on the entire entity. If the users are analyzing the financial statements, they are interested in the profit the assets can generate. If the entity is in the process of trying to sell some of the assets, the users will find this information helpful.

Disclosures

The entity should disclose:

1 The net cash flows, classified as operating, investing and financing, attributable to a **discontinued operation** for the current and comparative period on the face of the statement cash flows or in the notes.
2 A single amount on the statement of comprehensive income that shows the total of:
   (a) after-tax profit or loss from discontinued operations
   (b) the after-tax gain or loss recognized on the re-measurement to fair value less costs to sell or on disposal.

> **discontinued operations**
>
> A discontinued operation is a component of an entity that either has been disposed of or is classified as held for sale and both represents a separate line of business or geographical area of operations and is part of a single co-ordinated plan to dispose of a separate major line of business
>
> *Based on IFRS 5, Appendix A*

The entity should also disclose on the face of the income statement or in the notes the revenue, expenses, pre-tax profit or loss and the related income tax expense of the discontinued operation.

The classification, presentation and measurement requirements of IFRS 5 also apply to a non-current asset (or disposal group) classified as held for *distribution to owners*.

The 'component' in the definition of a discontinued operation is easily identifiable. It is part of an entity where the operations and cash flows can be clearly distinguished, operationally and for financial reporting purposes, from the rest of the entity. They are cash-generating units or a group of cash-generating units while being held for use.

The discontinued operation may be a single non-current asset or a group of non-current assets. In addition to non-current assets there may also be liabilities directly associated with the component.

At the end of the financial year, the entity has either disposed of the component or intends to. The reasons for the disposal could be many. They may be strategic, if the entity is shifting the focus of its operations, political if the component is in a region that the entity does not regard as favourable, or simply that the entity believes it can obtain more by disposal than by continuing to operate the component.

At the end of the financial year, the entity will be in one of the positions shown in Diagram 15.3.

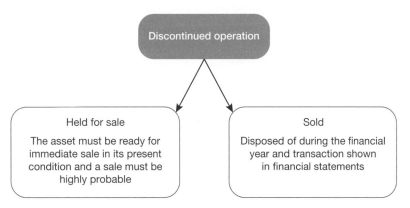

▲ **Diagram 15.3** *Discontinued operations accounting treatments*

Company example 15.3 is taken from the annual report and accounts of ENI. The company is one of the world's leading international oil and gas companies. It is the second largest company in Italy and among the world's top 50 by revenue. The company publishes an Integrated Annual Report. We discuss these types of reports in Chapter 21.

Company example 15.3

Discontinued operations

As far as the chemical business managed by Eni's wholly-owned subsidiary Versalis SpA is concerned, at December 31, 2015, negotiations were underway to define an agreement with an industrial partner who, by acquiring a controlling stake of Versalis, would support Eni in implementing the industrial plan designed to upgrade this business.

Therefore, effective for the full year, likewise Saipem, Versalis' assets and liabilities, revenues and expenses and cash flow have been classified as discontinued operations. In addition, Eni's net assets in Versalis have been aligned to the lower of their carrying amount and their fair value based on the transaction that is underway.

ENI, Integrated Annual Report, 2015, p. 61

Non-current assets held for sale

An asset is held-for-sale when an entity does not intend to use it for its ongoing business. The entity will make this decision by comparing the asset's carrying amount to the proceeds from a sale transaction and its value through continuing use. If the proceeds from the sale transaction are higher than both the carrying amount and the amount from continuing use, the entity may decide to sell. This is the immediate business rationale, although the entity may consider other factors such as its strategic plans and future trends in the market.

The criteria required for an entity to determine an asset or disposal group is held-for-sale are:

1   The asset is available for immediate sale in its present condition. The terms of the sale should be usual for sales of such assets (or disposal groups); and
2   The sale must be highly probable. To be highly probable:
    o   management must be committed to a plan to sell the asset (or disposal group);
    o   there must be an active programme to locate a buyer and complete the plan;
    o   the asset (or disposal group) must be actively marketed for sale at a reasonable price;
    o   the sale should be expected to be completed within one year from the date of classification unless events or circumstances beyond the entity's control delay it;
    o   it is unlikely that there will be significant change or withdrawal of the plan.

All of these criteria must be satisfied for classification of the asset as held-for-sale. For example, if it is evident that what the entity believes is a reasonable price is too high to attract buyers, management may decide not to continue with the plan. They may decide to keep using the asset and it will remain on the balance sheet similar to other assets. If an entity is unable to sell a disposal group and decides to abandon the disposal group, the entity will classify it as a discontinued operation.

An entity must satisfy all the criteria for classification as a held-for-sale asset at the end of the reporting period. The key to this requirement is timing. The asset may not meet the criteria until after the end of the reporting period. However, some weeks later, before the authorization of the financial statements, the asset may meet the criteria. This does not allow classification of the asset as held-for-sale. The asset must meet the criteria before the end of the financial period.

Once an entity has determined that a non-current asset or disposal group is held-for-sale, it calculates the amount based on the lower of its carrying amount and the fair value less costs to sell. Costs to sell are the incremental costs that the entity will incur because of the disposal of the assets. Examples may include costs to advertise the assets, costs to transport the assets and costs to uninstall the assets from their present location. Any depreciation on the asset should cease.

An entity should recognize any difference between the carrying value and the fair value less costs to sell. The difference is disclosed in the income statement as an impairment loss. This is an exception to IAS 36 *Impairment of Assets* (see Chapter 5), as this requires a comparison of the carrying amount to the recoverable amount. By applying this exception under IFRS 5, the entity recognizes immediately any anticipated losses from the sale of the assets as soon as the decision to sell the assets has taken place.

An entity may reverse the classification of held-for-sale of a non-current asset or disposal group. If so, the entity will measure the asset or disposal group at the lower of:

●   its carrying amount before the held-for-sale classification, adjusted for any depreciation that would have been charged if the asset had not been held-for-sale;
●   its recoverable amount at the date of the decision not to sell.

This regulation means that an entity cannot write up an asset past its original carrying value prior to the decision to sell the asset or disposal group. Worked example 15.1 will clarify some of these requirements.

Worked example 15.1   Farewell plc

A hypothetical company, Farewell plc, has a year-end at 31 December 2014. It holds a non-current asset it wishes to sell with a carrying amount of £100,000. It was classified as held-for-sale in September 2014. Its fair value less costs to sell at that time was considered to be £70,000. In the statement of financial position, the asset is recorded at £70,000 on a separate line item from ordinary assets held for use. Therefore, an impairment loss is required of £30,000 in profit or loss to record the asset at its new value of £70,000. Impairment losses are recorded as part of income from continuing operations in profit or loss unless the specific criteria for discontinued operations are also met.

If the company decided not to sell the asset, the measurement of £70,000 would be reversed to the lower of its carrying amount when it was classified as held-for-sale less any subsequent depreciation.

IFRS 8
OPERATING SEGMENTS

▼ **Table 15.7** *Timeline of IFRS 8*

Date	Comment
2006	Standard first issued
2013	Latest amendment

operating segment

An operating segment is a component of an entity:

- that engages in business activities that may earn revenue and incur expenses;
- whose operating results are regularly reviewed by the chief operating decision maker. The term 'chief operating decision maker' is not as such defined in IFRS8 because it refers to a function rather than a title. In some entities the function could be fulfilled by a group of directors rather than an individual; and
- for which discrete financial information is available.

Based on IFRS 8, Appendix A

The examples that we have shown in this book demonstrate the size and complexity of some companies. They can have thousands of employees, in different countries and with a wide range of products and services. It is impossible for a Board of Directors or a senior management team to have direct control and knowledge of every part of the organization.

To ensure good planning, control and decision making, the management may decide to identify different parts of the organization as **operating segments**. This allows the management to obtain useful information on the activities of the different operating segments. The information that is useful to managers is also of interest to investors and other users of financial reports.

To meet the needs of users, IAS 14 *Segment Reporting* was issued in 1997 to be effective from 1998. It required reporting of financial information by business or geographical area. The standard contained disclosure requirements for primary and secondary segments. The primary segments were based on whether the entity's risks and returns were affected predominantly by:

- the products and services it produces; or
- its operating in different geographical areas.

As part of the convergence project with the US, IAS 14 was withdrawn and replaced by a new standard IFRS 8 *Operating Segments in 2006*. An entity must comply with the standard if:

- its debt or equity instruments are traded in a public market; or
- it is seeking to issue any class of instruments in a public market.

There is nothing to prevent an entity that does not meet the above criteria from voluntarily providing the segment information IFRS 8 requires. If it does so, it should describe the disclosures as 'segment information'.

Although IFRS 8 requires the disclosure of segmental information it does not define what it considers a segment to be. Instead, the standard relies on the entity to identify the segments. This is done by the entity's 'chief operating decision maker'. This is not necessarily one person with that title but can be the person or group of managers whose responsibility is to allocate resources to and assess the performance of an entity's operating segments.

Relying on the entity to determine the segments to be disclosed has resulted in some criticisms. It means that the management decides what a segment is and therefore the information it should disclose. It also impairs comparability between financial statements of different entities, as the users do not know the criteria the entity used in identifying the segments.

Although the European Securities and Markets Authority (ESMA 2011) and others have queried the entities' level of discretion when they decide the operating segments, the standard setters have problems in setting criteria to identify segments. If the entity does not consider an activity to be a separate segment and therefore does not collect data, it cannot disclose information.

IFRS 8 does have percentage criteria for those segments that the chief operating decision maker identifies. We discuss these later in this section. At this stage, we wish to consider the identification of segments. Company example 15.4 demonstrates the approach that CRH plc adopts. CRH is a leading global building materials group employing over 89,000 people at around 3,900 locations worldwide. From these numbers, it is evident that the company must have separate segments.

Company example 15.4

Identification of segments

The principal factors employed in the identification of the six segments reflected in this note include the Group's organisational structure in 2014, the nature of the reporting lines to the Chief Operating Decision-Maker (as defined in IFRS 8 *Operating Segments*), the structure of internal reporting documentation such as management accounts and budgets, and the degree of homogeneity of products, services and geographical areas within each of the segments from which revenue is derived.

The Chief Operating Decision-Maker monitors the operating results of segments separately in order to allocate resources between segments and to assess performance.

continued

> ## Company example 15.4 *continued*
>
> Segment performance is predominantly evaluated based on operating profit. As performance is also evaluated using operating profit before depreciation and amortisation (EBITDA (as defined)*), supplemental information based on EBITDA (as defined)* is also provided below. Given that net finance costs and income tax are managed on a centralised basis, these items are not allocated between operating segments for the purposes of the information presented to the Chief Operating Decision-Maker and are accordingly omitted from the detailed segmental analysis below. There are no asymmetrical allocations to reporting segments which would require disclosure.
>
> ** EBITDA is defined as earnings before interest, taxes, depreciation, amortisation, asset impairment charges, profit on disposals and the Group's share of equity accounted investments' result after tax.*
>
> CRH plc, Annual Report and Accounts, 2014, p. 115

This extract shows us that:

- the entity has identified six operating segments;
- the Chief Operating Officer is responsible for allocating resources and assessing performance;
- segment performance is based on operating profit and EBITDA.

We would emphasize that the extract is in full compliance with the standard and CRH's report has over three pages showing considerable detail.

Disclosures of segmental information

An entity may have identified several separate operating segments but disclosure is required only if a segment meets any of the following quantitative thresholds:

- its reported revenue (external and inter-segment) is 10% or more of the combined revenue, internal and external, of all operating segments;
- its reported profit or loss is 10% or more of the greater, in absolute amount, of (i) the combined profit of all operating segments that did not report a loss and (ii) the combined loss of all operating segments that reported a loss; or
- its assets are 10% or more of the combined assets of all operating segments.

There is a threshold for disclosure of operating segments. If the total external turnover reported by the operating segments identified by size criteria is less than 75% of total entity revenue, there is identification of additional segments until the 75% level is reached. If there are several segments with similar economic characteristics an entity can aggregate them into a single operating segment for the purposes of the size criteria.

An entity must report consistently both current period and comparative segment information. It is possible that an entity reports a segment in the current period but did not report it in the previous period, possibly because it did not meet the size criteria at that time. In such a case, the entity must provide equivalent comparative information unless it would be prohibitively costly to obtain.

Entities can, if they wish, disclose information even if the segment meets the size criteria. This could occur where the management considers information about the segment would be useful to users of the financial statements.

Detailed disclosures

Main disclosures:

- General information on such matters as the method entities have used to identify the reportable segments and the segments' types of products or services from which it generates its revenue.
- A measure of profit or loss and total assets for each reportable segment.
- If the chief operating decision maker is regularly provided with information on liabilities, these liabilities should also be reported on a segment basis.

Disclosures for profit or loss and assets where the amounts are included in the measure of profit or loss and total assets are:

- Revenues – internal and external.
- Interest revenues and interest expense. The general rule is that these must not be netted off. However, they may be netted off if the majority of a segment's revenues are from interest and the chief operating decision maker assesses the performance of the segment based on net interest revenue.
- Depreciation and amortization.
- Material items of income and expense disclosed separately.
- Share of profit after tax of, and carrying value of investment in, entities accounted for under the equity method.
- Material non-cash items other than depreciation and amortization.
- The amount of additions to non-current assets other than financial instruments, deferred tax assets, post-employment benefit assets and rights arising under insurance contracts.

The measurement basis for each item separately reported should be the one used in the information provided to the chief operating decision maker. Where the internal reporting system uses more than one measure of an operating segment's profit or loss, or assets or liabilities, the measure used in the segment report should be the one that management believes is most consistent with those used to measure the corresponding amounts in the entity's financial statements.

Required reconciliations are:

- the total of the reportable segments' revenues to the entity's revenue;
- the total of the reportable segments' profit or loss to the entity's profit or loss;
- the total of the reportable segments' assets to the entity's assets;
- the total, where separately identified, of the reportable segments' liabilities to the entity's liabilities; and
- the total of the reportable segments' amounts for every other material item disclosed to the corresponding amount for the entity.

Entity-wide disclosures

If the information is not given in the segment report, an entity should disclose information on:

- its revenue on a geographical and 'class of business' basis; and
- non-current assets on a geographical basis, but not on a 'class of business' basis.

If revenues from a single external customer amount to 10% or more of the total revenue of the entity then the entity needs to disclose that fact plus:

- the total revenue from each customer (although the name is not needed); and
- the segment or segments reporting the revenues.

The 'entity-wide disclosures' are required even where the entity has only a single operating segment, and therefore does not effectively segment report.

A comprehensive view of the literature and their own analysis led Nichols et al. (2013) to conclude that the impact of IFRS 8, at least in European countries, resulted in a significant decrease in the average number of disclosures for operating segments.

If the standard leads to a lower level of disclosures, there is the question whether the replacement standard meets the needs of users. A study by Leung and Verriest (2015) concluded that IFRS 8 does not strongly affect analysts' forecast accuracy, forecast dispersion, market liquidity and cost of equity capital. This includes instances where IFRS 8 improved segment reporting.

Although the standard only becomes applicable in certain circumstances, segmental reporting is a valuable disclosure. The question arises whether IFRS 8 is sufficiently robust or whether the standard setters need to revisit it.

CONCLUSIONS

In this chapter, we have discussed standards that apply to specific entities and activities. You need a good understanding of the activities that occur in particular industries to understand the standards fully.

IAS 40 addresses the accounting treatment of investment properties. The standard is concise and clear. The standard makes a clear distinction between property that an entity acquires for its own use and one the entity acquires for investment purposes. There are important differences with investment property coming under IAS 40 and owner occupied property under IAS 16.

The measurement model an entity chooses has accounting implications. An entity can record investment property either at:

- fair value: this is the amount at which the property could be exchanged between knowledgeable and willing parties in an arm's length transaction;
- cost less accumulated depreciation and any accumulated impairment losses as prescribed by IAS 16.

Agriculture is a large industry and we all enjoy its outputs. IAS 41 addresses some interesting issues about identifying and accounting for items that are growing, whether they be cattle or plants. The IASB has removed bearer plants from the standard's requirements and additionally does not cover agricultural produce after harvesting.

The recognition and measurement criteria are clear. The entity controls the asset because of past events and considers that it is probable it will enjoy future economic benefits associated with the asset. The standard requires initial and subsequent measurement at fair value or cost and argues that cost can approximate to fair value.

We do not consider that IFRS 6 *Exploration for and Evaluation of Mineral Assets* is a robust standard. Research indicates that the operators in the industry had significant influence on the development of the standard and its requirements may represent a compromise. Added to this, the huge costs of exploration and extraction of mineral assets, and the turbulence that there can be in market prices, bring additional pressures to the operators and the users of financial statements. It may be that standard setters will be persuaded to return to the accounting requirements for this industry.

Apart from having the longest title of all standards, IFRS 5 *Non-current Assets Held for Sale and Discontinued Operations* is an unremarkable standard. Its purpose is to require the disclosure of certain information that is of value to the users of financial statements. The criteria required for an entity to determine an asset or disposal group is held-for-sale are that the asset is available for immediate sale and the sale must be highly probable.

IFRS 8 *Operating Segments* has been criticized. The main reason is that the entity decides the operating segments and this method could be abused. However, we cannot see a more practical solution to this problem. The main purpose of the standard is to require disclosures on an entity's operating segments. The requirements set specific percentage limits for disclosures. The standard functions well and we do not see any changes being imminent.

IN THE PIPELINE

IFRS 8 Operating segments

The Board commenced a review on the operation of the standard in 2012. It intends to publish an Exposure Draft towards the end of 2016.

IAS 40 Investment property

The IASB published the Exposure Draft *Transfers of Investment Property* (Proposed amendment to IAS 40) to propose a narrow-scope amendment to clarify the guidance on transfers to, or from, investment properties. The Interpretations Committee considered a summary of the comment letters and recommended that the Board should issue the proposed amendments subject to certain reservations. The Board is considering the Interpretations Committee's recommendation.

ADDITIONAL RESOURCES

Go online to the companion website for this book to access further teaching and learning materials for this chapter.

www.palgravehighered.com/hussey-cfr

BUSINESS COMBINATIONS AND CONSOLIDATED FINANCIAL STATEMENTS

IFRS 3 Business Combinations
IFRS 10 Consolidated Financial Statements

LEARNING OBJECTIVES

At the end of this chapter, you should be able to:

- Identify the main requirements of IFRS 3 for business acquisitions
- Explain the acquisition method under IFRS 3
- Explain the application of fair value
- Describe the accounting treatment for goodwill and intangible assets in an acquisition
- Explain the preparation of consolidated accounts under IFRS 10

INTRODUCTION

There are many types of relationships in the business world. One entity may own another entity completely or hold a majority of the equity. Two or more entities may act together on a particular joint venture. An entity may have only a small investment in another entity.

This chapter focuses on acquisitions and the preparation of consolidated accounts. This prepares a foundation for considering all the other types of relationships in the next chapter.

The acquisition of one entity by another leads to the requirement for a set of financial statements for the combined entity in addition to those for the two separate entities. Although the two entities may be legally independent, if one entity owns all or most of the shares in the second entity, then the second entity is an asset from which the first entity expects future economic benefits. There is an additional reporting entity comprising the two separate entities.

The separate financial statements for each of the two entities are inadequate for all of the activities of the acquiring entity. The two entities form one reporting entity and consolidated financial statements are required. These consolidated financial statements show assets, liabilities, equity, income, expenses and cash flow of the parent and its subsidiaries as if it were a single economic entity.

The acquiring entity – the parent – may own many other entities – the subsidiaries – to form a large group. Some subsidiaries may be fully owned and others partly owned. There may even be cases where ownership is difficult to identify.

As part of the convergence project with the FASB, in 2002 the IASB commenced a comprehensive project to address inconsistencies in the existing regulations. Although several accounting standards addressed different forms of organizational relationships, there were inconsistencies and situations where the regulations did not 'fit'.

Because of the various changes, the introduction of new standards and the significant amendments to some existing standards, we list in Table 16.1 the situation in 2016. The standards in bold have either been withdrawn or replaced by a significantly amended standard with the same number.

▼ Table 16.1 *Business combination standards*

Accounting standard	History
IAS 27 Consolidated and Separate Financial Statements	**Originally issued in 2003, it was superseded by IFRS 10 and IFRS 12, effective 1 January 2013**
IAS 27 (2011) Separate Financial Statements	As part of the reorganization, the original IAS 27 was withdrawn and replaced by this 2011 standard
IAS 28 Investments in Associates	**Originally issued in 2003, it was superseded by IFRS 12 and IAS 28 (2011)**
IAS 28 (2011) Investments in Associates and Joint Ventures	The original standard was withdrawn and replaced by this 2011 standard
IAS 31 Interests in Joint Ventures	**Originally issued in 2003, it was superseded by IFRS 11 and IFRS 12**
IFRS 3 Business Combinations	
IFRS 10 Consolidated Financial Statements	
IFRS 11 Joint Arrangements	These three standards were issued in 2011
IFRS 12 Disclosure of Interests in Other Entities	

In this chapter, we discuss IFRS 3 *Business Combinations* and IFRS 10 *Consolidated Financial Statements*. We discuss IFRS 11 and IFRS 12 in Chapter 17.

IFRS 3 and IFRS 10 are not isolated from other standards, and Diagram 16.1 demonstrates the linkages.

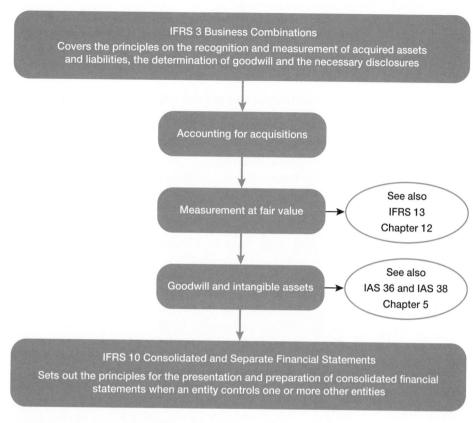

▲ **Diagram 16.1** *Structure of Chapter 16*

IFRS 3

BUSINESS COMBINATIONS

▼ Table 16.2 *Timeline of IFRS 3*

Date	Comment
2004	Standard first issued, the agreement date is on or after 31 March 2004
2008	Revised standard issued, effective where the acquisition date is on or after the beginning of the first annual reporting period beginning on or after 1 July 2009
2010	Amendment issued, effective for annual periods beginning on or after 1 July 2010
2013 (May)	Amendment issued, effective for business combinations for which the acquisition date is on or after 1 July 2014
2013 (December)	Two amendments issued, both effective for annual periods beginning on or after 1 July 2014

IFRS 3 (2008) seeks to enhance the relevance, reliability and comparability of information provided about business combinations (e.g. acquisitions and mergers) and their effects. It sets out the principles on the recognition and measurement of acquired assets and liabilities, the determination of goodwill and the necessary disclosures.

Accounting for acquisitions

The standard concentrates on explaining the acquisition method that entities must follow for all business combinations. The application method requires the entity to:

1   Identify the acquirer.
2   Identify the acquiree and acquisition date.
3   Recognize and measure the identifiable assets acquired, the liabilities assumed and any non-controlling interest in the acquiree.
4   Recognize and measure intangible assets and goodwill.

In Chapters 4, 5 and 6 we discussed assets, liabilities and goodwill and, if necessary, you should refresh your understanding of these topics.

Following the issue of IFRS 3, the IFRS Foundation (IFRS Foundation 2015) published a research document entitled *Post-implication Review* (PIR) which identified certain issues.

The IFRS Foundation assessed the comments it received and referred to other sources of information, such as academic research. From these sources, the IFRS Foundation gave an indication of the actions it contemplates taking. In this chapter, we refer to the PIR to clarify certain parts of the standard and to illustrate where entities are identifying problems.

For simplicity, our explanations assume that one single entity is acquiring another single entity. This rarely happens in practice with major companies. These companies can be very active in the disposal and acquisition of businesses in a financial year. There were 93 successful domestic and cross-border merger and acquisition transactions involving UK companies in April to June 2015. This compares to 110 in January to March of that year.

We analyze these totals in Table 16.3 which shows the number of domestic acquisitions, the inward acquisitions where foreign companies are acquiring UK companies and outward acquisitions where UK companies are acquiring foreign companies.

▼ Table 16.3 *Acquisitions in 2015*

Date	UK internal	Inward acquisitions	Outward acquisitions	Total
January to March	43	19	48	110
April to June	46	21	26	93

Source: ONS, 2015.

To provide one single example of a major company's activity, we have selected the record of Unilever plc during 2014 (see Company example 16.1). This exemplifies the international nature of its activities and demonstrates that there are frequently more than one acquisition in a financial year.

The size of the company must be borne in mind when considering the high level of activity in Company example 16.1. Unilever is an Anglo-Dutch multinational consumer goods company co-headquartered in Rotterdam and London. Its products include food, beverages, cleaning agents and personal care products. Unilever owns over 400 brands, many with an international recognition. It has research and development facilities in the UK, the Netherlands, China, India and the US.

Company example 16.1

Acquisitions and disposals

2014

On 16 January 2014 the Group signed an agreement to sell its Royal pasta brand in the Philippines to RFM Corporation, for US $48 million.

On 7 March 2014 the Group acquired a 55% equity stake in the Qinyuan Group, a leading Chinese water purification business for an undisclosed amount.

On 1 April 2014 the Group completed the sale of its meat snacks business, including the Bifi and Peperami brands, to Jack Link's for an undisclosed amount.

On 30 June 2014 the Group completed the sale of its global Ragu and Bertolli pasta sauce business to Mizkan Group for a total cash consideration of approximately US $2.15 billion.

On 10 July 2014 the Group sold its Slim.Fast brand to Kainos Capital for an undisclosed amount. Unilever will retain a minority stake in the business.

On 2 December 2014 the Group acquired Talenti Gelato & Sorbetto for an undisclosed amount.

On 22 December 2014 the Group announced the purchase of the Camay brand globally and the Zest brand outside of North America and the Caribbean from The Procter & Gamble Company. The transaction, for an undisclosed amount, is expected to close during the first half of 2015 subject to necessary regulatory approvals.

Unilever plc, Annual Report and Accounts, 2014, pp. 125–126

Identifying the acquirer

business

A business is an integrated set of activities and assets that is capable of being conducted and managed for the purpose of providing a return in the form of dividends, lower costs or other economic benefits directly to investors or other owners, members or participants.

Based on IFRS 3, Appendix A

The standard applies to the acquisition or merger of one **business** by another to form a business combination. We need to know what the terms 'business' and 'business combination' mean and the standard provides definitions.

The PIR research (IFRS Foundation 2015) revealed that respondents considered that the definition of a business is broad and that there is insufficient guidance in distinguishing between an acquired set of assets and a business. This is because the structure of large businesses is usually complex and the inter-entity transactions can be accordingly difficult.

In discussing corporate acquisition, we may be referring to either 'asset purchases' in which the buyer buys specific business assets from a selling entity or 'equity purchases' in which the buyer purchases equity interests in a target entity from one or more shareholders who are willing to relinquish their ownership.

For example, one entity may purchase several assets from another entity. It would show these on the balance sheet as assets. However, the entity must comply with the requirements of IFRS 3 if the acquisition falls within the broad definition of a business. The distinction between a set of assets and a business can also be very important because the acquisition of a business may result in the purchase of goodwill whereas the acquisition of an asset does not. We explain the issue of goodwill later in the chapter.

The IFRS agrees that defining a business is extremely difficult in industries such as real estate, extractive industries, pharmaceutical, technology and shipping. Their response is to encourage research to ascertain whether it is possible to improve the definition of a business and the related application guidance (IFRS Foundation 2015: 17).

The actual formation of a **business combination** has two distinct elements, as we illustrate in Diagram 16.2.

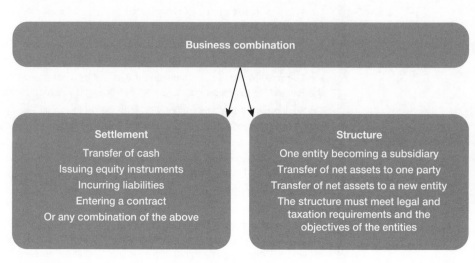

▲ **Diagram 16.2** *Elements of a business combination*

business combination

A business combination is a transaction or other event in which an acquirer obtains control of one or more businesses. Transactions sometimes referred to as 'true mergers' or 'mergers of equals' are also business combinations.

Based on IFRS 3, Appendix A

The standard does not apply to:

- The accounting for the formation of a joint venture in the financial statements of the joint venture itself (refer to IFRS 11, discussed in Chapter 17).
- The acquisition of an asset or group of assets that is not a business, although general guidance is provided on how to account for such transactions.
- Combinations of entities or businesses under common control.
- Acquisitions by an investment entity of a subsidiary that is required to be measured at fair value through profit or loss (refer to IFRS 10 later in this chapter).

The standard identifies a business as activities that are being conducted to convert inputs into outputs. There are processes, employees, plans to produce outputs, and there is the prospect of customers willing to purchase the output.

Where one business acquires another business on an agreed date, either by offering shares or cash or a combination of both, the acquirer must apply the acquisition method to the transaction. The acquirer (parent) gains control of the acquiree (subsidiary). This may be either a 100% acquisition where the parent holds all the equity in the subsidiary or where the acquirer holds only part of the equity but has gained control. In a partial ownership there will be other owners called 'non-controlling interests', previously known as 'minority interests'.

The concept of control is important but IFRS 3 does not explain the term. To understand the concept of control we must refer to IFRS 10. The details are complex and we explain them later in the chapter.

Identifying the acquiree and acquisition date

The basic principles in a business combination are that there will always be an **acquirer** and an **acquiree** and that it is possible to identify the acquirer. You will see references in business newspapers from time to time about the 'merger' of two companies. From an accounting perspective, this is more than likely to be an acquisition. The standard requires the application of the acquisition method for all business combinations.

The IFRS3 definitions assume that it is always possible to identify the acquirer, and the main indicator will be whether the acquirer has obtained control of the other entity. Where control is not easy to demonstrate, the standard offers guidance to determine which entity is the acquirer in different circumstances.

acquiree

The acquiree is the business or businesses that the acquirer obtains control of in a business combination.

Based on IFRS 3, Appendix A

acquirer

The acquirer is the entity that obtains control of the acquiree.

Based on IFRS 3, Appendix A

acquisition date

The acquisition date is the date on which the acquirer obtains control of the acquiree.

Based on IFRS 3, Appendix A

1 The acquiring entity is usually the one that transfers cash or other assets where this is the agreed method.

2 The acquiring entity is usually the largest entity measured by assets, revenue or profit.

3 The acquiring entity is usually the one that issues equity interests where this is the agreed method. The following factors may influence the conclusion:

   o relative voting rights in the combined entity after the business combination;

   o the existence of any large minority interest if no other owner or group of owners has a significant voting interest;

   o the composition of the governing body or management of the combined entity;

   o the terms on which equity interests are exchanged.

4 Where there are multiple entities involved in the business combination, the entity initiating the combination and the relative sizes of the combining entities are important.

Recognizing and measuring assets and liabilities

The general principle is that the cost of a business combination is the total of the fair values of the consideration given by the acquirer plus any directly attributable costs of the business combination. The acquirer should charge expenses, such as fees of lawyers and accountants acting as advisers, to the income statement. These costs are not part of the consideration.

IFRS 13 regulates the determination of fair value, and we discussed this standard in Chapter 12. We can regard fair value as the price an entity would receive on selling an asset or pay to transfer a liability. The transaction should be orderly and between market participants at the measurement date.

Although IFRS 13 applies to various transactions, in this chapter we discuss its application and the issues involved specifically concerning business combinations.

As far as the payment is concerned, the consideration paid may be:

- cash or other assets transferred to the acquire;
- liabilities assumed by the acquirer, e.g. taking on the liability for a bank loan of the acquiree;
- the issue of equity instruments, such as ordinary shares.

There are instances where only a provisional fair value is possible at the acquisition date. If there are adjustments arising within 12 months of the acquisition date they can be set back to the acquisition date and the goodwill recalculated (see Worked example 16.1).

Worked example 16.1   Provisional fair value

An entity may have made an acquisition of 100% of another entity on 1 January 2014 for the sum of £650,000. A provisional fair value of the net assets at that time was £500,000. The goodwill would be £150,000 at that stage. On 1 July, a final fair value is set at £620,000 so the goodwill is recalculated to £120,000. These would be the amounts reported in the parent's financial statements at the year-end. If there are any further adjustments to the fair value after the year-end, these are recognized in profit or loss.

Contingent consideration

There are business combinations where the acquirer and acquiree agree that, if some future specific events occur, the acquiree is entitled to further payment. One possibility is that the acquirer has the right to the return of previously transferred consideration if specified conditions occur.

The agreement for further payments by the acquirer to the acquiree, or for the acquirer to have previously made payment returned, introduces the term 'contingent consideration'. This term means that the potential payment is dependent on the acquiree achieving certain agreed financial targets.

With an acquisition, the acquirer usually believes that the acquired business will continue to make profits in the future, and even increase those profits. In some businesses, for example in the advertising industry, the value of the business acquired is mostly the creative abilities of the employees and the loyalty of the clients of the business.

The acquirer does not want to lose these benefits and may insert a clause in the agreement that specifies the targeted future profits for the next 3–6 years. If these are achieved, or surpassed, the acquirer agrees to pay further consideration.

Company example 16.2 of contingent consideration is taken from Fyffes plc. The company is listed on the Enterprise Securities Market (ESM) in Dublin and the Alternative Investment Market (AIM) in London. Its primary activities include production, procurement, shipping, ripening, distribution and marketing of bananas, pineapples and melons.

The advantage of contingent consideration agreements is that the acquirer has some reassurances on the future success of the business but any future payment they make is contingent on that success. For the previous owners, they have the possibility of receiving a much higher consideration in total than if they had settled for one amount at the time of the acquisition.

The standard requires the acquirer to recognize, at the date of acquisition, the fair value of the contingent consideration as part of the consideration for the acquiree. The application of this definition to contingent consideration is not easy and may result in problems for some entities.

In Scenario 16.1, the problem is the measurement of the contingent consideration in the number of shares instead of a specific financial sum. In making the agreement, InterAD has to predict the share price at the end of the period to know the full amount of the payment. A specified payment amount in financial terms is easier to manage and presents less risk.

Company example 16.2

Deferred contingent consideration

Deferred contingent consideration liabilities represent full provision for the net present value of the amounts expected to be payable in respect of acquisitions which are subject to earn out or other deferred payment arrangements. Total payments of €92,000 were made in 2015 (2014: €2,481,000) in relation to prior year acquisitions. The remaining consideration payable in respect of prior year acquisitions of €1,370,000 is no longer contingent on earnings and consequently was transferred to other payables during the year. As set out in note 26, a deferred contingent consideration liability of €1,126,000 arose in connection with the acquisition of a business in late 2015. This amount was subsequently paid in January 2016 following finalisation of certain outstanding matters related to the acquisition.

Fyffes, Annual Report and Accounts, 2015, p. 86

Scenario 16.1   Contingent consideration

InterAD plc acquires completely the business of EuroAd. The acquisition agreement states that there is a contingent consideration to be paid of 100,000 shares in two years' time. This is based on EuroAD achieving certain levels of profit. Both parties agree that these are achievable. At the acquisition date, the published share price of InterAD plc quoted shares is £1.00 per share.

However, EuroAd may be bargaining to receive the shares in the belief that the share price will increase in two years' time.

We return to the topic of contingent consideration later in this chapter. At this stage, we discuss what the acquirer obtains for its money. At the acquisition date, the acquirer must recognize the acquiree's assets, liabilities and contingent liabilities at their fair value if they meet the following criteria.

- Assets other than intangible assets should be recognized where it is probable that the associated future economic benefits generated by the use of the assets will flow to the acquirer and their fair value can be measured reliably.
- Liabilities, other than contingent liabilities, should be recognized where it is probable that an outflow of economic benefits will be required to settle the obligation and their fair value can be measured reliably.
- Intangible assets or contingent liabilities at fair value should be recognized where they can be measured reliably. Recognition can only occur where they meet the definition of an intangible asset complying with IAS 38 *Intangible Assets* and their fair value is capable of being measured reliably.

Not surprisingly, respondents to the IFRS's call for feedback stated that they confronted several difficulties in the concept of fair value in acquisitions, as well as practical difficulties.

Although agreeing that fair value measurement provided useful information to investors, the respondents identified the following concerns:

- It does not facilitate the comparison of trends between companies that grow organically and those that grow through acquisitions.
- Upward revaluations of acquired inventory to fair value reduce profitability in the first period following the acquisition. In other words, the inventory is measured by the acquired entity at the price it was originally purchased and this may have increased by the acquisition date.
- Measuring the fair value of contingent consideration is highly judgemental and difficult to validate. In the pharmaceutical industry the research and development period of a drug can take more than 10 years and it is common for acquisition agreements to have multiple success-based contingent consideration payments linked to stages of successful completion.
- The fair value of contingent liabilities is difficult to measure because it depends on a number of assumptions and because of a general lack of guidance. We discussed contingent liabilities in Chapter 13 with reference to IAS 37.

Recognizing and measuring intangible assets and goodwill

A major problem revolves around the recognition of intangible assets and their separation from goodwill. The acquiree may have on its balance sheet identifiable intangible assets. The acquiree also may have developed its own intangible assets such as a brand name or a list of customers.

Under IAS 38, the acquiree cannot recognize these on its balance sheet because it generated these intangible assets internally. You may find it helpful to refer to the sections on goodwill and intangible assets in Chapter 5 before continuing with this chapter.

When the acquirer pays for the business, it is acquiring these previously unidentified intangible assets. The acquirer can therefore place them on its balance sheet. The difficulty confronting the acquirer is determining the fair value of such intangibles.

The participants providing feedback to the IFRS's PIR expressed difficulties in determining the recognition and measurement of intangible assets that are separable from goodwill. The particular intangible assets causing problems are customer relationships, non-contractual intangible assets, those for which there is no active market, and those in the 'early stage' of development.

The Application Guidance of IFRS 13 provides some clarification and we summarize the main points below.

There must be separate recognition of identifiable intangible assets and goodwill. The intangible asset is identifiable if it meets either the separability criterion or the contractual legal criterion as we explain below.

Separability criterion

The acquired *intangible asset* can be separated or divided from the *acquiree*. It can be sold, transferred, licensed, rented or exchanged, either individually or together with a related contract, *identifiable* asset or liability.

Contractual legal criterion

An *intangible asset* that meets the contractual legal criterion is *identifiable* even if the asset is not transferable or separable from the *acquiree* or from other rights and obligations. The

Guidance gives examples of the contractual legal criterion. One example is where the acquiree owns and operates a nuclear power plant under licence. The licence cannot be sold or transferred separately from the power plant. An acquirer can recognize the fair value of the licence and the operating plant as a single asset for financial reporting purposes if the useful lives of these assets are similar. A separate calculation is made for any goodwill.

Having gone through the exercise of determining the fair value of the identifiable net assets (assets – liabilities), including intangible assets, the acquirer is likely to find that the amount it is paying is higher than the fair value of the net assets it is acquiring.

The critical factor in the calculation is that only identifiable assets are included. The acquiring company is, in all probability, acquiring the reputation of the business, loyal customers, procedures and processes that are established. These characteristics all contribute to the future economic benefits the acquirer hopes to enjoy but cannot identify them specifically and individually. The acquirer will group them together under the general description of 'Goodwill'.

In Chapter 5, we explained the standard IAS 38 *Intangible Assets*. Those regulations require an intangible asset to be identifiable to distinguish it from goodwill. Intangible assets can be rights under licensing agreements for items such as motion picture films, video recordings, plays, manuscripts, patents and copyrights.

The IFRS Foundation in its response recognizes the problems with identifying intangible assets and goodwill. It recommends research to explore whether particular intangible assets are part of goodwill. It is also considering whether additional guidance on the recognition and measurement of different types of intangible assets is necessary.

Until there is that guidance, entities must comply with the existing requirements. When one entity acquires another it will expect to pay for all the tangible non-current assets such as property, plant and equipment. It will also expect to pay for the identifiable intangible assets that it acquires.

The acquirer will usually pay more than the value of the tangible assets and intangible assets added together. The reason for this is that it wishes to acquire an operating, and a profitable business or one with the promise to be so. It is not just acquiring assets but all those other ingredients that make up that business such as reputation of the business, experience and knowledge of workforce, contacts with suppliers, customer base, and established systems and procedures.

All of these ingredients fall under the heading of goodwill. Goodwill is therefore an integrated part of the business that cannot be separated from it.

If it is so difficult to identify and classify the ingredients of goodwill, the question arises as to how one places a value on goodwill at the acquisition of another business. The standard requires that the acquirer recognize goodwill at the acquisition date. The acquirer arrives at the amount of the goodwill by:

1 Calculating and aggregating the consideration transferred and the amount of any non-controlling interests.

2 Deducting from the aggregate amount in Step 1, the net of the acquisition-date amounts of the *identifiable* assets acquired and the liabilities assumed.

Step 1 calculates the consideration, so the deduction in Step 2 means that the resulting balance is goodwill. We demonstrate this transaction with Worked example 16.2 overleaf.

You can see from Worked example 16.2 that goodwill is a balancing figure. Some would argue that, because there is no method for separately measuring goodwill, reliance cannot be placed on the amount. The acquirer should write it off immediately as an expense. The counter argument is that the acquirer has paid for it and the expectation is that it will bring future benefits.

Worked example 16.2   Calculation of goodwill

Acquirer

Balance sheet before acquisition

	£000		£000
Non-current assets	3,000	Equity	2,400
Cash	2,000	Liabilities	2,600
	5,000		5,000

Acquirer agrees to pay £1,800,000 cash to acquire the acquiree. Acquirer calculates the fair value of the assets it has acquired. Normally, there would be an extensive list of assets and liabilities but, in this example, we have simplified the information. Acquirer's calculations, at fair value, are as follows:

	£000
Assets acquired	
Premises	1,200
Machinery	300
	1,500
Less liabilities	100
Total	1,400

Acquirer has agreed to pay £1,800,000 cash and has calculated the net assets of the acquiree at fair value as £1,400,000. The acquirer recognizes the difference of £400,000 in its balance sheet as goodwill. Having made the payment in cash, the acquirer's cash balance declines from £2,000,000 to £200,000.

Acquirer

Balance sheet after acquisition

	£000		£000
Non-current assets	4,500	Equity	2,400
Goodwill	400		
Cash	200	Liabilities	2,700
	5,100		5,100

The payment made for the acquisition allows the calculation of the value of goodwill, even though it is only a balancing figure. Given the ephemeral nature of goodwill, understandably IAS 36 requires the annual testing of goodwill from a business for impairment.

If you refer to Chapter 5 on impairment, you will see that, where there is an impairment of a cash-generating unit, the entity must write off any goodwill immediately. The standard does not permit the reinstatement of goodwill in the financial statements even if the impairment no longer applies.

The standard assumes that, because the acquirer has paid more than the value of the net assets, the excess must have value. The acquirer must recognize goodwill on acquisition. However, an entity may make an acquisition for various reasons and may be willing to pay more than net assets. It is possible that an acquirer seeks to make the purchase not in the expectation of future benefits but for strategic reasons, as demonstrated in Scenarios 16.2 and 16.3.

> ### Scenario 16.2
>
> A small start-up business has developed a new technology that may pose a threat to the acquirer's present business. One solution may be to acquire control of the start-up through acquisition. The payment would be high, but the question is whether the excess amount is goodwill or due to the strategic decision to control or even prevent the new technology.

> ### Scenario 16.3
>
> A company is aware that a competitor is attempting to move into a market where it is already the biggest operator. It may attempt to stop the competitor by acquiring smaller businesses in the market.
>
> Another example could be a competitor attempting to move into a new business or marketing area through acquisitions. The acquirer may purchase a business to block the competitor.

Negative goodwill or bargain purchases

An acquiring entity may make a bargain purchase where the cost of acquiring the entity is less than the fair value of the identifiable net assets acquired. In these circumstances, there is a 'negative' goodwill and the acquirer has made a gain that it will record in the income statement.

However, prior to the recognition of a gain from a bargain purchase, the entity must re-assess the identification and measurement of the following:

- the identifiable assets acquired and liabilities assumed;
- the non-controlling interest in the acquiree, if any;
- or, for a business combination achieved in stages, the acquirer's previously held equity interest in the acquiree.

The required accounting treatment of intangible assets and goodwill does not meet with the satisfaction of everyone. Although the IFRS PIR found some agreed with the impairment approach to goodwill, there were several criticisms and proposed changes. The main points raised are:

(a) over time, internally generated goodwill will replace acquired goodwill;
(b) estimating the useful life of goodwill is possible and is no more difficult than estimating the useful life of other intangible assets;
(c) goodwill has been paid for and so, eventually, it should affect profit or loss;
(d) amortizing goodwill would decrease volatility in profit or loss when compared to an impairment model;
(e) amortizing goodwill would reduce pressure on the identification of intangible assets, because both goodwill and intangible assets would be amortized.

The IFRS Foundation, although recognizing the issues, is not favourably disposed to a combined amortization and impairment approach. It argues that there is evidence demonstrating that the impairment model is operating effectively. However, the Foundation accepts that there can be improvements to the impairment test and recommends further research. Any future changes are likely to be directed at IAS 36 and not IFRS 3.

Non-controlling interest

Non-controlling interest

The non-controlling interest is that part of the equity in a subsidiary that is not attributable, directly or indirectly, to a parent. The control of the subsidiary rests with the holder of the greatest share of the equity – the parent. Where another party holds a minor part of the equity, this is a non-controlling interest.

We discuss more fully **non-controlling interests** when we examine IFRS 10 later in this chapter. At this stage, we can assume that, with the acquisition, the acquirer owns all the equity in the acquiree or owns sufficient equity to control the acquiree. The acquirer is the parent and the acquiree is a subsidiary.

It is possible that the acquirer does not own all the equity and others own a minority proportion. These are termed 'non-controlling interests' (NCIs). IFRS 3 allows the acquirer a choice in the accounting policy it uses to measure the non-controlling interest. The acquirer can make this choice on a transaction-by-transaction basis. The acquirer can measure the non-controlling interest in one of two ways.

1   Fair value at the acquisition date (sometimes referred to as the full goodwill method). If the acquiree's shares are quoted on an active market, this price can be used, as long as the acquirer's and NCI's fair value per share does not differ. If there is no quoted share price the acquirer must resort to other valuation methods.

2   The NCI's proportionate share of the acquiree's net assets. The net assets, as explained earlier in the chapter, are tangible assets plus intangible assets minus liabilities.

We have three possible situations with an acquisition:

1   The acquirer has 100% ownership of the acquiree.

2   The acquirer does not have full control and there are NCIs. The aquiree opts to use the fair value of the acquiree at the acquisition date.

3   The acquirer does not have full control and there are NCIs. The acquirer opts to use the NCI's proportionate share of the acquiree's net asset.

In Worked examples 16.3, 16.4 and 16.5, we use the same basic figures for calculating goodwill but show the amount if there is a 100% acquisition, the fair value method using a 75% acquisition, and the proportionate share method with a 75% acquisition.

Worked example 16.3   100% acquisition

Grabber plc acquires 100% ownership of Minor plc for £1,600,000. The fair value of the assets and liabilities acquired is £1,200,000.

	£000
Consideration	1,600
Less net assets	1,200
Goodwill	400

Worked example 16.4   75% acquisition using NCI based on fair value

	£000
Consideration (75%)	1,200
Non-controlling interest	400
	1,600
Less net assets	1,200
Goodwill	400

> ### Worked example 16.5   75% acquisition using NCI based on net assets
>
> | | £000 |
> |---|---|
> | Consideration (75%) | 1,200 |
> | Non-controlling interest (25% of fair value) | 300 |
> | | 1,500 |
> | Less net assets | 1,200 |
> | Goodwill | 300 |

The feedback from participants to the IFRS PIR exercise was largely favourable, although some respondents pointed out that the option of two methods on a transaction-by-transaction basis reduced the comparability of financial statements. The IFRS will consider this issue with one possibility being the introduction of a one-time accounting policy choice for all business combinations instead of the current transaction-by-transaction choice.

The extract from the 2014 Annual Report and Accounts of GSK (see Company example 16.3), provides an overview of an entity's compliance with the standard's requirements.

> ## Company example 16.3
>
> ### Business combinations
>
> Business combinations are accounted for using the acquisition accounting method. Identifiable assets, liabilities and contingent liabilities acquired are measured at fair value at acquisition date. The consideration transferred is measured at fair value and includes the fair value of any contingent consideration. Where the consideration transferred, together with the non-controlling interest, exceeds the fair value of the net assets, liabilities and contingent liabilities acquired, the excess is recorded as goodwill. The costs of acquisition are charged to the income statement in the period in which they are incurred. Where not all of the equity of a subsidiary is acquired the non-controlling interest is recognised either at fair value or at the non-controlling interest's share of the net assets of the subsidiary, on a case-by-case basis. Changes in the Group's ownership percentage of subsidiaries are accounted for within equity.
>
> *GSK, Annual Report and Accounts, 2014, p. 141*

This extract complies with the standard by stating clearly:

1   Assets, liabilities and contingent liabilities are measured at fair value on the acquisition date.
2   Consideration is measured at fair value.
3   Where 2 is greater than 1, the excess is recorded as goodwill.

IFRS 3 provides additional guidance on the acquisition method. This provides assistance to entities where circumstances in the acquisition have some differences to the normal transaction. One of the examples is of a stepped transaction and two are where there is no transfer of consideration.

Stepped transaction

An acquirer may already hold equity but subsequently gains control of an acquiree immediately before the acquisition date. The standard refers to this as a business combination achieved in stages or as a step acquisition. The acquirer owned equity previously but then acquires more equity to give control. The stage of obtaining control requires remeasurement of previous investments (equity interests). The acquirer remeasures its previously held equity interest in the acquiree at its acquisition-date fair value and recognizes any resulting gain/loss in profit or loss.

Non-transfer of consideration

There are two situations that can arise. It could be that the acquirer and acquiree agree to combine their businesses with no consideration being transferred. The agreement for the combination is solely by contract. Another situation would be the acquiree repurchasing a number of its own shares. In doing so, it allows an existing investor to hold a sufficient proportion of equity to gain control. The standard requires the application of the acquisition method in both these circumstances.

IFRS 10

CONSOLIDATED AND SEPARATE FINANCIAL STATEMENTS

▼ **Table 16.4** *Timeline of IFRS 10*

Date	Comment
2011	Standard first issued. Effective for periods starting on or after 1 January 2013
2014	Latest amendment issued
Interpretations issued	None

consolidated financial statements

Consolidated financial statements are the financial statements of a group in which the assets, liabilities, equity, income, expenses and cash flows of the parent and its subsidiaries are presented as those of a single economic entity.

Based on IFRS 10, Appendix A

The objective of IFRS 10 is to establish principles for the presentation and preparation of **consolidated financial statements** when an entity controls one or more other entities. The standard has a single consolidation model, based on control, applicable to all entities regardless of the nature of the investee.

It is important to note that IFRS 10 has no disclosure requirements. These are contained in IFRS 12 *Disclosure of Interest in other Entities*, that we discuss in the next chapter. IFRS 12 addresses all disclosures in other entities and not only those under IFRS 10.

Although most people have some understanding of the term subsidiary companies, we believe it is useful to provide some depth to the term. A group of companies can consist of a large number of subsidiaries. For example, one of our sample companies, CRH plc, an International Building Materials group, lists over 120 principal subsidiary companies operating in many different countries.

Key principles of IFRS 10

The purpose of IFRS 10 is to set the requirements for the presentation and preparation of *consolidated financial statements*. These apply whether an entity controls only one subsidiary or several. To achieve this, the standard has the following five main ingredients.

1 It is the responsibility of the parent entity to compile consolidated financial statements.
2 The definition of control and the principle of control to determine consolidation.
3 The application of control to establish whether the investor controls the investee.
4 The accounting requirements for the preparation of consolidated financial statements.
5 The definition of an investment entity and the exceptions to consolidation of particular entities.

The concepts of control and power are the basis of the regulatory requirements. These two concepts are linked. Consolidated financial statements are only required where the investor (the parent) has control and power over the investee, as Diagram 16.3 shows.

The notions of control and power are central to the standard, and we examine these in more detail in the next section.

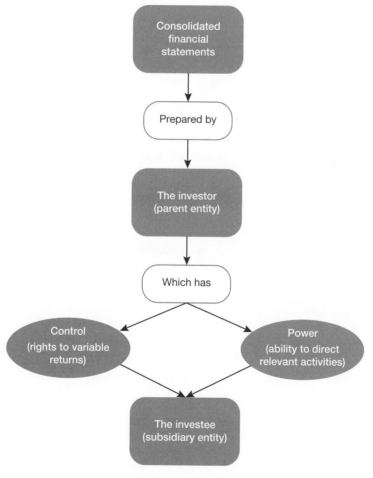

▲ **Diagram 16.3** *Control and power*

Control and power

An investor has a right to variable returns from the investee when the investor's returns may fluctuate because of the investee's performance. The returns could include dividends and remuneration. There are also other forms of returns that are not available to other interest holders. Examples are:

● access to scarce products;
● the ability to develop cost reductions;
● synergies by combining certain activities;
● economies of scale because of the increased size;
● proprietary knowledge through access to restricted information.

Control should be assessed on a continuous basis. Significant judgement may be required to determine whether an investor has control over an investee. The investor must consider the following factors (IFRS 10, Appendix B, para. B3):

(a) The purpose and design of the investee.
(b) The *relevant activities* and making decisions on those activities. Relevant activities are activities of the investee that significantly affect the investee's returns.
(c) Whether the rights of the investor give it the current ability to direct the relevant activities.
(d) Whether the investor is exposed, or has rights, to variable returns from its involvement with the investee.
(e) Whether the investor has the ability to use its *power* over the investee to affect the amount of the investor's returns.

> **power**
>
> Power is defined as existing rights that give the current ability to direct the relevant activities.
>
> *Based on IFRS 10, Appendix A*

> **control**
>
> An investor controls an investee when the investor is exposed, or has rights, to variable returns from its involvement with the investee and has the ability to affect those returns through its power over the investee.
>
> *IFRS 10, Appendix A*

An investor must have the ability to use its **power** to affect its returns from the investee. By having the ability to direct relevant activities, the investor has that power. In some cases, identifying the investor's power may be straightforward; for example, through voting rights granted by equity instruments. In other cases, the assessment may be complex; for example, when power results from contractual arrangements such as the rights to appoint key personnel or decision-making rights.

When the investor has **control** of the investee, consolidated accounts must be prepared. It is possible that the investor does not hold all the equity and other parties hold a minor part. These are non-controlling interests and consolidated accounts are not required.

Where the parent entity loses control of a subsidiary, it must carry out the following actions:

● Derecognition of the subsidiary's assets and liabilities from the consolidated statement of financial position.
● Recognition of any investments retained in the former subsidiary.
● Recognition of the gain or loss associated with the loss of control.

Consolidation

Following the acquisition, the parent entity will have to bring all the separate financial statements of the individual subsidiaries together to prepare consolidated financial statements. Formerly, IAS 27 provided guidance, but IFRS 10 has replaced it.

The requirements themselves are straightforward but we have supplied some worked examples to demonstrate their application.

The first stage of consolidation is to determine the assets, liabilities, income, expenses and cash flows of the parent and combine these with like items of the subsidiaries. The next stage is to eliminate the carrying amount of the parent's investment in each subsidiary and the parent's portion of equity of each subsidiary. This may give rise to an amount for goodwill. IFRS 3 sets out the accounting regulations in these circumstances.

The final stage is the most complex. In all probability, the entities in the group will have conducted some transactions among themselves. As these transactions have not been conducted with outside entities, the group has made neither a profit nor a loss. Profits or losses that individual entities recognized at the time of the transaction must be eliminated in full. We provide some examples of such transactions below.

Non-current asset transfers

One group entity may have transferred non-current assets such as machinery to another group entity at a price higher than the written-down amount in its own accounts. This transaction may have given rise to a profit. Using the single entity concept, the consolidated accounts should show the non-current asset in the consolidated group accounts at the amount as if the transfer had not been made. In other words, you must remove the profit element because a profit cannot be made between two members of the group of companies. This removal of the profit element will also involve an adjustment to depreciation (see Worked example 16.6).

Worked example 16.6   Inter-group profits

On 1 January, a subsidiary sells equipment that had cost £20,000 to its parent for £25,000. The parent depreciates equipment at 10% each year. For the group accounts at the year-end both the profit of £5,000 and the additional depreciation of £500 (£2,500 – £2,000) must be eliminated.

Intercompany balances

Members of a group usually trade with each other. One subsidiary may show accounts receivable in the set of financial statements. This amount is due from another subsidiary. The other subsidiary will have an equal accounts payable in its own financial statements. For the individual entities that is correct, but it is misleading to show the group owing cash to and from itself. On consolidation, the inter-company amounts are cancelled.

Unrealized profit

A member of a group may hold inventory at year-end purchased from another member at market price. The group member that bought the goods will record the inventory at the cost to itself, but this is not the actual cost to the group. The group entity making the sale will show a profit in its accounts – but the group has not made a profit. For the consolidated accounts, the inventory in the balance sheet and the closing inventory in the income statement are reduced to the cost without the 'internal' profit (see Worked example 16.7).

Worked example 16.7   Inventory adjustments

At the year-end, the parent has £250,000 of inventory that it purchased from its wholly owned subsidiary. The cost to the subsidiary of manufacturing these goods was £220,000 and it correctly shows in its own accounts a profit of £30,000. For the group accounts the 'profit' on the inventory must be eliminated by showing the inventory in the balance sheet and the income statement at its cost of £220,000.

We will explain some of these transactions further by looking at a simple example of a consolidated balance sheet with one wholly owned subsidiary (see Worked example 16.8). The holding entity is the trading entity and the wholly owned subsidiary manufactures the goods. To illustrate the transactions more clearly, we use tables instead of the usual balance sheet format.

Worked example 16.8   The consolidated balance sheet

Northern Trading has a fully owned subsidiary, Muggles Manufacturing. All of the output of Muggles is sold to Northern Trading. Below are the balance sheets, in table format, of Northern and Muggles at 31 December 2015.

	Northern	Muggles
	£000	£000
Tangible assets	350	450
Investment in Muggles (shares at cost)	400	
Inventories	160	120
Accounts receivable	80	90
Cash at bank	10	–
Total assets	1000	660
Equity	700	400
Retained earnings	150	200
Accounts payable	150	60
Total equity and liabilities	1000	660

Notes
1 Northern has £50,000 in its accounts receivable that is due from Muggles. This amount is shown in Muggles' accounts payable.

We draw up the consolidated financial statements by adding the two balance sheets together. We cancel items that appear as assets in one statement of financial position and as liabilities in the other statement of financial position.

In this example, there are two such items. The first is the shares held by Northern in Muggles. This amount appears as an asset in Northern's balance sheet, and is included in Muggles' equity of £400,000.

The second item is the accounts receivable of £50,000 in Northern's statement of financial position matched by the accounts payable of Muggles. The accounts receivables for the two entities total £170,000. We deduct the inter-company debt of £50,000 to give a total accounts receivable of £120,000. Similarly, we add the two accounts payable together to give a total of £210,000 and deduct the £50,000 for the consolidated total of £160,000.

continued

Worked example 16.8 *continued*

Consolidated statement of financial position at 31 December 2015

	£000	£000
Non-current assets		800
Current assets		
Inventories	280	
Accounts receivable	120	
Cash	10	410
Total assets		1,210
Equity		700
Retained earnings		350
Accounts payable		160
Total equity and liabilities		1,210

In Worked example 16.8, the subsidiary is wholly owned. Now, let us take the same figures but assume that Northern owns 80% of Muggles' shares that it bought at cost. We need to make the following adjustments to draw up the consolidated balance sheet (see Worked example 16.9).

1 The adjustment is made for the minority interests. We adjust for Northern's ownership of the shares that is 80%. We repeat the above example but we reduce Northern's investment to £320,000 (80% of £400,000).

2 We have increased Northern's inventory by £80,000 to compensate for the decrease in Northern's investment. We have made this mathematical adjustment so that we retain consistency and comparability between the two examples as far as all the other items are concerned.

3 We will assume, once again, that £50,000 in Northern's accounts receivable is due from Muggles and shown in that entity's accounts payable.

Worked example 16.9

	Northern	Muggles
	£000	£000
Tangible assets	350	450
Investment in Muggles (80% shares at cost)	320	
Inventories	240	120
Accounts receivable	80	90
Cash at bank	10	–
Total assets	1,000	660

continued overleaf

Worked example 16.9 *continued*

	Northern	Muggles
	£000	£000
Equity	700	400
Retained earnings	150	200
Accounts payable	150	60
Total equity and liabilities	1,000	660

Before we construct the consolidated statement, we will calculate the non-controlling interest. The non-controlling interest is 20% of Muggles' capital (£80,000) and 20% (£40,000)
of the retained earnings. The total for non-controlling interests is therefore £120,000, and in
the following statement we show it after retained earnings.

Consolidated statement of financial position at 31 December 2015

(80% owned subsidiary)

	£000	£000
Non-current assets		800
Current assets		
Inventories	360	
Accounts receivable	120	
Cash	10	490
Total assets		1,290
Equity	700	
Retained earnings (150,000 + 80% of £200,000)	310	1,010
Non-controlling interests		120
Accounts payable		160
Total equity and liabilities		1,290

The consolidated income statement

Our final topic in this section on consolidated accounts is the income statement. We will use
the example of Northern, the parent, having an 80% investment in Muggles. You may have
realized at this point that 80% of the consolidated profit will belong to Northern and 20% will
belong to the non-controlling interests.

The only complication we will include is that Muggles made £12,000 of sales to Northern
during the year. These goods had been purchased from an outside supplier for £8,000. You will
remember from our earlier discussions in this chapter that a group cannot make a profit by
member companies trading with one another. We will assume taxation is 33.3% (see Worked
example 16.10).

Note that we have calculated the tax on an arbitrary basis to demonstrate this example and
not according to the requirements of IAS 12 that we discussed in Chapter 14.

Worked example 16.10 Inter-group transactions

	Northern	Muggles	Adjustment	Consolidated
	£000	£000	£000	£000
Sales	150	76	(12)	214
Cost of sales	60	40		
Gross profit	90	36	(4)	122
Admin expenses	30	6		36
Profit before taxation	60	30		86
Tax	20	10		30
Profit after taxation	40	20		56
Non-controlling interest				4

Comments

1 The sales figure is reduced by £12,000, the amount of the sales that Muggles made to Northern.
2 Gross profit must be reduced by £4,000, being the amount that Muggles would have taken in its own income statement.
   The cost of sales figure can be calculated by deducting the consolidated gross profit from the consolidated sales.
3 The non-controlling interest share of the profit is calculated at 20% of Muggles' profit after tax because the shares are held in that entity.

Investment entities

An investment entity obtains funds from one or more investors and provides investment management services to them. The investment entity has the business purpose of investing funds solely for returns from capital appreciation, investment income or both. The entity will measure and evaluate the performance of substantially all of the investments on a fair value basis.

IFRS 10 requires a qualifying investment entity to account for investments in controlled entities, associates and joint ventures at fair value through profit or loss. This does not apply if the investee is a subsidiary that provides investment related services or engages in investment related activities with investees. In this instance, the investment entity has to prepare consolidated financial statements.

IFRS 10 requires a parent to determine whether it is an investment entity. To do this the entity must comply with three essential tests.

● It obtains funds from one or more investors to provide those investors with investment management services.
● Its declared business purpose is to invest for returns solely from capital appreciation and/or investment income.
● It measures and evaluates the performance of substantially all investments on a fair value basis.

The parent as an investment entity should have one or more of the following characteristics:

- It has more than one investment.
- It has more than one investor.
- It has investors that are not related parties of the investee.
- It has ownership interests in the form of equity or similar interests.

ACCOUNTING ISSUES

Business relationships are complex and they are numerous. Large entities frequently make agreements for different types of business relationships with others. These corporate activities involve not only strategic and managerial decisions but also are subject to legal, tax and accounting requirements.

The standards now in issue have resolved many of the difficulties for business combinations. However, there remain many areas where accountants must make substantial estimates and judgements. We have explained the requirements of IFRS 3 and IFRS 10 but here we highlight the main practical issues. These are separated into those pertaining at the time of acquisition and those occurring during the preparation of consolidated financial statements.

The practical issues at the time of the acquisition are:

- Whether one business has acquired another or merely purchased assets.
- The date on which the acquisition is made and identifying the acquirer.
- Identifying and placing a fair value on the assets acquired and the liabilities so that the deduction of net assets from the acquisition price correctly identifies goodwill.
- Identifying separate intangible assets so that they are not subsumed into goodwill.
- Measuring the consideration given by the acquirer for the acquiree. Consideration may include shares where there is no active market to price them. There may also be contingent consideration.

The practical issues at the time of preparing the consolidated statements are:

- Deciding any adjustments that should be made if the parent and subsidiary have different year-ends.
- Identifying asset classification of the subsidiaries' assets at the group level.
- Deciding which items should be disclosed separately in the corporate financial statements and those items that can be aggregated because they are immaterial at the group level.
- Amalgamating financial information measured in different currencies.

CONCLUSIONS

Business relationships are extensive and vary in their structure and operation. As part of the convergence project with the FASB, in 2002 the IASB commenced a comprehensive project to address inconsistencies in the existing regulations. Although there were several accounting standards addressing different forms of organizational relationships, there were inconsistencies and situations where the regulations did not 'fit'.

The project has produced IFRS 3 and IFRS 10, both concerned with mergers and acquisitions and consolidated financial statements.

IFRS 3 covers the principles on the recognition and measurement of acquired assets and liabilities, the determination of goodwill and the necessary disclosures. The emphasis is on the application of the acquisition method. Entities must use this for all business combinations. There are four stages:

1   Identifying the acquirer.
2   Determining the acquisition date.
3   Recognizing and measuring the identifiable assets acquired, the liabilities assumed and any non-controlling interest in the acquiree.
4   Recognizing and measuring goodwill or a gain from a bargain purchase.

The general principle is that the cost of a business combination is the total of the fair values of the consideration given by the acquirer plus any directly attributable costs of the business combination. IFRS 13 covers the application of fair value.

A major problem is the correct recognition and measurement of intangible assets and their separation from goodwill. The acquiree may be acquiring a business that has internally generated intangible assets that are not recognized on the balance sheet.

The acquiring company can place them on its own balance sheet but there is the issue of the fair value of these intangibles. The main problems are customer relationships, non-contractual intangible assets, those for which there is no active market, and those in the 'early stage' of development.

IFRS 10 explains the principles for the presentation and preparation of consolidated financial statements when an entity controls one or more other entities. The standard has a single consolidation model, based on control, applicable to all entities regardless of the nature of the investee. The standard contains no disclosure requirements. We discuss in the next chapter, the requirements for disclosure contained in IFRS 10.

IN THE PIPELINE

IFRS 3 does not apply to group restructurings and reorganizations, including those related to preparations for initial public offerings. This is because the same party controls the combining entities. The Board is currently assessing the best method for regulating these transactions.

ADDITIONAL RESOURCES

Go online to the companion website for this book to access further teaching and learning materials for this chapter.
www.palgravehighered.com/hussey-cfr

CHAPTER 17

ACCOUNTING FOR
ENTITY RELATIONSHIPS

IAS 28 Investments in Associates and Joint Ventures
IAS 27 Separate Financial Statements
IFRS 11 Joint Arrangements
IFRS 12 Disclosure of Interests in Other Entities
IAS 24 Related Party Disclosures

LEARNING OBJECTIVES

At the end of this chapter, you should be able to:

- Describe the different types of business relationships
- Explain the requirements for accounting for associates and joint ventures in IAS 28
- Discuss the concept of 'significant influence' in IAS 28
- Identify the three methods under IAS 27 for measuring investments
- Describe the requirements under IAS 27 for investment entities and a new parent
- Differentiate between joint ventures and joint operations as identified in IFRS 11
- Summarize the disclosure requirements in IFRS 12
- Explain the disclosure requirements for related parties under IAS 24

INTRODUCTION

In this chapter, we examine the different relationships that entities may have with each other that do not fall under the requirements of IFRS 3 *Business Combinations* and IFRS 10 *Consolidated Accounts*. We discussed both of these standards in the previous chapter. There are several types of relationships and the five standards we discuss have connections to each other and to other standards, including IFRS 3 and IFRS 10, as shown in Diagram 17.1.

The objectives of the standards are to define the types of relationships that can exist and to establish the accounting regulations. IAS 28 *Investments in Associates and Joint Ventures* and IFRS 11 *Joint Arrangements* concentrate on the types of relationships and we explain these first. IAS 27 *Separate Financial Statements* and IFRS 12 *Disclosure of Interests in Other Entities* concentrate on the provision of information.

The final standard IAS 24 *Related Party Disclosures*, we describe as a 'mopping up' standard. Essentially, if an entity is unable to define the relationship according to the requirements of IAS 28 and IFRS 11, the other entity becomes a related party. The standard explains the nature of related parties and the disclosures required.

There is a temptation to assume that standards address all possible eventualities. This is not the case. Corporate relationships are complex. It is not always easy for entities to decide the standard that applies to a particular relationship. It is also possible that no standard currently exists that regulates a particular relationship. We conclude this chapter with a specific example of such a case.

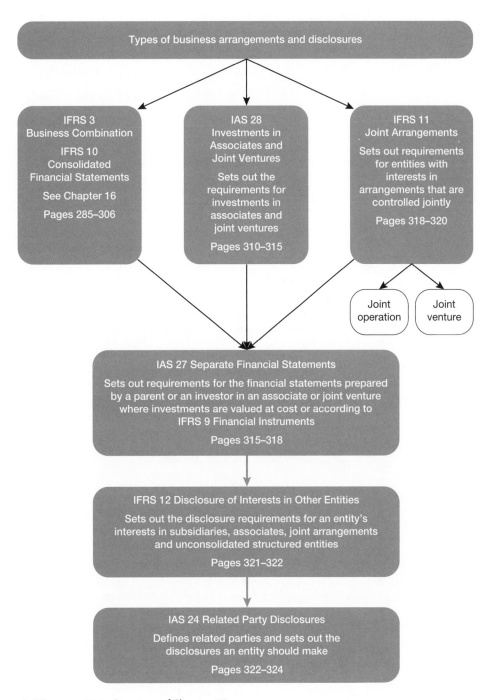

▲ Diagram 17.1 *Structure of Chapter 17*

IAS 28

INVESTMENTS IN ASSOCIATES AND JOINT VENTURES

▼ **Table 17.1** *Timeline of IAS 28*

Date	Comment
1989	IAS 28 Accounting for Investments issued, effective 1 January 1990
2003	IAS 28 Investments in Associates issued, effective 1 January 2005
2011	IAS 28 Investments in Associates and Joint Ventures issued, effective 1 January 2015
2014	Latest amendment
Interpretations issued	None

An investor may have a significant influence in another entity that is not a subsidiary. In this case, the entity does not appear in the consolidated financial statements under the provisions of IFRS 3 and IFRS 10 but under another standard. It is important that the users of financial statements are aware of the nature and implications of this investment.

IAS 28 applies to all entities that are investors with joint control of, or significant influence over, an investee. Investors must use the equity method to account for these investments.

The important points of the standard are that it:

- only applies to investments in associates and joint ventures;
- requires the investor to show the investments in its balance sheet;
- provides definitions of associates and joint ventures;
- requires the investor to apply the equity method;
- does not contain disclosure requirements as these are in IFRS 12.

Joint ventures and associates

joint venture

A joint venture is a joint arrangement whereby the parties that have joint control of the arrangement and the joint venturers have rights to the net assets of the arrangement.

Based on IAS 28, para. 3

associate

An associate company is an entity over which the investor has significant influence.

IAS 28, para. 3

By definition, no one party can control a **joint venture**. There must be two or more parties. An entity's investment in joint ventures is an investment that does not meet the criteria of IFRS 3. Therefore, the investing entity does not prepare consolidated financial statements but it must show the investments in its balance sheet.

Both of the above types of arrangements fall under the general heading of joint arrangements, but IAS 28 only regulates joint ventures and **associates**. IFRS 11 applies to **joint operations** and we discuss this standard in a later section. At this stage, we concentrate on accounting for joint ventures and associates under IAS 28.

It is more difficult to identify an investment in an associate company than an investment in a joint venture. You can compare the definition of an associate company to IFRS 3 in the previous chapter that requires the acquiring entity to have control over the acquiree.

The key to understanding the importance of the two definitions is the meaning of the term 'significant influence'. Unfortunately, this is not straightforward. The basic principle is the 20% rule and we explain this in the next section.

> **joint operation**
>
> A joint operation is an arrangement of which two or more parties have joint control.
>
> *Based on IAS 28, para. 3*

Significant influence

IAS 28 establishes the concept and the criteria for significant influence. If the investing entity has significant influence, its investment in another entity defines the investee as an associate company.

Significant influence occurs if the two following criteria are met:

- the investor has the power to participate in the financial and operating policy decisions of the investee;
- the investor does not have control or *joint control* of those policies.

Joint control is the contractually agreed sharing of control of an arrangement. This agreement exists only when decisions about the relevant activities require the unanimous consent of the parties sharing control.

The definition gives the break point for significant influence by stating the level at which the investing entity is deemed to have significant influence. This normally arises where the investor has 20% or more of the voting power. Although the standard gives a breakpoint, the investor may be able to demonstrate that it does not have significant influence although its holding is above this level.

Equally, an entity with a holding that is less than 20% may be able to prove that it does have significant influence.

In determining the 20% level, the existence and effect of potential voting rights that are currently exercisable or convertible, including potential voting rights held by other entities, are considered. In assessing whether potential voting rights contribute to significant influence, the entity examines all facts and circumstances that affect potential rights.

For example, an investor may hold more than 20% of the voting rights, but is unable to exercise significant influence because another investor holds the remaining voting rights.

However, a substantial or majority ownership by another investor does not necessarily preclude an entity from having significant influence.

The reverse situation can occur where the investor has less than 20% of the voting rights, but circumstances permit it to apply significant influence.

The standard (IAS 28, para. 6) provides the following examples of evidence that an entity does have significant influence:

- representation on the board of directors or equivalent governing body of the investee;
- participation in the policy-making process, including participation in decisions about dividends or other distributions;
- material transactions between the entity and the investee;
- interchange of managerial personnel; or
- provision of essential technical information.

An entity loses significant influence over an investee when it loses the power to participate in the financial and operating policy decisions of that investee. The loss of significant influence can occur with or without a change in absolute or relative ownership levels.

Before we examine the method of accounting investing entities should use, we show in Company example 17.1 the associates and joint ventures of Associated British Foods.

Company example 17.1

Joint ventures and associates

Interest in joint ventures and associates

A list of the group's significant interests in joint ventures and associates is given below:

Country of incorporation	Group %
Joint ventures	
Levaduras Collico S.A. Chile	50
Roal Oy Finland 50	
Qingdao Xinghua Cereal Oil & Foodstuff Co., Ltd China	25
Frontier Agriculture Limited UK	50
Vivergo Fuels Limited UK	47
Stratas Foods LLC US	50
Uniferm GmbH & Co. KG Germany	50
Associates	
C. Czarnikow Limited UK	43
New Food Coatings Pty Ltd Australia	50
Murray Bridge Bacon Pty Ltd Australia	20
Gledhow Sugar Company (Pty) Limited South Africa	30

Associated British Foods, Annual Report, 2014, Note 28, p. 130

Associated British Foods has invested in associates and joint ventures in many different countries. Its consolidated balance sheet for 2014 reveals that it has £180 million invested in joint ventures and £32 million in associate companies. What is of interest to us is how they account for this total investment of £212 million, and we discuss the accounting requirements in the next section.

The equity method of accounting

equity method

The equity method is a method of accounting whereby the investment is initially recognised at cost and adjusted thereafter for the post-acquisition change in the investor's share of the investee's net assets. The investor's profit or loss includes its share of the investee's profit or loss and the investor's other comprehensive income includes its share of the investee's other comprehensive income.

Based on IAS 28, para. 3

Entities with a significant influence or joint control over an investee must use the **equity method** to account for its investment. The investing entity is not required to use the equity method if it is exempt from preparing consolidated financial statements or if it meets all of the following conditions, as stated in IAS 28, para. 17:

- It is a wholly-owned subsidiary, or is a partially-owned subsidiary of another entity and its other owners, including those not otherwise entitled to vote, have been informed about, and do not object to, the entity not applying the equity method.

- Its debt or equity instruments are not traded in a public market (a domestic or foreign stock exchange or an over-the-counter market, including local and regional markets).
- It did not file, nor is it in the process of filing, its financial statements with a securities commission or other regulatory organisation, in order to issue any class of instruments in a public market.
- The ultimate or any intermediate parent of the entity produces consolidated financial statements available for public use that comply with IFRSs.

We can view the equity method in the following two stages.

Stage 1 Initial recognition

An investor recognizes at cost in the statement of financial position any investment in an associate or a joint venture. The investor uses the equity method from the date on which it becomes an associate or a joint venture. Any difference between the cost of the investment and the entity's share of the net fair value of the investee's identifiable assets is included in the carrying amount of the investment.

There may be an excess of the entity's share of the net fair value of the investee's net assets over the cost of the investment. If so, this excess is included as income in the determination of the entity's share of the associate or joint venture's profit or loss. This is actioned in the period in which the investment is acquired.

Stage 2 Subsequent financial periods

The investor adjusts the initial carrying amount subsequently to recognize post acquisition changes. The subsequent changes to the carrying amount can arise for several reasons. The investor will adjust the carrying amount to recognize the investor's share of the profit or loss of the investee. The investor recognizes its share of the profit or loss of the investee in its own profit or loss. Distributions received from an investee reduce the carrying amount of the investment.

The investor may also find it necessary to adjust the carrying amount because of changes in the investor's proportionate interest in the investee arising from changes in the investee's other comprehensive income. Examples of such changes are revaluations of property, plant and equipment and foreign currency translations which the investor recognizes in its statement of other comprehensive income.

An investor continues to use the equity method until the investment in the associate or joint venture ends. The reasons for termination and the action the investor should take are:

1 The investee becomes a subsidiary of the investor. The investor then accounts for the investment in accordance with IFRS 3 *Business Combinations* and IFRS 10 *Consolidated Financial Statements.*
2 The entity loses significant influence. In these circumstances, the investor treats the investment as a financial asset. The entity measures the retained interest at fair value, and the fair value of the retained interest is regarded as its fair value on initial recognition as a financial asset in accordance with IFRS 9 *Financial Instruments*. An investor may dispose of part of its interest in an investee. If so, the entity accounts in its profit or loss for any difference between (a) the fair value of any retained interest plus proceeds from the part disposal, and (b) the carrying amount of the investment at the date the equity method ended.

Other circumstances may occur that do not lead to the abandonment of the equity method:

1   An investment in an associate may change to an investment in a joint venture or an investment in a joint venture may change to an investment in an associate. The entity continues to use the equity method because there has only been an exchange in the concepts of significant influence and joint control. The investment remains and the underlying criterion of standard IAS 28 remains applicable.
2   An entity's ownership interest in an associate or a joint venture may be reduced, but the entity continues to have significant influence. In these circumstances, the entity continues to apply the equity method. There is no change in the way the entity accounts for investments, except for the reduction of its proportionate share of the investment income.

Applying the equity method

Once the investing entity has decided to use the equity method, there are some issues to be resolved. We have separated these into procedural issues and technical issues.

Procedural issues

The procedural issues for applying the equity method are straightforward and are as follows:

1   Unless it is unpractical to do so, the investing entity should ensure that the financial statements of the associate or joint venture share the same financial dates as itself. If it is not practical, the investing entity uses the most recent financial statements. The investor must adjust these statements for any significant transactions or events occurring between the accounting period ends. The reporting dates of the investor and associate should not differ by more than three months.
2   The accounting policies of the associate or joint venture should not differ from those of the investor. Where they do so, the associate or joint venture must adjust their policies so they comply with the investor's accounting policies.
3   The investing entity must account for an investment in an associate or a joint venture in its entity's separate financial statements (IAS 27 *Separate Financial Statements*).

Technical issues

Technical issues are more complex and we have arranged them in what we consider to be their order of complexity. We emphasize that not all investing entities will confront these problems.

1   If the investor is a non-investment entity and the investee is an investment entity, the investor can retain the fair value measurement used by the associate or joint venture to its interests in subsidiaries. In other words, the associate or joint venture is itself an investor with investments in subsidiaries. The main investing entity can retain the fair value measurement used by the investee.
2   The circumstance can arise where an investor's or joint venturer's share of losses of an associate or joint venture equals or exceeds its interest in the associate or joint venture. In these circumstances, the investor or joint venturer discontinues recognizing its share of further losses. After the investor or joint venturer's interest reduces to zero, it recognizes a liability only to the extent that it has incurred legal or constructive obligations or made payments on behalf of the associate.
     If the associate or joint venture subsequently reports profits, the investor or joint venturer resumes recognizing its share of those profits only after its share of the profits equals the share of losses not recognized.

3   The final technical issue concerns transactions between the investor and the associate or joint venture. The standard refers to upstream and downstream transactions. Upstream transactions are from the associate to investor, or joint venture to joint venturer. Downstream transactions are from the investor to associate, or joint venturer to joint venture.

Profits and losses resulting from transactions are eliminated to the extent of the investor's interest in the associate or joint venture. Unrealized losses are not eliminated to the extent that the transaction provides evidence of a reduction in the net realizable value or in the recoverable amount of the assets transferred.

As from 1 January 2016, an amendment entitled *Sale or Contribution of Assets between an Investor and its Associate or Joint Venture* came into effect. This amendment is concerned only with gains or losses from downstream transactions. If such transactions involve assets that constitute a business between an entity and its associate or joint venture, the investor must recognize the assets in full in its financial statements.

Application of other standards

We mentioned at the beginning of the chapter that investments in associates and joint ventures come under the requirements of other standards. From the investor's point of view, once it applies the equity method, IAS 39 *Financial Instruments: Recognition and Measurement* (see Chapter 13) regulates accounting for the investment. The investment entity must decide if it is necessary to recognize any additional impairment loss with respect to its net investment in the associate or joint venture.

If the investor decides that there is impairment, it calculates what the amount is by reference to IAS 36 *Impairment of Assets* (see Chapter 5). The entire carrying amount of the investment is tested for impairment as a single asset including any goodwill. The investor must assess the recoverable amount of an investment for each individual associate or joint venture. This does not apply if the associate or joint venture does not generate independent cash flows.

An impairment loss is not allocated to any identifiable asset. This includes goodwill because it is an integral part of the carrying amount of the investment in the associate or joint venture. If there is a reversal of the impairment loss, it is recognized in accordance with IAS 36.

IAS 27
SEPARATE FINANCIAL STATEMENTS

Students may find the term 'separate financial statements' confusing. It means non-consolidated financial statements and the standard applies to a parent, or an investor in a joint venture or associate. In the case of an investor, the standard only applies where it accounts for its investments either at cost or in accordance with IAS 39 *Financial Instruments: Recognition and Measurement* or IFRS 9 *Financial Instruments*.

IAS 27 has the objective of setting the requirements to be applied in accounting for investments in subsidiaries, joint ventures, and associates when an entity elects, or is required by local regulations, to present separate financial statements. The standard also outlines the accounting requirements for dividends, and there are some important disclosure requirements that we discuss at the end of this section.

In the previous chapter, we discussed consolidated financial statements. We need to return to this discussion and the requirements of IFRS 10 to clarify the types of entities that must

▼ **Table 17.2** *Timeline of IAS 27*

Date	Comment
1989	IAS 27 Consolidated Financial Statements and Accounting for Investments in Subsidiaries issued, effective 1 January 1990
2003	IAS 27 Consolidated and Separate Financial Statements issued, effective 1 January 2005
2011	IAS 27 Separate Financial Statements 2011 issued, effective 1 January 2013
2014	Latest amendment
Interpretations issued	None

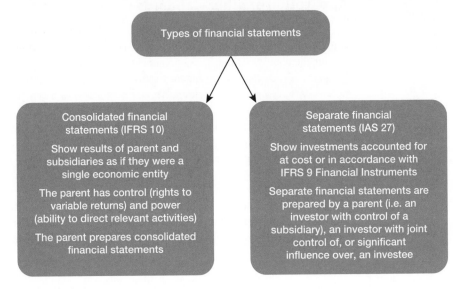

▲ **Diagram 17.2** *Types of financial statements*

prepare consolidated accounts and those that must prepare separate accounts. We contrast the two types of financial statements in Diagram 17.2.

Diagram 17.2 illustrates that the combination of IAS 27 and IFRS 10 results in the parent company with subsidiaries having to prepare consolidated financial statements for the group of companies and **separate financial statements** for itself.

IAS 27 contains important guidance concerning its appropriate application. The standard does not itself mandate which entities should produce separate financial statements. However, entities with investments in subsidiaries, joint ventures and associates may elect, or be required by local regulations, to produce separate financial statements.

Although we focus on IFRSs in this book, the relationship of parent and subsidiary companies in the UK comes under Financial Reporting Standards as issued by the Financial Reporting Council (FRC).

separate financial statements

Separate financial statements are the financial statements presented by a parent (i.e. an investor with control of a subsidiary), an investor with joint control of, or significant influence over, an investee, in which the investments are accounted for at cost or in accordance with IFRS 9 Financial Instruments.

Based on IAS 28, para. 4

consolidated financial statements

Consolidated financial statements are the financial statements of a group in which the assets, liabilities, equity, income, expenses and cash flows of the parent and its subsidiaries are presented as those of a single economic entity.

Based on IFRS 10, Appendix A

The UK's IFRS regulations require a listed group of companies to prepare **consolidated financial statements** complying with *EU-adopted IFRSs*. Any other entity or group, including parent and subsidiary companies within a listed group should comply with FRS 102 issued by the FRC. This standard has certain disclosure exemptions and a parent company or subsidiary wishing to take advantage of these must be an entity within a group that prepares publicly available consolidated accounts that give a true and fair view.

You will find that the consolidated financial statements of a group of companies comply with IFRSs but it is usual for a UK parent company to prepare its own financial statements in accordance with the UK FRS 102. This standard was issued in September 2015, and we do not discuss it further in this book.

The accounting method

An entity preparing separate financial statements has a choice of three methods under IAS 27 for measuring the investments:

1 At cost unless they are held for sale. In this case, the entity applies the regulations in IFRS 5 *Non-current Assets Held for Sale and Discontinued Operations* (see Chapter 15). Investments carried at cost are measured at the lower of their carrying amount and fair value less costs to sell.

2 In compliance with the requirements of IFRS 9 *Financial Instruments*. Some entities may not yet have adopted IFRS 9 and therefore must comply with IAS 39. We discussed both of these standards in Chapter 13.

3 In compliance with the equity method in IAS 28 that we discussed earlier in this chapter.

There are two situations where different requirements are required: investment entities and where an entity establishes a new parent.

Investment entities

The IASB introduced a consolidation exemption for **investment entities** that became effective for annual periods beginning on or after 1 January 2014. IFRS 10 requires a parent investment entity to measure its investment in a subsidiary at fair value through profit or loss. IFRS 9 and IAS 39 illustrate the methods. The investment entity must also account for its investment in a subsidiary in the same way as in its separate financial statements.

investment entity

An investment entity is one that:

a) obtains funds from one or more investors for the purpose of providing those investor(s) with investment management services;

b) commits to its investor(s) that its business purpose is to invest funds solely for returns from capital appreciation, investment income, or both; and

c) measures and evaluates the performance of substantially all of its investments on a fair value basis.

Based on IFRS 10, Appendix A

It is possible for an investment entity that is a parent to cease being an investment entity and no longer meet the definition. In these circumstances, the entity has a choice. It can either account for an investment in a subsidiary at cost (based on fair value at the date of change or status) or in accordance with IFRS 9. Conversely, a parent entity may become an investment entity. If so, it must account for any investment in accordance with IFRS 9 which requires accounting for a subsidiary at fair value through profit or loss.

A new parent

Different accounting requirements are also required where a parent reorganizes the structure of its group by establishing a new entity as its parent. There are variations on this. There could be the establishment of an intermediate parent in addition to a new ultimate parent. Alternatively, the entity may not be a parent but establishes a new parent.

All of these reorganizations must comply with the accounting requirements of IAS 27 (para. 13) if they satisfy the following criteria:

- the new parent obtains control of the original parent by issuing equity instruments in exchange for existing equity instruments of the original parent;
- the assets and liabilities of the new group and the original group are the same immediately before and after the reorganization; and
- the owners of the original parent before the reorganization have the same absolute and relative interests in the net assets of the original group and the new group immediately before and after the reorganization.

If the above criteria apply then the new parent:

- accounts for its investment in the original parent at cost;
- measures the carrying amount of its share of the equity items shown in the separate financial statements of the original parent at the date of the reorganization.

A parent entity, under IFRS 10, may elect not to prepare consolidated financial statements but instead prepare separate financial statements. The standard contains a lengthy list of the disclosures required in the separate financial statements. For our discussions the most relevant are:

- the fact that the financial statements are separate financial statements;
- that the exemption from consolidation has been used;
- a description of the method used to account for the foregoing investments.

IFRS 11

JOINT ARRANGEMENTS

▼ **Table 17.3** *Timeline of IFRS 11*

Date	Comment
2011	IFRS 11 Joint Arrangements issued, effective from 1 January 2013
2014	Latest amendment
Interpretations issued	None

Where there is joint control, IFRS 11 defines two types of joint arrangements: joint operations and joint ventures. A joint operation falls under IFRS 11, and we discuss the requirements of the standard in this section. A joint venture falls under IAS 28 that we discussed earlier in the chapter.

The first stage in the application of IFRS 11 is to determine whether there is a joint arrangement. There are two determining factors:

1 A contractual arrangement binds the parties together.
2 The contractual arrangement gives two or more of those parties joint control of the arrangement.

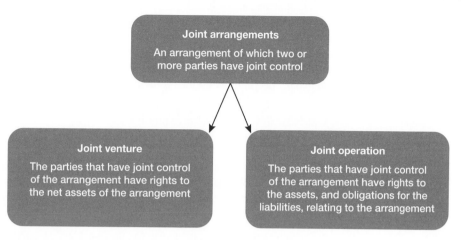

▲ Diagram 17.3 *Classification of joint arrangements*

The contract normally incorporates such issues as (IFRS 11, para. B4):

- The purpose, activity and duration of the joint arrangement.
- How the members of the Board of Directors, or equivalent governing body, of the joint arrangement are appointed.
- The decision-making process: the matters requiring decisions from the parties, the voting rights of the parties and the required level of support for those matters. In a joint arrangement, the decision-making process in the contractual arrangement establishes joint control of the arrangement.
- The capital or other contributions required of the parties.
- How the parties share assets, liabilities, revenues, expenses or profit or loss relating to the joint arrangement. The rights and obligations established by the contractual arrangement related to the assets, liabilities, revenue, expenses or profit or loss arising from the arrangement will determine how the arrangement is classified (as a joint operation or a joint venture).

decisions

Jointly made decisions concern matters such as the operating and capital arrangements. This includes budgets.

relevant activities

Relevant activities are those activities that significantly affect the returns of the arrangement. Examples are the selling and purchasing of goods or services, researching and developing new products.

unanimous consent

Unanimous consent exists where any one of the parties concerned could block the decision.

Contractual arrangements need to be enforceable and will often, but not always, be in writing. Generally, they will be in the form of a contract or documented discussions, such as minutes of meetings, between the parties.

Where a separate vehicle is set up, the articles, charter or by-laws of that vehicle may set out some aspects of the contractual arrangement, for example voting rights and percentage required to reach a decision.

For there to be joint control, the parties should have agreed a contract that shares control of the arrangement. The joint control exists only when decisions about the relevant activities require the unanimous consent of the parties sharing control.

Joint control does not mean that each party must have the same percentage share. Imagine that there are four parties. Three hold a 30% share and one holds the remaining 10% share. If the contractual agreement states that a decision requires 70% of the votes, any combination of three of the four parties could pass the decision. Such an arrangement does not meet the requirements of IAS 11 unless the agreement specifies which parties are required to agree unanimously.

For example, the agreement may specify that Parties 1, 2 and 4 must vote in favour for the arrangement to be considered joint. If Party 4 is against the decision, the motion will not be passed. The requirement in IFRS 11 for unanimous consent means that any of the parties with joint control of the arrangement can prevent a decision and thus can prevent the other parties from making decisions without its consent.

The financial statements for joint operations

IFRS 11 sets out the requirements for the parties involved in joint operations. The parties must recognize their involvement in the joint operations in their own financial statements. The requirements for disclosure under IAS 28 *Investments in Associates and Joint Ventures* are as follows.

Income statement

- the share of the revenue from the sale of the output by the joint operation;
- the share of the expenses, including the share of any expenses incurred jointly.

Statement of financial position

- the assets, including the share of any assets held jointly;
- the liabilities, including the share of any liabilities incurred jointly.

The initial investment in the joint operation is also shown on the balance sheet of the parties.

In including the above items in their own financial statements, the parties must use the appropriate IFRSs unless they conflict with IFRS 11. There are no specific requirements in IFRS 11.

Disclosure

IFRS 11 does not specify any disclosure requirements. IFRS 12 *Disclosure of Interests in Other Entities* outlines the disclosures required. We discuss this standard in the following section, but for completeness, we summarize the relevant requirements of IFRS 12 in this section.

IFRS 12 requirements

Disclosures required:

- Where an entity has made significant judgements and assumptions in determining that it has joint control.
- If the joint arrangement has been structured through a separate vehicle, such as an incorporated entity, the significant judgements and assumptions made in determining whether the arrangement is a joint operation or a joint venture.
- The nature, extent and financial effects of its interests in joint arrangements, nature and effects of contractual relationships, and nature of, and changes in, risks associated with joint ventures.

IFRS 12

DISCLOSURE OF INTERESTS IN OTHER ENTITIES

▼ Table 17.4 *Timeline of IFRS 12*

Date	Comment
2011	IFRS 12 Disclosure of Interest in Other Entities issued, Effective 1 January 2013
2014	Latest amendment
Interpretations issued	None

The objective of IFRS 12 is to require the disclosure of information that enables users of financial statements to evaluate:

● the nature of, and risks associated with, its interests in other entities;
● the effects of those interests on its financial position, financial performance and cash flows.

IFRS 12 does not refer to any particular accounting treatments for different economic transactions and events but confines itself solely to the disclosure of financial information. This involves several accounting standards. We noted these when discussing the individual standards, and we provide Diagram 17.4 as a revision tool.

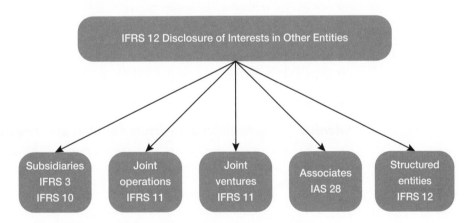

▲ Diagram 17.4 *Impact on other standards and entities*

Note: A structured entity is purposely constructed so that voting or similar rights are not the dominant factor in deciding who controls the entity. For example, any voting rights may refer only to routine administrative procedures. The entity has a narrow and well-defined objective and relevant activities are directed by means of contractual arrangements. Structured entities include such arrangements as securitization vehicles, asset-backed financings and some investment funds.

Entities with interests detailed in Diagram 17.4 must comply with IFRS 12. If compliance with IFRS 12 does not give sufficient disclosure, an entity must disclose whatever additional information is necessary to provide the appropriate information to users.

The following list summarizes the main disclosure requirements in IFRS 12 (para. 2).

Significant judgements and assumptions made in deciding:

- that it controls another entity;
- that it has joint control of an arrangement or significant influence over another entity;
- the type of joint arrangement (i.e. joint operation or joint venture) when the arrangement has been structured through a separate vehicle.

Interests in subsidiaries to assist users of consolidated financial statements to:

- understand the composition of the group;
- understand the interest that non-controlling interests have in the group's activities and cash flows;
- evaluate the nature and extent of significant restrictions on its ability to access or use assets, and settle liabilities, of the group;
- evaluate the nature of, and changes in, the risks associated with its interests in consolidated structured entities;
- evaluate the consequences of changes in its ownership interest in a subsidiary that do not result in a loss of control;
- evaluate the consequences of losing control of a subsidiary during the reporting period.

Interests in unconsolidated subsidiaries by investment entities disclosing:

- the fact the entity is an investment entity;
- information about significant judgements and assumptions it has made in determining that it is an investment entity;
- details of subsidiaries that have not been consolidated;
- details of the relationship and certain transactions between the investment entity and the subsidiary;
- information where an entity becomes, or ceases to be, an investment entity.

Interests in unconsolidated structured entities assisting users to:

- understand the nature and extent of its interests in unconsolidated structured entities;
- evaluate the nature of, and changes in, the risks associated with its interests in unconsolidated structured entities.

IAS 24

RELATED PARTY DISCLOSURES

We explained at the beginning of the chapter that business relationships could be very complex. For the user of financial statements, these relationships can be extremely important because they may influence the activities and financial performance of an entity.

The standards that we discussed in the previous chapter and in this chapter have identified and defined specific relationships. IAS 24 is a 'mopping up' standard that attempts to ensure

▼ **Table 17.5** *Timeline of IAS 24*

Date	Comment
1984	IAS 24 Related Party Disclosures issued, effective 1 January 1986
2003	IAS 24 Related Party Disclosures issued, effective 1 January 2005
2009	IAS 24 Related Party Disclosures issued, effective 1 January 2011
2013	Latest amendment
Interpretations issued	None

that all business relationships are covered. It states that its objective is to ensure that an entity's financial statements contain the disclosures necessary to draw attention to the possibility that its financial position and profit or loss may have been affected by the existence of related parties and by transactions and outstanding balances with such parties.

The standard defines a related party as a person or entity that is related to the reporting entity. The standard has an exhaustive list of those persons and entities that may be related to the reporting entity. It also has a much smaller list of those who are not related.

The definition of a related party transaction is equally broad. It is a transfer of resources, services, or obligations between related parties, regardless of whether a price is charged.

The standard contains disclosure requirements that are too comprehensive to include in this book. Possibly, the most relevant to our discussions is the relationship between parent and subsidiaries. An entity must disclose the name of its parent and, if different, the ultimate controlling party.

If neither the entity's parent nor the ultimate controlling party produces financial statements available for public use, the name of the next most senior parent that does so must also be disclosed. These disclosures are required even if no transactions have taken place in the financial period.

On a more general basis, where transactions with related parties excluding subsidiaries have taken place, the entity must disclose the nature of the related party relationship as well as information about the transactions. This standard (IAS 24, para. 18) requires disclosures separately for each category of related parties. The information must show:

- the amount of the transactions;
- the amount of outstanding balances, including terms and conditions and guarantees;
- provisions for doubtful debts related to the amount of outstanding balances;
- expenses recognized during the period in respect of bad or doubtful debts due from related parties.

We illustrate the information provided by companies in Company example 17.2 overleaf. We have only shown the current year for clarity.

Wisdom Marine Lines Co., Limited (Cayman) was incorporated in the Cayman Islands on 21 October 2008. On 1 December 2010, the Company was approved and listed on Taiwan Stock Exchange (TWSE). The company and its subsidiaries primarily provide marine cargo transportation services, related to the maintenance, vessel leasing, and shipping agency and management services.

The auditors confirm that the financial statements comply with IFRSs. There is a note to readers stating that the financial statements are in accordance with accounting principles and practices generally accepted in the Republic of China and not those of any other jurisdiction.

Company example 17.2

Related parties

For the years ended 31 December, 2015 and 2014, the Group received service from (rendered service to) related parties as follows:

Related party	Item	Amount
For the year ended 31 December 2015	US dollars	
Other related parties	Vessel management service	(2,971,425)
	Commissions	1,369,190
	Commissions and agency fees	1,537,428
	Business travel expenses and entertainment exp.	262,013
	Entertainment expenses and miscellaneous expenses	72,348
	Management revenue	(3,466)
	Other expenses	18,000
	Commission income	(24,827)
	Port charges, Agency fees, Travel	31,739
	Passenger Ticket revenue, Other revenue	(231,342)

Wisdom Marine Lines Co., Limited (Cayman), Consolidated Financial Statements, 2015

COMPLEX RELATIONSHIPS

We have a cluster of standards that attempt to identify and establish the accounting treatments for different types of business relationships. In the previous chapter, we explained business combinations and the requirements under IFRS 3. In many ways, this is the simplest arrangement from an accounting viewpoint. We establish that there is an acquirer and an acquiree. Both the acquirer and acquiree prepare separate financial statements but the acquiree also prepares consolidated financial statements.

In this chapter we have discussed other types of arrangements and the accounting requirements. These business relationships become more difficult to identify. However, companies enter arrangements that cannot be identified under any of the existing standards.

The fact that they cannot be identified under existing standards makes it impossible for us to list these standards. However, we have the good fortune to be able to provide an excellent example in Company example 17.3.

The company has explained clearly the nature of the business relationship. It identifies the features of the arrangements and has analyzed them in the context of IFRSs and other accounting standards. The company has concluded that no standard addresses the arrangement and has developed an accounting treatment that it considers best reflects the arrangements.

Company example 17.3

Corporate relationships

RISK AND REVENUE SHARING ARRANGEMENTS (RRSAs)

RRSAs with key suppliers (workshare partners) are a feature of our Civil aerospace business. Under these contractual arrangements the key commercial objectives are that: (i) during the development phase the workshare partner shares in the risks of developing an engine by performing its own development work, providing development parts and paying a non-refundable cash entry fee; and (ii) during the production phase it supplies components in return for a share of the programme revenues as a 'life of type' supplier (ie as long as the engine remains in service). The share of development costs borne by the workshare partner and of the revenues it receives reflect the partner's proportionate cost of providing its production parts compared to the overall manufacturing cost of the engine. The share is based on a jointly agreed forecast at the commencement of the arrangement.

These arrangements are complex and have features that could be indicative of: a collaboration agreement, including sharing of risk and cost in a development programme; a long-term supply agreement; sharing of intellectual property; or a combination of these. In summary, and as described below, the directors' view is that the development and production phases of the contract should be considered separately in accounting for the RRSA, which results in the entry fee being matched against the non-recurring costs incurred by the Group.

Having considered the features above, the directors considered that there is no directly applicable IFRS to determine an accounting policy for the recognition of entry fees of this nature in the income statement. Consequently, in developing an accounting treatment for such entry fees that best reflects the commercial objectives of the contractual arrangement, the directors have analysed these features in the context of relevant accounting pronouncements (including those of other standard setters where these do not conflict with IFRS) and have weighed the importance of each feature in faithfully representing the overall commercial effect. The most important considerations that need to be balanced are: the transfer of development risk; the workshare partner receiving little standalone value from the payment of the entry fee; and the overall effect being collaboration between the parties which falls short of being a joint venture as the Group controls the programme. Also important in the analysis is the fact that, whilst the Group and the workshare partner share risks and rewards through the life of the contract, these risks and rewards are very different during the development and production phases.

In this context, the entry fee might be considered to represent: an amount paid as an equalisation of development costs; a payment to secure a long-term supply arrangement; a purchase of intellectual property; or some combination thereof. The accounting under these different scenarios could include: recognition of the entry fee to match the associated costs in the income statement; being spread over the life of the programme as a reduction in the cost of supply during production; or being spread over the time period of the access to the intellectual property by the workshare partner.

Rolls-Royce plc, Annual Report and Accounts, 2014, p. 102

CONCLUSIONS

Corporate relationships arise in different types of industries and for various reasons. The IASB has issued standards intended to capture the essence of these relationships and to establish the accounting regulations.

In the previous chapter, we discussed business combinations. IFRS 3 *Business Combinations* relies on the concepts of control and power to determine the entities that are subsidiaries. IFRS 10 *Consolidated Financial Statements* establishes the principles for the presentation and preparation of consolidated financial statements when an entity controls one or more other entities.

Neither IFRS 3 nor IFRS 10 discuss disclosures. The regulations are contained in IFRS 12 which covers the regulations for all disclosures in other entities. The standard is simple but it does apply to all interests in other entities. This is a broad remit and we have explained in this chapter the relevant standards covering other types of relationships.

One key issue for entities is to determine the nature of the relationship that exists. The choices are:

IAS 28 *Investments in Associates and Joint Ventures*. The standard distinguishes between joint operations and joint ventures and describes the concept of significant influence. The standard only regulates associates and joint ventures and requires the application of the equity method of accounting.

IAS 27 *Separate Financial Statements* identifies three methods for measuring investments for an entity preparing separate financial statements. It also identifies the requirements for investment entities and a new parent.

IFRS 11 *Joint Arrangements* establishes the accounting requirements for entities that jointly control an arrangement. Joint control involves the contractually agreed sharing of control. Such arrangements can be either a joint venture or a joint operation.

IFRS 12 *Disclosure of Interests in Other Entities* contains the disclosure requirements for all these standards. In this chapter, we have summarized the main disclosure requirements.

IAS 24 *Related Party Disclosures* defines related parties and the disclosures an entity should make.

Our discussions have demonstrated that the task is difficult for both the standard setters and the entities that must comply with the regulations. If you have an arrangement, regardless of what the contractual agreement states, a charismatic person may well control or significantly influence decisions.

We would argue that it is impossible to regulate every type of relationship. There are times when entities must examine their activities and determine for themselves how best to account for them. If the entity takes this route, it must explain the decision to the users. Our Company example 17.3 from Rolls-Royce demonstrates how this can be achieved.

IN THE PIPELINE

On 17 December 2015 the IASB announced that it had postponed the date when entities must change some aspects of how they account for transactions between investors and associates or joint ventures.

The postponement applied to changes introduced by the IASB in 2014 through narrow-scope amendments to IFRS 10 *Consolidated Financial Statements* and IAS 28 *Investments in Associates and Joint Ventures*. Those changes affect how an entity should determine any gain or loss it recognizes when assets are sold or contributed between the entity and an associate or joint venture in which it invests. The changes do not affect other aspects of how entities account for their investments in associates and joint ventures.

The reason for making the decision to postpone the effective date was that the IASB is planning a broader review that may result in the simplification of accounting for such transactions and other aspects of accounting for associates and joint ventures.

ADDITIONAL RESOURCES

Go online to the companion website for this book to access further teaching and learning materials for this chapter.
www.palgravehighered.com/hussey-cfr

INTERIMS AND YEAR-ENDS

IAS 34 Interim Financial Reporting

IAS 10 Events After the Reporting Period

At the end of this chapter, you should be able to:

- Explain the timing issues in preparing an interim report
- Identify the requirements of IAS 34
- Explain the rationale for IAS 10
- Differentiate between adjusting and non-adjusting events and explain their accounting treatment

INTRODUCTION

In many countries, stock exchanges rules or legislation require listed companies to issue financial information either quarterly or half-yearly. These reports are referred to as 'interims'. It is unrealistic to expect investors to wait twelve months before receiving corporate information. Users want disclosures that are more frequent. The interims contain much less information than the annual report but address the issue of timeliness.

In the UK, stock exchange rules require a half-yearly report or interim. Where an entity issues such reports, they must comply with IAS 34 *Interim Financial Reporting*. This is a disclosure standard with the emphasis on providing timely information.

Unfortunately, the reduction of the reporting period from twelve months to six months introduces issues of recognition and measurement. The standard addresses these, but there are some problems, that we discuss in this chapter, that seem insoluble.

The second section of this chapter examines the regulations for a transaction or event that is outside the 12-month reporting period or the information is not available when the financial statements are prepared. For example, a tornado may damage a hotel. This could happen in the financial period but there is no estimate for repairs until after the financial statements have been completed but not yet authorized by the Directors. The question arises as to whether shareholders should be informed.

IAS 10 *Events After the Reporting Period* answers these and similar questions. The standard has been in force for many years.

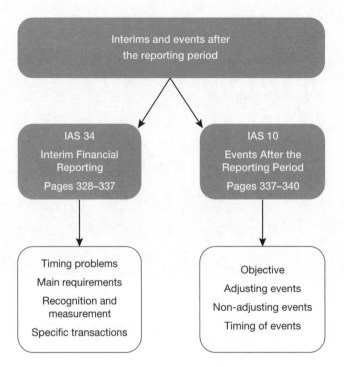

▲ Diagram 18.1 *Structure of Chapter 18*

IAS 34

INTERIM FINANCIAL REPORTING

▼ Table 18.1 *Timeline of IAS 34*

Date	Comment
1999	Standard first issued
2014	Latest amendments
Interpretation issued 25 September 2014	IFRIC 10 Interim Financial Reporting and Impairment

The requirement for entities to publish interim reports was a response to the perceived need of users. The 12-month gap between annual reports did not meet their need for information on a more regular basis.

IAS 34 specifies the *content* of an interim financial report that conforms to International Financial Reporting Standards (IFRSs). The standard does not state which entities must publish interim financial reports or how frequently. National governments, securities regulators, stock exchanges, and accountancy bodies decide these requirements. The standard is essentially about the accounting treatment for the contents of the document.

Most stock exchanges around the world require their listed companies to issue interim financial reports to produce timely and reliable information. The stock exchange may require companies to issue these at the six-month stage (half-yearly) as in Canada and the UK, or to issue them every three months (quarterly) as in Australia and the US.

Where the stock exchange regulations are for half-yearly interims, entities should issue an interim for the first six months of the financial year but not for the second six months because the entity will be producing an annual report. For quarterly interims, the stock exchanges normally require entities to produce interim financial statements for the first three quarters of the year. There is no requirement for fourth quarter interims because an entity issues the annual financial statement.

Timing problems

The requirement for entities to produce annual financial statements may not reflect the timing of their activities. Some entities may be in retailing where there is a rapid turnover in stock daily. Others may be involved in heavy manufacturing with jobs lasting over 12 months. Some may have revenue and costs peaking at different times in the same financial year. If we consider agriculture, timing may be even more variable (we discussed IAS 41 *Agriculture* in Chapter 15).

Standard setters and entities have been able to resolve most of the issues for annual reporting. When we come to half-yearly reporting, the recording and measurement of some transactions and events can become very difficult. We describe three scenarios to highlight them.

Scenario 18.1

A company has a year-end at 31 December. An **annual** maintenance programme in the factory takes place on 1 September at a cost of £60,000. How should the company account for this?

1 Ignore it at the half year because the event has not taken place.
2 Charge £30,000 in the interim report because the charge of £60,000 reflects the maintenance charge for the entire year.

Scenario 18.2

A company's financial year begins on 1 April. It intends to launch a large advertising campaign in April 2017. The company plans for the campaign to last for 6 months. The total cost will be £500,000. It is anticipated that the benefits in increased revenues will last until 31 March 2018. How should the company account for this?

1 Charge the full cost of the campaign in the interim statement at 30 September 2017 because the expenditure is incurred in that period.
2 Spread the total cost over the 12 months because the benefits are for the full year. This would mean that £250,000 would show in the interim statement.

Scenario 18.3

A company manufactures Christmas decorations. Manufacturing occurs throughout the year but the main sales only take place in November and December. Consequently, the company has costs for the six months to June but a very low sales figure. How should the company account for this? Would it be useful to users for the company to make a prudent proportional estimate of the sales it anticipates making for the year in the interim statement?

We can generalize from these three examples and identify the transactions and events that give rise to accounting dilemmas at the half year:

(a) Seasonal fluctuations of revenue.
(b) Substantial fixed costs in some periods but applying to the full year.
(c) Costs/expenses incurred at infrequent intervals during the year which relate to a full year's activities.
(d) Infrequent or unusual events or transactions that have a substantial effect on the results of operations for an interim period.

There is also the basic problem of assembling information. There is a limited time to obtain the information for the interim period, which leads to numerous estimates. Entities must rectify any misleading estimates in subsequent periods, which may distort the year-end results.

The main decision for the regulators when developing a standard was whether to use a discrete, integral or composite approach (a mixture of the two) for interim reporting.[1] The differences in the approaches are significant:

- With the discrete approach, an entity treats each half-yearly or quarterly period as a self-contained period. Costs and revenues are matched in each period and the same accounting policies and treatments are used for the interim period as for the annual accounts.
- With the integral approach, an entity treats each shorter period as part of the longer period. This approach recognizes that business activity may be cyclical with profits generated unevenly throughout the year. The integral approach attempts to match planned costs and profits on a basis relating to the year as a whole.
- The composite approach considers the nature of the transactions and events to determine the appropriate accounting treatment.

There are criticisms of all three approaches. The discrete approach can lead to successive six-month periods becoming distorted. Large fluctuations in revenues and expenses in one period can be misleading. For example, an annual charge for maintenance will appear in one six-month period, although the entire year has benefited. The discrete approach may not provide information for the user to predict what the results will be for the full year.

The integral approach also has its weaknesses. The spreading of costs to different periods can be misleading. It is a judgement that management is making. This could be incorrect by design or accidentally. There is also the danger that management is making adjustments based on its prediction of operations for subsequent periods. These predictions may be wrong.

The composite approach permits managers to determine whether it should use the discrete or integral approach for transactions. This method appears to reflect the weaknesses with both of the other methods.

Given these conceptual challenges, the standard setters decided to require the same accounting policies for the interim financial statements as for annual financial statements. This represents a 'discrete period' approach to interim reporting. This pronouncement leads to conflicts with certain transactions. At the end of this section, we list the standard's guidance for specific transactions.

Some companies that experience seasonal fluctuations may bring this to the notice of readers of the interim report. Pirelli is a good example (see Company example 18.1). The company was founded in 1872, and is a leading global manufacturer of car, motorcycle, truck, bus and agricultural tyres. The Group is represented in more than 160 countries.

Pirelli issues quarterly reports complying with IAS 34 in which the company addresses the issue of seasonality. Pirelli's interim report for the first quarter of 2016 contains 96 pages.

Company example 18.1

Interims and seasonality

We note seasonality factors with respect to trade receivables, which involved an increase in the values at the end of the quarter compared to the corresponding values at year-end. Revenue performance instead is not affected by significant trends connected to seasonality factors. (p. 46)

Trades receivable

The increase compared to December 31, 2015 was due to the usual seasonality linked to sales, with an increase in trade receivables in proportion to revenues. The value of trade receivables at March 31, 2015 amounted to euro 1,063,743 thousand. (p. 60)

PIRELLI & C. Società per Azioni (Joint Stock Company), Interim Report, 2016

Main requirements

IAS 34 *Interim Financial Reporting* prescribes the minimum content for an interim financial report, and the principles for recognition and measurement in complete and condensed financial statements for an interim period.

The standard has been effective since 1 January 1999. The IASB made the 2014 amendment as a consequential amendment of IAS 1 (2007) *Presentation of Financial Statements*. These changes impacted terminology, the titles and layout of the financial statements.

IAS 34 encourages entities to provide interim financial statements at least at the end of the first six months of their trading year, and to make these statements available no later than 60 days after the end of the interim period. The standard only encourages, and a country's legislation or stock exchange determines whether a company should publish interim reports and whether this should be quarterly or half-yearly.

An entity can decide to issue either a complete set of financial statements for interim reporting purposes or a condensed set of financial statements. IAS 34 defines the minimum content of an interim financial report as a:

- condensed balance sheet;
- condensed income statement;
- condensed statement showing changes in equity;
- condensed cash flow statement;
- selected explanatory notes.

The interim financial reports must show each of the headings and the sub-totals as illustrated in the most recent annual financial statements and the explanatory notes as required by IAS 34. Additional line items should be included if their omission would make the interim financial information misleading. If the annual financial statements were consolidated (group) statements, the interim statements should be group statements as well.

The notes to the interim financial statements are essentially an update. They include disclosures about changes in accounting policies, seasonality or cyclicity, changes in estimates, changes in outstanding debt or equity, dividends, segment revenue and results, events occurring after balance sheet date, acquisition or disposal of subsidiaries and long-term investments, restructurings, discontinuing operations, and changes in contingent liabilities or contingent assets.

Although IAS 34 is specific to interim financial statements, other standards regulate an entity's actual transactions and events. Where an entity considers that complying with a particular IFRS could be misleading, it can ignore the requirements of that IFRS. There must not be any other regulation preventing this departure and the entity must provide additional disclosures to demonstrate that its aim was to achieve a fair presentation.

Interim reports are not usually subject to a full audit. Nevertheless, entities frequently desire some seal of approval and we show below an extract from the interim report of Air China. KPMG issued the review (Company example 18.2).

Company example 18.2

Scope of Review

We conducted our review in accordance with Hong Kong Standard on Review Engagements 2410, 'Review of interim financial information performed by the independent auditor of the entity', issued by the Hong Kong Institute of Certified Public Accountants. A review of the interim financial report consists of making enquiries, primarily of persons responsible for financial and accounting matters, and applying analytical and other review procedures. A review is substantially less in scope than an audit conducted in accordance with Hong Kong Standards on Auditing and consequently does not enable us to obtain assurance that we would become aware of all significant matters that might be identified in an audit. Accordingly, we do not express an audit opinion.

Conclusion

Based on our review, nothing has come to our attention that causes us to believe that the interim financial report as at 30 June 2015 is not prepared, in all material respects, in accordance with IAS 34.

Air China, Interim Report, 2015, KPMG, p. 29

Air China is listed in Hong Kong and the review has been conducted in accordance with Hong Kong regulations. The interim financial report complies with IAS 34. This is an example of local regulations in a country having certain requirements and an international accounting standard regulating the financial statement.

Recognition and measurement

An entity should use the same accounting policy throughout the financial year with the same policies for interim reporting and annual financial statements. The exceptions are accounting policy changes made after the date of the most recent annual financial statements, as an entity will incorporate these in the next annual financial statements. If an entity decides to change a policy mid-year, it implements the change retrospectively, and restates the previously reported interim data.

The principles for recognizing, assets, liabilities, income and expenses are the same as those used for the annual financial statements. However, the standard recognizes that there are situations needing guidance and identifies three key points:

- Revenues received seasonally, cyclically or occasionally within a financial year should not be anticipated or deferred at the interim date if this practice is not used at the financial year-end.
- Costs that are incurred unevenly during a financial year should be anticipated or deferred if this practice is appropriate at the end of the financial year.
- Estimates should be reasonable in both the annual and interim reports but the interim reports need a greater use of estimates than the annual report.

The accounting policies applied in the interim financial statements should be consistent with those applied in the most recent annual financial report. Companies must state in the interim report that they have met this requirement. This is to ensure that companies do not change their accounting policies at the interim stage to make their results look more favourable. We discussed the importance and nature of accounting policies in Chapter 13.

However, an entity may intend to change the accounting policies for the next annual financial statements and knows this at the interim stage. These changes may be because the IASB is issuing a new or revised IFRS. Preparers of interim financial statements must consider any changes in accounting policies it intends to apply for the next annual financial statements, and to implement the changes for interim reporting purposes.

Where there is a change in accounting policy, the entity should restate the financial statements of the interim period of the current financial year and the comparable interim periods of prior financial years. However, the concept of impracticability applies where an entity cannot make the changes after every reasonable effort to do so.

Specific transactions

The standard provides guidance for specific transactions.

Revenues

Where the entity receives revenues seasonally, cyclically or occasionally within a financial year, it should not anticipate or defer them at the interim date. It is only acceptable to do so if anticipation or deferral is appropriate at the end of the financial year. For example, a retailer does not divide forecasted revenue for the entire year by two to arrive at its half-year revenue figures. It must report its actual revenue for the first six months.

To assist the user in appreciating the cyclical nature of its business, the retailer could include additional information on the actual revenue for the 12 months up to the end of the interim reporting period and comparative information for the corresponding previous 12-month period.

Uneven costs

An entity can incur costs unevenly during its entity financial year. It should not anticipate or defer such costs for interim reporting purposes. In other words, an entity cannot spread its costs evenly over the entire year. In Scenario 18.2, we gave the example of the entity that incurred large advertising costs in the first part of the year. An entity must recognize these costs in full in the period in which they are incurred. There is an exception to this. If the entity's policy is to anticipate or defer that type of cost at the end of the financial year, it can apply this policy at the interim stage.

The above two examples are contained in the main body of the standard and establish the principles for recognizing and measuring revenue and costs. Section B of the standard is an illustrative example demonstrating the application of the principles. We discuss the main items to provide a general picture of the requirements.

Employer payroll taxes and insurance contributions

It is usual for an employer to estimate payroll taxes or contributions to government-sponsored insurance on an annual basis. If this is its normal practice, it should recognize related expense in interim periods. The method for making this estimate is to use an estimated average annual effective payroll tax or contribution rate. Even if an entity makes an actual payment of a large proportion in the first six months, it must still make an estimated average for the interim report.

Major planned periodic maintenance or overhaul

An entity cannot anticipate in the interim report the cost of a planned major periodic maintenance or overhaul or other seasonal expenditure that it expects to occur later in the year.

There is an exception to this requirement, and that is where an event has caused the entity to have a legal or constructive obligation. For example, the entity may have a leasing contract to use some expensive machinery. The contract may contain a clause that the entity must carry out annual maintenance; a legal obligation. The mere intention or necessity to incur expenditure related to the future is not sufficient to give rise to an obligation.

Provisions

In Chapter 13, we discussed IAS 37 that regulates the making of provisions. There have been abuses of this standard in the past and the IASB is strengthening the requirements. IAS 34 requires an entity to recognize a provision when it has no realistic alternative but to transfer economic benefits because of an event that has created a legal or constructive obligation.

IAS 34 requires an entity to apply the same criteria for recognizing and measuring a provision at an interim date as it would at the end of its financial year. The existence or non-existence of an obligation to transfer benefits is not a function of the length of the reporting period. It is a question of fact.

Year-end bonuses

In some organizations, employees may receive a bonus at the year-end based on the profitable performance of the entity or some other measures of performance. Some entities may grant bonuses based on continued employment during a time. These may be purely discretionary, contractual, or due to years of historical precedent. An entity can anticipate a year-end bonus only if:

- the bonus is a legal obligation, or past practice would make the bonus a constructive obligation and the entity has no realistic alternative but to make the payments; and
- a reliable estimate of the obligation can be made.

Contingent lease payments

We discussed accounting for leases, and the recent changes, in Chapter 14. The IASB has made significant amendments in the regulations that will affect lease accounting. Currently, contingent lease payments are an example of a legal or constructive obligation that, under IAS 34, an entity recognizes as a liability.

For example, a retailer may lease premises and the lease payments depend on the level of sales achieved annually. If this is the case, an obligation can arise in the interim period of the financial year before the achievement of the required annual level of sales. However, if that required level of sales is expected to be achieved the entity has no realistic alternative but to make the future lease payment.

Intangible assets

We discussed IAS 38 *Intangible Assets* in Chapter 5. Entities cannot defer expenses at the interim stage in the belief or hope that these expenses will meet later the criteria to permit capitalization as an intangible asset. An entity should recognize intangible assets when they meet the recognition criteria.

Vacations, holidays, and other short-term compensated absences

We explain IAS 19 *Employee Benefits* in Chapter 19. That standard requires an entity to measure the expected cost of and obligation for accumulating compensated absences at the amount the entity expects to pay because of the unused entitlement that has accumulated at the end of the reporting period. That principle also applies at the end of interim financial reporting periods.

Irregularly occurring and discretionary costs

An entity may budget to incur such costs as charitable donations and training of employees at some time during the financial year. Although the entity may plan and intend to incur these costs, they are usually discretionary and an entity can avoid them if it decides not to make the payments. An entity cannot recognize at the end of the interim period that it intends to make these payments later in the year.

Volume rebates

In some industries, it is practice for suppliers to give a reduction on its charges to a customer based on the volume purchased during a financial period. This is known as a volume rebate and is frequently made at the year-end. An entity can anticipate these rebates in the interim financial statement where they are contractual in nature, not discretionary, and it is probable that they will be earned or will take effect.

This is contrary to what you may have thought would be the position but one suspects that these practices were established long before the standard was issued. The IASB may well have decided that it was not worthwhile to change established normal business practice. We have taken the following extract from GSK (Company example 18.3 overleaf).

Inventories

An entity measures inventories for interim financial reporting using the same principles as at the financial year-end. In Chapter 8, we described the recognition and measurement criteria of IAS 2 *Inventories*. The valuation of inventories is a large task and, to save cost and time, companies often use estimates to measure inventories at interim dates. IAS 34 explains the method for applying estimates in different situations.

Company example 18.3

Turnover

Revenue is recognised when title and risk of loss is passed to the customer, reliable estimates can be made of relevant deductions and all relevant obligations have been fulfilled, such that the earnings process is regarded as being complete. Gross turnover is reduced by rebates, discounts, allowances and product returns given or expected to be given, which vary by product arrangements and buying groups. These arrangements with purchasing organisations are dependent upon the submission of claims some time after the initial recognition of the sale. Accruals are made at the time of sale for the estimated rebates, discounts or allowances payable or returns to be made, based on available market information and historical experience.

GSK, Annual Report, 2014, Note 3, p. 132

Impairment of assets

IAS 34 requires at the interim stage that an entity conducts the same procedure for impairment of assets as it would at the year-end. However, the entity is relieved of making detailed calculations. It should review indications of significant impairment since the end of the most recent financial year. If it appears that impairment has taken place, the entity must make detailed calculations. We discussed the requirements of IAS 36 *Impairments* in Chapter 5.

*   *   *

IAS 34 has been a useful standard with little criticism despite the uncertain accounting transactions it covers. It is appropriate to ask whether IAS 34 is effective in view of the growth of internet reporting – a subject we discuss in Chapter 21.

If you visit a company's website, a printed document of a restricted number of pages is only a small part of a company's disclosures. We have extracted the main half-yearly disclosures on the website of J. Sainsbury in Company example 18.4. These disclosures are reasonably typical of many websites. The items can be downloaded or viewed.

Company example 18.4

Interim Results Announcement

Interim results announcement
Interim Results Booklet
Interim results presentation webcast
Analyst presentation
Full Transcript

www.j-sainsbury.co.uk/investor-centre/results-and-presentations/2015/ interim-results-announcement/ (accessed 14 September 2016)

The announcement in Company example 18.4, made on Sainsbury's website on 11 November 2015, referred to the six months ended 26 September 2015. As well as booklets and webcasts, interested users can obtain a copy of the presentation that was made to analysts. This is a considerable amount of information and the company has given guidance on how users can easily download the files. All this information is only concerned with the specified six months, and the website carries substantial information on annual reporting for many years.

The Sainsbury example is very similar to many other companies. To assume that corporate financial reporting is restricted to a printed annual report is far from current practice. The expansion in the requirements for disclosure of financial information, the growth in narrative reporting and the aim of many companies to voluntarily provide a wide range of information has been made possible by the internet. In Chapters 20 and 21, we examine present communication practices and explore the possible future of corporate reporting.

IAS 10

EVENTS AFTER THE REPORTING PERIOD

▼ **Table 18.2** *Timeline of IAS 10*

Date	Comment
1978	Standard issued as Events Occurring After the Balance Sheet Date
1999	Reissued as Events After the Balance Sheet Date
2003	Latest revision effective
2007	Retitled as Events After the Reporting Period

An entity cannot issue its financial statements before the directors sign (authorize) them. This formal attestation can occur several weeks, or even months, after the year-end. This delay before authorization can give rise to problems.

First, there is the issue of information not becoming available until after the year-end but before the directors authorize the financial statements. The other possibility is that significant events occur after the year-end but before the directors authorize the financial statements. The question is what action the directors should take. We demonstrate the dilemma with Scenarios 18.4 and 18.5.

Scenario 18.4

It is 18 February 2016. The Directors have met in the boardroom to approve the financial statements to 31 December 2015. The Production Manager looks out of the window and shouts, 'Stop. The factory is burning and we are not insured. We must change the financial statements. We have no factory. We are finished'. The Sales Manager replies, 'The factory was there at the year-end so the financial statements are correct. What happens now will be reported in the next year's accounts – if there are any'.

Scenario 18.5

An entity, with the year-end at 31 December, owns a large luxury hotel on a tropical island. In November there had been a large storm severely damaging the hotel. The local manager makes an approximate estimate of the cost so that the financial accounts can be prepared. However, a final valuation for damage repair is received after the year-end but before the financial statements are authorized. How does the company account for this?

With both of these scenarios, and similar ones, the company needs guidance. That guidance is given in IAS 10 *Events After the Reporting Period*.

It is possible for many events to take place between the date of the year-end and the signing of the financial statements. In addition, some events of substance occur before the year-end but the entity does not know the full financial consequences for some considerable time later.

IAS 10 establishes the proper accounting treatment for events that occur, or information becoming available, after the end date but before the directors authorize the financial statements.

Note that the events can be either favourable or unfavourable. These events can be of great interest to the user of the financial statements. The events may have taken place after the year-end, but the information may assist the user in assessing the financial performance and position of the entity. The standard addresses the users' needs by identifying the accounting requirements for both favourable and unfavourable events. The standard defines both types of events as either adjusting events or non-adjusting events.

It is critical that entities correctly identify adjusting events and non-adjusting events. The former changes the financial statements for the reporting period. Non-adjusting events appear as a note. We summarize the position in Diagram 18.2.

> **events after the reporting period**
>
> Events after the reporting period are those events, both favourable and unfavourable, that occur between the reporting date and the date on which the financial statements are authorized by the directors for issue.
>
> *Based on IAS 10, para. 3*

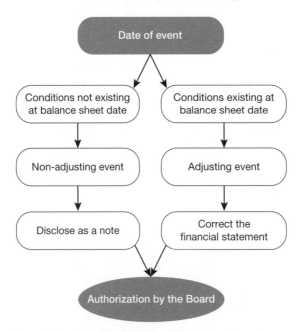

▲ **Diagram 18.2** *IAS 10 Events After the Reporting Period*

Adjusting events

Adjusting events give new evidence on conditions as at the date of the balance sheet. Where an entity has an adjusting event, it must alter the financial statements to show this new information before their authorization.

For example, the balance sheet may record office premises at a carrying amount of £15 million. Shortly after the year-end, an independent valuator informs them that this valuation is incorrect and the office premises are only valued at £12 million as at the balance sheet date. Evidence has therefore become available that shows the original valuation to be incorrect and the financial statements must be restated before they can be authorized.

Typical examples of adjusting events are:

- Discovery of fraud or errors.
- Information about the value or recoverability of an asset at the year-end.
- Settlement of an outstanding court case; that is, a case that was in court before the year-end has been settled after the year-end.

Worked example 18.1   An adjusting event

An entity's financial statements for the year ended 31 December 2015 were completed on 18 February 2016. Before the directors could authorize the financial statements they discovered that fraud had been committed at one of the entity's major warehouses. Inventory was overstated by 15%. What action should the directors take?

As the fraud took place before the end of the year, although not known until later, this is an adjusting event. Before the financial statements have been released, the correct amount of inventory is known. The entity must restate the financial statements before the directors can authorize them.

Non-adjusting events

Significant events can occur after the balance sheet date but before the directors sign the financial statements. The amounts shown on the financial statements are correct so there is an argument that there is no need to inform the shareholders. The standard takes the position that the financial statements are correct and no change is required but, if the events are significant, the entity should inform shareholders.

For example, premises correctly valued at the year-end but subsequently severely damaged by floods before the authorization date is a non-adjusting event. The financial statements are correct as at the year-end and do not have to be restated. However, a non-adjusting event has occurred that is of significant importance and disclosure should be made. An entity would include this information in its notes to the accounts in its annual report.

Examples of non-adjusting events are:

- fire, floods or other catastrophes after the balance sheet date that destroy or damage non-current assets;
- announcements of a major restructuring plan;
- major purchases of items such as property, plant and equipment;
- purchase of another entity;
- major disposal of property plant and equipment.

Company example 18.5

Events after the reporting period

In November 2015, Siemens announced the extension of its seven-year IT outsourcing contract with AtoS through December 2021, with minimum committed volumes increasing by €3.23 billion to €8.73 billion. Furthermore Siemens announced the extension of its current lock-up shareholder commitment in AtoS through September 2020.

Also in November 2015, Siemens announced the sale of its 49% stake in Unify to AtoS. While ownership of the Unify stake has adversely affected Siemens' financial results in fiscal 2015 and prior fiscal years, the transaction is not expected to result in a material effect. Closing of the transaction is subject to the approvals of the regulatory and antitrust authorities. Closing is expected in the second quarter of fiscal 2016.

Siemens Aktiengesellschaft, Berlin and Munich, Annual Report, 2015, Note 33, p. 107

The company featured in Company example 18.5, Siemens (Berlin and Munich), is a global corporation in electrical engineering and electronics with 348,000 employees. The company develops and manufactures products, designs and installs complex systems and projects, and tailors a wide range of services for individual requirements.

In Company example 18.5, Siemens notes that it had announced these events in November, prior to the year-end. Although the impact of these events will not show in the financial statements until subsequent years, the company has correctly, in compliance with IAS 10 provided the information in its annual report.

Timing of events

In determining the appropriate classification of the event, it is essential to consider all the surrounding circumstances. For example, the reduction in value of a property after the balance sheet date but before the authorization date is usually identified as a non-adjusting event. However, information received after the balance sheet date that demonstrated that the property had lost its value before the balance sheet date is an adjusting event.

The standard also requires that an entity should not prepare financial statements on a going concern basis if events occur between the balance sheet date and the date of authorization that indicate that the entity is not a going concern. Entities should disclose the authorization date for financial statements. It is essential that users know this date as the financial statements and disclosures will not report any events occurring after the authorization date.

The critical aspect of this standard is the timing of the event and the date of authorization of the financial statements. The standard offers the following guidance:

1   An entity may have to submit its financial statements for approval after the issue of financial statements to shareholders. It is usual for the board to authorize the financial statements for issue prior to submitting them to the shareholders. The date of issue will be the date of authorization and not the date of the shareholders' approval.

2   The management of an entity may have to issue its financial statements to a supervisory board (made up solely of non-executives) for approval. The financial statements are authorized when the board issues them to the supervisory board.

NOTE

1   A study by Hussey and Woolfe (1994) reported on these various issues prior to the release of the standard.

CONCLUSIONS

An entity's activities do not flow regularly into a twelve-month period, starting on 1 January and ending on 31 December. Production continues with sales made and raw materials ordered for payments at future dates. Entities enter into long-term agreements and launch advertising programmes anticipating benefits at some future time.

Standards IAS 34 and IAS 10 attempt to resolve the issues arising from the conflict of operational continuity and users' needs for regular and reliable financial information.

One timing issue is the annual reporting cycle. Most jurisdictions have decided that 12 months is too long for users not to receive financial information, and either legislation or the national stock exchange requires interim financial statements from listed companies. These may be half-yearly or quarterly depending on the country.

Where entities are required to issue interim statements they should comply with IAS 34. There are conceptual and practical problems that the standard has not been able to resolve fully. This results in a number of economic transactions where entities must use a considerable amount of estimation and judgement to decide on the nature of the disclosure.

There can also be timing issues at the date of the year-end financial statements. There are events that occur after the year-end and events that occur during the reporting period with the financial consequences not known until later.

The question arises as to whether the entity should inform users of these events. IAS 10 has addressed the issue by identifying the conditions where an event is an adjusting one and requires amended financial statements before the Board can authorize them. Other events are non-adjusting and, if they are sufficiently significant, shareholders must be informed.

ADDITIONAL RESOURCES

Go online to the companion website for this book to access further teaching and learning materials for this chapter.
www.palgravehighered.com/hussey-cfr

THE ANALYSIS OF CORPORATE REPORTS

INTRODUCTION

Ratios are widely used by various groups and individuals to analyze the financial data in corporate reports. Present and potential investors, managers, lenders, trade unions, suppliers and other trade associations, credit rating agencies, investment analysts and financial journalists analyze the financial statements of a company by calculating ratios. Governments also use ratios to help assess the economic environment, and tax authorities calculate ratios as a means of detecting fraud.

Students can fall into the trap of thinking that, because they can calculate financial ratios, they can conduct an analysis of a company. This is far from the truth. There are three distinct but related stages in the process of conducting an analysis:

1 The selection of appropriate data, both financial and narrative.
2 The calculation of ratios.
3 The analysis and interpretation of the results.

We start this chapter by explaining the range of data you need to select before you commence your analysis. We identify the sources of the information and the context in which to interpret the data you have. There is also an explanation of some basic methods you can use to analyze data.

The second part of the chapter is entitled 'Calculating ratios'. The purpose of this section is to introduce the advantages of using ratios. Companies' revenue figures, amounts of profit and details of their assets and liabilities have more meaning if you can identify the relationships.

The third section of the chapter is 'Financial statement analysis'. We demonstrate a range of ratios that determine the profitability and liquidity of a company. We also explain how you can examine a company's cash strengths or weaknesses.

The penultimate section is entitled 'Investor analysis'. We demonstrate and explain the range of ratios used by those who are investing in a business operation. These ratios are calculated by those who make loans and those who purchase shares.

We give a few words of caution before we begin to explain the details. There are usually no set definitions of the various terms used in ratio analysis, and there are various approaches to calculating them. There is one ratio, earnings per share (EPS), that has its own standard, IAS 33.

In this chapter, we explain the main ratios and use the most common definitions of terms and methods of calculation. Where there are frequently used alternatives, we refer to them in the text.

Additionally, there are alternative names for some of the data and terms drawn from the financial statements. For example, the terms 'profit' and 'earnings' mean the same. We have used mainly 'profit' for consistency, but applied the term 'earnings' where that is more common. You must be alert to whether we are referring to profit before interest and tax (also known as 'earnings before interest and tax') or profit after interest but before tax.

The term 'capital' is part of some of the ratios. Generally, capital means equity and retained earnings. The term 'capital employed' usually means equity plus long-term debt. When we explain the individual ratios, we make evident the term we are using.

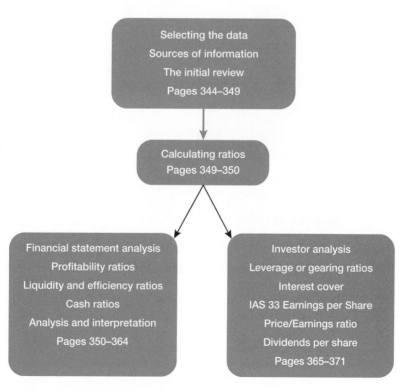

▲ **Diagram 19.1** *Structure of Chapter 19*

SELECTING THE DATA

It is important that you do not rush into selecting, calculating and analyzing ratios without an exploration of the context in which your study is taking place. This prior investigation is essential if you are to understand the factors external to your chosen company. These factors contribute towards shaping its financial performance and position, and are shown in Diagram 19.2.

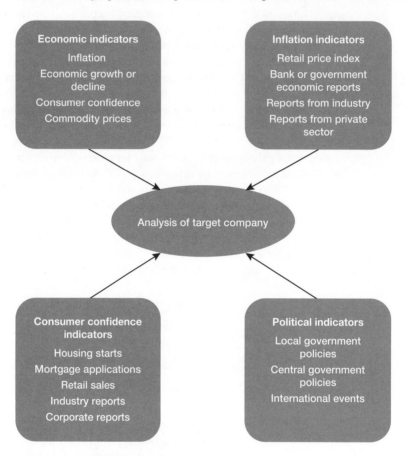

▲ **Diagram 19.2** *Selecting the data*

Sources of information

The main sources for contextual information will be:

- Daily newspapers, e.g. *Wall Street Journal*, *Financial Times*, for an overview and immediate information.
- 'Investment' magazines specifically related to the activities of the share markets.
- General business magazines, e.g. *Forbes*, *Business Week*, *The Economist*.
- Newsletters issued by various government and industry bodies and departments.
- The internet and various websites.
- Companies that provide a substantial amount of information both in hard copy and on their websites. Use caution because they are likely to present information that favours their financial activities.

From these sources, you will be aiming to extract indicators of past performance, current events and predictions of future trends. Once the context is established, you can use the following procedure to analyze the target company.

1 Acquire financial statements for several years, preferably a minimum of three years although five to ten years would be preferable. This collection should include annual and interim financial statements. It is helpful to obtain any internal financial documents if possible.

2 Scrutinize all the documents to see if there have been any significant changes over a period. Putting the key figures for the main items, such as revenue and earnings, on a spreadsheet helps the comparison. It is also useful to include aggregations such as total assets, net current assets and working capital.

3 If you have the published documents, you must review the notes. You are looking for information on changes in accounting policies or accounting treatments that do not comply fully with the standards.

4 Examine the balance sheet, income statement and cash flow statement without calculating ratios. Your objective is to detect any items that look particularly large or unusual.

5 Identify and calculate the ratios you consider the most important for your task and relevant to the company you are investigating.

6 If possible, obtain the ratios for a competitor and the industry averages. These are usually available in most libraries or on the internet. Ensure that the definitions of terms and methods of calculation are comparable to your own.

7 Analyze and interpret the ratios using all the information you have collected. The process of interpretation may reveal additional information you require to complete your task.

8 If the management of the company has discussed their financial results, and in the annual report they will have done so, compare it to your own interpretation. If there are differences, investigate them.

In addition to the above indicators, there are also data and information that influence change as much as they indicate change. The information not only captures what has happened but also sets off a series of other changes. As far as share prices and stock markets are concerned, the main influencers are:

- company results
- results of competitors
- revisions in broker forecasts
- opinion on market and industry
- exchange rates
- political upheavals
- rumours
- greed

The published financial results of a company and its competitors can do much to influence share prices. If the company has poor results and the competitors' are good, its share prices go down. Analysts comment on company performance, and frequently predict a company's earnings for the current year. If the company exceeds those earnings, its share price goes up.

Political and economic upheavals can affect share prices. Finally, there are rumours and there is greed. Most people buy shares because they want to see a good return on their investment. Sometimes rumour in the market place encourages speculators to purchase shares that do not perform as well as the rumours suggested.

It is sometimes difficult to differentiate between good and poor information. Individuals and groups hope either to make money or to ensure that they do not lose money. They need information to make their decisions and sometimes speculation and rumour can be more exciting than good, sound evidence.

One major source of comparisons is the financial statements of the companies themselves. Large companies incorporate ratios in their annual report and accounts. They also have key performance indicators (KPIs), that we discuss in Chapter 20. You need to compare these to the ratios that you are calculating. Is the company calculating the same answers as you? Is the company using different ratios, such as KPIs? If so, you should calculate the same ratio if the base data is available.

The initial review

Before commencing a detailed analysis using ratios, it is worthwhile to conduct an initial review. This provides some hard numbers to compare to the information you collected in establishing the context. The two following approaches are simple and quick to apply. Frequently, they provide enough information for you to decide whether you wish to proceed further:

- Trend analysis
- Vertical analysis

Trend analysis

With this technique, we are looking at data either with a simple comparison with the previous period or over an extended period. This could be years, months, weeks or even hours and minutes. The change could be in one item only or it could be in several items.

In Worked example 19.1, we are looking at the sales figure for one company. The comparison is the current year to the previous year, and we show the change in pounds and percentages.

Worked example 19.1   Year to year analysis

	Current year	Previous year	£ change	% change
Revenue	£70,100	£59,200	£+10,900	+18.4%

The above table shows a simple analysis in which we are comparing only two years. The obvious question we need to answer is the reason that revenue increased by such a large amount.

A trend analysis usually takes two or three related items and compares them over several years. We show a trend analysis for eight years in Worked example 19.2.

It is often helpful to show the data in the form of a chart. Using the data in Worked example 19.2, we have used a two-line graph (see Diagram 19.3). This makes the message very clear. Although the gross profit was complementary to the revenue for the first few years, in recent years the gross profit has been declining, although the revenue has been increasing.

Worked example 19.2   Trend analysis of revenue and gross profit

	2008	2009	2010	2011	2012	2013	2014	2015
Revenue	96	102	112	105	108	110	115	118
Gross profit	56	60	72	65	70	65	62	55

Over an eight-year period we have more data, but it is not so easy to understand immediately the significance. The above figures demonstrate an increasing trend in revenue until 2011 when it drops but gradually recovers. The gross profit follows the increase in revenue but drops in 2011 with a slight recovery in 2012. This is followed by a decline.

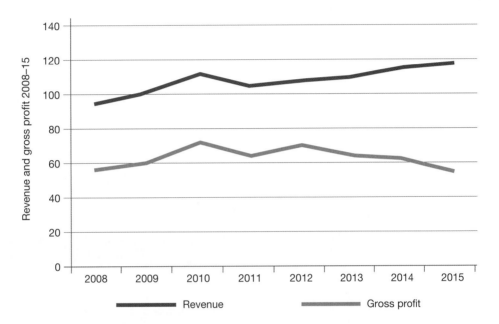

▲ **Diagram 19.3** *Line graph showing trends*

Of course, neither the table in Worked example 19.2 nor the graph in Diagram 19.3 give the answers, but they show us where to look. If you have collected the contextual data, you can investigate whether the indicators shown in Diagram 19.2 provide any evidence. Analysts have the advantage of being able to contact the company and seek answers. If possible, try to procure analysts' briefings.

Same size or vertical analysis

Worked example 19.3 is known as either a same size analysis or a vertical analysis. Revenue is 100% and all the costs and the profit are expressed as a percentage of that amount. We could express all the separate assets on the statement of financial position as a percentage of the total assets or the separate liability accounts as a percentage of total liabilities. The presentations and analyses of data are improved where comparative figures for the previous financial period are available.

Worked example 19.3   Vertical analysis

	Income statement for 2015	
	£000	%
Revenue	1,000	100
Cost of sales	750	75
Salaries	120	12
Rent	20	2
Admin	10	1
Depreciation	40	4
Interest	10	1
Profit before tax	50	5

To interpret the data in Worked example 19.3, we need comparisons. Companies usually have their own targets. They will know that for every £1,000 of revenue, their operating costs will be about £750. If you do not have any internal information, you must use other companies as comparisons.

You will also find that most companies have several pages discussing their financial highlights. These are often in graphical format, but Company example 19.1 from Associated British Foods plc's Annual Report 2014 provides various data. As with all data from any source, you must check the definitions carefully.

Company example 19.1

Financial Highlights

Group revenue
£12.9bn
Actual: –3%
Constant currency: +1%

Adjusted operating profit*
£1,163m
Actual: –1%
Constant currency: +2%

Adjusted profit before tax**
£1,105m
Up 2%

Adjusted earnings per share**
104.1p
Up 6%

Dividends per share
34.0p
Up 6%

Net capital investment
£691m

Net debt reduced to
£446m

Operating profit
£1,080m
Down 1%

Profit before tax
£1,020m
Up 18%

Basic earnings per share
96.5p
Up 30%

NB Asterisked notes not reproduced here.

Associated British Foods plc, Annual Report, 2014, p. 2

If you obtain the annual reports for Associated British Foods plc for several years, you can construct your own comparisons. Alternatively, you can search for comparative data from companies in a similar industry. As with all data from any source, you must check carefully the definitions of terms.

CALCULATING RATIOS

ratio analysis

Ratio analysis is a technique for evaluating the financial performance and stability of an entity, with a view to making comparisons with previous periods, other entities and industry averages over a period of time.

In the previous sections, we discussed the collection of data and the calculation of simple ratios. **Ratio analysis** is not only about calculating the ratios but also their analysis and their interpretation. A simple spreadsheet model will calculate as many ratios as you want. Only you can conduct the analysis and interpretation. Experience will help you produce a more sophisticated analysis. This section provides you with all the tools, and advice on how to select and calculate ratios and on how to analyze and interpret your findings.

As with the previous examples, we keep the calculations simple in Worked example 19.4. At this stage, we concentrate on the analysis. Our first example uses only two sets of data: the revenue and gross profits for two companies for one year. Gross profit is usually defined as the difference between revenue and the cost of making a product or providing a service, before deducting overheads, payroll, taxation, and interest payments. Most people regard gross profit as a good measure of how successful a company is in what are its core activities.

Worked example 19.4

There are two companies in the same industry. Their revenue and gross profits for 2015 are:

	Company A £000	Company B £000
Sales	80	160
Gross profit	40	60

From the above it is clear that company B makes the highest gross profit. This is to be expected because it is twice the size of A as measured by sales. The question is, which company is the most profitable?

To answer this question we calculate a ratio known as the gross profit margin by expressing the gross profit as a percentage of sales.

Gross profit margin

Company A	Company B
$\dfrac{40}{80} \times 100 = 50\%$	$\dfrac{60}{160} \times 100 = 37.5\%$

Company B is the larger company in terms of both revenue and gross profit. However, Company A is the more profitable since the gross profit margin is 50%. If Company A could increase its revenue to £160,000 whilst maintaining a gross profit margin of 50% it would make a gross profit of £80,000.

The next step in our analysis would be to use all of the contextual information we have collected to try to explain the differences in the gross profit margin percentages. We would pursue such factors as whether the companies are paying different prices for their goods inwards or operating in different markets.

We would also consider whether it is possible to increase the revenue of Company A whilst maintaining the gross profit margin, or whether it is possible to improve the gross profit margin of company B.

We could extend our analysis by comparing the performance of these two companies against the average for the industry in which they are operating. We could also calculate the ratios for a number of previous years and ascertain whether the ratios for 2015 are part of a trend or unusual in some way.

In Worked example 19.4, we calculated only one ratio. Although one ratio can be helpful, ratios are related and it is the appropriate combination of ratios that makes for a good analysis.

Analyses must use comparative figures. An analysis can be for one company over several years, or for several companies, for just one year or for several years. Because they are audited, the annual reports and accounts are the most easily obtained and the most credible sources of information. If you can obtain a company's internal documents, they may be more revealing but be cautious on the definitions used.

Companies usually show ratios in their annual report and accounts. Take care in understanding the definitions they have used.

If you are doing an analysis over several years, there will have been changes in accounting standards. You must adjust your calculations to allow for these.

FINANCIAL STATEMENT ANALYSIS

We calculate most ratios from a company's financial statements. If you are making comparisons with another company, you must ensure that the data is consistent. The presence of International Financial Reporting Standards (IFRSs) has greatly improved comparability but there are items where different accounting treatments may be used.

Numerous ratios can be calculated. We have selected the most common ones and grouped them into profitability ratios, liquidity and efficiency ratios, and cash ratios. There are no set definitions of these ratios. Different terms are used to identify them and the data for calculating the ratio may be different. You should always check when you are making comparisons that you are using the same terms and definitions.

In Diagram 19.4, we show the three groupings with the purpose of the ratios in each group and the ratios we discuss.

Profitability ratios

People buying shares or loaning money to a company do so in anticipation that the company is making and will continue to make profits. One can also argue that if you are going to work for a company, you want it to be profitable. If you supply goods or services to a company, you want it to be successful.

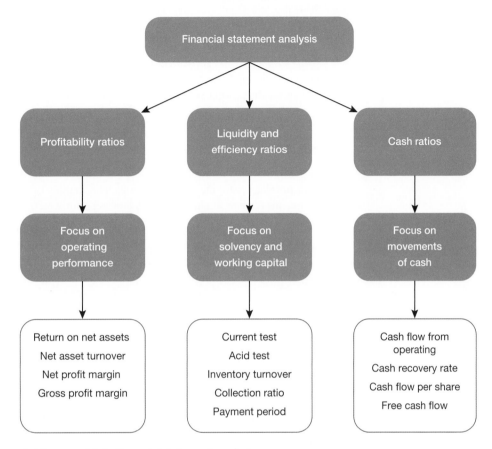

▲ **Diagram 19.4** *Financial statement analysis*

Many users of financial statements are interested in a company's profitability and need a way to measure this. The profitability ratios concentrate on financial performance. The main ratios are:

- Return on capital employed – ROCE (also known as return on net assets employed – RONA)
- Net asset turnover (also known as capital turnover)
- Net profit margin (also known as return on sales – ROS)
- Gross profit margin

As there are no standard definitions, we use the following explanations of the terms.

Return. This term usually means profit before interest and tax (PBIT). Larger companies may identify this as operating profit or earnings (EBIT). Smaller companies may use the terms 'net profit' or 'net earnings'.

Net assets. These are the total assets minus the current liabilities. Some analysts prefer to use the total asset amount without deducting current liabilities.

Return on net assets. This ratio measures the percentage return on the investment of funds in the business. It provides information on how effective the business is in generating revenue from resources and management's ability to control costs. An alternative title is the 'prime ratio'. It is regarded as the main indicator of the success or otherwise of a company.

Net asset turnover. This ratio measures the number of times the net assets been used (i.e. turned over) during the year to achieve the sales revenue. Generally, the more frequently the net assets are 'turned over' the more successful the business is.

Net profit margin or *PBIT.* This is the profit before interest and tax expressed as a percentage of the sales figure. It shows the percentage profit a company makes on sales after deducting all expenses but before interest charges and tax.

Gross profit margin. This measures gross profit as a percentage of sales and is a good indicator of how successful the business is in its basic trading operations. For managers and investors, this is a key ratio in assessing business performance.

You will note that we are using the profit figure before interest and tax in our calculations because interest and tax do not reflect the operating performance of a company. Interest charges are a financing decision and tax, as we explained in Chapter 14, is a separate calculation. That is not to say that they are not important and we examine interest in detail later in the chapter.

Liquidity and efficiency ratios

In Chapter 10, we discussed the need for a statement of cash flows. A company can appear profitable but it must also be able to manage its cash. The ratios in this section demonstrate the ability of a company to manage cash.

The main ratios are:

- Current test
- Acid test
- Inventory turnover
- Collection ratio or accounts receivable period
- Payment ratio or accounts payable period

The *current test* calculates the solvency of the company in the short term by comparing current assets and current liabilities, usually expressed as x:1. It demonstrates whether the company can pay its current debts.

The *acid test* shows the relationship between liquid assets and current liabilities, and is usually expressed as x:1; x being the liquid assets defined as current assets minus inventory. It is a more stringent test than the current test in assessing the solvency of a business. Liquid assets are all current assets except stock (inventories), as these take longer to convert into cash.

Inventory turnover. Manufacturing and retail companies normally hold a stock of goods for future sale. This stock is referred to as inventory and comprises the goods that the company holds at any time (see Chapter 8). The ratio 'inventory turnover' shows the efficiency of the company at converting manufactured or purchased goods into sales revenue.

The *collection ratio* is an efficiency ratio that measures the average time, in days, trade debtors (accounts receivable), usually customers, have taken to pay the business for goods and services over the year.

The *payment ratio* measures the average time, in days, the entity is taking to pay its own debts. The purchases amount on the income statement is the most appropriate figure, but if this is not available, the sales figure is an alternative.

In discussing liquidity and efficiency ratios, the phrase 'working capital' is used. This is the amount of funding required for the company's day-to-day operations. It is the total of the current assets (e.g. inventories, accounts receivable and cash) less current liabilities (e.g. accounts payable, bank overdrafts).

In Worked example 19.5, we calculate the profitability and liquidity ratios. We exclude interest and tax from our calculations. The ratios are only to one decimal place. We find this is normally sufficient for most analyses. The worked example shows a summary income statement and balance sheet for the fictional Lakeview Ltd. This is followed by Table 19.1 that demonstrates the calculation of the main ratios.

Worked example 19.5

Lakeview Ltd

Summary Income Statement to 31 December 2015

	£000	£000
Revenue		230
Cost of sales:		
Opening inventory	88	
Purchases	160	
	248	
less Closing inventory	110	138
Gross profit		92
Operating expenses		50
Profit before interest and tax		42

Summary Balance Sheet as at 31 December 2015

	£000	£000
Non-current assets:		96
Current assets:		
Cash	2	
Accounts receivable	36	
Inventory	110	148
Total assets		244
Current liabilities: Accounts payable		24
Long-term liabilities		80
Total liabilities		104
Owners' equity:		
Capital	94	
Profit for the year	46	140
		244

▼ **Table 19.1** *Calculation of main ratios*

PROFITABILTY RATIOS	Formula	Ratio
Return on net assets %	$\dfrac{\text{PBIT}}{\text{Net assets}}$	$\dfrac{42}{220} = 19.0\%$
Gross margin %	$\dfrac{\text{Gross profit}}{\text{Sales}}$	$\dfrac{92}{230} = 40.0\%$
Return on sales %	$\dfrac{\text{PBIT}}{\text{Sales}}$	$\dfrac{42}{230} = 18.3\%$
Net assets turnover	$\dfrac{\text{Sales}}{\text{Net assets}}$	$\dfrac{230}{220} = 1.04$ times
LIQUIDITY RATIOS		
Current test	$\dfrac{\text{Current assets}}{\text{Current liabilities}}$	$\dfrac{148}{24} = 6.2{:}1$
Acid test (Quick ratio)	$\dfrac{(\text{Current assets} - \text{Inventories})}{\text{Current liabilities}}$	$\dfrac{38}{24} = 1.6{:}1$
WORKING CAPITAL MANAGEMENT		
Collection period	$\dfrac{\text{Receivables} \times 365}{\text{Sales}}$	$\dfrac{36}{230} \times 365 = 57$ days
Payment period	$\dfrac{\text{Payables} \times 365}{\text{Purchases}}$	$\dfrac{24}{160} \times 365 = 55$ days
Inventory turnover	$\dfrac{\text{Sales}}{\text{Inventory}}$	$\dfrac{230}{110} = 2.1$ times

To assess the profitability of this company, we apply the profitability and liquidity ratios. Without comparators, it is difficult to conduct a comprehensive analysis but we can add some comments.

The profitability ratios

Everybody has their own favourite profitability ratios but most will focus on the 'Big Three'. The return on net assets shows the profit the company made from the net assets it held. This main ratio is supported by two subsidiary ratios, the return on sales and net asset turnover. By multiplying the return on sales ratio by the net asset turnover, you calculate the return on net assets ratio. This relationship is very important and we show it in Diagram 19.5.

Allowing for rounding up of decimal places, the relationship of the ratios is that the return on sales multiplied by the net asset turnover equals the return on net assets. In Diagram 19.5, the 18.3% for return on sales multiplied by the 1.04 net asset turnover gives the 19.0% return on net assets.

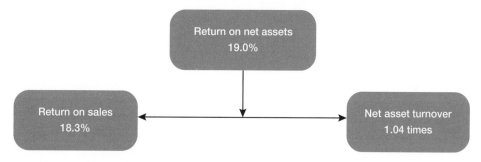

▲ Diagram 19.5 *Main profitability ratios*

Let us put those calculations into a business perspective using the company in Worked example 19.5 and the ratios in Table 19.1.

1 The company strives to improve its return on net assets, as that is the key measure of its performance. It can only improve that ratio by improving one or both of the subsidiary ratios.

2 The net assets turnover is a guide to the efficiency of the company in using its net assets. The ratio can indicate that some assets are not being fully employed, which needs further investigation. Machinery may be idle or under used, a building may be partly empty or too large for the level of activity. If the company could reduce its net assets, it may be able to achieve a turnover figure of 1.5 times. Multiply this by the return on sales ratio of 18.3% and the return on net assets jumps to an impressive 27.4%.

3 Another avenue may be to increase the sales volume without requiring additional net assets to meet the increased demand. If the company can increase sales to £300,000 without requiring a further investment in net assets, the net asset turnover would be 1.36. Multiplying this by the return on sales ratio of 18.3% gives a return on net assets of 24.8%, which is a considerable improvement on the 19.0% currently being achieved. Such an action may require the company to expand its working hours by adding another work shift or other strategies to increase production without investing in more assets.

4 The return on sales ratio is the profit expressed as a percentage of the sales figure. Improving this ratio requires either an increase in the selling price of the products or a reduction in the costs incurred. An increase in volume of sales will not by itself increase the return on sales ratio unless the company strictly controls its operating costs.

5 The stage before the return on sales ratio is the gross profit margin. A company should direct its attention to the impact on final profit. The gross profit represents the difference between the selling price and the costs of the goods sold. If the gross profit margin is 40%, it will be that for £1, or £1 million, of sales. An increase in volume will not change the ratio. Companies should investigate an increase in the selling price or a reduction in the cost of sales.

A major issue with these calculations is that our figure of net assets does not take into account operating leases. A company may be using a substantial amount of non-current assets but, if these are leased instead of owned, they do not appear in our calculations. As explained in Chapter 14, the new standard on leases will resolve this problem.

Working capital ratios

Working capital is calculated by deducting current liabilities from current assets:

Working capital = Current assets – Current liabilities

It represents the investment by the company in its trading cycle. A company must be alert to the amount of investment in non-current assets, such as buildings and machinery; it must be even more aware of its investment in working capital.

Insufficient working capital can cause a company to become bankrupt. The use of ratios assists a company to manage its working capital. It also reveals to investors the immediate financial health of the company.

The premise underpinning these ratios is that companies should be able to pay their current liabilities from their current assets. If they are unable to do this, they must seek more finance, which can be difficult.

To put figures on this dilemma we provide Worked example 19.6.

Worked example 19.6

Company A has a current ratio of 1.4:1. In other words it has £1.40 of current assets for every £1.00 of current liabilities. This suggests that if the company has to pay its current liabilities it should be able to do so from its current assets.

Company B has a current ratio of 0.9:1. If the creditors want immediate payment, the company cannot do so because it only has 90 pence for every £1.00 it owes. This means it must try to obtain more funding, sell off some of its non-current assets or go bankrupt.

The weakness of the current test is that a company may hold a very large inventory. This can be very difficult to sell in a hurry. The proof is the number of advertisements you see in newspapers where bankrupt stock is offered at very low prices. The acid test omits inventories from current assets and is therefore more rigorous then the current test.

Worked example 19.7 uses data from the fictional Lakeview Ltd, the company we analyzed previously, and the ratios calculated in Table 19.1.

Worked example 19.7

Lakeview Ltd has a current test of 6.2:1 and the acid test is 1.6:1. At first glance, one may conclude that this company is financially very healthy because it has such significant coverage of its current liabilities. This is not the case.

The ratios reveal that the management is very poor at managing the finances of the company. Management must be funding the £148,000 of current assets in some way, presumably through the long-term liability on which it pays interest.

Looking at the composition of the current assets, there is a modest amount of cash. The accounts receivable amount is larger but the collection period is 57 days and the payment period is 55 days, both of which seem reasonable. For a company giving a month's credit, the average time is 45 days.

The only remaining figure is £110,000 for inventory, and that looks high compared to the other current assets. The inventory turnover is 2.1 times. This indicates that the company

continued

> **Working example 19.7** *continued*
>
> sells its inventory about twice in the year. If you consider that a supermarket will sell a tin of beans every few seconds the ratio looks poor. However, we need the following information:
>
> 1 What would be the usual turnover figure in this industry?
> 2 Does the company have to hold a large number of different products?
> 3 Is the amount of inventory being increased because a busy period is expected, e.g. Christmas?
> 4 Does the balance sheet represent the usual level of inventory or is there some other factor influencing the amount?
> 5 Is the figure accurate? There could be obsolete inventory that the company should write off. We discussed in Chapter 8 how companies could manipulate profit by altering the closing inventory figure.
>
> We have examined the current assets in detail but we have not investigated the non-current assets of £96,000. Unfortunately, we do not have a breakdown of this amount, and there could be problems. If the company purchased property 40 years ago, it is probably worth much more now. If it were to be revalued this would have a negative effect on the return on net assets. In addition, we do not know whether the company has any intangible assets and the accounting treatment it uses. This is further information we require in order to make a full analysis.

Cash ratios

We discussed the statement of cash flows in Chapter 10. It supports the income statement and the balance sheet and provides information that these two statements do not contain. There are several cash flow ratios and we show the main ones in Tables 19.2 to 19.5.

▼ **Table 19.2** *Cash flow from operating activities to current liabilities*

Purpose	To determine the amount of cash available to pay current liabilities
Source of data	The net cash flow from operations comes from the statement of cash flow and the current liabilities from the balance sheet. Where possible, calculate the average liabilities by adding the figure from last year's balance sheet to this year's and dividing by two.
Formula	$\dfrac{\text{Net cash flow from operating activities}}{\text{Average current liabilities}} \times 100$

▼ **Table 19.3** *Cash recovery rate*

Purpose	To determine the amount of cash generated by assets. A long-term investment has been made in assets and we need to assess whether these assets generate more cash than they cost
Source of data	The cash flow figure comes from the cash flow statement. Some people take the total assets and others only the non-current assets from the balance sheet.
Formula	$\dfrac{\text{Net cash flow from operations}}{\text{Average total assets}} \times 100$

▼ **Table 19.4** *Cash flow per share*

Purpose	To ascertain the amount of cash each share earns
Source of data	Some users will take the earnings before interest, tax, depreciation and amortization (EBITDA) as the 'cash flow' amount. Others prefer to take the net cash flow from operating activities as shown on the cash flow statement but may adjust it by adding any cash received from the disposal of assets.
Formula	$$\frac{\text{Cash flow}}{\text{Weighted number of ordinary shares in issue}}$$

▼ **Table 19.5** *Free cash flow ratio*

Purpose	To determine the amount of cash flow available for expansion and acquisitions or to survive a difficult economic period
Source of data	The operating cash flow comes from the cash flow statement. Some analysts deduct capital expenditures as these are necessary to maintain the company's activities
Formula	This can be shown either as an amount or as a ratio: $$\frac{\text{Free cash flow}}{\text{Operating cash flow}}$$ The higher the percentage of free cash flow embedded in a company's operating cash flow, the greater the financial strength of the company.

A useful explanation of free cash flow is given by Barrick Gold Corporation in Company example 19.2. It not only explains the purpose of the measure but also points out its deficiencies. Barrick Gold Corporation is the largest gold mining company in the world, with its headquarters in Canada.

Company example 19.2

Free Cash Flow

Free cash flow is a measure which excludes capital expenditures from operating cash flow. Management believes this to be a useful indicator of our ability to operate without reliance on additional borrowing or usage of existing cash.

Free cash flow is intended to provide additional information only and does not have any standardized definition under IFRS and should not be considered in isolation or as a substitute for measures of performance prepared in accordance with IFRS. The measure is not necessarily indicative of operating profit or cash flow from operations as determined under IFRS. Other companies may calculate this measure differently. The following table reconciles this non-GAAP measure to the most directly comparable IFRS measure.

continued

Company example 19.2 *continued*

Reconciliation of Operating Cash Flow to Free Cash Flow

($ millions)	For the years ended Dec. 31			For the three months ended Dec. 31	
	2015	2014	2013	2015	2014
Operating cash flow	$2,794	$2,296	$4,239	$698	$371
Settlement of currency and commodity contracts	–	–	64	–	–
Non-recurring tax payments	–	–	56	–	–
Adjusted operating cash flow	$2,794	$2,296	$4,359	$698	$371
Capital expenditures	(1,713)	(2,432)	(5,501)	(311)	(547)
Free cash flow	$1,081	$(136)	$(1,142)	$387	$(176)

Barrick Gold Corporation, Financial Report, 2015, p. 78

Worked example 19.8, showing a comparison between two hypothetical companies, emphasizes the interpretation of the ratios and uses simple calculations. We would apply the same procedures for a large, listed company but the volume of data and the variety of the transactions would be much greater. We are using the financial statements representing two small companies.

Worked example 19.8 is in three parts: the financial statements, the calculation of the ratios and the analysis and interpretation.

Worked example 19.8

Financial statements – Matcon and SuperIns

Company Matcon has been in business for over 25 years but company SuperIns has been in business for only 7 years. Both companies supply vegetables to restaurants.

Their income statements are given overleaf.

Note that we have deducted the cost of the goods sold from the total revenue to give the gross profit. This calculation was explained in Chapter 8. The purchase of materials for the 2015 year were Matcon £169,000 and SuperIns £44,800. The two companies would have had opening and closing inventories that would have been used in the calculation of the cost of goods sold in 2015.

continued overleaf

Worked example 19.8 *continued*

Income Statements 2015
Matcon and SuperIns

	Matcon	SuperIns
	£	£
Revenue	240,000	80,000
Less: cost of goods sold	129,600	47,200
Gross profit	110,400	32,800
Delivery costs	8,800	–
Wages	72,000	24,000
Advertising	12,000	2,200
Office expenses	1,060	380
Depreciation	5,000	1,300
Interest on loan	500	–
Operating costs total	99,360	27,880
Net profit	11,040	4,920

Matcon Balance Sheet as at 31 December 2015

	£	£	£
Non-current assets:			
Premises at cost		65,000	
Vehicle cost	12,000		
Less depreciation	8,000	4,000	
Total non-current assets			69,000
Current assets:			
Cash	1,500		
Accounts receivable	35,000		
Inventory	144,500		181,000
Total assets			250,000
Liabilities and equity: Current liabilities:			
Accounts payable		28,960	
Long-term loan		50,000	
Total liabilities			78,960
Owners' equity:			
Capital	160,000		
Profit for the year	11,040		171,040
			250,000

continued

Worked example 19.8 *continued*

SuperIns Balance Sheet as at 31 December 2015

	£	£
Non-current assets:		
Premises at cost		113,000
Current assets:		
Bank	4,400	
Inventory	23,600	
		28,000
Total assets		141,000
Current liabilities:		
Accounts payable		12,080
Owners' equity:		
Share capital	124,000	
Profit for the year	4,920	128,920
Total liabilities & owners' equity		141,000

Calculation of ratios – Matcon and SuperIns

We demonstrate the calculation of the main profitability and liquidity/efficiency ratios in Table 19.6. It is always helpful when preparing an analysis to do it in a tabular form.

▼ **Table 19.6** *Ratios – Matcon and SuperIns*

PROFITABILTY RATIOS		Matcon	SuperIns
Return on net assets %[1]	$\dfrac{\text{PBIT}}{\text{Net assets}}$	$\dfrac{11,540}{171,040} = 6.75\%$	$\dfrac{4,920}{128,920} = 3.82\%$
Gross margin %	$\dfrac{\text{Gross profit}}{\text{Sales}}$	$\dfrac{110,400}{240,000} = 46.00\%$	$\dfrac{32,800}{80,000} = 41.00\%$
Return on sales %	$\dfrac{\text{PBIT}}{\text{Sales}}$	$\dfrac{11,540}{240,000} = 4.81\%$	$\dfrac{4,920}{80,000} = 6.15\%$
Net assets turnover[1]	$\dfrac{\text{Sales}}{\text{Net assets}}$	$\dfrac{240,000}{171,040} = 1.40 \text{ x}$	$\dfrac{80,000}{128,920} = 0.62 \text{ x}$
LIQUIDITY RATIOS			
Current test	$\dfrac{\text{Current assets}}{\text{Current liabilities}}$	$\dfrac{181,000}{28,960} = 6.25{:}1$	$\dfrac{28,000}{12,080} = 2.32{:}1$
Acid test (Quick ratio)	$\dfrac{(\text{Current assets} - \text{inventories})}{\text{Current liabilities}}$	$\dfrac{36,500}{28,960} = 1.26{:}1$	$\dfrac{4,400}{12,080} = 0.36{:}1$

Table 19.6 continued overleaf

Worked example 19.8 *continued*

▼ **Table 19.6** *continued*

WORKING CAPITAL MANAGEMENT		Matcon	SuperIns
Collection period	$\dfrac{\text{Receivables}}{\text{Sales}} \times 365$	$\dfrac{35,000}{240,000} \times 365$ $= 53$ days	N.A.
Payment period	$\dfrac{\text{Payables}}{\text{Purchases}} \times 365$	$\dfrac{28,960}{169,000} \times 365$ $= 63$ days	$\dfrac{12,080}{44,800} = 98$ days
Inventory turnover	$\dfrac{\text{Sales}}{\text{Inventory}}$	$\dfrac{240,000}{144,500} = 1.66 \text{ x}$	$\dfrac{80,000}{23,600} = 3.39 \text{ x}$

Notes

1 We calculate the profit before interest and tax (PBIT) for Matcon by adding back the interest. This provides the total amount of profit from both the investment of the owners' capital and the long-term loan. If Matcon has a return of 6.75% but is paying a higher interest on the loan then this is a poor position. If we were only interested in the return the owner is receiving on the capital they have invested, we would have used the profit after interest.

2 We have expressed the payment period and the collection period in number of days, although some prefer to express it as a percentage or a ratio.

3 For this exercise we have taken only the closing inventory amounts to calculate inventory turnover. Some claim that by calculating the average inventory (opening inventory plus closing inventory, divided by 2) you obtain a more accurate reflection of performance.

Analysis and interpretation – Matcon and SuperIns

This is the most important part of the process. In this section, we offer some guidance on the interpretation of the ratios and the further action you can take. These are only suggestions and do not apply to all investigations. You should find that any contextual analysis you conducted at the beginning will help in the interpretations of the ratios.

Gross margin ratio

Matcon's ratio at 46% is higher than SuperIns' 41%. This suggests that Matcon is either able to charge more for its goods or buys them at a lower price than SuperIns from the suppliers.

Interpretation

The financial statements suggest that Matcon offers delivery (cost in profit and loss account) and allows its customers credit (accounts receivable on balance sheet). SuperIns does not do this. Matcon must recover the costs of these services in its prices. It is also possible that Matcon offers a higher quality product.

Action

Telephone calls to determine whether Matson offers delivery/credit and SuperIns does not.

Obtain their price lists to ascertain whether one charges more than the other for the same product.

continued

Return on sales

Although Matcon's gross margin ratio is higher, the return (i.e. PBIT) on sales is lower at 4.81% compared to SuperIns' 6.15%.

Interpretation

Appears to confirm that Matcon is recovering delivery and credit costs. SuperIns may therefore be competing more on price rather than services to customers.

Action

Search for any industry averages or market reports that provide pricing information.

Return on net assets

This ratio gives you the overview of the profitability performance. If we take Matcon's figure, we get a return of 6.75%. In other words, the money invested by shareholders and lenders long term in the business to acquire the net assets receives a return of 6.75%. SuperIns is not doing quite as well as Matcon with a return on net assets of 3.82%.

Interpretation

SuperIns should investigate the reasons for its lower performance. The next two ratios provide explanation.

Action

Ascertain current market rates on an investment. These may be lower than the companies' returns but the investment is safe. The higher the level of risk then the greater the return you would expect.

Return on sales and net asset turnover

SuperIns wishes to improve its return on net assets so the company must look at these other two ratios. SuperIns' return on sales is 6.15% and the net asset turnover is 0.62 x. If we multiply these two amounts together, the result is the prime ratio of 3.82%. If Super-Ins wishes to improve the prime ratio, the answer is in improving one or both of the other ratios.

Interpretation

We have explained the possible reasons for SuperIns' gross margin ratio being lower than Matcon's but the return on sales is higher. This indicates that the problem may be with the non-current assets.

We need to look at the components of our non-current assets. The balance sheets reveal that the largest component for both companies is premises. SuperIns, the smaller company, has premises in the balance sheet at £113,000. Matcon, the larger company is much lower at £65,000. This needs investigation. SuperIns appears to own premises that are much bigger than its current needs.

Action

Visit both premises and ascertain the space occupied.

Ascertain whether SuperIns is occupying all of the premises or letting a part.

Matcon purchased its premises many years ago. Check if it is in the balance sheet at the original cost with no revaluation.

Investigate whether SuperIns' premises are in a much better location.

Telephone estate agents and find out average square foot cost for such premises.

continued overleaf

Worked example 19.8 *continued*

Current test and acid test

These two tests should be used in conjunction. Usually the interpretation is highly dependent on the financial statements. As far as action is concerned, the most important matter is to ensure that the financial statements have credibility.

Interpretation

Matcon has a very high current test of 6.25:1 and even the acid test is relatively high at 1.26:1. There are no perfect ratios because the interpretation depends on the circumstances but, for the current test, usually a ratio between 1.6:1 to 2:1 is considered healthy. The reason for this is that a value of 1.6:1 means that for every £1 of current liability the company has £1.60 of current asset. In other words, if the company had to pay everyone to whom it owed money by tomorrow, it should be able to do so.

SuperIns has a slightly high current test at 2.3:1 but the acid test is worrying at 0.36:1 SuperIns does not allow credit to its customers so there is no category of accounts receivable. Although there is cash in the bank, this is insufficient to pay debts in the short term. Its payment period of 98 days is considerably higher than Matcon's, which indicates financial stress.

An apparent issue with both companies is inventory turnover. To be able to investigate this we need to know the external factors.

Action

Telephone calls to reliable contacts to see if there are any rumours on the financial strength of the two companies.

Visit both premises and judge whether any goods are in poor condition.

Ascertain whether both companies are building up their inventories in expectation of a large demand.

Investigate the usual ratios in the industry.

Caution

Accounting ratios are easy to calculate but you must be aware of some of the problems. There are no set definitions for the ratios. This means that if you compare your ratios to those calculated by someone else you must ensure you are using the same definitions. In the next chapter we discuss key performance indicators and the conclusion is that you must understand how ratios have been calculated.

The second issue is the financial statements themselves. Even if you are calculating ratios from statements that comply with IFRSs, companies may take different approaches. Some IFRSs can be interpreted in different ways by companies so check the notes accompanying the financial statements to look for explanations of calculations and examine the auditors' report for any comments.

Finally, compare like with like. If you take the financial statements of a mining company in Canada and compare them with those of an Australian agricultural company, you are going to find large differences. Your comparisons must be of companies in the same industry. If you are doing international comparisons you must interpret the ratios in regard to the economic and political position in the different countries.

INVESTOR ANALYSIS

Shareholders are interested in the share price and the return they are receiving on their investment. They can measure their return both in the increase in the share price – a capital gain, and in the dividend they receive.

Although the financial statements may provide information on the company, it depends on what the market thinks of the shares. These opinions are based on the financial statements and an analysis of external factors. One must also accept that rumour and greed may play a part in determining share prices.

One term that is frequently used to 'measure' companies is 'market capitalization'. This is calculated to ascertain the value the stock market puts on a company. The formula is:

Current share price **x** Number of ordinary shares in issue

Since share prices fluctuate, even on a daily basis, the 'value' of the company is always changing. At no stage is it possible to match the market valuation with the 'book value' of the company. You will find that many large companies often have the current share price displayed on their website.

For an in-depth analysis we use the ratios in Diagram 19.6.

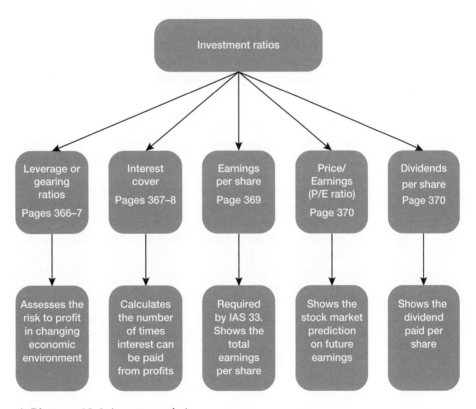

▲ **Diagram 19.6** *Investor analysis*

Leverage or gearing ratios

The terms 'gearing' and 'leverage' both refer to the same ratio. The ratio analyzes the financial structure of the business by comparing the amount of equity compared to long-term debt. The ratio indicates the risk attached to the return on the investment. These risks arise because of fluctuations in profit.

Businesses fund their activities with the capital invested by the owners plus any retained earnings giving the amount of total equity. They may also have to borrow funds from banks and other financial institutions and these will form the long-term liabilities, frequently referred to as debt.

As with all ratios, definitions of these terms vary but equity is normally the risk capital and debt is the total of all liabilities over 12 months old. We discussed this accounting equation previously. As we are using these terms in a variety of ways, we show below the composition of the equation. We have inserted numbers to demonstrate the relationship.

Equity (capital invested by owners plus retained profits)	£10,000
Long-term debt (borrowings)	£10,000
Total of capital employed	£20,000
Total assets (non-current and current assets)	£22,000
Deduct current liabilities	£2,000
Net assets	£20,000

Leverage or gearing refers to the relative proportions of equity and debt that a company has in its financial structure. In our example above, it is 50% of each. A highly leveraged company is one that has a high proportion of debt in relation to equity. A company that has a low proportion of debt in relation to equity is a low leveraged company. Whether a company has a high or low proportion of debt is deduced by looking at the trend over several years and by comparison with other companies in a similar industry.

In the example above we have used the ratio Debt/Equity. Some analysts prefer to calculate the ratio using Debt/Debt + Equity. The conclusions drawn from the different approaches should be the same.

The relative proportions of equity and debt that a company has in its financial structure has an impact on profit in different economic conditions. A highly leveraged company is one that has a high proportion of debt in relation to equity. In times of increasing profit, this is of great benefit to shareholders. A decline in profits will cause those shareholders grief. A company that has a low proportion of debt in relation to equity is a low leveraged company. This will not be so exciting to shareholders but is less risky when there is an economic downturn.

The two ratios that capture the potential financial risk to investors due to leverage are the return on net assets and the return on equity. Return on net assets, or capital employed, has already been discussed in this chapter. This is the amount of profit before interest and tax expressed as a percentage of the net assets. With the return on equity ratio, we are going to define return as the earnings *after* interest but before tax. In other words, we are calculating what the shareholders receive on their investment, excluding long-term liabilities, from our considerations. The formula is:

$$\frac{\text{Profit after interest but before tax}}{\text{Equity}} \times 100$$

In Worked example 19.9, we compare a highly leveraged company with a low leveraged company. It is assumed that they are in similar industries.

Worked example 19.9

Upside plc is a low leveraged company and Downside plc is a highly leveraged company. In 2015, they both have the same amount of earnings before interest. The details for the two companies are as follows.

	Upside plc	Downside plc
Equity	£600,000	£300,000
Long-term debt	£300,000	£600,000
Profit before interest and tax	£60,000	£60,000
Interest charge on debt at 5%	£15,000	£30,000
Profit after interest but before tax	£45,000	£30,000

We can now analyze these two sets of figures by calculating the return (profit before interest and tax) on net assets (debt + equity) and the return (profit after interest but before tax) on equity.

	Upside plc	Downside plc
Return on net assets	6.6%	6.6%
Return on equity	7.5%	10%

Although the two companies have the same profit before interest and tax (6.6%) the return that the shareholders receive is very different because of the amount of debt that Downside holds. If a company is enjoying high profits, the shareholders in the highly leveraged company will get a better return. This is because, once the interest is paid, the profit after interest relates to the much smaller amount of equity.

If there is an economic recession, the shareholders in the highly geared company are the ones who are going to suffer. If profit before interest and tax is £30,000 the results would be:

	Upside plc	Downside plc
Equity	£600,000	£300,000
Debt	£300,000	£600,000
Profit before interest and tax	£30,000	£30,000
Interest charge on debt at 5%	£15,000	£30,000
Profit after interest but before tax	£15,000	£0
Return on net assets	3.3%	3.3%
Return on equity	2.5%	0%

If you are a risk taker you may wish to invest in a highly geared company because in a booming economy you will do very well. The more pessimistic person may decide to invest their funds in a less spectacular low geared company.

Interest cover

Leverage ratios is a valuable technique in highlighting the risks to investors where the economy is turbulent. As with most ratios, there can be definitional issues. A simpler technique is interest cover. The purpose of the ratio is to determine the number of times current interest charges can be paid out of current profits before interest and tax. Instead of PBIT, you may see the acronym EBIT meaning 'earnings before interest and tax'.

$$\frac{\text{Profit (Earnings) before interest and tax}}{\text{Interest charge}} = \text{Number of times}$$

The calculation of the ratio shows the number of times a company can pay its interest charges from its current profits before interest and tax. If the interest charge can be paid (i.e. it is covered) several times from the profits, investors can be confident that they will receive their return. Lenders will receive their interest and existing shareholders should receive some form of dividend.

In an economic decline the low leveraged company is less risky than a highly leveraged company. With a highly leveraged company, the number of times that profits can cover interest charges will be very few. If the profits are insufficient to cover the interest charges, the company is insolvent. In the worst situation, there are insufficient profits to cover interest and there is the danger that the company will go into bankruptcy.

When the economy is booming, profits are higher and a company should be able to pay its interest charges and the increased profits should permit it to pay higher dividends.

Using the same companies as for the calculation of the leverage ratios, Worked example 19.10 shows the interest cover for both companies in good and poor economic situations.

Worked example 19.10   Calculating interest cover

Upside plc is a low leveraged company and Downside plc is a highly leveraged company. In 2015, they both have the same amount of earnings before interest.

The details for the two companies are as follows.

	Upside plc	Downside plc
Equity	£600,000	£300,000
Long-term debt	£300,000	£600,000
Profit before interest and tax	£60,000	£60,000
Interest charge on debt at 5%	£15,000	£30,000
Profit after interest but before tax	£45,000	£30,000

The following table shows the calculation of interest cover for both companies in a good and a poor economy.

	Upside		Downside	
	Calculation	Interest cover	Calculation	Interest cover
Good economy	$\dfrac{£60,000}{£15,000}$	4 times	$\dfrac{£60,000}{£30,000}$	2 times
Poor economy	$\dfrac{£30,000}{£15,000}$	2 times	$\dfrac{£30,000}{£30,000}$	1 time

In a good economy, both companies have the same profit before interest of £60,000. Upside has interest cover of four times but downside's interest is only covered twice. In a poor economy, Downside manages to pay only its interest charge and there is no remaining profit to distribute to shareholders.

The lower the interest cover, the weaker the company's financial position looks. If the company can only pay its interest, shareholders will not receive a dividend. If the interest falls below 1.0, lenders are not going to receive all the interest they are due in that financial period. The company has significant financial problems and it is probable that it will not be able to continue without taking some major actions.

Earnings per share

Shareholders are interested in the financial performance of a company because this is a guide to the dividend they may receive. If a company is paying high dividends, the shareholder not only has an immediate return but the share price may increase because it is a successful company.

A company does not usually pay all its profit out as dividends. The aim of the company is to grow, and it can do this by retaining some of the profit for expansion. The shareholder may not receive such a high dividend but if the company is growing, the shareholder's shares will be more valuable; that is, there is capital growth.

The financial statements disclose the total profits for the financial period. Shareholders are interested in this but are more interested in how their own shares have benefited. To ensure that the EPS disclosed by companies is the one that shareholders receive, we have a standard that regulates this important calculation.

▼ **Table 19.7** *Timeline of IAS 33*

Date	Comment
1997	Standard first issued
2003	Latest revision
2009	Latest amendment

IAS 33 *Earnings per Share* requires companies to calculate and to disclose the basic earnings per share (EPS) on the face of their income statement. The information that a company must provide is:

- details of basic and diluted EPS on the face of the income statement;
- the amounts used as the profit or loss for ordinary shareholders in calculating basic and diluted EPS;
- the weighted average number of ordinary shares used in calculating basic and diluted EPS;
- a description of those ordinary share transactions or potential ordinary share transactions that occur after the balance sheet date and would have had a significant effect on the EPS.

The basic EPS is calculated by dividing the profit or loss attributable to ordinary equity holders of the parent entity by the weighted average number of ordinary shares outstanding during the period (that is, all ordinary shares in issue during the year). Worked example 19.11 illustrates the calculation if a company has not issued further shares during the year.

Worked example 19.11

A company has earnings for the year of £7,000,000. For the year, the weighted average number of shares is 60,000,000. The calculation is:

Earnings for year ended 31 December 2015	£7,000,000
Weighted average number of shares in issue	60,000,000

$$\text{Basic EPS} = \frac{£7,000,000}{60,000,000} = 11.7 \text{ pence}$$

The other disclosure is the diluted EPS. Dilution arises where some individuals have the right to receive ordinary shares in the future in exchange for another type of investment. For example, they may have preference shares or convertible debt and they have the right to convert into ordinary shares in the future. Where conversion takes place, there are more ordinary shares in issue and the EPS declines.

The diluted EPS is a warning to existing shareholders that there is the risk of an issue of more ordinary shares in the future. If that is the case the earnings per share they currently enjoy is not necessarily a good guide to the benefit they may receive in the future.

Price/earnings ratio (P/E ratio)

Shareholders are interested in their current earnings per share but they are also interested in the future performance of the company and thus their shares. Although an analysis of the financial statements can assist shareholders to make predictions on a company's future, a perspective can be gained of the stock market's opinion of the shares.

The P/E ratio reflects the stock market's opinion on the possible future earnings of the company. The ratio calculates the number of times it will take to recover the cost of the share from current profits. The ratio uses the earnings per share and the current market price of one share, the formula being:

$$\frac{\text{Current price of one share in the market}}{\text{Earnings per share}}$$

The current price of a share is easily obtained from stock market information. For this example, we assume that the current price is £2.34. We use the example in the previous section, for which we calculated an EPS of 11.7 pence. Applying the above formula the P/E ratio is:

$$\frac{£2.34}{£0.117} = 20$$

The number 20 is usually interpreted as the number of years it will take to recover the payment for one share at the current price of £0.117. This assumes that the company will continue to make the current profit each year for the next 20 years.

You may think that waiting 20 years to recover the outlay on the share is not attractive. You may consider that a company with a P/E ratio of about 5 years would be a better investment. However, the share with a high P/E ratio may be a good investment.

The P/E ratio uses current facts. With current profits, it would take 20 years but this may be an incomplete analysis. The market may be willing to pay more for the share than the current level of earnings would justify because it believes the company will make much higher profits in the future.

Dividends per share

Dividends are paid from profits. The financial statement shows the total amount paid in dividends. The individual shareholder is more interested in the dividend they receive for each share they hold. The following two ratios can be calculated.

- The *dividend net* is the amount of dividend per share for the financial year.
- The *dividend yield* measures the dividend yielded on a share in relation to the current market price.

We demonstrate the calculation in Worked example 19.12.

Worked example 19.12

Dividend per share

A company has 50,000 shares in issue and for 2015 it declares dividends of £10,000. Its current share price is £5.00 per share.

$$\text{Dividend per share} = \frac{\text{Total dividends}}{\text{Number of ordinary shares}} = \frac{£10,000}{50,000} = 20 \text{ pence per share}$$

Once again, comparison with other companies or previous years will reveal whether this level of dividend is acceptable.

continued

> **Worked example 19.12** *continued*
>
> **Dividend yield**
>
> The shareholder may have purchased the share several years ago at a lower price than the current market price. The dividend yield ratio reflects the dividend as a return on the current price of the share. The formula is:
>
> $$\frac{\text{Dividend per share}}{\text{Current share price}} \times 100 = \frac{20 \text{ pence}}{\pounds 5.00} \times 100 = 4\%$$
>
> The investor has the choice of retaining the share and receiving a return of 4% or selling the share and reinvesting the proceeds. If investors believe that a higher return than 4% can be obtained and the P/E ratio does not indicate that the stock market expects earnings to increase in future years, investors may decide to place their money elsewhere.

LIMITATIONS OF RATIO ANALYSIS

Ratios are widely used to analyze the financial statements that form part of the corporate report. In conducting this analysis, it is essential to put the ratios in the context of all the additional information in the corporate report. It is also essential to have comparisons.

One ratio, by itself, is neither good nor bad. You can compare it to those from previous years, to industry averages or to similar companies. With new companies or those operating in niche markets, there may not be comparable companies or industry averages. One option is to look at related companies or industries. Does the new company have suppliers or linked businesses that you can investigate to assess its strengths and weaknesses?

Many companies calculate their own ratios for use as comparators. However, companies may choose to use terms and calculations that present a different analysis from the one you have made. You need to investigate such differences.

In this chapter, we have used the terms and definitions that we consider commonly used. Unfortunately, there are no universal definitions and terms that have some authorized support. This means that any comparisons with ratios from other sources must be treated with caution.

Ratios calculated on published financial statements do not take account of non-financial factors. To support your interpretation of the ratios you should review the other indicators we identified in Diagram 19.2.

CONCLUSIONS

Corporate financial reports and websites provide users with a mass of information. A method needs to be found to analyze and interpret all this data. For many years, analysts and others have used accounting ratios. Data is extracted from the financial statements and formulae are applied to calculate ratios.

There are three stages in the analysis of corporate reports. Although, the financial statements are the source for the calculations, the analysis and interpretation requires information about the state of the industry, economic outlooks and social and political changes. A broad range of information is required to provide the context in which the analysis and interpretation is conducted.

The second stage is the calculation of relevant ratios. It is also necessary to understand the relationship of the ratios. We grouped the ratios under two main headings: financial statement analysis and investor analysis.

Financial statement analysis examines profitability, liquidity and efficiency, and cash management. Investor analysis looks at profit per share, dividends and the influence of the stock market.

The final stage is the analysis and interpretation. This involves reflecting on the ratios within the context you have developed. It also requires action. This involves seeking explanations for differences between the ratios you have calculated and those from other sources. It also requires reflection on the picture that your ratios portray and the one that is being promoted by the company.

Increasingly, companies are calculating, disclosing and commenting on their activities both with numbers and with narrative data. In the next chapter, we examine the information that is contained in the corporate reporting package.

ADDITIONAL RESOURCES

Go online to the companion website for this book to access further teaching and learning materials for this chapter.
www.palgravehighered.com/hussey-cfr

THE CORPORATE REPORTING PACKAGE

At the end of this chapter, you should be able to:

- Describe the structure and main contents of a corporate reporting package
- Discuss the disclosure requirements in the strategic report
- Explain the purpose and content of the business model
- Explain the corporate governance statement and the objectives of the stewardship report
- Describe the factors influencing sustainability and social reporting
- Define key performance indicators and explain their use

INTRODUCTION

Legislation and voluntary disclosures by companies have greatly expanded the length of the traditional annual report and accounts. The highly regulated financial section now occupies about one-third of the document. Legislation has required information additional to that communicated by the financial statements.

Companies also provide substantial narrative information voluntarily. Companies now issue what is better described as a corporate reporting package (CRP). In this chapter, we use the term 'annual report and accounts' when discussing specific companies or instances. We use the term 'corporate reporting package' where we wish to emphasize the additional information being disclosed.

Legislation requiring additional information varies from country to country. In this chapter, we discuss the requirements in the UK. Other countries require similar disclosures and we include some relevant examples.

In the UK, strategic report and corporate governance disclosures are required. We discuss the contents in this chapter. Several countries require annual reports and accounts to contain a management discussion and analysis section requiring similar information. For most countries, the emphasis in the past has been on the explanation of the results and the manage-ment of the directors and the remuneration they receive. This has expanded to contain infor-mation on the environment and other social concerns.

Voluntary disclosures – that is, information other than that required by legislation or ac-counting standards – are decided by the company. In this chapter, we concentrate on disclosures in the printed annual report and accounts (see Diagram 20.1). However, the most significant growth in disclosures has been on company websites. We discuss this topic in the next chapter.

▲ Diagram 20.1 *Structure of Chapter 20*

THE CORPORATE REPORTING PACKAGE (CRP)

In the early days of companies publishing an annual report and accounts, the document was limited in length and content. There would be less than 10 pages, and the information would essentially be the financial statements.

Over the decades, there has been an increase in both the amount and nature of corporate disclosures. The reasons for this growth have been:

- legislation requiring additional financial and non-financial information;
- IASs and IFRSs requiring more detailed financial information;
- user and societal demands for increased disclosures;
- companies choosing to provide a wider range of information.

Understandably, there has been a growth in financial disclosures because of the impact of accounting standards. Another factor has been the growth in narrative or non-financial reporting. Narrative reporting is part voluntary and part required by legislation.

To capture some indication of growth of disclosures in the CRP we analyzed 10 annual reports and accounts chosen at random from our sample of 25 companies. We categorize the reported information into four headings: audit report, financial statements, notes to the accounts and general narrative reporting, which some describe as non-financial reporting. Under those headings, we selected the lowest and highest number of pages, comparing reports from 2005, when the European Union (EU) adopted international standards, with those from 2014 (Table 20.1).

▼ Table 20.1 *Length of sections in annual reports and accounts*

	2005		2014	
	Lowest no. of pages	Highest no. of pages	Lowest no. of pages	Highest no. of pages
Audit report	1	1	3	6
Financial statements	3	5	4	5
Notes to the accounts	22	67	39	70
Narrative reporting	34	115	89	153

Table 20.1 does not show the weightings of the various sections of the annual report and accounts, as we retrieved the selection from different reports. For example, our longest annual report of 172 pages in 2005 did not have the longest section on narrative reporting. Table 20.1 is constructed to indicate the growth in the various types of disclosures, particularly narrative reporting.

However, the 2005 data emphasizes the wide range for company disclosures in the various sections in one year. The comparison of the two years demonstrates substantial growth in disclosures. The results for the audit report and financial statements are as might be expected, but the difference in the length of the notes to the accounts is significant. The reasons for this are the requirements of accounting standards for greater disclosures and the increase in the number of standards.

As one may have anticipated, the main growth is due to narrative reporting. The term 'narrative reporting' refers to the contextual and non-financial information reported in addition to the required financial information. The narrative information assists users' understanding of a company's business, its market position, strategy, and performance and future prospects – including quantified metrics.

For most companies, narrative reporting has divided itself into two main sections: strategic review and corporate governance. Later in this chapter, we examine both the legal requirements and entity practices for these two sections.

As an update and extension on existing disclosure practices, we conducted a broad analysis of the page lengths of 22 of the 25 documents in our sample of annual reports and accounts. We explain the omission of three of the reports later in this section.

In Table 20.2 we show the lowest, highest and average number of pages for what we consider to be the three main sections of the 22 annual reports examined. We also give the percentage share of the total of the three sections identified.

▼ Table 20.2 *Content analysis of 2014 corporate reports*

	Number of pages			Percentage of the three sections
	Highest	Lowest	Average	
Strategic report	70	29	47	31%
Corporate governance	58	30	42	27%
Financial statements plus notes	97	39	65	42%

The total of the average number of pages of the three sections differs from the average of 163 total pages for the 22 annual report and accounts. This is because many companies provide additional information in their Summary that falls outside of the three main sections.

The first conclusion to be drawn from our survey is that there is not a typical annual report and accounts. Those companies with the lowest number of pages in any one section did not necessarily have the lowest number of pages in another section. As a generality, reports with a high number of total pages tended to have the highest number of pages in each section. Sometimes the lengths of the sections depended on the layout and design rather than substantive content.

The second conclusion is that mainly narrative information, as contained in the strategic report and corporate governance sections, outweighs the number of pages in the financial statements section. Once again, the balance depended on how the company decided to provide the information.

The above analysis gives a general indication of the weighting of the content in corporate reports. We provide greater insight by examining the three corporate reports that were not included in the above analysis (see Company examples 20.1, 20.2 and 20.3). We consider that these three reports – from TUI, Unilever and WPP – have some unique features that are worthy of separate discussion.

These three company examples emphasize that there is not a regimented format for CRPs and that companies have considerable opportunity to determine what information to disclose and how to present it.

Company example 20.1

TUI AG is the world's leading integrated tourism group. It has 1,800 travel agencies, 300 own brand hotels and 12 cruise vessels. The auditor's report states that the consolidated financial statements comply, in all material respects, with IFRSs as adopted by the EU, and the additional requirements of German commercial law.

The annual report and accounts has three parts:

Section 1 – To our shareholders (pp. 10–46), which incorporates a corporate governance report.
Section 2 – Management Report (pp. 47–284), which incorporates the financial statements and supporting notes.
Magazine of 70 pages.

TUI AG, Annual Report, 2013/14

Company example 20.2

Unilever plc issues its annual report and accounts in two parts: the Strategic Report and the Governance and Financial Report.

The Strategic Report (pages 1–41) 'contains information about us, how we make money and how we run our business. It includes our strategy, business model, markets and Key Performance Indicators, as well as our approach to sustainability and risk.' It also incorporates a number of photographs and diagrams.

The Governance section has 37 pages and the Financial Report takes up 62 pages. Together, the 'Governance and Financial Report contains detailed corporate governance information, how we mitigate risk, our Committee reports and how we remunerate our Directors, plus our Financial Statements and Notes.' It also has an index that is very useful for a document with 140 pages.

Unilever plc, Annual Report and Accounts, 2014

Company example 20.3

WPP plc

With a company that offers internationally everything from advertising services to public relations and specialist communications, a report of over 240 pages is not unexpected. Every year their annual report and accounts is embellished with famous artwork. For their 2014 report, they focussed on Africa to feature (mostly) contemporary artists from Tanzania, Kenya and South Africa.

We show the opening contents with page numbers below (without the many colours used in the original).

The fast read
1   A six-minute read

Who we are
12   Our companies & associates

Why we exist
14   Our mission
     Our 4 strategic priorities
16   New markets, new media, data investment management & application of technology, horizontality

WPP: a global company
18   Our growth markets

How we're doing
21   Financial summary
24   Strategic report to share owners
45   Reports from our company leaders

All of the legally required information, plus much more is contained in the remaining (almost) 200 pages.

WPP plc, Annual Report and Accounts, 2014

▼ Table 20.3 *Usual segments of printed CRPs*

Segment	Disclosures
Summary/Introduction	Picks out key information such as growth in profits, board changes, mergers, markets
Chairman's statement	The success, or otherwise, over the past year in achieving the company's strategy
Strategic report	We discuss this topic in detail later in this chapter
Corporate governance	We discuss this topic in detail later in this chapter
Directors' report	Legal disclosures
Directors' remuneration report	The payments made to directors. This report is usually very detailed
Directors' responsibility statement	A statement that the directors have fulfilled their responsibilities
Auditor's report	Legal requirement
Main financial statements	We discussed in previous chapters
Notes to the accounts	We discussed in previous chapters

Quoted companies usually provide a wide range of information. The volume in each segment can vary depending on the amount of information the entity is compelled to disclose and the amount it wishes to provide voluntarily.

In Table 20.3, we indicate the various sections you will find in many printed CRPs.

If we consider international practices of large companies, we find similar disclosures, although titled differently. Our first example (Company example 20.4) is from the annual report and accounts of China Petroleum & Chemical Corporation (Sinopec Corp.).

Company example 20.4

Page
  2   Company Profile
  3   Principal Financial Data and Indicators
  6   Changes in Share Capital and Share Holdings of Principal Shareholders
  8   Chairman's Statements
 11   Business Review and Prospects
 19   Management's Discussion and Analysis
 31   Significant Events
 39   Connected Transactions
 43   Corporate Governance
 51   Report of the Board of Directors
 56   Report of the Board of Supervisors
 58   Directors, Supervisors, Senior Management and Employees
 71   Principal Wholly Owned and Controlled Subsidiaries

Sinopec, Annual Report and Accounts, 2014

Sinopec is registered in Beijing, the People's Republic of China. It is a listed company on domestic and international stock exchanges including the London Stock Exchange. In Company example 20.4, we show the first section of its 2014 annual report and accounts illustrating the types of information communicated, in addition to the financial statements and their accompanying notes.

Company example 20.4 has some different headings from those you would find in the annual report and accounts of a company incorporated in the UK. Although there are differences in the headings, the contents are broadly similar. The Management's Discussion and Analysis section covers material that UK companies place in separate sections.

With companies incorporated outside the UK, the financial statements may comply with IFRSs, but the narrative information reflects the legislation and practices in their own country. Two sections that you are unlikely to find with UK based company disclosures are the Report of the Board of Supervisors and information on directors, supervisors, senior management and employees.

THE STRATEGIC REPORT

Most companies start the annual report with narrative information. This may be a chair's statement, an overview of the financial results or even information on their products. The main narrative section that is most informative about the company is the strategic report. There have been several legislative stages that brought about the disclosure of this information.

The UK Companies Act 2006 introduced the requirement that companies should include a business review in their director's report in the annual report and accounts. The reason for the disclosure is to provide information on how the directors have performed their duty to promote the success of the company. This requirement now usually comes within the strategic report in the CRP.

Remember that the Companies Act 2006 applies to UK companies, and practices in other countries may differ. In the US, Canada and some other countries there is a management discussion and analysis section that addresses similar material to the business review.

The disclosure requirements placed on quoted companies are extensive. In addition to reporting on the main trends and factors likely to affect the future development, performance and position of the company's business, the Act required the business review to include information on:

- environmental matters (including the impact of the company's business on the environment);
- the company's employees;
- social and community issues.

The legislation also required an analysis using financial and other key performance indicators. Key performance indicators (KPIs) enable a company to measure effectively and communicate the development, performance and position of the business.

The introduction of KPIs raises some interesting issues. One conclusion may be that the financial information generated by compliance with IFRSs is insufficient or inadequate for users' needs. It may be that KPIs add dimensions not captured by the traditional financial measures. Later in this chapter, we discuss KPIs in detail.

The UK government, in 2011, consulted on new proposals for narrative reporting as an improvement on the business review. In August 2013, the Government approved The Companies Act 2006 (Strategic Report and Directors' Report) Regulations 2013.

The main change in the new regulations was that companies, apart from those using the small companies' exemption, needed to prepare a strategic report as part of their annual report. This replaced the previous requirement for entities to include a business review within the directors' report.

To support the legislation, the Department for Business, Innovation and Skills (BIS) requested the Financial Reporting Council (FRC) to prepare non-mandatory guidance supporting the new legal requirements for the strategic report. The FRC considered this an opportunity to make the annual report a more cohesive document; in other words, to encourage the linking of narrative and financial disclosures.

The final guidance (FRC 2014c) provides advice on the strategic report but also emphasizes its links with other parts of the annual report. Although the FRC document does not have mandatory force, it establishes best practice. It also identifies significant issues regarding the strategic report and some of the failures of the previous business review.

The objective of the strategic report is to provide information for shareholders so that they can assess the directors' performance in promoting the success of the company. The FRC states that, in meeting the needs of shareholders, the information in the annual report may also be of interest to other stakeholders.

The content elements for the strategic report set out in the guidance are derived from the Companies Act 2006, and include:

- description of the entity's strategy, objectives and business model;
- explanation of the main trends and factors affecting the entity;
- description of its principal risks and uncertainties;
- analysis of the development and performance of the business;
- analysis using key performance indicators.

In addition to the above, where material, an entity should disclose information on:

- the environment;
- employees, social, community and human rights issues;
- gender diversity.

The communication principles adopted by the FRC suggest that the strategic report should have the following characteristics:

- fairness, balance and understandability;
- conciseness;
- forward-looking;
- inclusion of entity-specific information;
- links to information in different parts of the annual report.

enterprise risk management

Enterprise risk management is a process, effected by an entity's board of directors, management and other personnel, applied in strategy setting and across the enterprise, designed to identify potential events that may affect the entity, and manage risk to be within its risk appetite, to provide reasonable assurance regarding the achievement of entity objectives.

Based on Committee of Sponsoring Organizations of the Treadway Commission (COSO), 2004

Of course, the directors decide the depth and scope of information they will disclose in compliance with the regulations. One issue is that information of importance in managing a business reflects the directors' opinions. This may not necessarily meet the information needs of the users. The information required for assessing an entity for investment purposes reflects the opinions of investors. This may differ from the opinion of managers. There are additional complications in that there are different types of investors. We will return to these issues in the next chapter.

One section that has been increasing considerably is the description of the company's principal risks and uncertainties. Financial risk is clearly important and we discussed strategies to manage this in Chapters 11 and 12. The trend, however, is a movement away from only giving the financial perspective and allocating more attention to **enterprise risk management.**

The Committee of Sponsoring Organizations of the Treadway Commission (COSO) has a risk management framework providing key principles and concepts, and clear direction and guidance.

Other organizations have issued advice and guidance on risk management, seeking to identify the issues arising when management wishes to improve its financial return but can only do so by accepting greater risks. The increase in the 'risk appetite' has revealed the responses that management are or should be undertaking. The themes that have emerged are:

1 The necessity for companies to accept the need for clear risk management.
2 The development of enforceable risk policies.
3 A range of risk identification techniques including scenario analysis.
4 Integration of the different types of risk and the unintended consequences, e.g. outsourcing to third parties in other countries.
5 The difficulties in identifying where the risk lies in the value chain.
6 The increasing use and complexity of technology. Technology not only offers opportunities but it brings with it risks.
7 Assessing the costs of failure.

The business model

It is probably inescapable that not all users' information needs can be satisfied. The legislation has increased the amount of disclosure and the nature of the information provided. Since 2010, the UK Corporate Governance Code, which is mandatory for listed companies under Stock Exchange rules, requires directors to include an explanation of their business model in the annual report (FRC 2010).

In general terms, a business model describes the *activities* of a *business*. This covers the components of the business, the functions of the business, and the *revenues* and *expenses*.

The regulations state that the entity should disclose:

- How it generates or preserves value over the longer term, and how it captures that value.
- What it does and why it does it.
- How it is structured.
- The markets in which it operates.
- How it engages with those markets.

Underpinning these requirements is the recognition that entities operate as a part of the value chain. An entity often creates value through its activities at several different parts of its business process. The legislation requires that the portrayal of the business model should focus on the parts of the business processes that are most important to the generation, preservation or capture of value.

Although the business model is an important part of the annual report and accounts, it is not usually lengthy. Companies use diagrams and financial information to accompany the text. Most companies take only two or three pages for the text and any diagrams they wish to use.

To demonstrate the approach companies adopt, we use a brief extract of the introductory text from two companies in different industries (see Company examples 20.5 and 20.6). These demonstrate that there is no standard business model, but the model depends on the nature of the company. The first example is Sage plc which has a relatively straightforward business model. The second is Rolls-Royce, the company that we examined in Chapter 8 where we demonstrated the complexity of their closing inventory valuation.

Sage plc was formed in 1981 and was listed on the LSE in 1989. Sage provides small and medium-sized companies with a range of business management software and services. This includes accounting and payroll, enterprise resource planning, customer relationship management and payments. It has over 13,000 employees in 23 countries covering the UK and Ireland, mainland Europe, North America, South Africa, Australia, Asia and Brazil.

Company example 20.5

The business model

What we do…

Growing economies rely on successful SME businesses. We're committed to helping them achieve this success by being their most trusted supporter.

We've been dedicated to the success of SME businesses for over 30 years through the provision of localised products and services that help our customers to run their businesses with confidence.

Our support offering is a key strength and is highly valued because it gives our customers somewhere to turn if they have a technical problem, an accounting question or when they're affected by legislative changes. Our commitment to supporting our customers in this way, where we look to maintain ongoing and active relationships with them, differentiates us from other software vendors.

It also means we've built a strong base of recurring revenue that underpins 73% of our total revenue, which is derived from 1.8 million support, subscription and payments relationships that we have with customers across the world.

Ultimately, we have the resources, vision and resilience to be there for our customers over the long term as their businesses grow.

Sage plc, Annual Report and Accounts, 2014, p. 6

Company example 20.6

Business model

We bring advanced technology to market through integrated power and propulsion systems and services for use in the air, on land and at sea.

Engineering excellence is a fundamental source of competitive advantage across the Group. Our methods, processes and experience enable us to deliver complex, high-value programmes. Our ability to optimise and integrate entire systems is a core competence informed by a close understanding of customer needs and decades of domain knowledge.

continued

Company example 20.6 *continued*

Addressing complementary markets from a shared capability and technology base brings breadth and scale, diversity and balance, enabling us to invest efficiently, and providing the resilience required to offset new project risk. Our manufacturing model is consistent across the Group; we only produce parts ourselves where we can create and sustain a competitive advantage.

The balance of our supply chain is built around close and long-standing relationships with key partners and suppliers, a model that provides flexibility of capacity and secures access to world-class capability. Some partners, as well as supplying parts, share in the risks and rewards of the whole programme from research and development to manufacture, through risk and revenue sharing arrangements.

Services are an essential part of our business, building customer relationships and providing revenue stability by moderating the effects of new equipment order cycles. Services offer strong growth potential and the opportunity to align incentives through long-term service contracts, providing visibility of costs to our customers and helping us secure future revenues. This is particularly the case in Civil aerospace where contractual and air safety considerations mean that we have rights that secure a large part of the aftermarket spare parts business even where we do not have a TotalCare® agreement.

The operation of our business model over decades has resulted in a substantial and growing installed base of engines at all stages of the product life cycle. Cash flows today from investments made, in some cases many years ago, support investment for the future.

We are focused on making this proven business model more effective through relentless focus on costs to generate the funds to sustain the investment necessary to remain competitive.

Rolls-Royce, Annual Report and Accounts, 2014, p. 24

These examples illustrate how the type of industry shapes the contents of the business model. Rolls-Royce is large with complex production facilities. Sage is smaller with different processes and outputs.

In addition to the text shown in the example, Rolls-Royce's annual report includes diagrams, and statistical and financial information. However, the section on the business model, in most cases, does not refer specifically to the financial statements. The sections are stand alone and not integrated. We discuss integrated reporting in the next chapter.

There is serious debate in the UK, Europe and worldwide regarding how to develop and regulate narrative reporting. Commentators have identified several issues and offered potential solutions as follows.

- The present annual reports are too long and complicated. In the UK, the FRC (2011) is encouraging the removal of 'clutter' by eliminating immaterial and unimportant disclosures.
- Much of the information is in separate unrelated segments. On the international level, integrated reporting is being proposed and we discuss that in the next chapter.
- The business model explains how the business 'operates' but does not show clearly the economic consequences. There have been suggestions in the academic literature that companies should demonstrate the connection between their business models and their financial results.

A comprehensive review of the literature by Nielsen and Roslender concluded that 'business model informed financial reporting is particularly appropriate for providing information that is explicitly focused on the creation and delivery of value to customers' (2015: 14). Although the argument is persuasive, there are substantial problems.

A major difficulty is that the Conceptual Framework (CF) that we discussed in Chapter 2 would require a complete revision. Experience shows that obtaining agreement on the present CF is elusive. Some commentators argue that the present disclosures of business model do not demonstrate a sufficiently robust theoretical basis, and a strong link with financial reporting has yet to be demonstrated.

CORPORATE GOVERNANCE AND STEWARDSHIP CODE

corporate governance

Corporate governance is the system by which companies are directed and controlled. Boards of directors are responsible for the governance of their companies. The shareholders' role in governance is to appoint the directors and the auditors and to satisfy themselves that an appropriate governance structure is in place. The responsibilities of the board include setting the company's strategic aims, providing the leadership to put them into effect, supervising the management of the business and reporting to shareholders on their stewardship. The board's actions are subject to laws, regulations and the shareholders in general meeting.

Cadbury Committee Corporate Governance Code, 1992, para. 2.5

Towards the end of the twentieth century, greater attention was being paid to the conduct of companies in addition to their financial performance. There were accusations of corporate greed with directors enjoying inflated bonuses. Questions were also being asked about the environmental damage caused by some industrial practices, work conditions and product safety. These criticisms finally led to several reports and documents offering advice.

The first report to offer advice in a formal matter was the Cadbury Code in 1992. The Greenbury Report followed in 1995. This report was a response to the public outcry on excessive executive remuneration. The Hampel Report was published in 1998 and led to the Combined Code being issued in the same year. This brought together the issues addressed by Cadbury and Greenbury. Much later the Stewardship Code was added.

The various reviews of the operation of the Combined Code resulted in a redraft in 2003 and a revision in 2008. In that year, the FRC published the Combined Code on Corporate Governance. Their objective was not to provide a rigid set of rules but a guide to good board practice.[1]

The FRC anticipated that companies would comply with the code, but accepted that non-compliance may take place for valid reasons such as the unavailability of data or concerns over confidentiality. Where there was non-compliance, the company had to explain the reasons to shareholders. This 'comply or explain' approach commenced with the 1992 Code. This is fundamental to the present code that applies to accounting periods beginning on or after 1 October 2014.

All companies with a Premium listing of equity shares on the London Stock Exchange should comply with the Code regardless of whether the company was incorporated in the UK or elsewhere. The Listing Rules require companies to apply the Main Principles and report to shareholders on how they have done so.

The principles are the foundation of the Code and there are five main principles and several supporting principles. Rather than duplicate the section of the Code that covers main principles, we summarize those in Table 20.4 with a brief explanation of each.

The code (FRC 2014e) that applies to accounting periods beginning on or after 1 October 2014 introduced some key changes, as described below.

▼ Table 20.4 *Main principles of the combined code*

Principle	Explanation
Leadership	There should be an effective board responsible for the company's success. The Chairperson is responsible for the leadership and effectiveness of the board.
Effectiveness	The board should have the requisite balance of skills, experience and knowledge of the company. Directors must give sufficient time to their responsibilities and be submitted for re-election at regular intervals.
Accountability	The board is responsible for deciding the application of corporate reporting, risk management and internal control principles.
Remuneration	No director can set his or her own remuneration. Performance related packages are acceptable but should be transparent, stretching and rigorously applied.
Shareholders	The board is responsible for ensuring that there is a satisfactory dialogue with shareholders with a clear understanding of objectives.

Going concern, risk management and internal control

- Companies should state whether they consider it appropriate to adopt the going concern basis of accounting and identify any material uncertainties in their ability to continue to do so.
- Companies should robustly assess their principal risks and explain how they are being managed or mitigated.
- Companies should state whether they believe they will be able to continue in operation and meet their liabilities taking account of their current position and principal risks, and specify the period covered by this statement and why they consider it appropriate. It is expected that the period assessed will be significantly longer than 12 months.
- Companies should monitor their risk management and internal control systems and, at least annually, carry out a review of their effectiveness, and report on that review in the annual report.
- Companies can choose where to put the risk and viability disclosures. If placed in the strategic report, directors will be covered by the 'safe harbour' provisions in the Companies Act 2006.

Remuneration

- Greater emphasis should be placed on ensuring that remuneration policies are designed with the long-term success of the company in mind, and that the lead responsibility for doing so rests with the remuneration committee.
- Companies should put in place arrangements that will enable them to recover or withhold variable pay when appropriate to do so, and should consider appropriate vesting and holding periods for deferred remuneration.

Shareholder engagement

- Companies should explain when publishing general meeting results how they intend to engage with shareholders when a significant percentage of them have voted against any resolution.

Stewardship Code

Stewardship Code

The Stewardship Code assists the quality of engagement between the owners of the company and the managers by requiring investors to apply effective stewardship, thus improving long-term risk-adjusted returns to shareholders.

In September 2012, the FRC issued the **Stewardship Code** which specified that directors do not have the ultimate responsibility for all of a company's decisions. The directors are responsible to the owners. With large companies, the most powerful owners are the institutional investors.

The FRC stated that: 'The UK Stewardship Code sets out the principles of effective stewardship by investors. In so doing, the Code assists institutional investors better to exercise their stewardship responsibilities, which in turn gives force to the "comply or explain" system.' (FRC 2012b: 1).

The Code is aimed at institutional investors comprising asset owners and asset managers with equity holdings in UK listed companies. Asset owners include pension funds, insurance companies, investment trusts and other collective investment vehicles. Asset managers have responsibility for managing investments. The aim of the Code is to encourage institutional investors to play an influential role in the governance of the company.

As with the UK Corporate Governance Code, the UK Stewardship Code has a 'comply or explain' basis. In other words, if you comply with the Code, no explanations are necessary. If you do not comply you have to disclose the reasons.

The Code is not rule based but principles based and institutional investors should:

1. publicly disclose their policy on satisfying their stewardship responsibilities.
2. have a robust policy on managing conflicts of interest in relation to stewardship.
3. monitor their investee companies.
4. establish clear guidelines on when and how they will escalate their stewardship activities.
5. be willing to act collectively with other investors where appropriate.
6. have a clear policy on voting and disclosure of voting activity.
7. report periodically on their stewardship and voting activities. (FRC 2102b: 5)

Lansdowne Partners have a useful example of their approach to the above principles on their website.[2]

SUSTAINABILITY AND CORPORATE SOCIAL REPORTING

sustainability

Sustainability is development that meets the needs of the present without compromising the ability of future generations to meet their own needs.

Based on World Commission on the Environment and Development, 1987, p. 43

Increasingly, the terms '**sustainability**' and '**corporate social responsibility**' (CSR) have been appearing in companies' annual reports and accounts, usually included either as part of the strategic report or in the corporate governance section. Other terms, such as 'social and environmental reporting', 'social responsibility reporting' and 'environmental accounting', are also used. These disclosures attempt to bridge the possible divide between economic growth and protection of the environment or societal interests.

A broader view of sustainability is 'the generation, analysis and use of monetarised environmental and socially related information in order to improve corporate environmental, social and economic performance' (Bent and Richardson 2003). This incorporates economic viability, social

corporate social responsibility (CSR)

Corporate social responsibility is defined as the voluntary activities undertaken by a company to operate in an economic, social and environmentally sustainable manner.

Government of Canada

responsibility and environmental responsibility. Elkington (1998) coined the phrase 'the Triple Bottom Line', and it is frequently used in relation to CSR.

The term 'corporate social responsibility' includes many different corporate activities. The Government of Canada has given a broad definition.[3]

The Global Reporting Initiative (2011) has proposed a sustainability reporting framework for organizations of any size, sector, or location. The adoption of this framework would help companies to report sustainability information in a way that is similar to financial reporting.

The GRI *Reporting Framework* contains general and sector-specific content. A wide range of stakeholders around the world has agreed that it is generally applicable for reporting an organization's sustainability performance. Standard disclosures are proposed, with performance indicators and other items. In 2015, the GRI established a Sustainability Reporting Standards Board (SRSB).

There is also a Sustainability Accounting Standards Board (SASB) based in the US. It aims to develop and disseminate sustainability accounting standards. The purpose is to enable public corporations to disclose material, decision-useful information to investors. SASB Sustainability Accounting Standards provide disclosure guidance and accounting standards on sustainability topics. Both US companies and foreign public companies can use them.

SASB standards customized for specific industries identify sustainability topics at that level. The standards provide companies with standardized metrics designed to communicate performance on sustainability topics. The standards have the following attributes:

- *Objectivity* – Criteria should be free from bias.
- *Measurability* – Criteria should permit reasonably consistent measurements, qualitative or quantitative, of subject matter.
- *Completeness* – Criteria should be sufficiently complete so that those relevant factors that would alter a conclusion about subject matter are not omitted.
- *Relevance* – Criteria should be relevant to the subject matter.

There has also been interest in Canada in promoting sustainability reporting. The Chartered Professional Accountants of Canada, in 2015, issued *A Starter's Guide to Sustainability Reporting*. In conjunction with the Toronto Stock Exchange, it also published *A Primer for Environmental and Social Disclosures*.

In Australia, the legal requirements come under the Corporations Act 2001. The main ones require companies to include details of breaches of environmental laws and require providers of financial products with an investment component to disclose. However, guidelines have been published specifically for the Australian market.[4]

In 2010, the European Commission renewed its efforts to develop CSR to encourage long-term employee and consumer trust. The Commission considered that environmental issues were a priority subject for greater disclosures. This is not a compulsory standard but a guidance document providing advice and recommendations to those organizations wishing to embrace CSR. It discusses the following subjects:

- Organizational governance
- Human rights
- Labour practices
- The environment
- Fair operating practices
- Consumer issues
- Community involvement and development

The EU then decided to move from the voluntary approach to a legal one. The European Parliament adopted two resolutions in 2013:

- Corporate Social Responsibility: promoting society's interests and a route to sustainable and inclusive recovery;
- Corporate Social Responsibility: accountable, transparent and responsible business behaviour and sustainable growth.

In December 2014, the *Directive on disclosure of non-financial and diversity information by certain large companies* came into force. Member states had two years to transpose it into national laws. The Directive introduces measures that will strengthen the transparency and accountability of approximately 6,000 companies in the EU. These so-called 'public interest entities' with more than 500 employees will be required to:

- report on environmental, social and employee-related, human rights, anti-corruption and bribery matters;
- describe their business model, outcomes and risks of the policies on the above topics, and the diversity policy applied for management and supervisory bodies.

Companies will be encouraged to rely on recognized frameworks such as GRI's Sustainability Reporting Guidelines, the United Nations Global Compact (UNGC), the UN Guiding Principles on Business and Human Rights, OECD Guidelines, International Organization for Standardization (ISO) 26000 and the International Labour Organization (ILO) Tripartite Declaration.

It is expected that the first company reports will be published in 2018 covering financial year 2017–2018.

Given the numerous bodies offering encouragement and advice on sustainability reporting, we find it difficult to summarize what companies are doing in practice. However, we show short extracts from the annual report and accounts of two of our 25 sample companies (see Company examples 20.7 and 20.8). We have selected these because they demonstrate some existing practices.

Company example 20.7 is from CRH – an international building materials group. The heading for the piece is Sustainability and Governance. Company example 20.8 is from an Australian company Incitec Pivot Limited – an international manufacturer of industrial explosives and fertilisers. The extract is the opening of their sustainability report.

Company example 20.7

Sustainability and Governance

CRH's strategy and business model is built around the principles of sustainable, responsible and ethical performance. The Group's organisational culture is rooted in a daily commitment to core values of honesty, integrity and respect in all business dealings.

CRH believes that combining these principles and values with best international practice, promotes good governance and provides a platform for the business to deliver superior returns over a sustained period of time, while also being sensitive and responsive to stakeholders and the environment in which the Group operates.

CRH has therefore placed sustainability and corporate social responsibility at the heart of its business model, strategy and activities worldwide.

CRH, Sustainability Report, 2014, p. 7

> ## Company example 20.8
>
> ### Sustainability Strategy
>
> Incitec Pivot defines Sustainability as 'the creation of long term economic value whilst caring for our people, our communities and our environment'. This commitment to Sustainability is driven by the Company's Values and is core to the way Incitec Pivot operates its business.
>
> Incitec Pivot's Sustainability Strategy was formally adopted by the Board in September 2010. During the 2014 financial year, a formal review of the Company's sustainability performance to date was undertaken. The review included two independent peer benchmarking reviews: one investor focused (Dow Jones) and one customer focused (Eco Vadis). As a result of this review the existing strategy for operational sites was re-affirmed. It was also determined that Incitec Pivot should seek to influence suppliers to promote alignment with the Company's corporate values and continue the sustainable development of its supply chain
>
> *Incitec Pivot Limited, Annual Report and Accounts, 2014, p. viii*

Both of the extracts demonstrate a commitment to sustainability and exemplify the stated sustainability objectives and activities of many companies. For a more general view of company practices, we provide the results of an international survey of large companies by KPMG (2011):

Ninety-five per cent of the 250 largest companies in the world (G250 companies) now report on their corporate responsibility (CR) activities, two-thirds of non-reporters are based in the US.

Traditional CR reporting nations in Europe continue to see the highest reporting rates, but the Americas and the Middle East and Africa region are quickly gaining ground. Only around half of Asia Pacific companies report on their CR activities.

For the 100 largest companies in each of the 34 countries we studied (N100 companies), CR reporting by the consumer markets, pharmaceuticals and construction industries more than doubled since KPMG's last survey in 2008, but overall numbers in some sectors – such as trade and retail and transportation – continue to lag stubbornly behind.

Of the N100 companies, 69 per cent of publicly traded companies conduct CR reporting, compared to just 36 per cent of family-owned enterprises and close to 45 per cent for both cooperatives and companies owned by professional investors such as private equity firms.

KPMG's survey was conducted in 2011 and we expect that company practices have increased since that time. Although some may regard sustainability and corporate reporting as a marketing and public relations exercise, such evidence there is suggests that it is expanding. This is being encouraged by a number of initiatives that we have addressed in this section.[5]

PERFORMANCE INDICATORS AND MEASURES

It is impossible to summarize all of the types of voluntary disclosures of information that companies make in their annual report and accounts. Frequently, the voluntary disclosures are related to legally required disclosures and it is difficult to separate them. It is also difficult to deduce the intended audiences for some of the information provided.

Although much of the literature, particularly in the US, refers to shareholders and investors as the users, there is a recognition in some quarters that there may be a range of potential users. A press release from the FRC on the strategic report noted, 'In meeting the needs of shareholders, the information in the annual report may also be of interest to other stakeholders. The annual report should not, however, be seen as a replacement for other forms of reporting addressed to other stakeholders' (FRC 2015c). Whether, in providing information voluntarily, companies are purposefully communicating to other stakeholders is doubtful. We assume that it is highly unlikely that seasoned financial analysts are swayed by the colourful photos of groups of happy employees, depictions of products and views of company premises. However, it may be good public relations and should not be criticized because of that.

The distinctly typical voluntary information is usually in the first few pages. There is normally an 'overview' of the financial results. This is in a diagrammatic form and may cover several years. There may be a statement from the chairman, although some companies prefer to use this as the lead for the strategic report.

One 'semi-voluntary' disclosure is the **key performance indicators** (KPIs) we referred to earlier. Although required by legislation, companies have flexibility in the information they provide and the method of calculation. Some companies also provide alternative measurement indicators that may be labelled as such or included with other KPIs. We include these in our discussion.

> **key performance indicators (KPIs)**
>
> Key performance indicators comprise a set of quantifiable measures that a company calculates to demonstrate and explain its financial performance.

Key performance indicators are an important component of the disclosures used to describe the information needed to explain a company's progress in achieving its strategy. We would emphasize that KPIs provide additional information to that found in the financial section of the annual report and accounts.

The recommendation of the FRC (2014c) is that shareholders should be able to understand each KPI used in the strategic report. To achieve this, the company should identify and explain where relevant:

(a) its definition and calculation method;
(b) its purpose;
(c) the source of underlying data;
(d) any significant assumptions made; and
(e) any changes in the calculation method used compared to previous financial years, including significant changes in the underlying accounting policies adopted in the financial statements that might affect the KPI.

The FRC discusses the disclosure of non-financial KPIs. These may include, for example, measures related to product quality and customer complaints. They may be indicators of future financial prospects and progress in managing risks and opportunities.

KPIs are mainly closely related to the industry in which a company operates. The literature is replete with suggestions and examples of KPIs suitable for specific types of industry. An indication of the types of KPIs that are appropriate for three different industries is shown in Table 20.5.

There are also KPIs for different issues. In 2012, the Department for Environment, Food & Rural Affairs (Defra) commenced an informal consultation to seek views on revised guidance for how UK organizations should measure and report on their environmental impacts. This guidance was intended to replace the existing guidance which was published in 2006.

▼ Table 20.5 *KPIs in different industries*

Banking	Petroleum	Retail
Customer retention	Capital expenditure	Capital expenditure
Customer penetration	Exploration success rate	Store portfolio changes
Asset quality	Refinery utilization	Expected return on new stores
Capital adequacy	Refinery capacity	Customer satisfaction
Assets under management	Volume of proven and probable reserves	Same store/like-for-like sales
Loan loss	Reserve replacement costs	Sales per square foot/metre

Source: PricewaterhouseCoopers, 2007, p. 5.

The guidance sets out general principles for how to measure and report on environmental KPIs. It suggests a structured means for reporting those indicators and covers the five areas:

- air pollution and other emissions;
- water;
- biodiversity/ecosystem services;
- materials;
- waste.

If we look at individual companies and the information disclosed, Whitbread provides an example explaining their philosophies and how they are measured (see Company example 20.9 overleaf).

Whitbread's measures for the creation of shareholder value are the ones most closely connected to the financial statements. But you must use caution in drawing conclusions too quickly. Whitbread, like many other companies, in addition to providing an income statement, also provides its own calculation of profit. In this case, it is referred to as 'underlying profit'.

Such measures may be named KPIs but some companies and commentators refer to them as additional (or alternative) performance measures (APMs). There are no regulations preventing companies from providing APMs as long as they have provided, in addition, audited financial statements complying with IFRS.

In Canada, there is a management discussion and analysis section that includes similar information. The Canadian company, Loblaw, includes numerous and useful measures of performance in its management discussion and analysis section under the heading 'Key Financial Performance Indicators'. We show an extract from a long list in Company example 20.10.

Loblaw has identified key financial performance indicators to measure the progress of short- and long-term objectives. With the completion of the acquisition of Shoppers Drug Mart, the Company's 2014 results include the consolidation of Shoppers Drug Mart and the associated acquisition-related accounting adjustments. Certain key financial performance indicators are set out in Company example 20.10 overleaf.

The company states the circumstances affecting the measures and there are comprehensive explanations as to their importance in both the short term and the long term. The information can assist users in better understanding the financial performance of the company because it is detailed and specific to Loblaw's particular activities.

Company example 20.9

Whitbread KPIs

Business philosophy	Measures
We build highly engaged teams who make everyday experiences special for our millions of customers – by recruiting the best people, investing in training and development, growing talented leaders and recognising and rewarding success.	• Team engagement • Team turnover • Health and safety
We put the customer at the heart of everything we do, as well as developing innovative new products and services to meet and exceed customer expectations, building brand preference and winning market share. We are committed to maintaining the quality of our estate through ongoing refurbishment.	• Net guest scores • Brand performance • Brand standards
We create shareholder value by growing profits and delivering good returns through focused investment in Premier Inn (including our unique joint site restaurant model) and Costa, where we pursue organic growth in domestic and selected international markets. We maximise Group synergies through a focus on delivering a consistently good customer experience in a service and people-intensive environment and utilising our central property expertise.	• Growth milestones • Underlying profit • Underlying basic EPS • Returns on investment • Like for like sales growth • Market performance
We aim to be a force for good within the communities in which we operate by embedding our CSR principles into the way we do business. Our plan has three main pillars: Teams and Community; Customer Wellbeing; and Environment.	• Good Together targets • Carbon consumption • Waste diverted from landfill

Whitbread plc, Annual Report and Accounts, 2013/14, p. 8

Company example 20.10

Revenue growth
Adjusted EBITDA
Adjusted EBITDA margin
Adjusted net earnings
Basic net earnings per common share
Adjusted basic net earnings per common share
Same-store sales growth

Loblaw, Annual Report and Accounts, 2014, p. 5

KPIs and APMs supply useful information. They usually provide data that is not easily extracted from the audited financial statements. However, the unsophisticated user may not be aware that some measures are recalculations of the profit that was shown on the IFRS-compliant financial statements. They are essentially alternative performance measures. The user may also not realize that some measures, as well as not being financial but quantitative, have not been audited.

Companies provide this information, presumably, because they consider that the profit calculation under accounting standards does not give a complete picture of management's method of measuring financial performance. We provide an extract in Company example 20.11 from the annual report and accounts of Diageo that gives a clear explanation of the rationale.

Company example 20.11

Non-GAAP measures

Diageo's strategic planning process is based on the following non-GAAP measures. They are chosen for planning and reporting, and some of them are used for incentive purposes.

The group's management believes these measures provide valuable additional information for users of the financial statements in understanding the group's performance. These non-GAAP measures should be viewed as complementary to, and not replacements for, the comparable GAAP measures and reported movements therein.

Organic movements

In the discussion of the performance of the business, organic information is presented using pounds sterling amounts on a constant currency basis, excluding the impact of exceptional items and acquisitions and disposals. Organic measures enable users to focus on the performance of the business which is common to both years and which represents those measures that local managers are most directly able to influence.

Diageo, Annual Report and Accounts, 2014, p. 50

Diageo's statement makes it clear that these measures are not GAAP measures but provide additional information deemed of value to the users of financial statements. However, there are drawbacks with APM and Holt (2014a) has identified these. Although most companies are careful in their explanations, there could be:

- bias in the calculations;
- inconsistency in the calculations from year to year;
- inaccurate classification of items;
- insufficient information on the basis for the calculations;
- no reconciliation with the audited profit figure;
- inadequate definition of terms.

NOTES

1 A comprehensive guide to corporate governance is J. Solomon (2013) *Corporate Governance and Accountability*, 4th edn, Wiley.
2 This can be found at *https://www.lansdownepartners. com/home/uk-stewardship-code/* (accessed 15 September 2016).
3 *http://www.international.gc.ca/trade-agreements-accords-commerciaux/topics-domaines/other-autre/csr-rse.aspx?lang=eng* (accessed 15 September 2016).
4 The Department of Environment and Heritage (now the Department of Environment, Water, Heritage

and the Arts) released *Triple Bottom Line Reporting in Australia: A Guide to Reporting Against Environmental Indicators* in June 2003. The *Group of 100* (which represents the Chief Financial Officers of large business enterprises in Australia) released in 2003 *Sustainability: A Guide to Triple Bottom Line Reporting*.
5 A series of useful case studies are given in A. Hopwood, J. Unerman and J. Fries (eds) (2010) *Accounting for Sustainability*, Earthscan.

CONCLUSIONS

There has been substantial growth in the annual report and accounts, both in the detail of the disclosures and the nature of the information given. Legislation is responsible for some of the growth, but there are also initiatives in voluntary disclosures by companies.

The question arises as to who are considered to be the 'users' of all this information. It may be investors but we can envisage that others could also be interested. Indeed the FRC frequently adopts the term 'stakeholders' and this takes us back to the arguments in Chapter 1 about who are, or should be, the users of corporate reports and what is the role of the modern corporation in society?

In addition to these all topics, there is the debate on whether all the information provided by companies in their annual report and accounts should be more closely

legislated. There is a considerable amount of information that may be useful but is not regulated, may not be reliable and does not give comparisons to other companies that are not disclosing similar information. The FRC has given its answer to the question of regulation:

> However, I think we should avoid standardisation of reporting requirements for a while longer. I think we should encourage innovation and a degree of diversity. Standardisation helps comparability but it also encourages boilerplate reporting and that undermines the exercise of judgement. Narrative reporting is in transition and at the FRC we are keen within legal requirements to let the best ideas emerge. We have developed the framework of law, codes and standards significantly since the financial crisis. (Haddrill 2016)

ADDITIONAL RESOURCES

Due to the nature of the content, there are no multiple choice questions for this chapter. The accompanying website has case studies, projects and references to other materials that address the issues that we have raised.
www.palgravehighered.com/hussey-cfr

THE FUTURE OF CORPORATE REPORTING

At the end of this chapter, you should be able to

- Describe the regulatory processes and identify the problems changes in regulation raise for preparers and users of corporate reports
- Discuss the use of the internet by companies for corporate reporting
- Explain integrated reporting and suggest how it may develop
- Explain XBRL and the advantages it offers both the preparers and users of information.
- Predict how the activities discussed in this chapter may affect corporate reports

INTRODUCTION

In earlier chapters, we have considered in depth the regulations placed on corporate financial reporting. In the UK, the Companies Act, the London Stock Exchange and the International Accounting Standards Board determine financial accounting and reporting by companies. Other countries have similar structures. We have also explained the growth in non-financial information, known as narrative reporting, and the move towards companies providing information voluntarily.

In this chapter, we wish to take a broader view of corporate reporting and suggest the direction in which it is going. First, we discuss possible changes in regulation. Regulations change as do company practices. Our snapshot will enable us to identify particular issues and serve as the foundation for considering new regulatory developments that will take effect in the future.

The second section examines companies' increasing use of the internet to communicate financial and narrative information. In the third section, we examine the arguments for integrated reporting. This promotes an entirely new approach to corporate reporting. It is not about the accounting methods that fall under IFRSs. It is about communicating corporate reporting in a way that draws the various strands together. Our penultimate section explains eXtensible Business Reporting Language (XBRL) and the work of the IFRS.

Our final section reviews past developments in corporate reporting and reflects on the pressures that bring about change. We consider opinions on the users of corporate reports and the types of information they want. This includes both financial and narrative information. We also look at a subject that is infrequently addressed – what information do companies wish to give?

This final chapter is being written as Britain is withdrawing from the EU and Donald Trump is competing with Hillary Clinton to be the next President of the US. We are certain that in other countries equally momentous events are occurring. These events can have an impact on corporate reporting and the regulation of corporate reporting that we have not foreseen.

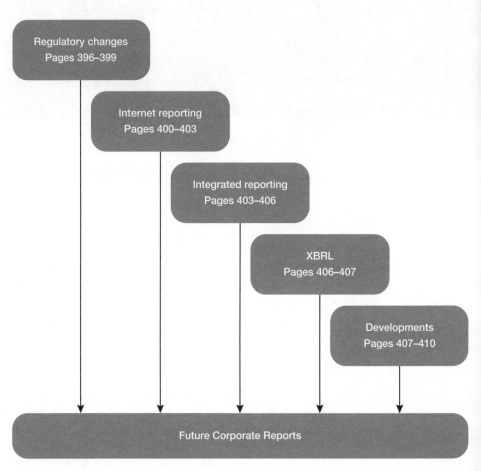

▲ **Diagram 21.1** *Structure of Chapter 21*

REGULATORY CHANGES

There are no major changes in company law envisaged in the near future. In the UK, the Financial Reporting Council (FRC), however, has the legal responsibility for financial accounting and reporting and may recommend changes in practices. We discussed their role in Chapter 2. The FRC is very active in monitoring and advising on a continuous basis, and we consider the projects they have that will have future impacts.

The International Accounting Standards Board (IASB) carries out its amendments programme annually. These are usually minor changes to some standards. More importantly, the IASB may decide to make significant changes to some standards, remove a standard or issue a new one. This process usually takes years. Not only is the decision process very extended but companies must be given time to understand and apply the new standard.

Legislation

In every country, legislation takes a long time to develop. It can take years to go through the various processes and consultations. Not all government initiatives relating to corporate reporting are concerned only with the disclosure of financial information. For example, in 2015, the UK Government issued a consultation paper 'Closing the Gender Pay Gap' that seeks to increase transparency around gender pay differences.

This led on to a follow-up consultation inviting feedback on the details of draft regulations to introduce mandatory gender pay gap reporting for private and voluntary sector employers in England, Scotland and Wales with at least 250 employees.[1] This is not financial information, but clearly the Government considers that it is both a desirable policy and that companies should disclose their own practices.

Once a government passes any legislation requiring financial or other disclosures by companies there needs to be some delegated body to monitor the effectiveness and compliance with the legislation on a regular basis. In the UK, it is the FRC.

In 2011, the Financial Reporting Lab was launched to enable investors and companies to develop solutions to reporting needs. The Lab has worked with 65 different companies, 60 investment organizations and over 300 retail investors to bring insight and understanding to a number of key areas of disclosure. It has produced numerous reports on different aspects of corporate reporting.

A good method for checking the effectiveness of the legislation, company compliance and issues that need resolving is to read the publications issued by the FRC. In addition to many other documents, the FRC has published the following reports that relate to issues we have discussed previously.

- Clear and Concise: Developments in Narrative Reporting, 17 December 2015
- Lab Project Report Disclosure of Dividends – policy and practice, 24 November 2015
- Summary Lab Project Report – Digital Present, 29 May 2015
- Developments in Corporate Governance and Stewardship 2014, 15 January 2015

Although these reports do not call for changes in either company legislation or International Financial Reporting Standards (IFRSs), they point to areas where change may be contemplated in the future.

The FRC also publishes an annual Corporate Reporting Review. The summary of their findings for large companies in the October 2015 document included the following points. We have inserted the chapters in this book where we discuss each topic.

- The overall quality of corporate reporting is generally good but the application of the 'materiality' concept can be a problem. The FRC advised companies to consider materiality in the context of what the investors expect to see (Chapter 3).
- Application of the new consolidation, joint venture and associate accounting regulations was generally successful (Chapters 16 and 17).
- Most companies effectively explained their strategy and described their business model (Chapter 20).
- Accounting for pension deficit funding commitments requires explanations of judgements made around pension assets or excess deficit funding liabilities (Chapter 9).

- There were improved disclosures on complex supplier arrangements.
- Narrative disclosures had improved.
- The effect of changes in estimates needs to be better explained (Chapter 13).

The FRC has also investigated narrative reporting (FRC 2015c). Once again, we summarize some of the main points in the document.

- The introduction of the strategic report has improved the overall quality of corporate reporting but there remains room for improvements (Chapter 20).
- Companies should take a longer time frame in their strategic reports and not limit it to one year (Chapter 20).
- There are opportunities for more concise reporting if companies apply the concept of materiality (Chapter 3).
- There is scope for improvement in the disclosure of key performance indicators. Companies should explain their relevance to the business and relationship to GAAP measures (Chapter 20).

The large firms of accountants also survey or comment on corporate practices. Ernst & Young (2015) sought the opinions of 1,000 CFOs or heads of reporting of large organizations. This was an international survey and a major conclusion was that, while the expectations and scope of corporate reporting have increased, finance leaders' confidence in reporting is falling. They are also concerned about reporting effectiveness.

Main findings

- The objective of investors (valuation or stewardship) does matter.
- Investors favour the income statement.
- Investors have strong reservations about the representational faithfulness of bottom line figures.
- Regardless of its shortcomings, financial accounting information is a key input factor for investors' decision making.
- The quality of corporate governance, including audit, influences investors' assessment of the representational faithfulness.

Implications of the research

- One size does not fit all, suggesting that standard setters need to clearly prioritize the different objectives for financial reporting.
- Investors seem to be strongly anchored on the income statement, which appears to conflict with the balance sheet view promoted by the IASB's existing framework.
- There is a need for development of more standardized performance measures for the income statement.
- Investors' perceptions of corporate governance significantly affect their views of representational faithfulness. Standard setters therefore need to consider costs of corporate governance and enforcement of accounting standards when setting standards. For preparers, investment in high-quality governance, including audit, may well pay off in the form of enhanced investor confidence.

If we reduce the above summary into two main messages, they would be:

- The income statement (profit or loss account) is the most important financial statement for investors.
- Good corporate governance enhances investors' trust in financial statements.

International Financial Reporting Standards

Before we continue this section, we would like to remind you:

- Not all countries have adopted IFRSs.
- Those countries that have adopted IFRSs may not follow all the requirements.
- Some countries do not have monitoring and enforcement procedures to ensure company compliance.
- Not all companies in a country must comply with IFRSs. Usually, only the larger companies list their shares on a stock exchange. Smaller companies follow national accounting standards or the IFRS for Small and Medium-sized Companies.

IFRSs are not static. Amendments are made, some standards are withdrawn and new standards are issued. In addition, the International Financial Reporting Committee (IFRIC) issues interpretations which provide guidance on the application of particular standards. We discussed the work of IFRIC in Chapter 2.

Changes to standards present problems, both to the preparers of financial statements and to the users. Preparers have to comply with the new regulations. This may necessitate changes in their accounting procedures to collect the relevant data. Standard setters are aware of this and allow sufficient time for the conversion. For example, IFRS 16, the new standard for leasing, was issued on 13 January 2016, and companies must apply the standard for annual reporting periods beginning on or after 1 January 2019.

The IASB does not tackle amendments to standards one at a time. It has a continuing work plan that is shown on the IFRS website. The work plan is in several stages and a useful guide to future changes is the research project stage. This is divided into the assessment stage that considers the nature of the problem and the identification of any financial reporting problem, and the development stage where the assessment has been made and the IASB is developing proposals. In mid-June 2016 the development stage included:

- Business combinations under common control
- Disclosure Initiative
- Dynamic risk management – a portfolio revaluation approach to macro hedging
- Equity methods of accounting
- Financial instruments with characteristics of equity.

For those projects that will go ahead, the next stage is likely to be a Discussion Paper issued for public comment.

The Disclosure Initiative seeks to improve existing guidance in IFRS that helps entities determine the basic structure and content of a complete set of financial statements. It is concerned mostly with the general disclosure guidance in IAS 1 *Presentation of Financial Statements* and IAS 8 *Accounting Policies, Changes in Accounting Estimates and Errors*. The aim is to develop a disclosure standard that improves and brings together the principles for determining the basic structure and content of the financial statements, in particular the notes.

Although IFRSs to some extent provide uniformity in the provision of financial information there remain differences as countries vary in their adoption. In addition, many disclosures are not required by IFRSs, but by the national legislation. The issue has grown to be such a problem that the influential International Federation of Accountants (2016) has called for governments around the world to stop issuing a patchwork set of regulations that are stifling economic growth.

As discussed above, the FRC and the IASB have launched several initiatives to make the information in corporate reports more accessible to users, but the increasing pressures for greater disclosures may lead to conflict. Two solutions may be internet reporting and integrated reporting which we discuss in the following sections.

INTERNET REPORTING

Company example 21.1

Internet reporting

Investor Relations app

Our Marks & Spencer Investor Relations app provides information to investors and the financial media in an iPad™ optimised format. The app displays the latest share price information and corporate news. It also contains financial reports, presentations and videos.

For more information visit marksandspencer.com/investors

Marks & Spencer, Annual Report and Accounts, 2015, p. 1

Company example 21.1 illustrates how far we have moved away from the annual report and accounts as the main source of information. Using the Marks & Spencer Investor Relations app you can get immediate information on your smart phone. This includes not only the annual financial statements but also presentations by senior management, videos, up-to-date share prices and news.

Commercial usage of the internet has grown at a tremendous pace over the last few years. Various forms of business communication, in particular for product/service marketing, have adopted the technology. It allows companies to communicate text, graphics, sound and video.

Not surprisingly, companies have also grasped the opportunity to use the internet for corporate reporting, both financial and narrative. We can trace this growth in usage from its earliest days to the present. Lymer (1997) conducted a survey of the top 50 UK listed companies showing the practice of internet reporting. The results are illustrated in Table 21.1 opposite.

Before 1995, there was nothing. In 1996, the practice seemed to have commenced and then grew rapidly. Slightly later research by Craven and Marston (1999) expanded the number of companies to the largest 200 companies as listed by market capitalization in the *Financial Times*, 22 January 1998. They also included six companies that Lymer (1997) had used. Table 21.2 shows the types of disclosures.

It is surprising that even within the last 20 years only the minority (32.5%) of the sample companies had detailed annual reports on line. One-quarter of the sample did not even have a website. Our present investigations demonstrate that the practice of using the internet as a communication tool for company financial and non-financial information is widespread.

The Craven and Marston research not only captured the types of information disclosed but also sought to explain the variations in disclosure by companies. The researchers identified two independent variables: company size and industry type. There were four size variables – turnover, number of employees, total assets employed and average market value – and six different industrial categories.

▼ Table 21.1 *Early internet practices*

	Number of sites	Percentage (of 50 companies)
Websites (active)	46	92
Accounts or reports on web	26	52
Full accounts	7	14
Before 1995	0	0
1995	6	12
1996	6	12
Summary Accounts	6	12
Before 1995	0	0
1995	1	2
1996	6	12
Interim Accounts (unaudited)	13	26
Before 1995	0	0
1995	7	14
1996	14	28
Highlights	16	32
Additional information on web	13	26
Use of graphics	10	20
Depth from home page		
Link on page	15	30
One level down	10	20
Two levels down	1	2
More than two	0	0

Source: Lymer, A. (1997) 'The Use of the Internet in Company Reporting: A Survey and Commentary on the Use of the WWW in Corporate Reporting in the UK'. Paper presented at the 1997 BAA National Conference, 21–25 March 1997, Birmingham. Table 1 reproduced with permission.

▼ Table 21.2 *Summary of financial reporting on the internet by the sample of top UK companies 1998*

Financial disclosure	Number	Percentage
Detailed annual report	67	32.5
Parts or summaries of annual report	42	20.4
Website but no financial information	44	21.4
No website	52	25.2
Unclear/ambiguous	1	0.5
Total	206	100

Source: B.M. Craven and C.L. Marston (1999) 'Financial Reporting on the Internet by leading UK companies', *European Accounting Review*, 8(2), pp. 321–333. Table 1 reprinted by permission of the publisher (Taylor & Francis Ltd, *http://www.tandfonline.com*) and the authors.

The researchers conducted statistical analysis and we summarize the main findings.

- For each one of the four size variables, companies with a website had a median size about twice as large as companies without a website.
- There were positive associations between the size variables and the extent of financial disclosure on the internet.
- There was no relationship between industry type and the extent of financial disclosure on the internet based on the sample of 206 large companies.

To give some form of comparison with the 1998 study, we identified some main trends on the 'investor websites' of our sample of 25 companies. They all had websites and all contained the annual report and accounts and interim statements. We list in Table 21.3 the main headings of additional information separately displayed at the first level.

▼ Table 21.3 *Corporate reporting on the internet*

Disclosure	Number of companies
Share information	25
Financial calendar	22
Results and presentations	21
Corporate performance	20
Investor information	17
Corporate governance	14
Regulatory news	10
Analysts' coverage	10
Annual general meeting	6
Dividends	5
Advisers	3
Debt instruments	2
Brokerage cover	1
Credit rating	1
Directors' names	1
Pension governance	1

Table 21.3 gives an indication of the main items disclosed. Companies may have aggregated and grouped information under separate headings. We did not investigate this detail. The table demonstrates, however, the great expansion there has been in internet usage for corporate reporting.

Much of the research has examined the disclosures by companies on their web pages. One interesting study sought to ascertain what corporate information internet users seek (Rowbottom et al. 2005). They measured online information using activity logs from the web server of a UK FTSE 100 company which fulfils user requests for information over the internet.

The researchers carefully explain the limitations of the methodology and the issues in the interpretation of the results. The web log analyses do not provide absolute levels of online information usage. They measure what information is demanded online. They do not indicate whether the information has been used or read. They provide a proxy measure of online internet reporting (IR) information usage and are not an appropriate proxy for general IR information usage.

Having given those disclaimers, we summarize some of Rowbottom et al.'s findings that are most relevant to this chapter. We emphasize that this research concentrated on the annual report and accounts. Data on all the other information that users place on their investors' website was not included.

The financial section of the annual report and accounts

- The most visited financial reporting information is the profit or loss account.
- The notes to the accounts and the balance sheet come second.
- The cash flow statement and the statement of total recognized gains and losses are among the least requested parts of the report.

The narrative section of the annual report and accounts

The most requested information is the remuneration report and the statement on compliance with the Combined Code for Corporate Governance.

* * *

This research gives some insights as to what information users seek on the internet. This study is over 10 years old and present activity may have changed. Certainly, the amount and range of information on the websites has increased. In the next section, we discuss current attempts to bring the disparate amounts of financial and narrative information into a logical structure.

The expansion in the use of technology for corporate reporting is supported by the IFRS and the FRC. The IFRS is working on an eXtensible Business Reporting Language (XBRL) that converts printed financial statements into something that is computer readable. We discuss this later in the chapter.

In 2014, the Financial Reporting Lab launched a project examining the impact technology might have on corporate reporting. They argued that the volume of data generated by and about companies was increasing significantly. Stakeholders needed to understand these developments so that the advantages of technology could improve the effectiveness of corporate reports

The first report from the project was *Digital Present* released in 2015. This examined investors' views on the current state of digital corporate reporting by companies. The next stage of the project, entitled *Digital Future* will investigate the impact of technology advancements on corporate reporting.

INTEGRATED REPORTING

Annual reports and accounts usually contain three distinct sections: Strategic report; Governance; Financial statements. Usually, there are not strong links between these sections, although key performance indicators do provide a bridge between the Strategic report and Financial statements. The 2007/8 economic crisis revealed that financial reporting by itself does not provide sufficient information on short-term and long-term business performance. Organizations should provide a full disclosure of how they create value.

Commentators have argued that companies should attempt to make the relationships between the three sections stronger. They complain that too much of the document is 'boiler plate' material, that is it is merely repeated year after year. The notes to the financial statements contain text that is copied direct from the standard, and the emphasis is too often on mere disclosure and not explanation. It would be unfair to criticize all companies for these practices, but there has been enough concern for proposals to revise corporate reports.

The International Integrated Reporting Council (IIRC) is a global coalition of regulators, investors, companies, standard setters, the accounting profession and NGOs. The coalition is promoting communication about value creation as the next step in the evolution of corporate reporting. The first few words of its website state that integrated reporting has been created to 'enhance accountability, stewardship and trust'.

In February 2013, the IASB and IIRC agreed that the two organizations would deepen their cooperation on the IIRC's work to develop an integrated corporate reporting framework.

The IIRC Framework, dated December 2013, provides companies with a starting point for driving thinking and reporting in an integrated way.[2] The Framework has the following four sections:

- Using the framework
- Fundamental concepts
- Guiding principles
- Content elements

An integrated report is far broader than the present financial statements. It contains details of how an organization's strategy, governance, performance and prospects lead to the creation of value over the short, medium and long term. The primary audience of integrated reports are the providers of financial capital, but they contain information of interest to a wide range of stakeholders.

The fundamental concepts of integrated reporting are concerned with the various capitals that the organization uses and affects, the organization's business model, and the creation of value over time. In using the word 'capital', the IIRC departs from the way that we use the term in financial accounting. Capital usually refers to equity, but the Integrated Reporting Model has identified six different capital inputs. We list the six inputs in Diagram 21.2 with a brief summary of their nature.

Not all organizations have the same capitals or the same balance. In some organizations, the relationships with some of the capitals are so minor that they are not disclosed in the integrated report. This information can provide an input into the analysis of the financial statements that the user is making.

If you review the examples in the previous chapter, you will see similar terms and phrases in some annual reports or on companies' websites. Those of you who have studied management accounting will recognize similar concepts in the Balanced Scorecard and Total Quality Management approaches.

Companies can encounter issues in preparing an integrated report and the communication of the information. The IIRC has offered guiding principles and these are:

A   Strategic focus and future orientation
B   Connectivity of information

C   Stakeholder relationships
D   Materiality
E   Conciseness
F   Reliability and completeness
G   Consistency and comparability

These terms have appeared before in this book, and take us back to the discussions on a conceptual framework. The Framework lists the following content elements:

A   Organizational overview and operating context
B   Governance
C   Business model
D   Risks and opportunities
E   Strategy and resource allocation
F   Performance
G   Outlook
H   Basis of preparation and presentation
I   General reporting guidance

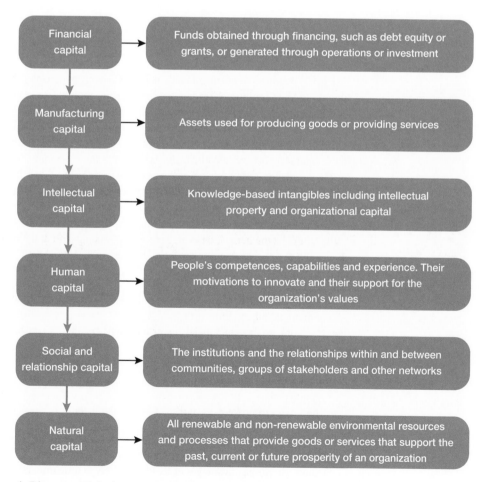

▲ Diagram 21.2 *An organization's capital inputs*

This is not necessarily the order in which the elements should be presented, and the Framework proposes that the information should be arranged in a way that makes the interconnections between the content elements apparent. In the Framework, each one of the seven content elements is stated in the form of a question rather than a list of specific items. It is for management to determine what should be reported.

Initiatives similar to the IIRC's proposal have been made previously and have not won overwhelming support. However, Dzinkowski (2013) argues that there is evidence that this time may be different for the following reasons:

1   The IIRC's Framework is the work of the world's leading accounting associations.
2   The International Organization of Securities Commissions, a powerful body representing security regulators, supports it.
3   There are an increasing number of examples around to demonstrate how it can be done.

We would add to this that the major firms of accountants are beginning to issue reports extolling the benefits of integrated reporting. It is too early to know whether the proposals will be successful, but the actions by the EU and the proposals by the IIRC show where corporate reporting is moving, and accountants are fully involved in these developments.

XBRL

eXtensible Business Reporting Language (XBRL) converts printed financial statements into something that is computer readable. It does this by applying an identifying tag for each individual item of data. Items such as revenue, inventories and income have their own unique tags. These tags are computer readable and allow the interactive use of financial information.

The first stage in the process is to produce a list of tags to identify specific financial items in the annual report and accounts. This is known as the 'taxonomy'. The tags are represented in the taxonomies as elements, such as 'cash and cash equivalents' and 'inventories'. The data items reported by a company are mapped to the matching elements of the appropriate taxonomy.

At that stage, software processes these mappings to create the instance documents.

These documents contain all of the information included in the taxonomy elements, such as the nature of the item, the language in which it is presented, the manner in which it is disclosed, and the accounting standard used to prepare it.

The benefits of using XBRL are claimed to be:

- For companies, there are cost savings and the streamlining of the collection and reporting of financial information.
- Investors, analysts, financial institutions and regulators can find, compare and analyze data more efficiently.
- The development of other taxonomies can be applied to a range of data including the management discussion and analysis report, executive compensation and sustainability reports.
- There is an improvement in the information efficiency of the capital markets.

Despite the claimed benefits of XBRL, there does not currently seem to be great enthusiasm to adopt it. A major questionnaire survey in the UK (Dunne et al. 2013) found that key champions understand the advantages of XBRL but there is little understanding outside this group. The result is that the technology is not being used effectively in the UK.

Although the authors of the study put forward proposals for extending the use of XBRL, they believe that, without greater regulatory commitment, XBRL will fade and die. However, our experience of corporate reporting on the internet demonstrates that it can take several years before the widespread adoption of a new technology. When this does occur, there is a large and rapid growth in its use, and there are signs that digital or electronic reporting will become a fact.

Many countries have introduced electronic depositories of financial statements to improve access. Some have also introduced the use of XBRL to tag data inside these reports to make smaller parts of the financial statement searchable and accessible.

The IFRS Foundation believes that the structured electronic reporting of IFRS financial statements is in accord with its own mission statement in three main ways:

Assists transparency: increases accessibility of information for all market participants.

Assists accountability: structured electronic data supports market enforcement of IFRS by regulators.

Assists efficiency: accessible data may reduce costs to process IFRS information allowing users to focus on analysis.

(*http://www.ifrs.org/XBRL/Pages/XBRL.aspx*, accessed 16 September 2016)

The IFRS Foundation produces the IFRS Taxonomy in XBRL. It has also launched a research project to map current requirements for filing and the use of structured electronic filing around the world. The project is making progress and analysts undoubtedly will take advantage of these developments.

PAST AND FUTURE DEVELOPMENTS

Developments and improvements in corporate reporting have occurred since the first Companies Act. Some of the changes have been driven by the need to ensure the credibility of information and to prevent fraud. Other drivers have been the need to identify:

- the users of corporate information;
- the information they want;
- the information companies should give.

Users of corporate reports

There have been movements away from thinking only of investors as the users of corporate reports. The IASB, possibly influenced by US thinking, tends to concentrate on investors who require information for making investment decisions. The FRC has a wider brief and the term 'stakeholder' is frequently used in its literature.

Even if we concentrate on investors, there are highly sophisticated investors and less sophisticated investors. It could be argued that the introduction of key performance indicators into annual reports targets unsophisticated investors and those with a general interest in a company. The sophisticated investor is well able to extract from the annual accounts the data to calculate a range of ratios.

To identify other users, we could use the exhaustive list in the corporate report (1975). There have been past examples of companies recognizing other groups as recipients of financial information. There have been surges of interest in producing special financial reports for employees and, in the UK, the legal permission allowing companies to issue summary financial statements recognized the unsophisticated investor.

Present legal moves in the UK and elsewhere suggest that some disclosures being required on governance, stewardship and sustainability stem from the Companies Act 1948 which held the concept that companies had a responsibility to society.

Information users want

As we move from the narrow focus on sophisticated users being the only users to society generally, this question becomes more difficult to answer. The FRC's research has produced some very good insights into the information needs of investors. Their research has primarily been centred on financial information and gives the IASB solid input into the weaknesses of some IFRSs.

This input is not restricted to financial information and investors. The FRC currently has a Culture Project with the following themes:

- *Delivering sustainable success* – the role of an effective board.
- *People issues* – delivering alignment between culture, values, human resource practices and performance reward systems.
- *Stakeholder issues* – relationships between culture and business models, with shareholders, customers and suppliers, and the impact on the wider community and environment.
- *Embedding and assurance* – measuring and monitoring culture, the role of internal audit, risk management and public reporting of cultural indicators.
- *Engagement and evidence gathering.*

We can anticipate that their findings will influence the information provided by companies.

The information companies should give

Obviously public limited companies must comply with the legislation of the country in which they were incorporated, the requirements of the stock exchange on which they are listed and the requirements of the appropriate accounting standards. In this book, we have concentrated on IFRSs.

Companies also disclose other information that reflects the interests and concerns of society. Some of these concerns have been in existence for many years. Although environmental concerns seem to be a current interest, it was in 1991 that the Association of Chartered Certified Accountants launched an Environmental Award for corporate reporting. There are awards being given by various bodies for sustainability disclosures and integrated reporting.

To a large extent, it would seem that company legislation follows company practices.

The range of disclosures has moved away from only financial to narrative reporting. This has caused some concern because some commentators consider that words and diagrams, particularly if voluntarily offered, can be manipulated and misleading, particularly as they are not audited. We do not disagree but offer some context.

The argument that narrative reporting can be manipulated assumes that financial reporting is rigorous, robust and complete. That is not the case. All annual reports and accounts state that companies had to use assumptions and estimates in compiling the financial data. These estimates and assumptions could be misleading but still evade the scrutiny of an auditor.

The financial statements themselves could also mislead the unwary, or at least not provide the most useful information. We offer a few comments that we have raised in earlier chapters.

1   The valuation of closing inventory can be difficult for large companies, especially where items are still in process. A small difference in closing inventory valuation can have a substantial impact of profit. Additionally, we discussed in Chapter 8, the treatment of fixed production overheads. By increasing closing inventory, the fixed overheads are not treated as a period cost.

2 The balance sheet does not show the current values of non-current assets. It is the original cost less the depreciation charged to date (an estimate). If current values were given it could dramatically change such ratios as return on net assets. Companies can, if they wish, revalue net assets and they must adjust for impairments, if the directors consider there has been impairment.

3 Intangible assets and goodwill present significant problems. If a company pays for them, they are shown on the balance sheet. If a company generates them itself, they may not always appear on the balance sheet.

There are other weaknesses and the IASB is constantly attempting, and succeeding, in resolving many of these issues. But financial statements are not as rigorous as some would suggest, and narrative reporting is not as weak as others would claim.

Narrative reporting adds a broader canvas to assist all users in understanding a company's activities. It is also well established and not as fragile as some would believe. We conclude this section by quoting from Adelberg (1979) who researched narrative reporting in the US. He was referring to narrative reporting but his remarks can also apply to the assumptions and estimates that underpin financial reporting:

> Given human behaviour, the placing of managers in complete control of the accounting communication process which monitors their performance breeds a situation wherein it is perfectly natural to expect that some managers would obfuscate their failures and underscore their success.

The Brexit effect

In this section we concentrate on the potential impact of the UK's exit from the European Union on international financial reporting standards. We complete the section with comments on Brexit's impact on corporate financial reporting.

In Chapter 2, we discussed briefly the immediate impact of Brexit on accounting regulations, and our conclusion was that it would be minor. We stated that there were potential economic issues with the financial statements themselves, and some of these could be immediate and others longer term.

The immediate effect on financial statements could be changes in asset and liability amounts because of changes in foreign exchange rates, interest rates or market prices. Assets may become impaired and disclosures made by companies that rely on future predictions may need revising.

If we look to several years hence, we hold to our conviction that Brexit will not have a major effect on international accounting regulations. Our opinion is based on the following three factors.

1 Adoption of standards

The present position is that the EU 'adopts' international standards and the 28 member countries apply them nationally. If the UK does leave the EU, one suspects that the remaining 27 countries will continue with the present procedure. The UK would use its own mechanisms to adopt international standards. This responsibility may fall on the FRC or a separate body may be established.

2 The UK commitment

The UK has a long record of setting accounting standards at the national level, as discussed in Chapters 1 and 2. It was one of the countries that established the original International

Accounting Standards Committee and it has always been active in accounting regulation at the international level. We consider it unlikely that the UK will abandon international accounting standards.

3 The importance of accounting internationalization

The IFRS Foundation has recently issued an analysis that demonstrates that the stability of international accounting is not dependent on events in the EU. It estimates that more than 25,000 of the approximately 48,000 domestic listed companies on the 85 major securities exchanges in the world use IFRSs (*http://www.ifrs.org/Use-around-the-world/Pages/listed-companies-using-ifrs-standards-globally.aspx, accessed 16 September 2016*).

The IFRS Foundation also regularly updates information on the jurisdictions using IFRSs. The following overall observation can be made about the information in the profiles describing how domestic companies apply IFRSs in each of the 143 jurisdictions: the IFRS claims that 133 jurisdictions have made a public commitment supporting a single set of high-quality global accounting standards.

As a final note, although we argue that Brexit will not have a direct effect on international accounting standards, it may well have an indirect effect. Brexit raises economic issues and increased market volatility in the weeks following the referendum. The one area that remains controversial is financial instruments (Chapter 11 and 12).

Although the IASB issued a number of new standards, some companies will experience stress if fair values of financial instruments are in severe decline. This may not lead to major demands for new standards but some companies, particularly banks and financial institutions, may be looking for relaxations in the application of the standards.

Brexit is likely to have a significant effect on Corporate Financial Reports. In Chapter 1 we explained that companies were increasing their disclosures on various subjects and that financial information regulated by IFRSs was no longer the main item of reporting. Most of the regulations on environmental and social disclosures are required by legislation passed in the EU. We consider that the UK will be at the forefront of such disclosures and may even be in advance of future regulations passed by the EU.

NOTES

1 The link to the ongoing position is *https://www.gov.uk/government/consultations/mandatory-gender-pay-gap-reporting* (accessed 16 September 2016).

2 The IIRC Framework is available as a download on their website *http://integratedreporting.org/resource/international-ir-framework/* (accessed 16 September 2016).

CONCLUSIONS

The ever-expanding growth in corporate reporting by companies may not be as beneficial as one would think. We may suffer from information overload! The main growth does not come from IFRSs and financial reporting. Certainly, the regulations change, but the actual amount of financial information that entities should disclose has not grown substantially.

The growth is in narrative reporting. We have strategic reports, business models, governance, and stewardship as part of the printed annual report and accounts. In addition, companies understandably wish to communicate additional information about their successes, if not their failures.

Some of the narrative information is not directed, apparently, only to investors. It is noticeable that the FRC in some of its literature refers to stakeholders. There is a trend, backed in part by recent legislation, to demonstrate that a company is a good citizen. This takes us back to Chapter 1 and the debate on the users of corporate reports.

It is now being acknowledged, at least in the UK, that other groups are interested in the activities of a company.

The availability of the internet supports the issue of a complete range of information – financial and narrative.

Future developments are uncertain, but one possible scenario is a divide between the structured financial information and general corporate reporting. The structured financial information is accessible, but one suspects that investors and analysts would be the primary users.

General corporate reporting would contain a summary of the main financial statements but would primarily be concerned with the narrative reporting, both that legally required and that voluntarily provided. Given that divide, companies could concentrate on integrated reporting.

Whether our predictions will become reality is questionable. There are criticisms that it is difficult to compare companies on a global basis because of the differences in information disclosures. IFRSs provide a common language but it is a country's decision to the extent that it adopts fully IFRSs. More importantly, the legislation in a country determines all the other corporate reporting disclosures that a company should make. We cannot envisage countries reaching agreement on a common global disclosure policy.

ADDITIONAL RESOURCES

Due to the nature of the content, there are no multiple choice questions for this chapter. The accompanying website has case studies, projects and references to other materials that address the issues that we have raised.

www.palgravehighered.com/hussey-cfr

GLOSSARY

Accounting policies   These are the specific principles, bases, conventions, rules and practices applied by an entity in preparing and presenting financial statements. (*IAS 8, paragraph 5*)

Accounting profit   Profit or loss for a period before deducting tax expense. (*IAS 12, paragraph 5*)

Accounting standards   Regulations issued by a recognized body setting out the rules and procedures relating to the recognition, measurement and disclosure of economic transactions and events. Either a national or an international standard-setting body issues standards. There is normally, at the national level, some mechanism to ensure that companies comply with the accounting standards.

Acquiree   The business or businesses that the acquirer obtains control of in a business combination. (*IFRS 3, Appendix A*)

Acquirer   The entity that obtains control of the acquiree. (*IFRS 3, Appendix A*)

Acquisition date   The date on which the acquirer obtains control of the acquiree. (*IFRS 3, Appendix A*).

Active markets   A market in which transactions for the asset or liability take place with sufficient frequency and volume to provide pricing information on an ongoing basis. (*IFRS 13, Appendix A*)

Agricultural activity   The management by an entity of the biological transformation and harvest of biological assets for sale or for conversion, into agricultural produce, or into additional biological assets. (*IAS 41, paragraph 5*)

Amortized cost   The amount at which the financial asset or financial liability is measured at initial recognition minus the principal repayments, plus or minus the cumulative amortization using the effective interest method of any difference between that initial amount and the maturity amount and, for financial assets, adjusted for any loss allowance. (*IFRS 9 Appendix A*)

Asset   An asset is 'a resource controlled by the enterprise as a result of past events and from which future economic benefits are expected to flow to the enterprise'. (*IASB Exposure Draft, 2015, paragraph 4.4*)

Associate   An associate company is an entity over which the investor has significant influence. (*IAS 28, paragraph 3*)

Borrowing costs   The interest and other costs that an entity incurs in connection with the borrowing of funds. (*IAS 23, paragraph 5*)

Business   An integrated set of activities and assets that is capable of being conducted and managed for the purpose of providing a return in the form of dividends, lower costs or other economic benefits directly to investors or other owners, members or participants. (*IFRS 3, Appendix A*)

Business combination   A transaction or other event in which an acquirer obtains control of one or more businesses. Transactions sometimes referred to as 'true mergers' or 'mergers of equals' are also business combinations. (*IFRS 3, Appendix A*)

Capital reduction   The process of decreasing an entity's shareholder equity through share cancellations and share repurchases.

Cash equivalents   A highly liquid investment having a maturity of three months or less. It must be unrestricted so that it is available for immediate use and there should be a minimal risk of change in value.

Cash-generating unit (CGU) A clearly identifiable group of assets that generates cash inflows mostly independent of the cash flows from other assets or groups of assets.

Closing rate The spot exchange rate at the balance sheet date.

Conceptual Framework The *Conceptual Framework* sets out the concepts that underlie the preparation and presentation of financial statements. It identifies principles for the IASB to use when it develops and revises its IFRS. (*IASB Discussion Paper, July 2012*)

Consolidated financial statements The financial statements of a group in which the assets, liabilities, equity, income, expenses and cash flows of the parent and its subsidiaries are presented as those of a single economic entity. (*IFRS 10, Appendix A*)

Contingent asset A contingent asset is a possible asset that arises from past events and whose existence will be confirmed only by the occurrence or non-occurrence of one or more uncertain future events not wholly within the control of the entity. (*IAS 37, Paragraph 10*)

Contingent liability A contingent liability is where there is significant uncertainty with a number of aspects regarding the liability. (*IAS 37, Paragraph 10*)

Contract An agreement between two or more parties that creates enforceable rights and obligations. (*IFRS 15, Appendix A*)

Control An investor controls an investee when the investor is exposed, or has rights, to variable returns from its involvement with the investee and has the ability to affect those returns through its power over the investee. (*IFRS 10, Appendix A*)

Corporate governance Corporate governance is the system by which companies are directed and controlled. Boards of directors are responsible for the governance of their companies. The shareholders' role in governance is to appoint the directors and the auditors and to satisfy themselves that an appropriate governance structure is in place. The responsibilities of the board include setting the company's strategic aims, providing the leadership to put them into effect, supervising the management of the business and reporting to shareholders on their stewardship. The board's actions are subject to laws, regulations and the shareholders in general meeting. (*Cadbury Committee Corporate Governance Code, 1992, paragraph 2.5*)

Corporate reporting The provision of information that describes the activities of a company. The range of information can include, but not be limited to financial statements and supporting explanations, directors' remuneration, corporate governance, sustainability reporting, ethical and environmental policies and other narrative reports. The information may be required by legislation, accounting standards, stock exchange rules or it may be provided voluntarily.

Corporate social responsibility (CSR) The voluntary activities undertaken by a company to operate in an economic, social and environmentally sustainable manner. (*Government of Canada, http://www.international.gc.ca/trade-agreements-accords-commerciaux/topics-domaines/other-autre/csr-rse.aspx?lang=eng, accessed 15 September 2016*)

Credit losses The difference between all contractual cash flows that are due to an entity in accordance with the contract and all the cash flows that the entity expects to receive (i.e. all cash shortfalls), discounted at the original effective interest rate (or credit-adjusted effective interest rate for purchased or originated credit-impaired financial assets). (*IFRS 9, Appendix A*)

Current tax The amount of income taxes payable (recoverable) in respect of the taxable profit (tax loss) for a period. (*IAS 12, paragraph 5*)

Customer A party that has contracted with an entity to obtain goods or services that are an output of the entity's ordinary activities in exchange for consideration. (*IFRS 15 Appendix A*)

Deductible temporary difference A temporary difference that will result in amounts that are tax deductible in the future when the carrying amount of the asset is recovered or the liability is settled. (*IAS 12, paragraph 6*)

Depreciation (Chapter 4) The systematic allocation of the depreciable amount of an asset over its useful life. (*IAS 16, paragraph 6*)

Depreciation (Chapter 8)   Depreciation is an annual charge to the income statement calculated by dividing the depreciable amount of an asset over its useful economic life. The annual depreciation charge is deducted from the carrying amount of the asset on the balance sheet.

Derecognition   The removal of all or part of a previously recognized asset or liability from an entity's statement of financial position. (*IASB Exposure Draft, ED/2015/3, 2015, paragraph 5.25*)

Derivative financial instruments   A contract, wherein the value is established (i.e. derived) from the performance of an underlying asset, index or interest rate. Derivative financial instruments are widely used in transactions and include options, futures, forwards and swaps.

Disclosure   The communication of financial information to those who have a right to receive it or an interest in the activities of the entity.

Discontinued operations   A component of an entity that either has been disposed of or is classified as held for sale and both represents a separate line of business or geographical area of operations and is part of a single coordinated plan to dispose of a separate major line of business. (*IFRS 5, Appendix A*)

Effective rate method   The rate that exactly discounts estimated future cash payments or receipts through the expected life of the financial asset or financial liability to the gross carrying amount of a financial asset. (*IFRS 9, Appendix A*)

Employee benefits   All forms of consideration given to an employee in exchange for the employee's services. Examples are cash bonuses, retirement benefits and private health care.

Enterprise risk management   A process, effected by an entity's board of directors, management and other personnel, applied in strategy setting and across the enterprise, designed to identify potential events that may affect the entity, and manage risk to be within its risk appetite, to provide reasonable assurance regarding the achievement of entity objectives. (*Committee of Sponsoring Organizations of the Treadway Commission (COSO), 2004*)

Equity (Chapter 6)   Equity is the residual interest in the assets of the entity after deducting all its liabilities. (*IASB, Exposure Draft, 2015, paragraph 4.4*)

Equity (Chapter 11)   In accounting, the word equity is used when referring to an ownership interest in a business. It is a contract that evidences a residual interest in the assets of an entity after deducting all of its liabilities.

Equity method   A method of accounting whereby the investment is initially recognized at cost and adjusted thereafter for the post-acquisition change in the investor's share of the investee's net assets. The investor's profit or loss includes its share of the investee's profit or loss and the investor's other comprehensive income includes its share of the investee's other comprehensive income. (*IAS 28, paragraph 3*)

Events after the reporting period   Those events, both favourable and unfavourable, that occur between the reporting date and the date on which the financial statements are authorized by the directors for issue. (*IAS 10, paragraph 3*)

Exchange differences   The differences resulting from translating a given number of units in one currency into another currency at a different exchange rate.

Fair value   The price that would be received to sell an asset or paid to transfer a liability in an orderly transaction between market participants at the measurement date. (*IFRS 13, Appendix A*)

Fair value other comprehensive income (FVOCI)   All gains and losses are recognized in the other comprehensive income statement (*IFRS 9, Appendix A*)

Fair value through profit or loss (FVTPL)   Financial assets at fair value through profit and loss are carried in the consolidated balance sheet at fair value with gains or losses recognized in the consolidated statement of income.(*IFRS 9, Appendix A*)

Finance lease   A finance lease is an agreement between two parties that transfers substantially all risks and rewards of ownership from the lessor to the lessee.

Financial accounting and reporting   The branch of accounting concerned with the recognition and measurement of economic transactions and events and their disclosure by organizations to external users.

Financial asset   An asset whose value is derived from a contractual claim, such as bank deposits and shares.

Financial instruments   Created by a contract between two parties. The contract gives one party a financial asset and the other party has a financial liability or equity. (*IAS 32, paragraph 11*)

Financial liability   A contractual obligation to deliver cash or another financial asset to another entity or to exchange financial assets or financial liabilities under potentially unfavourable conditions. It can also be a contract that will or may be settled in the entity's own equity. (*IAS 32, paragraph 11*)

Financial reporting   The communication of the financial information of the entity's business activities to external users. The communication is usually in the form of structured financial statements accompanied by notes.

Functional currency   The currency of the primary economic environment in which the company operates.

Generally Accepted Accounting Principles (GAAP)   A set of regulations with substantial authoritative support. GAAP is the framework that determines how accountants and businesses record their economic transactions and events to produce and disclose financial statements and other corporate information.

Goodwill   An intangible asset representing the future economic benefits arising from assets that are not capable of being individually identified and separately recognized.

Hedging   Hedging is reducing risk by taking action now to reduce the possibility of future losses, usually with the possibility of not enjoying any future gains.

Highest and best use   The use of a non-financial asset by market participants that would maximize the value of the asset or the group of assets and liabilities (e.g. a business) within which the asset would be used. (*IFRS 13, Appendix A*)

Impairment   Impairment of an asset takes place if the carrying amount shown in the organization's financial records is greater than the proceeds the organization considers would be received if the asset was retained in use or sold to an outside party.

Income (Chapter 7)   Increases in economic benefits during the accounting period in the form of inflows or enhancements of assets or decreases of liabilities that result in an increase in equity, other than those relating to contributions from equity participants. (*IFRS 15, Appendix A*)

Income (Chapter 9)   The definition of income encompasses both revenue and gains. Revenue arises in the course of the ordinary activities of an entity and is referred to by a variety of different names including sales, fees, interest, dividends, royalties and rent. (*Conceptual Framework, 2010, paragraph 4.29*)

Intangible asset   An identifiable non-monetary asset without physical substance. (*IAS 38, paragraph 8*)

Inventories   Assets in the form of finished goods, works in progress or raw materials.

Investment entity   An entity that:

    a) obtains funds from one or more investors for the purpose of providing those investor(s) with investment management services;

    b) commits to its investor(s) that its business purpose is to invest funds solely for returns from capital appreciation, investment income, or both; and

    c) measures and evaluates the performance of substantially all of its investments on a fair value basis. (*IFRS 10, Appendix A*)

Investment property   Land, a building, part of a building held by the owner or, if there is a finance lease, by the lessee to earn rentals or for capital appreciation or both.

Joint operation   An arrangement of which two or more parties have joint control. *(IAS 28, paragraph 3)*

Joint venture   A joint arrangement whereby the parties that have joint control of the arrangement and the joint venturers have rights to the net assets of the arrangement. *(IAS 28, paragraph 3)*

Key performance indicators (KPIs)   A set of quantifiable measures that a company calculates to demonstrate and explain its financial performance.

Lease   A contract that conveys to the customer the right-to-use an asset for a period of time in exchange for consideration. *(IASB, Project Update: Definition of a Lease, February 2014)*

Liabilities   A present obligation of the entity to transfer an economic resource as a result of past events. (*IASB Exposure Draft, 2015, paragraph 4.4*)

Limited liability   The liability of the shareholders of the company for its debts are limited to the amount they have agreed to invest. Generally, the liability of the shareholders is limited to the amount, if any, on any unpaid amount on their shares in the event of the company becoming bankrupt.

Loss allowance   The allowance for expected credit losses on financial assets measured according to the regulations in the standard.

Materiality   Information is material if omitting it or misstating it could influence decisions that the primary users of general purpose financial reports make on the basis of financial information about a specific reporting entity. (*IASB Exposure Draft, 2015, paragraph 2.11*)

Measurement   The process of quantifying, in monetary terms, information about an entity's assets, liabilities, equity, income and expenses. (*IASB Exposure Draft, ED/2015/3, 2015, paragraph 6.2*)

Mineral resources   The search for mineral resources, including minerals, oil, natural gas and similar non-regenerative resources after the entity has obtained legal rights to explore in a specific area, as well as the determination of the technical feasibility and commercial viability of extracting the mineral resource. (*IFRS 6, Appendix A*)

Most advantageous market   The market that maximizes the amount that would be received to sell the asset or minimizes the amount that would be paid to transfer the liability, after taking into account transaction costs and transport costs. (*IFRS 13, Appendix A*)

Net realizable value   The estimated sales value of the goods minus the additional costs likely to be incurred in completing production, if necessary, and any other costs necessary to make the sale. *(IAS 2, paragraph 6)*

Non-controlling interest   That part of the equity in a subsidiary that is not attributable, directly or indirectly, to a parent. The control of the subsidiary rests with the holder of the greatest share of the equity – the parent. Where another party holds a minor part of the equity, this is a non-controlling interest.

Objectives   The objective of general purpose financial reporting is to provide financial information about the reporting entity that is useful to existing and potential investors, lenders and other creditors in making decisions about providing resources to the entity. Those decisions involve buying, selling or holding equity and debt instruments, and providing or settling loans and other forms of credit. (*Exposure Draft, 2015, p. 22*)

Operating lease   An agreement that permits one party (the lessee) the use of an asset, but not the ownership. This remains with the owner (lessor) of the asset. An operating lease does not appear on the balance sheet as an asset. The rental expense appears on the income statement.

Operating segment   A component of an entity:
- that engages in business activities that may earn revenue and incur expenses;
- whose operating results are regularly reviewed by the chief operating decision maker;* and
- for which discrete financial information is available. (*IFRS 8, Appendix A*)

*The term 'chief operating decision maker' is not as such defined in IFRS8 because it refers to a function rather than a title. In some entities the function could be fulfilled by a group of directors rather than an individual.

Other comprehensive income   Other comprehensive income comprises items of income and expense (including reclassification adjustments) that are not recognized in profit or loss as required or permitted by other IFRSs. (*IAS 1*)

Performance obligation   A promise in a contract with a customer to transfer to the customer either

- a good or service (or a bundle of goods or services) that is distinct; or
- a series of distinct goods or services that are substantially the same and that have the same pattern of transfer to the customer. (*IFRS 15 Appendix A*)

Permanent difference   A one-off difference due to certain transactions not being taxable. (*IAS 12, paragraph 6*)

Power   Existing rights that give the current ability to direct the relevant activities. (*IFRS 10, Appendix A*)

Presentation currency   The currency in which the financial statements are presented.

Principal market   The market with the greatest volume and level of activity for the asset or liability. (*IFRS 13, Appendix A*)

Prior period errors   Prior period errors are omissions from, and misstatements in, the entity's financial statements for one or more prior periods arising from a failure to use, or misuse of, reliable information. (*IAS 8, paragraph 5*)

Profit or loss   Profit or loss is calculated by deducting the expenses for the financial period from the income. Transactions and events that are classified under the heading of other comprehensive income are excluded from the calculation.

Property, plant and equipment (PPE)   Tangible items used in the production or supply of goods or services, for rental to others, or for administrative purposes and expected to be used for more than one financial period.

Provision   A liability of uncertain timing or amount.

Ratio analysis   A technique for evaluating the financial performance and stability of an entity, with a view to making comparisons with previous periods, other entities and industry averages over a period of time.

Reclassifications   Reclassification adjustments are amounts reclassified to profit or loss in the current period that were recognized in other comprehensive income in the current or previous periods. (*IAS 1*)

Recognition   The process of capturing, for inclusion in the statement of financial position or the statement(s) of financial performance, an item that meets the definition of an element. (*IASB Exposure Draft ED/2015/3, paragraph 5.2*)

Recoverable amount   The higher of fair value less costs to sell and value in use. (*IAS 36, paragraph 6*)

Reporting entity   An entity that chooses, or is required, to prepare general purpose financial statements. A reporting entity is not necessarily a legal entity. It can comprise a portion of an entity, or two or more entities. (*Exposure Draft, 2015, paragraphs 3.11 and 3.12*)

Reserves   A part of the shareholders' equity excluding the amount of the basic share capital.

Revenue   Revenue arises from the sale of goods, the provision of services, and the use of assets yielding interest, royalties and dividends. It is the gross inflow of economic benefits, for example, cash, receivables, and other assets arising from the ordinary operating activities of an enterprise.

Separate financial statements   The financial statements presented by a parent (i.e. an investor with control of a subsidiary), an investor with joint control of, or significant influence over, an investee, in which the investments are accounted for at cost or in accordance with IFRS 9 Financial Instruments. (*IAS 28, paragraph 4*)

Share-based payments   A transaction where the entity transfers equity instruments (e.g. shares or share options) in exchange for goods or services supplied by employees or third parties (*IFRS 2 Appendix A*)

Share buyback or share repurchase   Where an entity purchases its own shares, thus reducing the number of shares on the open market.

Share capital   The amount that shareholders invest by purchasing shares from the issuing entity. The amount of share capital can increase if an entity issues new shares to the public in exchange for cash. Any price differences arising subsequently from price increases or decreases on the stock exchange are not reflected in the balance sheet.

Share option (US, stock option)   A benefit, given or sold by one party to another (in this case the employee), that gives the recipient the right, but not the obligation, to buy (call) or sell (put) a share at an agreed-upon price within a certain period or on a specific date.

Spot exchange rate   The exchange rate for immediate delivery.

Statement of changes in equity   A financial statement, sometimes referred to as 'Statement of retained earnings' in US GAAP, discloses changes over a financial period in the reserves comprising the owners' equity.

Statement of total comprehensive income   Total comprehensive income is all components of 'profit or loss' and of 'other comprehensive income'. It is reflected in the change of an entity's equity during a period due to transactions and other events. Changes as a consequence of transactions with owners in their capacity as owners are not included. (*IAS 1, paragraph 7*)

Stewardship Code   The Code assists the quality of engagement between the owners of the company and the managers by requiring investors to apply effective stewardship, thus improving long-term risk-adjusted returns to shareholders.

Stock exchange   A stock exchange is an institution, organization or association that serves as a market for trading financial instruments such as stocks, bonds and their related derivatives. Most modern stock exchanges have both a trading floor and an electronic trading system.

Sustainability   Development that meets the needs of the present without compromising the ability of future generations to meet their own needs. (*World Commission on the Environment and Development, 1987, p. 43.*)

Taxable profit (tax loss)   The profit (loss) for a period, determined in accordance with the rules established by the taxation authorities, upon which income taxes are payable (recoverable). (*IAS 12, paragraph 5*)

Taxable temporary difference   A temporary difference that will result in taxable amounts in the future when the carrying amount of the asset is recovered or the liability is settled. (*IAS 12, paragraph 6*)

Tax expense (tax income)   The aggregate amount included in the determination of profit or loss for the period in respect of current tax and deferred tax. (*IAS 12, paragraph 5*)

Temporary difference   A difference between the carrying amount of an asset or liability and its tax base. (*IAS 12, paragraph 6*)

Transaction price   The amount of consideration to which an entity expects to be entitled in exchange for transferring promised goods or services to a customer, excluding amounts collected on behalf of third parties. (*IFRS 15, Appendix A*)

Value in use   Value in use is the discounted future cash flows expected from an individual asset or a cash-generating unit. (*IAS 36, paragraph 6*)

REFERENCES

Abernathy, J.L., Beyer, B. and Rapley, E.T. (2014) 'Earnings Management Constraints and Classification Shifting', *Journal of Business Finance and Accounting*, 41(5) & (6), June/July, pp. 600–626.

AbuGhazaleh, N.M., Al-Hares, O.M. and Haddad, A.E. (2012) 'The Value Relevance of Goodwill Impairment: UK Evidence', *International Journal of Economics and Finance*, 4(4), pp. 206–216.

Adelberg, A.H. (1979) 'Narrative Disclosures Contained in Financial Reports: Means of Communication or Manipulation?', *Accounting and Business Research*, Summer.

Andriosopoulos, D., Andriosopoulos K. and Hoque, H. (2013) 'Information Disclosure, CEO Overconfidence, and Share Buyback Completion Rates', *Journal of Banking and Finance*, 37, pp. 5486–5499.

ASSC (Accounting Standards Steering Committee) (1975) *The Corporate Report*, A discussion paper published for comment by the Accounting Standards Steering Committee, London: The Institute of Chartered Accountants in England and Wales.

Barker, R. (2010) 'On the Definition of Income and Expenses', *Accounting in Europe*, 7(2), December, pp. 147–158.

Barkhausen, H.A. (2010) 'Winter Derivatives in Bankruptcy: Some Lessons from Lehman Brothers', *The Journal of Structured Finance*, pp. 7–10.

Barlev, B., Fried, D., Haddad, J.R. and Livnat, J. (2007) 'Reevaluation of Revaluations: A Cross-Country Examination of the Motives and Effects on Future Performance', *Journal of Business Finance & Accounting*, 34(7) & (8), September/October, pp. 1025–1050.

Bent, D. and Richardson, J. (2003) *The Sigma Guidelines: Toolkit Forum for the Future*, London: Sigma Project.

BIM (British Institute of Management) (1957) *Presenting Financial Information to Employees*, London.

Board of Trade (1925) *Minutes of Evidence.* Company Law Amendment Committee (Greene Committee). HMSO, London.

Board of Trade (1945) *Company Law Amendment Committee Report* (Cohen Committee). HMSO, Cmnd 6659, London.

Bromwich, M., Macve, R. and Sunder, S. (2010) 'Hicksian Income in the Conceptual Framework', *Abacus*, 46(3), pp. 348–376.

CFREF (Canadian Financial Executive Research Committee) (2013) *The Cost of IFRS Transition In Canada*, CFERF.

Ciartano, C. (2012) 'The Valuation of Investment Property Under Construction: UK REITs' Compliance with Disclosure Requirements', *The IUP Journal of Accounting Research and Audit Practices*, XI(3), pp. 31–41.

Committee of Sponsoring Organization of the Treadway Commission (1999) *Fraudulent Financial Reporting 1987–1997. An Analysis of U.S. Public Entities, 1999.*

Cortese, C. (2013) 'Politicisation of the International Accounting Standard Setting Process: Evidence from the Extractive Industries', *Journal of New Business Ideas and Trends*, 11(2), pp. 1–57.

Craven, B.M. and Marston, C.L. (1999) 'Financial Reporting on the Internet by leading UK companies', *European Accounting Review*, 8(2), pp. 321–333.

Dearing, R. (1988) *The Making of Accounting Standards*, Report of the Review Committee, ICAEW, London.

De George. E.T., Ferguson C., Spear, N. (2013) 'How much do IFRS cost? IFRS Adoption and Audit Fees', *Accounting Review*, 88(2), pp. 429–462.

dos Santos, O. and dos Santos. A. (2014) 'Lobbying on Accounting Regulation: Evidence from the Oil Industry', *Revista Contabilidade & Finanças. USP, São Paulo*, 25(65), pp. 124–144

Dunne, T., Helliar, C., Lymer, A. and Mousa, R. (2013) 'Stakeholder Engagement in Internet Financial Reporting: The diffusion of XBRL in the UK', *The British Accounting Review*, 45, pp. 167–182.

Dzinkowski, R. (2013) 'A New View from America?', *Accounting and Business*, June, p. 30.

Economist (1926) 12 June.

Elkington, J. (1998) *Cannibals with Forks: The Triple Bottom Line of 21st Century Business*, Capstone Publishing.

Ernst & Young (2015) *Are You Prepared for Corporate Reporting's Perfect Storm?*

ESMA (European Securities and Markets Authority), 'Review of European Enforcers on the Implementation of IFRS 8 Operating Segments'. Available at http://www.esma.europa.eu/system/files/2011_372.pdf (accessed 9 November 2011).

Farshadfar, S. and Monem, R. (2013) 'Further Evidence on the Usefulness of Direct Method Cash Flow Components for Forecasting Future Cash Flows', *The International Journal of Accounting*, 48, pp. 111–133.

FASB (Financial Accounting Standards Board) (1976) *Accounting for Leases, Statement of Financial Accounting Standard No. 13*, Stamford, Financial Accounting for Leases Standards Board.

FASB/IASB (2005) *Preliminary Views on an Improved Conceptual Framework for Financial Reporting: The Objective of Financial Reporting and Qualitative Characteristics of Decision-useful Financial Reporting Information.*

Financial Reporting Lab (2012) *Lab Project Report: Operating and Investing Cash Flows*, FRC.

Financial Reporting Lab (2014) *Lab Project Report: Accounting Policies and Integration of Related Financial Information*, FRC.

FRC (Financial Reporting Council) (2008) *The Combined Code on Corporate Governance*, June.

FRC (Financial Reporting Council) (2010) *Updated Corporate Governance Code.*

FRC (Financial Reporting Council) (2011) *Cutting Clutter. Combating Clutter in Annual Reports.*

FRC (Financial Reporting Council) (2012a) *FRS 100 Application of Financial Reporting Requirements.*

FRC (Financial Reporting Council) (2012b) *The UK Stewardship Code*, September.

FRC (Financial Reporting Council) (2013) *FRC Seeks Consistency in the Reporting of Exceptional Items*, Press Release PN 108, 13 December.

FRC (Financial Reporting Council) (2014a) *FRC Challenges the Reporting of Companies Classifying Pension Liabilities as Equity*, Press Release PN 002/14, 15 January.

FRC (Financial Reporting Council) (2014b) *The FRC and its Regulatory Approach*, January, pp. 10–13.

FRC (Financial Reporting Council) (2014c) *Guidance on The Strategic Report*, June.

FRC (Financial Reporting Council) (2014d) *True and Fair*, June.

FRC (Financial Reporting Council) (2014e) *The UK Corporate Governance Code*, September.

FRC (Financial Reporting Council) (2015a) *Conceptual Framework for Financial Reporting*, November.

FRC (Financial Reporting Council) (2015b) *Developments in Corporate Governance and Stewardship*, January.

FRC (Financial Reporting Council) (2015c) *FRC Promotes Clear and Concise Reporting Through Strategic Report*, Press Release PN 76/15, 17 December.

FRC (Financial Reporting Council) (2016) https://frc.org.uk/News-and-Events/FRC-Press/Press/2016/February/FRC-comments-on-new-IFRS-requirement-on-debt-discl.aspx (accessed 7 October 2016).

Global Reporting Initiative (2011) *Sustainability Reporting Guidelines*, available at www.globalreporting.org/Pages/default.aspx (accessed 15 September 2016).

Goyal, M.K. (2004) 'A Survey on Popularity of the Direct Method of Cash Flow Reporting', *Journal of Applied Management Accounting Research*, 2, pp. 41–52.

Haddrill, S. (2016) *Comply or Explain: Review of FTSE 350 Companies*, Speech by Stephen Haddrill, Chief Executive, Financial Reporting Council Climate Disclosure Standards Boards, 28 January.

Hicks, J.R. (1946) 'Income', Chapter XIV of *Value and Capital*, 2nd edn, Clarendon Press (Reprinted in R.H. Parker, G.C. Harcourt and G. Whittington (eds) (1986) *Readings in the Concept and Measurement of Income*, 2nd edn, Philip Allan).

Holt, G. (2014a) 'Catering to User Demand', *Accounting and Business*, June, pp. 49–51.

Holt, G. (2014b) 'Profit and Loss and OCI', *Accounting and Business*, July, pp. 49–51.

Holt, G. (2015a) 'Accounting for CBPs', *Accounting and Business*, March. pp. 49–51.

Holt, G. (2015b) 'Reconciliation?', *Accounting and Business*, June, pp. 49–51

Hussey, R. and Ong, A. (2014) *Pick a Number: Internationalizing U.S. Accounting*, Business Expert Press.

Hussey, R. and Woolfe, S. (1994) *Interim Statements and Preliminary Profit Announcements*, Institute of Chartered Accountants in England and Wales, London.

IASB (International Accounting Standards Board) (2010) *Conceptual Framework for Financial Reporting 2010*, September.

IASB (International Accounting Standards Board) (2013) *http://www.ifrs.org/Alerts/ProjectUpdate/Pages/IASB-publishes-a-Discussion-Paper-on-the-Conceptual-Framework.aspx* (accessed 21 September 2016)

IASB (International Accounting Standards Board) (2015a) *Exposure Draft ED/2014/6 Proposed Amendments to IAS 7*, April 17.

IASB (International Accounting Standards Board) (2015b) *Exposure Draft ED/2015/3.*

IASB (International Accounting Standards Board) (2016) *Disclosure Initiative Amendments to IAS 7 Statement of Cash Flows.*

ICAS (1998) *Making Corporate Reports Valuable,* Kogan Page/Institute of Chartered Accountants in Scotland.

IFRS Foundation (2014) *Project Summary: IFRS Financial Instruments,* July.

IFRS Foundation (2015) *Post-implication Review – IFRS 3 Business Combinations.*

IFRS Foundation (2016) *Effects Analysis: IFRS 16 Leases,* January.

IIRC (International Integrated Reporting Council) (2013) *The International Framework,* December.

International Federation of Accountants (2016) *From Crisis to Confidence: A Call for Consistent, High-Quality Global Regulation,* 3 February.

Kingston, B. and Schreiner, L. (2014) 'Corporate Tax: The Bigger Picture', *CPA Magazine,* October, pp. 50–51.

Kirsch R.J. (2012) 'The Evolution of the Relationship Between the US Financial Reporting Standards Board and the International Accounting Standard Setters 1973–2008', *Accounting Historians Journal,* 39(1), pp. 1–51.

KPMG (2011) *International Survey of Corporate Responsibility Reporting,* KPMG.

Leung, E. and Verriest, A. (2015) 'The Impact of IFRS 8 on Geographical Segment Information', *Journal of Business Finance & Accounting,* 42(3) & (4), April/May, pp. 273–309.

Lewis, N., Parker, L. and Sutcliffe, P. (1982) *Financial Reporting to Employees: Iterative Cycles of Development,* Monash University, Australia.

Lin, Y.C. and Peasnell, K.V. (2000) 'Fixed Asset Revaluation and Equity Depletion in the UK', *Journal of Business Finance Of Accounting,* 27(3 & 4) April/May, pp. 359–394.

Lloyd, S. (2014) 'IFRS 9: A Complete Package for Investors', *Investor Perspectives,* July.

Lloyd, S. (2015) 'Big Changes Ahead: Accounting for Financial Instruments', *Banking Magazine,* March.

LSE (London Stock Exchange) (2016) *http://www.londonstockexchange.com/traders-and-brokers/rules-regulations/rules-regulations.htm* (accessed 21 September 2016).

Lymer, A. (1997) 'The Use of the Internet in Company Reporting: A Survey and Commentary on the Use of the WWW in Corporate Reporting in the UK'. Paper presented at the BAA National Conference, 21–25 March, Birmingham.

McBarnet, D. and Whelan, C. (1991) 'The Elusive Spirit of the Law: Formalism and the Struggle for Legal Control', *Modern Law Review,* 54(6), pp. 848–873.

Meder, A., Schwartz, S.T., Spires, E.E. and Young, R.A. (2011) 'Structured Finance and Mark-to-Model Accounting: A Few Simple Illustrations', *Accounting Horizons,* 25(3), pp. 559–576.

Napier, C.J. (1993) 'Company Law and Accounting UK', *European Accounting Review,* 2, pp. 370–375.

Naylor, G. (1960) *Company Law for Shareholders,* Hobart Paper No. 7, Institute of Economic Affairs.

Nichols, N.B., Street, D.L. and Tarca, A. (2013) 'The Impact of Segment Reporting Under the IFRS 8 and SFAS 131 Management Approach: A Research Review', *Journal of International Financial Management & Accounting,* 24(3), pp. 261–312.

Nielsen, C. and Roslender, R. (2015) 'Enhancing Financial Reporting: The Contribution of Business Models', *British Accounting Review,* 47(3), September, pp. 262–274.

ONS (Office for National Statistics) (2015) *Mergers and Acquisitions Involving UK companies, Quarter 2 Apr to June 2015).* Available at http://www.ons.gov.uk/ons/rel/international-transactions/mergers-and-acquisitions-involving-uk-companies/q2-2015/index.html (accessed 6 September 2016).

Page, M. (2005) 'The Search for a CF: Quest for a Holy Grail, or Hunting a Snark?', *Accounting, Auditing & Accountability Journal,* 18(4), pp. 565–576.

Persons, O.S. (2012) 'Stock Option and Cash Compensation of Independent Directors and Likelihood of Fraudulent Financial Reporting', *Journal of Business & Economic Studies,* 18(1), Spring, pp. 54–74.

Pittis, D. (2013) 'Canada's Soaring Farmland Prices', November 11. Available at http://www.cbc.ca/news/canada/soaring-farmland-prices-a-crisis-in-the-making-don-pittis-1.2420223 (accessed 24 August 2016).

PricewaterhouseCoopers (2007) *Guide to Key Performance Indicators: Communicating the Measures that Matter,* June.

Richardson, A.J. (2011) 'Regulatory Competition in Accounting: A History of the Accounting Standards Authority of Canada', *Accounting History Review,* 21(1), pp. 95–114.

Rose, H. (1965) *Disclosure in Company Accounts,* The Institute of Economic Affairs Ltd., Paper 1. London.

Rowbottom, N., Allam, A. and Lymer, A. (2005) 'An Exploration of the Potential for Studying the Usage of Investor Relations Information Through the Analysis of Web Server Logs', *International Journal of Accounting Information Systems*, 6, pp. 31–53.

Waine, D. (2009) 'NZ 41 Neither Fair Nor Value for the Agricultural Sector', *Chartered Accountants Journal*, May, pp. 54–56.

Walker, R.G. (1987) 'Australia's ARSB: A Case Study of Political Activity and Regulatory Capture', *Accounting and Business Research*, 17(67), pp. 269–286.

Webb, S. and Webb, B. (1914–15) 'Cooperative Production and Profit Sharing', *New Statesman: Special Supplements*.

Zeff, S. (2013) 'The Objectives of Financial Reporting: A Historical Survey and Analysis', *Accounting and Business Research*, 43(4), pp. 262–327.

INDEX